MASTER VISUALLY®

by Julia Kelly

Visual

Excel 2003 VBA Programming

Master VISUALLY® Excel 2003 VBA Programming

Published by
Wiley Publishing, Inc.
111 River Street
Hoboken, NJ 07030-5774

Published simultaneously in Canada

Library of Congress Control Number: 2004117699

ISBN: 0-7645-7973-8

Manufactured in the United States of America

10 9 8 7 6 5 4 3 2 1

1K/RQ/QS/QV/IN

Trademark Acknowledgments

Contact Us

For general information on our other products and services please contact our Customer Care Department within the U.S. at 800-762-2974, outside the U.S. at 317-572-3993 or fax 317-572-4002.

For technical support please visit www.wiley.com/techsupport.

WILEY

U.S. Sales

Contact Wiley
at (800) 762-2974 or
fax (317) 572-4002.

Praise for Visual Books...

"If you have to see it to believe it, this is the book for you!"
—PC World

"A master tutorial/reference — from the leaders in visual learning!"
—Infoworld

"A publishing concept whose time has come!"
—The Globe and Mail

"Just wanted to say THANK YOU to your company for providing books which make learning fast, easy, and exciting! I learn visually so your books have helped me greatly – from Windows instruction to Web development. Best wishes for continued success."
—Angela J. Barker (Springfield, MO)

"I have over the last 10-15 years purchased thousands of dollars worth of computer books but find your books the most easily read, best set out, and most helpful and easily understood books on software and computers I have ever read. Please keep up the good work."
—John Gatt (Adamstown Heights, Australia)

"You're marvelous! I am greatly in your debt."
—Patrick Baird (Lacey, WA)

"I am an avid fan of your Visual books. If I need to learn anything, I just buy one of your books and learn the topic it in no time. Wonders! I have even trained my friends to give me Visual books as gifts."
—Illona Bergstrom (Aventura, FL)

"I have quite a few of your Visual books and have been very pleased with all of them. I love the way the lessons are presented!"
—Mary Jane Newman (Yorba Linda, CA)

"Like a lot of other people, I understand things best when I see them visually. Your books really make learning easy and life more fun."
—John T. Frey (Cadillac, MI)

"Your Visual books have been a great help to me. I now have a number of your books and they are all great. My friends always ask to borrow my Visual books - trouble is, I always have to ask for them back!"
—John Robson (Brampton, Ontario, Canada)

"I write to extend my thanks and appreciation for your books. They are clear, easy to follow, and straight to the point. Keep up the good work! I bought several of your books and they are just right! No regrets! I will always buy your books because they are the best."
—Seward Kollie (Dakar, Senegal)

"What fantastic teaching books you have produced! Congratulations to you and your staff."
—Bruno Tonon (Melbourne, Australia)

"Thank you for the wonderful books you produce. It wasn't until I was an adult that I discovered how I learn—visually. Although a few publishers claim to present the materially visually, nothing compares to Visual books. I love the simple layout. Everything is easy to follow. I can just grab a book and use it at my computer, lesson by lesson. And I understand the material! You really know the way I think and learn. Thanks so much!"
—Stacey Han (Avondale, AZ)

"The Greatest. This whole series is the best computer-learning tool of any kind I've ever seen."
—Joe Orr (Brooklyn, NY)

Credits

Project Editor
Jade L. Williams

Acquisitions Editor
Jody Lefevere

Product Development Manager
Lindsay Sandman

Copy Editor
Scott Tullis

Technical Editor
Namir Shammas

Editorial Assistant
Adrienne Porter

Editorial Manager
Robyn Siesky

Manufacturing
Allan Conley
Linda Cook
Paul Gilchrist
Jennifer Guynn

Book Design
Kathie Rickard

Project Coordinator
Nancee Reeves

Layout
Jennifer Heleine
Amanda Spagnuolo

Screen Artists
Elizabeth Cardenas-Nelson
Jill A. Proll

Illustrator
Ronda David-Burroughs

Proofreader
Sossity R. Smith

Quality Control
Brian H. Walls

Indexer
Steve Rath

Special Help
Microsoft Corporation

Vice President and Executive Group Publisher
Richard Swadley

Vice President and Publisher
Barry Pruett

Composition Director
Debbie Stailey

About the Author

Julia Kelly has been writing books about Microsoft Office programs and editing a wide variety of technical books and manuals since 1992. She holds a Master of Science degree from the University of Washington, and was a U.S. Air Force pilot before she began writing technical books. She lives in rural north Idaho with assorted horses, dogs, chickens, and one cat.

PART I
Creating Simple Macros

1) Recording Simple Macros

2) Running Macros

3) Recording Complex Macros

4) Simplifying and Protecting Macros

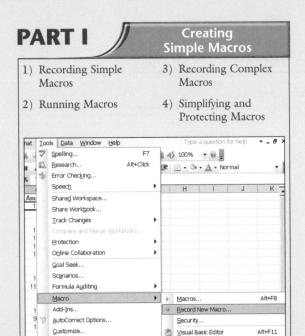

PART II
Exploring the Visual Basic Editor

5) Getting to Know the Visual Basic Editor

6) Using the Visual Basic Editor

7) Manipulating Modules and Projects

Options

| Editor | Editor Format | General | Docking |

Code Settings

☑ Auto Syntax Check
☐ Require Variable Declaration
☑ Auto List Members
☑ Auto Quick Info
☑ Auto Data Tips

☑ Auto Indent
Tab Width: 4

Window Settings

☑ Drag-and-Drop Text Editing
☑ Default to Full Module View
☑ Procedure Separator

OK   Cancel

PART III
Manipulating Workbooks and Worksheets

8) Writing Workbook Macros

9) Creating Worksheet Macros

10) Changing Worksheet Settings

Macro   ? ✕

Macro name:
OpenWB

PERSONAL.XLS!closeWbIndex
PERSONAL.XLS!closexl
PERSONAL.XLS!ConvertFormulas
PERSONAL.XLS!ConvertToValues
PERSONAL.XLS!CutPasteDynamic
OpenWB
PERSONAL.XLS!Sort
PERSONAL.XLS!subtotal
PERSONAL.XLS!ToggleDecimal

Run
Cancel
Step Into
Edit
Create
Delete

Macros in: All Open Workbooks

Options...

Description

PART IV
Working with Ranges

11) Selecting and Manipulating Ranges

12) Formatting Ranges

13) Entering Data and Formulas

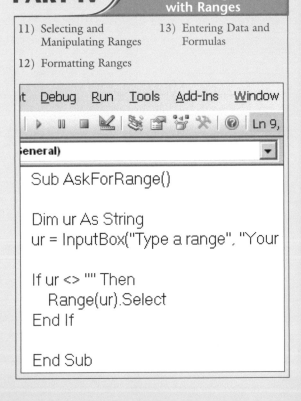

PART V
Making a Macro Smart

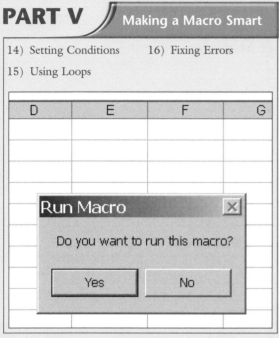

PART VI
Creating Chart and PivotTable Macros

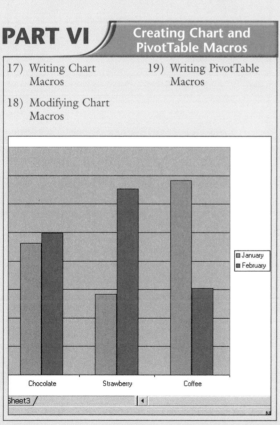

PART VII
Using Forms and Controls

PART I / Creating Simple Macros

① Recording Simple Macros

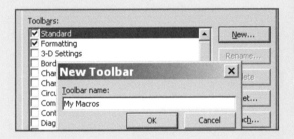

② Running Macros

③ Recording Complex Macros

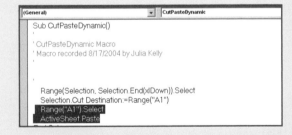

④ Simplifying and Protecting Macros

TABLE OF CONTENTS

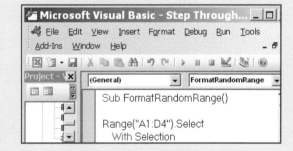

PART II — Exploring the Visual Basic Editor

5 Getting to Know the Visual Basic Editor

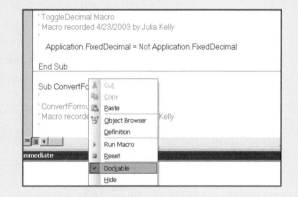

6 Using the Visual Basic Editor

7 Manipulating Modules and Projects

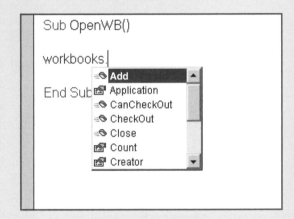

PART III

Manipulating Workbooks and Worksheets

8 Writing Workbook Macros

9 Creating Worksheet Macros

10 Changing Worksheet Settings

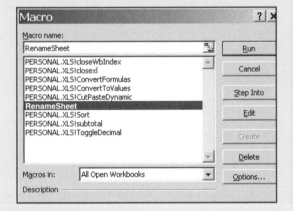

TABLE OF CONTENTS

```
Sub ProtectAllWs()
Dim ws As Worksheet

For Each ws In Worksheets
    ws.Protect Password:="aaa", AllowFormattingCells:=True
```

PART IV — Working with Ranges

⓫ Selecting and Manipulating Ranges

⓬ Formatting Ranges

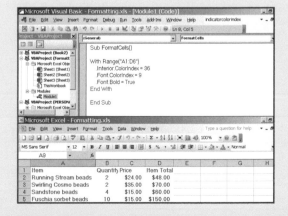

⓭ Entering Data and Formulas

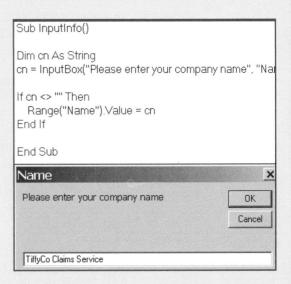

PART V — Making a Macro Smart

⓮ Setting Conditions

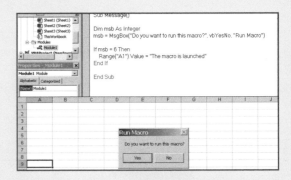

⓯ Using Loops

TABLE OF CONTENTS

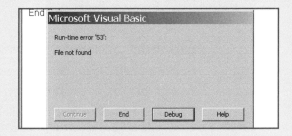

PART VI

Creating Chart and PivotTable Macros

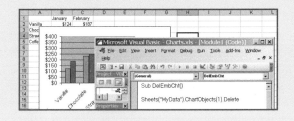

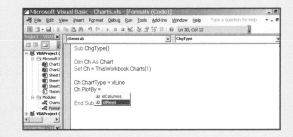

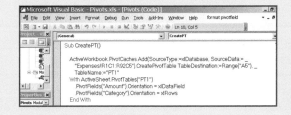

PART VII

Using Forms and Controls

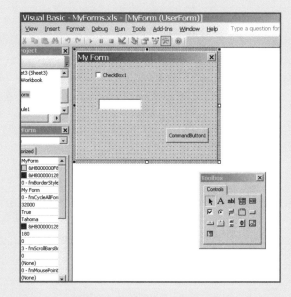

TABLE OF CONTENTS

How to Use this Master VISUALLY Book

Do you look at the pictures in a book or newspaper before anything else on a page? Would you rather see an image than read how to do something? Search no further. This book is for you. Opening *Master VISUALLY Excel 2003 VBA Programming* allows you to read less and learn more about how to create and run programs in Microsoft Excel using Visual Basic for Applications.

Who Needs This Book

This book is for the programming beginner, who is familiar with Microsoft Excel but unfamiliar with Visual Basic for Applications in Excel. It is also for more computer literate individuals who want to expand their knowledge of the different features that Visual Basic for Applications has to offer.

Book Organization

Master VISUALLY Excel 2003 VBA Programming has 23 chapters and is divided into seven parts. Each part contains three or more chapters. Each chapter is divided into tasks.

Chapter Organization

This book consists of sections, all listed in the book's table of contents. A *section* is a set of steps that show you how to complete a specific computer task.

Each section, usually contained on two facing pages, has an introduction to the task, a set of full-color screen shots and steps that walk you through the task, and a set of tips. This format allows you to quickly look at a topic of interest and learn it instantly.

Chapters group together three or more sections with a common theme. A chapter may also contain pages that give you the background information needed to understand the sections in a chapter.

Part I: *Creating Simple Macros* introduces you to Macros. Chapter 1 gives you an overview on Macros, showing you how to record, open, edit, and delete a Macro. Chapter 2 shows you how to run a macro from four locations as well as create a toolbar. Chapter 3 illustrates how to record complex macros. Chapter 4 demonstrates how to simplify and protect macros.

Part II: *Exploring the Visual Basic Editor* gives you a tour of how the editor works. Chapter 5 helps you to become familiar with the Visual Basic Editor. Chapter 6 shows you how to use the editor to create macros. Chapter 7 illustrates how you can manipulate modules and projects within the editor.

Part III: *Manipulating Workbooks and Worksheets* illustrates how to create and change workbook settings. Chapter 8 shows you how to write workbook macros. Chapter 9 demonstrates how to create worksheet macros. Chapter 10 shows you how to change worksheet settings.

Part IV: *Working with Ranges* demonstrates how to write, manipulate, and format ranges. Chapter 11 shows you how to create, build, and control ranges. Chapter 12 outlines how to format ranges by setting, adding, and changing conditions. Chapter 13 illustrates how to enter data and formulas into ranges.

Part V: *Making a Macro Smart* introduces you to loops and conditions that add efficiency to your macros. Chapter 14 demonstrates how to use conditional statements to add decision-making ability to a macro. Chapter 15 shows you how to use loops to write a macro that make long or repetitive tasks much more efficient. Chapter 16 helps you to resolve runtime errors, syntax errors, compile errors, and logical errors that can stop your macro from running or give incorrect results.

Part VI: *Creating Chart and PivotTable Macros* instructs you on how to write and modify chart macros and two-dimensional database macros. Chapter 17 shows you how to write chart macros. Chapter 18 illustrates how to modify chart macros. Chapter 19 walks you through writing complex PivotTables macros.

Part VII: *Using Forms and Controls* demonstrates how to create and program controls. Chapter 20 shows you how to create interactive worksheet controls. Chapter 21 instructs you on how to program controls. Chapter 22 walks you through controlling macros with events. The final chapter, Chapter 23, illustrates ways in which you can enhance a macro.

What You Need to Use This Book

This book is applicable to programming Visual Basic for Applications in Excel 2000, 2002, and 2003. It was written using Excel 2003 on a Windows 2000 operating system.

HOW TO USE THIS BOOK

Using the Mouse

This book uses the following conventions to describe the actions you perform when using the mouse:

Click

Press your left mouse button once. You generally click your mouse on something to select something on the screen.

Double-click

Press your left mouse button twice. Double-clicking something on the computer screen generally opens whatever item you have double-clicked.

Right-click

Press your right mouse button. When you right-click anything on the computer screen, the program displays a shortcut menu containing commands specific to the selected item.

Click and Drag, and Release the Mouse

Move your mouse pointer and hover it over an item on the screen. Press and hold down the left mouse button. Now, move the mouse to where you want to place the item and then release the button. You use this method to move an item from one area of the computer screen to another.

The Conventions in This Book

A number of typographic and layout styles have been used throughout *Master VISUALLY Excel 2003 VBA Programming* to distinguish different types of information.

Bold

Bold type represents the names of commands and options with which you interact. Bold type also indicates text and numbers that you must type into a dialog box or window.

Italics

Italic words introduce a new term and are followed by a definition.

Italics Code

Italicized code words indicate variables that the user must replace when writing your code.

Numbered Steps

To successfully complete a task and achieve a similar result, you must perform instructional numbered steps in order.

Bulleted Steps

These steps point out various optional features. You do not have to perform these steps; they simply give additional information about a feature.

Indented Text

Indented text tells you what the program does in response to you following a numbered step. For example, if you click a certain menu command, a dialog box may appear, or a window may open. Indented text may also tell you what the final result is when you follow a set of numbered steps.

Notes

Notes give additional information. They may describe special conditions that may occur during an operation. They may warn you of a situation that you want to avoid, for example, the loss of data. A note may also cross reference a related area of the book. A cross reference may guide you to another chapter, or another section within the current chapter.

Icons and Buttons

Icons and buttons are graphical representations within the text. They show you exactly what you need to click to perform a step.

 You can easily identify the tips in any section by looking for the Master It icon. Master It offers additional information, including tips, hints, and tricks. You can use the Master It information to go beyond what you have learn learned in the steps.

Conventions Assumed in this Book

This book assumes that you know how to navigate through the files in your computer and how to open, save, and close files. This book also assumes that you are familiar with Microsoft Excel but new to programming in Visual Basic for Applications.

Operating System Difference

This book is applicable to programming Visual Basic for Applications in Excel 2000, 2002, and 2003. It was written using Excel 2003 on a Windows 2000 operating system.

1 Recording Simple Macros

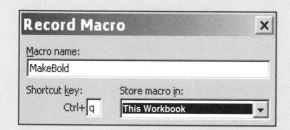

2 Running Macros

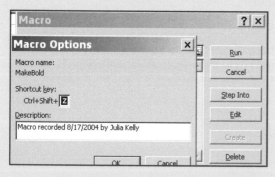

3 Recording Complex Macros

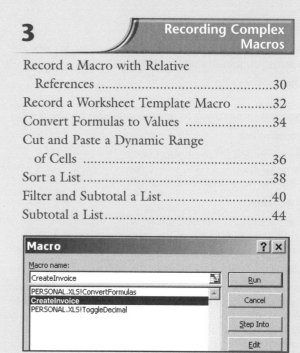

4 Simplifying and Protecting Macros

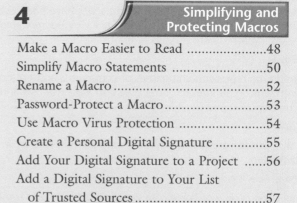

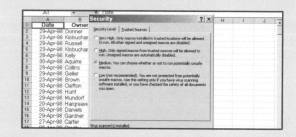

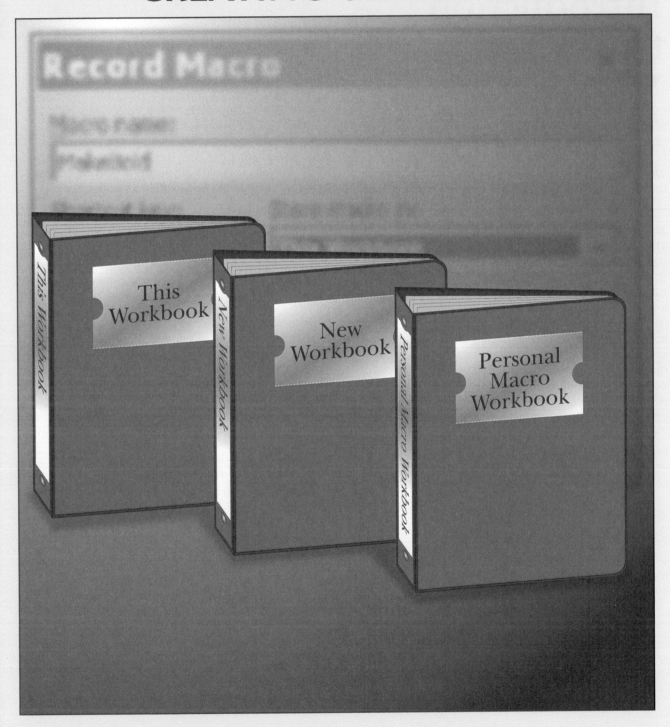

Introduction to Macros

You can record macros to automate tedious and repetitive tasks in Excel without writing programming code directly. Macros are efficiency tools that enable you to perform repetitive or tedious actions quickly with a single keystroke or button click. A macro can be very short. For example, by using the macro recorder and a little quick editing, you can create a one-line macro that turns fixed-decimal entry on or off with a single button click. Without a macro, the same procedure requires five button clicks. A macro can also be quite lengthy. You can record a macro to format and summarize some data, set up charts to present the data, and finally print the data. A single macro can do all of this with one click of a button, and much more rapidly than you can do it yourself.

Macro Recorder

The macro recorder works just like a tape recorder. When you turn it on, it records all of your actions in the worksheet and translates them into the VBA language. You do not have to hurry when you record a macro. The recorder records your actions, but not the time you take to perform them. Planning your actions and performing them carefully and in a logical order is more important than performing them quickly, because every mouse click, cell selection, and cell entry is recorded. If you make a mistake, either deleting the macro and recording it again, or opening the finished macro and editing your mistakes, is easy to do.

Because the recorder is limited to recording only the actions you perform, not all procedures can be written using this method alone. For example, the recorder cannot create a complex macro that repeats specific actions until a particular condition is met, or display a custom dialog box to take user input. On the other hand, the macro recorder is very useful for quickly recording many actions that you can edit manually to make them even more useful, or copy and paste into longer procedures that require additional written procedure code. The recorder is also a very useful method for learning the Visual Basic for Applications (VBA) language because you can record your actions, and then look at the VBA code the recorder wrote.

Macro Storage

All macros are stored in workbooks. When you record a macro, you must choose a storage workbook. You have three options for macro storage. When you record a macro, you can choose to store the macro in This Workbook, in a New Workbook, or in the Personal Macro Workbook. Store the procedure code for a macro somewhere that is easily accessible.

Store Macros in This Workbook

This Workbook stores macros in the currently active workbook, making them available to use in all open workbooks as long as this workbook is open. This is a good option to choose if you want to share the macro with other users, or if you want to send an automated workbook application with its macros to another user. When you send the workbook, its macros go with it.

Store Macros in the New Workbook

If you store a macro in New Workbook, Excel creates a new workbook and the macro stored there is only available when that workbook is open. This is useful if you want to create a new workbook to begin building an application, or create a new workbook just to store specific groups of macros, such as financial or budget macros.

Store Macros in the Personal Macro Workbook

A macro stored in the Personal Macro Workbook is always available to any workbook you have open. The Personal Macro Workbook is named PERSONAL.XLS and is saved in the XLSTART folder in your Microsoft folders. It always opens but remains hidden when Excel starts, so you never see it unless you unhide it. The first time you store a macro in the Personal Macro Workbook, Excel creates the workbook; every time you store another macro in the Personal Macro Workbook, the macro is added to the existing Personal Macro Workbook. These macros are only available in your copy of Excel. They do not travel with other workbooks you send to other users.

Record
a Macro

Y ou can save time by using the macro recorder and letting Excel write much of your programming code for you. You can also become familiar with the programming language more quickly by looking at the procedure code the macro recorder writes for the actions you perform.

When you record a macro, give the macro a recognizable name. Macro names must begin with a letter and are limited to 255 characters. The names cannot have spaces, but they can have letters, numbers, and underscore (_) characters. Names such as MakeBold and ToggleDecimal are good examples.

You must select a workbook in which to store the macro. The macro can run in any workbook as long as the workbook where the macro is stored is open. The Personal Macro Workbook is a hidden workbook that opens when you open Excel, so any macros you store in the Personal Macro Workbook are always available.

You can create an optional shortcut key to run the macro, and in the Description box add a comment to the macro that does not affect the macro actions. You can delete the description or enter a different description that more accurately describes what this macro does if you want to.

Record a Macro

① Click Tools.

② Click Macro.

③ Click Record New Macro.

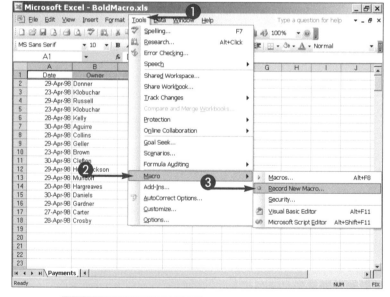

The Record Macro dialog box appears.

④ Click in the Macro name field and type a name for the macro.

⑤ Click in the Shortcut key box and type a letter if you want to create a shortcut key.

⑥ In the Store macro in box, click ▣ and select a workbook in which to store the macro.

⑦ Click OK.

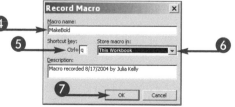

The Stop Recording toolbar appears. The macro recorder is recording all your actions.

⑧ Perform the actions you want the macro to perform.

In this example, the Bold button (**B**) is clicked and the selected cells are formatted bold.

⑨ Click the Stop Recording button (▣).

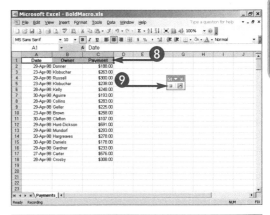

The Stop Recording toolbar disappears, and your macro is recorded.

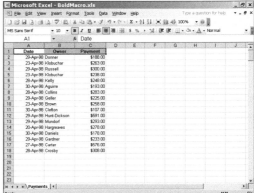

How can I test the recorded macro?

▼ You can test the macro immediately by using the shortcut key or the macros dialog box. To use the shortcut key, set up a worksheet to run your macro and press the macro shortcut key. To use the macro dialog box, set up a worksheet to run your macro. From the menu, click Tools, Macro, and then Macros. In the Macros dialog box, select the macro name from the Macro name list and then click the Run button.

How can I record the macro to run in any cells I choose rather than the same cells every time?

▼ If you select cells after you start the macro recorder, that cell selection is recorded. To run in any cells you select, select cells before you start the macro recorder, and then start the recorder and record your actions. For example, if you want to record entering a formula, select a cell before you start the recorder, and then record entering the formula.

Record a Macro to Turn on Decimal Entry

Recording a macro that turns on the Fixed Decimal setting is an efficiency tool because it does in one-step what would normally take five. Because it is stored in the Personal Macro Workbook, the macro is always available to any workbook.

If you enter fixed-decimal numbers in a worksheet, such as prices or expenses, you find yourself typing the decimal point repeatedly. Excel enters the decimal point automatically if you turn on the Fixed Decimal setting, enabling you to type the numbers without having to type the decimal points.

After you run the macro, type a number in a cell. The number is entered with fixed decimals even though you did not type a decimal point.

After the macro turns the Fixed Decimal setting on, you must either turn it off manually or create a second macro to turn it off for you. You can make this second macro even more efficient by making it a toggle, which turns the Fixed Decimal setting on and off with the same single keystroke or button click. To make the macro a toggle, see the section "Edit a Macro to Make It a Toggle."

Record a Macro to Turn on Decimal Entry

① Click Tools.

② Click Macro.

③ Click Record New Macro.

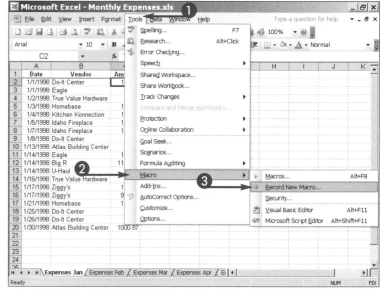

The Record Macro dialog box appears.

④ Click in the Macro name field and type an identifiable name for the macro.

⑤ Click in the Shortcut key box and type a letter for the Shortcut key.

⑥ In the Store macro in box, click ⊡ and select Personal Macro Workbook.

⑦ Click OK.

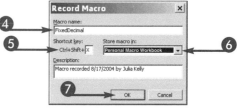

The Stop Recording toolbar appears, and the macro recorder is recording all your actions in the workbook.

⑧ Click Tools.

⑨ Click Options.

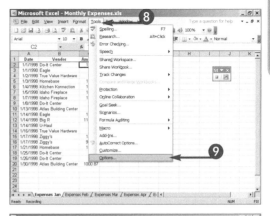

The Options dialog box appears.

⑩ Click the Edit tab.

⑪ Click the Fixed Decimal check box to select it (☐ changes to ☑).

⑫ Click OK.

⑬ On the Stop Recording toolbar, click ▣ to stop recording.

The Stop Recording toolbar disappears, and your recorded macro turns on fixed-decimal entry.

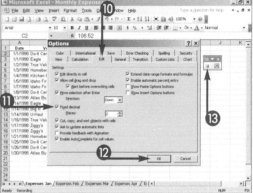

What if I want three decimal places instead of two?

▼ The macro only records the clicking of the check box. If you change the Fixed Decimal setting in the Edit dialog box to 3, the macro turns on three decimal places when you run it. Then from the menu, click Tools and Options. Select the Edit tab again and turn the Fixed Decimal setting off. The macro uses the changed setting.

How can I make this macro easier to run?

▼ You can attach this macro to a custom toolbar button or menu item, which makes the macro available in any workbook, or you can attach the macro to a graphic object in a specific workbook and run it by clicking the object. Because this macro turns on an Excel setting, the fixed decimal entry is turned on in all workbooks until you turn it off again. See Chapter 2 to assign macros to buttons, menus, and graphical objects.

Open a Macro

You can open a macro to see and edit the code the recorder wrote for the actions you performed. Macros open in the Visual Basic Editor. The Visual Basic Editor is a separate program from Excel. The Excel program window remains open behind the Visual Basic Editor program window. You can switch between the two open programs by clicking the program buttons on the Windows taskbar at the bottom of your screen.

You can edit an open macro to change what it does, make it easier to read, and simplify macro statements so the macro runs faster. You can also add code that is not recordable, such as loops.

When you open a macro, you see a procedure that begins with the keyword *Sub*, followed by the macro name and an empty set of parentheses, all on the first line. The code ends with the keyword *End Sub*. The statements, which are the lines in between the Sub line and the End Sub line, are the programmed actions in the macro. The green statements preceded by an apostrophe are informational comments entered by the macro recorder.

Open a Macro

1. Click Tools.

2. Click Macro.

3. Click Macros.

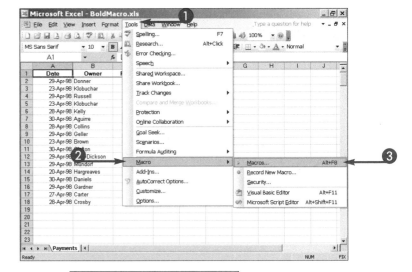

The Macro dialog box appears.

4. Click the name of the macro you want to see.

5. Click Edit.

The Visual Basic program window opens to show the macro you selected.

- The name of the macro is in the Sub line at the top of the code window.

- The procedure code you recorded is everything between the Sub line and the End Sub line.

⑥ Click the Close button ([x]).

You can also click File and then click Close and Return to Microsoft Excel.

The Visual Basic Editor window closes and you return to the Excel window.

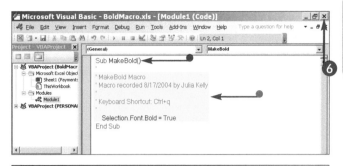

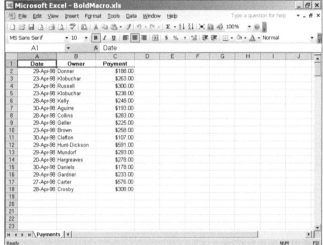

How can I open a macro in the Personal Macro Workbook?

▼ The Personal Macro Workbook is a hidden workbook, and you cannot open a macro using the Macro dialog box unless you unhide the workbook. To unhide the Personal Macro Workbook, click Window and then click Unhide. Click PERSONAL.XLS and then click OK. The PERSONAL.XLS workbook appears on your screen, and you can open macros using the Macro dialog box. Hide the Personal Macro Workbook again when you finish so it continues to open and run hidden in the background when you start Excel. To hide it, click Window, then click Hide.

Are there any other ways to open a macro?

▼ Yes, there are three more ways to open the Visual Basic Editor and look at a macro. You can click Tools, Macro, and then Visual Basic Editor; you can press Alt+F11; or you can click the Visual Basic Editor button on the Visual Basic toolbar. All of these methods open the Visual Basic Editor to the display it had when it was last closed. These methods also work in the Personal Macro Workbook without unhiding it.

Edit a Macro to Make It a Toggle

I f you create a macro for a feature that has two settings, you can edit the macro to enable a user to toggle the setting on and off as needed. Creating a single macro that acts as a toggle is not a process you can do by recording. However, you can record the initial procedure to get the structure in place quickly, and then edit the macro to make it a toggle.

To make a macro a toggle, you use a *keyword*, a word Excel understands, to change a setting in the workbook or the program. The keyword for a toggle is Not. The Not

keyword tells Excel that whatever the current value of this setting is, make the new setting *not* that value. In other words, if the setting is currently True, change it to False, and if the setting is currently False, change it to True. *True* is the VBA word for "on," and *False* is the VBA word for "off."

To edit a macro, you need to open the Visual Basic Editor. To open the Visual Basic Editor, see the section "Open a Macro."

Edit a Macro to Make It a Toggle

① Open the Visual Basic Editor to display your macro code.

The statement to edit is the line that ends in = True or = False.

② Select the statement object.

③ Click the Copy button (　).

④ Delete the keyword True.

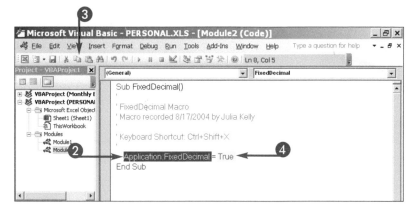

⑤ Type the keyword **not** in place of the word True.

⑥ Click Paste (　).

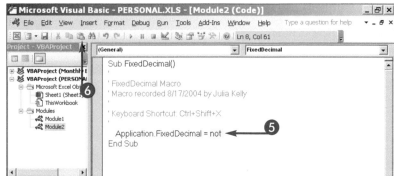

The copied phrase is pasted after the keyword.

7 Press Enter or click away from the statement.

The keyword is capitalized and blue.

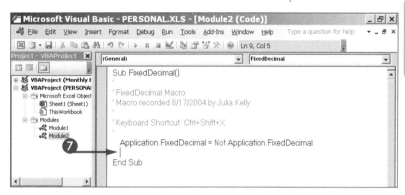

8 Click File.

9 Click Close and Return to Microsoft Excel.

The Visual Basic Editor closes.

The macro toggles the setting between on and off every time you run it.

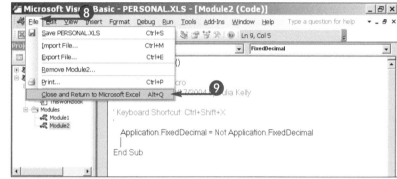

Why did my keyword not turn blue and get capitalized?

▼ If a keyword is spelled incorrectly, Excel does not capitalize it or turn it blue. That is an indication that you misspelled the keyword. The same is true for names, objects, properties, and any other words that Excel should recognize. All Excel keywords and code words use capital letters, so using capital letters in names is a good practice. Then, if you type all code in lowercase, you can find misspellings easily because Excel does not capitalize the word.

Is there a more efficient way to run my toggle macro?

▼ Yes, attaching the macro to a button for launching is more efficient, so you do not have to remember a keystroke or take the extra steps to open the Macro dialog box. If the macro changes an Excel setting such as the fixed decimal entry, you can make the macro quick to use in any workbook by assigning it to a custom toolbar button and displaying the button on your Standard toolbar.

Delete a Macro

You can eliminate clutter from your macro list by deleting the macros you no longer need. Then you can quickly select the macro you need without scrolling through an extensive list of macros.

When you delete a macro, Excel removes the macro so you can no longer run it, but changes made by that macro are unaffected. For example, if your macro created a worksheet template, all the worksheet templates already created by the macro remain unchanged.

You can delete a macro quickly by opening the Macro dialog box and deleting the macro name. If you select All Open Workbooks in the Macros in box, all the macro

names in all open workbooks can be deleted. However, if you try to delete a macro in the Personal Macro Workbook, you see a message that says you must first unhide the Personal Macro Workbook. To delete a macro from the Personal Macro Workbook through the Macro dialog box, see the section "Delete a Macro in the Personal Macro Workbook."

You can also delete a macro from within the Visual Basic Editor code window. You can delete macros from the Personal Macro Workbook without revealing (unhiding) them if you use the code window.

Delete a Macro from the Macro Dialog Box

1 Click Tools.

2 Click Macro.

3 Click Macros.

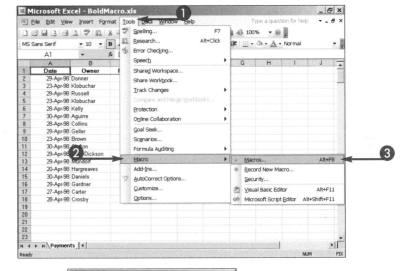

The Macro dialog box appears.

4 Click the name of the macro.

5 Click Delete.

6 If queried whether you want to delete the macro, click Yes.

The macro deletes.

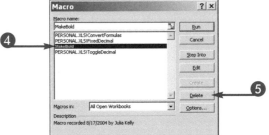

Delete a Macro from the Code Window

1 Open the macro in the Visual Basic Editor.

Note: To open the Visual Basic Editor, see the section "Open a Macro."

2 Select the entire macro, from the Sub line to the End Sub line.

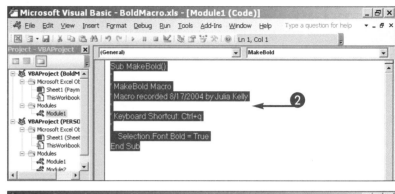

3 Press Delete.

The macro deletes.

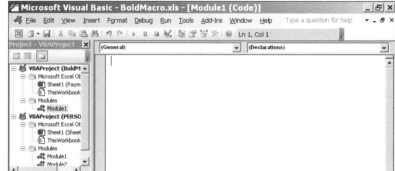

Will my toolbar button or menu still run the macro after I delete it?

▼ No. When you delete a macro, your toolbar buttons and menu commands retain the macro assignment. When you click the button or menu command, you get an error message that says the macro cannot be found. To remove a non-functional menu command or toolbar button, click Tools and then click Customize. While the Customize dialog box is open, drag the button or menu command away from the toolbar or menu bar and drop it on the worksheet. Then click Close in the Customize dialog box.

Can I get a macro back after I delete it?

▼ No. When you delete a macro, it is gone, which is why you are queried before deleting. You can save macro code in a text file by exporting the entire module, or you can save the macro code by copying the code and pasting it into any text file, such as Windows Notepad or Word. You can get the macro back by copying and pasting the code into a module, or by importing an exported module.

Delete a Macro in the Personal Macro Workbook

You can delete the macros in your Personal Macro Workbook quickly if you first unhide the Personal Macro Workbook. The Personal Macro Workbook is always hidden when you start Excel, and Excel does not allow you to delete macros from hidden workbooks through the Macro dialog box.

The Personal Macro Workbook is created the first time you store a macro in it. It exists to hold macros that are always available to any workbook. Macros that are stored in the Personal Macro Workbook are always displayed in the Macro dialog box as PERSONAL! followed by the macro name.

If you try to delete a macro in the Personal Macro Workbook through the Macro dialog box, you see a message that says you must first unhide the Personal Macro Workbook. After you delete the macro, you should hide the Personal Macro Workbook again so that it continues to open hidden and run in the background when you start Excel. If you do not hide it, the Personal Macro Workbook continues to open and display every time you start Excel. By hiding it, you eliminate clutter in your Excel window and any chance of making unwanted changes to the Personal Macro Workbook.

Delete a Macro in the Personal Macro Workbook

① Click Window.

② Click Unhide.

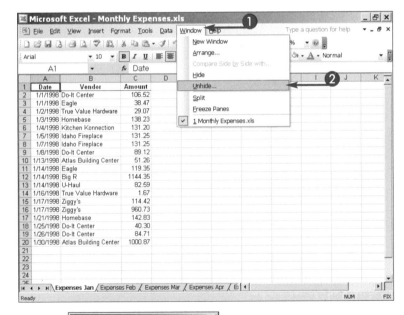

The Unhide dialog box displays a list of open, hidden workbooks.

③ Click PERSONAL.XLS.

④ Click OK.

The Personal Macro Workbook is unhidden and displayed in the Excel window.

⑤ Click Tools.

⑥ Click Macro

⑦ Click Macros.

The Macro dialog box appears.

⑧ Click the name of the macro.

⑨ Click Delete.

⑩ When asked if you want to delete the macro, click Yes.

⑪ Click Window.

⑫ Click Hide.

The macro deletes. The Personal Macro Workbook is safely hidden again.

Can I delete a macro from the Personal Macro Workbook in the code window?

▼ Yes, and you do not need to unhide the Personal Macro Workbook. Open the Visual Basic Editor. All macros in all open workbooks, including the Personal Macro Workbook, are available. In the Project Explorer window, expand the VBAProject (PERSONAL.XLS) project, and then expand the project's Modules. Double-click the module that contains the macro. Then select all the macro text, including the Sub and End Sub lines, and delete it. See the section "Delete a Macro" for the steps.

I deleted my Personal Macro Workbook. How can I get it back?

▼ You can get the Personal Macro Workbook back from the Windows Recycle Bin if you have not emptied the Recycle Bin since you deleted the workbook. Open the Recycle Bin, right-click the PERSONAL.XLS file, and click Restore. The workbook is returned to the XLSTART folder. If you already emptied the Recycle Bin, you cannot get the original Personal Macro Workbook back, but you can create a new one by recording a macro and storing it in the Personal Macro Workbook.

Run a Macro

Y ou can find and run a macro quickly, without having to remember a shortcut key or attach the macro to any objects, if you run the macro directly from the Macro dialog box.

The workbook where your macro is stored must be open for its macros to be available. The Personal Macro Workbook is always open, so its macros are always available.

You choose a macro source in the Macros in box. You can limit the list of macros to choose from by selecting either PERSONAL.XLS, which is the Personal Macro Workbook, or

This Workbook, which is the active workbook. To show all currently available macros, select All Open Workbooks in the Macros in box.

If the macro you want to run is stored in the active workbook, just the macro name is listed in the Macro name list. If the macro you want to run is stored in a workbook other than the active workbook, the workbook name is attached to the macro name. For example, if the MakeBold macro is stored in the open workbook BoldMacro.xls, the name you see in the Macros in box is BoldMacro.xls!MakeBold. Names of macros in the Personal Macro Workbook always start with PERSONAL.XLS!.

Run a Macro

① Click File.

② Click Open.

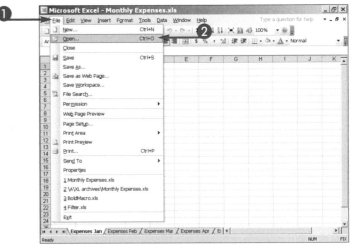

The Open dialog box appears.

③ Click the workbook containing the macro you want to run.

④ Click Open.

The workbook containing the macro opens.

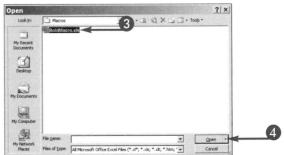

5 Click the cell in the workbook where you want the macro to run.

6 Click Tools.

7 Click Macro.

8 Click Macros.

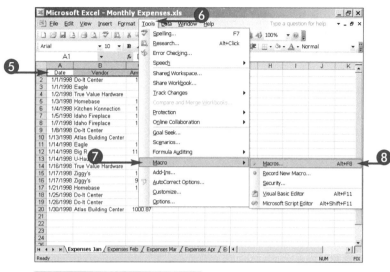

The Macro dialog box appears.

9 Click ⊡ and select the macro source.

10 Click the macro name.

11 Click Run.

The macro runs, and the Macro dialog box disappears.

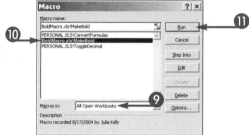

Why can't I run the macros in a specific workbook?

▼ Because your Security setting is set High or Very High and the workbook contains unsigned macros. If your Security setting is High or Very High, you can only run macros that are signed with a certificate from a Certificate Authority. To run the macros, change your Security setting to Medium or Low. To change the Security setting, see the section "Use Macro Virus Protection" in Chapter 4. To sign your own macros, see the sections "Create a Personal Digital Signature," and "Add Your Digital Signature to a Project" in Chapter 4.

What is the Options button in the Macro dialog box for?

▼ The Options button opens the Macro Options dialog box for the selected macro. In the Macro Options dialog box, you see the current Shortcut key and Description comment for the macro, both of which you created when you recorded the macro. You can change the Shortcut key or Description comment, or create a new Shortcut key if you didn't create one when you recorded the macro. Both the Shortcut key and the Description comment are optional. For more information about shortcut keys, see the section "Change a Keyboard Shortcut."

Create a New Toolbar

You can create a larger work area in your workbooks by creating your own custom toolbar and adding the buttons that you use all the time. Then you can hide all the built-in toolbars and display just your custom toolbar, creating more workbook area in which to work.

After you create a macro, running the macro with the click of a button is easier and more efficient than trying to remember the shortcut key you assigned or taking the extra steps to run the macro from the Macro dialog box. You can add custom buttons to built-in toolbars, but if you create

many different macros, you may end up with more custom buttons than fit comfortably on the Standard or Formatting toolbars. You can create a custom toolbar and add to that toolbar both built-in buttons and custom buttons that run macros.

You can create as many custom toolbars as you want and use them floating on the worksheet or docked to the top, bottom, or side of the worksheet. You can rename and delete custom toolbars, but you cannot delete or rename built-in toolbars.

Create a New Toolbar

① Click View.

② Click Toolbars.

③ Click Customize.

You can also right-click in the toolbar area and click Customize on the shortcut menu.

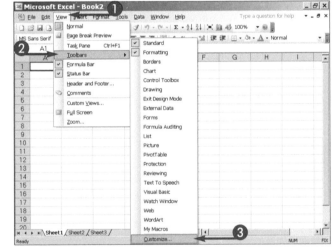

The Customize dialog box appears.

④ Click the Toolbars tab.

⑤ Click New.

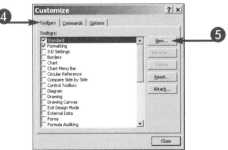

The New Toolbar dialog box appears.

6 Click in the Toolbar name field and type a name for the toolbar.

7 Click OK.

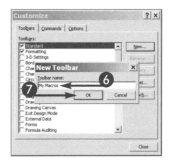

A small, empty toolbar appears.

The name of the new toolbar appears at the bottom of the list of toolbars.

8 Click Close.

● The new toolbar displays.

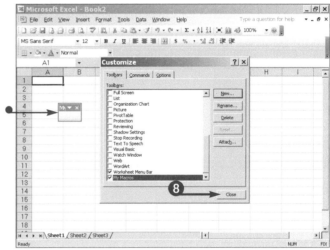

How do I delete or rename a custom toolbar?

▼ Click View, Toolbars, and then Customize. In the Customize dialog box, click the Toolbars tab. To delete a toolbar, click the name of the toolbar you want to delete and then click Delete. After you delete a custom toolbar, you cannot reset it; if you want to recover the toolbar you need to rebuild it. To rename a toolbar, click the name of the toolbar you want to rename and click Rename. Type a new name in the Rename Toolbar dialog box and click OK.

How can I send a custom toolbar to a colleague?

▼ You can attach the custom toolbar to a workbook and send the workbook to the colleague. After opening the workbook, open the Customize dialog box and click the Toolbars tab. Select the toolbar name and click Attach. In the Attach Toolbars dialog box, click the toolbar name in the Custom toolbars list. Click the Copy button and click OK. Save the workbook and send it. The toolbar travels with the workbook. If the buttons run macros, be sure the macros are also in the workbook.

Add Buttons to a Toolbar

You can make your Excel workspace more convenient by adding your favorite buttons to toolbars. You can create a custom toolbar and add just the buttons you use all the time. You can then hide all the built-in toolbars and display just your custom toolbar, creating a larger work area in your workbooks. You can add both built-in and custom buttons to both built-in and custom toolbars.

To make macros more convenient, you can attach them to custom toolbar buttons and then run the macros with just the click of a button. You can keep all your custom macro buttons in one place and easy to find by adding them to one custom toolbar.

To add buttons to a toolbar, click and drag the button command you want from the Customize dialog box onto the toolbar. In the Customize dialog box, the Categories list is equivalent to the built-in menus, and the Commands list shows all the commands in the selected category. Many useful commands in each category are not found on the built-in menus or toolbars, such as the Select Current Region command in the Edit category. The custom buttons for running macros are in the Macros category.

Add Buttons to a Toolbar

① Display the toolbar to which you want to add a button.

Note: To create a custom toolbar, see the section "Create a New Toolbar."

② Click View.

③ Click Toolbars.

④ Click Customize.

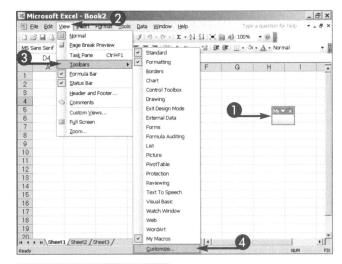

The Customize dialog box appears.

⑤ Click the Commands tab.

Note: To attach a macro to a custom button, see the section "Run a Macro from a Toolbar Button."

The Commands list shows all the buttons for the selected Category.

6 Click a Category.

7 Click and drag the button icon from the Commands list and drop it on the toolbar.

8 Click Close.

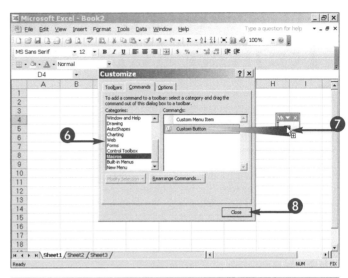

The Customize dialog box disappears.

● The button displays on the toolbar.

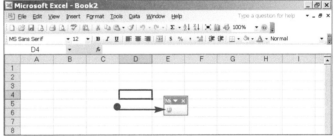

How do I delete a button from a toolbar?	If I delete a button from a toolbar, is it permanently gone?	How can I copy buttons from one toolbar to another?
▼ The easiest way to delete a button is to press and hold down the Alt key while you click and drag the button away from the toolbar. Release the mouse button to drop the toolbar button when you see an X next to the mouse pointer, and then release the Alt key.	▼ Not if the button is a built-in Excel button. You can replace it by adding it from the Customize dialog box or by resetting the built-in toolbar to its default configuration. But if you delete a custom button, it is gone permanently and you must re-create it from scratch.	▼ Display both toolbars. Press and hold down both the Alt key and the Ctrl key while you click and drag the button from one toolbar to the other. Release the mouse button to drop the toolbar button into position on the new toolbar, and then release the Alt and Control keys.

Run a Macro from a Toolbar Button

You can launch a macro quickly by assigning the macro to a custom toolbar button. Running a macro from a toolbar button is efficient because you do not have to remember a keyboard shortcut or click five times to run the macro from the Macro dialog box.

Excel provides a custom toolbar button to which you can assign macros. The Custom button is found in the Macros category in the Customize dialog box. You can create as many custom toolbar buttons as you want, and you can change the button faces or display text instead of a graphic image on the button. You can also give the button any name you want. You can add custom toolbar buttons to built-in toolbars or to custom toolbars you create.

After adding a custom button to a toolbar, you assign the macro to the custom button. When you assign a macro, the Customize dialog box must be open, but you do not use the Customize dialog box. It must remain open while you work on the button, and when you close the dialog box the button is no longer editable.

Run a Macro from a Toolbar Button

① Display the toolbar that holds the button to which you want to attach your macro.

Note: To create custom toolbars and buttons, see the sections "Create a New Toolbar" and "Add Buttons to a Toolbar."

② Click Tools.

③ Click Customize.

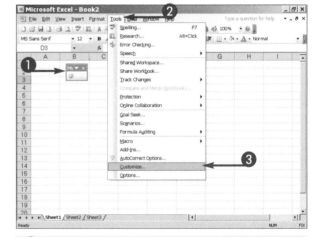

The Customize dialog box appears. You do not use it, but it must be open.

④ Right-click the custom button.

⑤ Click Assign Macro.

The Assign Macro dialog box appears.

6 Select the workbook where the macro is stored.

7 Click the macro name.

8 Click OK.

● The macro is assigned to the button.

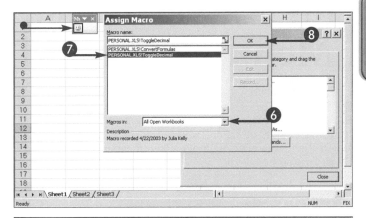

9 Click Close on the Customize dialog box.

● Clicking the button runs the macro.

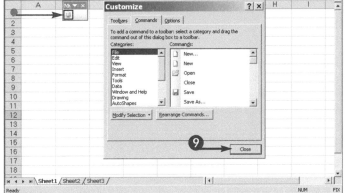

Will editing the macro affect the button that runs it?

▼ No. The button runs whatever code is in the macro. But if you change the macro name, you need to reassign the new macro name to the button. Follow the steps to assign a macro to the button and choose the new macro name in the Assign Macro dialog box.

How do I change the button face?

▼ Open the Customize dialog box and right-click the button on the toolbar. In the shortcut menu, click Change Button Image for a selection of custom faces. Click Edit Button Image to open the Button Editor and recolor or draw a new image. To display just the button name, choose Text Only (Always). The Default Style command displays just the button image.

How do I change the ToolTip label?

▼ Open the Customize dialog box and right-click the button on the toolbar. In the shortcut menu, type a new name in the Name box. The name is both the ToolTip label and the name displayed on the button if you select Text Only (Always). To add a hot key, type an Ampersand (&) left of the hot key character.

Run a Macro from a Menu Command

Y ou can launch a macro quickly by clicking a menu command to which you have assigned the macro. Running a macro from a menu command is convenient because you do not have to remember a keyboard shortcut or click five times to run the macro from the Macro dialog box.

You can assign macros to as many custom menu commands as you want, and you can position the commands on built-in menus or create a separate custom menu on the menu bar to hold all your macro menu commands.

After adding a custom menu command to a menu, you assign the macro to the menu command. When you work with custom menus and commands, the Customize dialog box must be open for the menus and commands to be editable. You do not actually do any work in the Customize dialog box after you drag the menu or command to its new location, but the dialog box must remain open while you work on the menus and commands. When you close the Customize dialog box, the menus and commands are no longer editable.

Run a Macro from a Menu Command

① Open the Customize dialog box.

Note: To show the Customize dialog box, see the section "Run a Macro from a Toolbar Button."

② Click Macros.

③ Click Custom Menu Item.

④ Drag the Custom Menu Item onto the menu name.

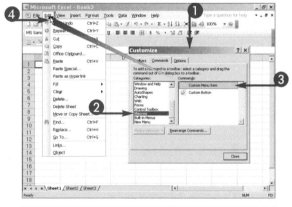

The menu opens.

⑤ Drag the Custom Menu Item into position on the open menu.

The horizontal bar across the menu shows the position of the item.

⑥ Release the mouse button.

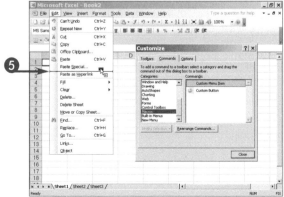

The Custom Menu Item is placed on the menu.

⑦ Right-click the Custom Menu Item.

⑧ Click Assign Macro.

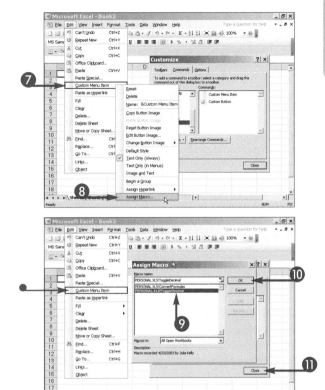

The Assign Macro dialog box appears.

⑨ Click the macro name.

⑩ Click OK.

● The macro is assigned to the menu command.

⑪ Click Close in the Customize dialog box.

Clicking the menu command runs the macro.

How do I create a new menu for the new menu command?

▼ Display the Customize dialog box. On the Commands tab, click the New Menu category and then drag the New Menu command to the menu bar. Release the mouse button when the vertical line is where you want it on the menu bar. This creates a new menu on the menu bar to which you can add custom menu commands.

How do I rename the new menu and commands?

▼ With the Customize dialog box open, right-click the new menu on the menu bar. Type a new name in the Name box and then click in the worksheet to close the shortcut menu and display the new name. Follow a similar procedure to rename custom menu commands by right-clicking on the custom menu command and typing a new name.

How do I create shortcut keys for menus and commands?

▼ A shortcut key enables you to run the command by pressing Alt+the underlined letter. To create shortcut keys for your menus and commands, type an ampersand (&) to the left of the shortcut key letter in the name. You cannot use a shortcut key that is already used by another menu or command.

Run a Macro from a Graphical Object

S ending a workbook in which a graphical object is stored is a convenient way to make a macro available to another user. You can assign a macro to any graphical object, including objects you draw using the Drawing toolbar buttons, clip art, or pictures you insert. After you create a graphical object on a worksheet, you assign the macro to the object.

Unlike toolbar buttons and menu commands, graphical objects are only available on the worksheet where they exist. However, if you copy a worksheet, any graphical

objects with macros attached are functional as long as the macro is available to the workbook where you paste the copy. You can also copy the graphical object itself to another worksheet or workbook, and the object keeps the attached macro.

To select the object without running the macro, right-click the object and then click on the dotted border. The shortcut menu disappears, and you can move, reshape, format, or change the text in the object. Click in the worksheet to deselect the object and make the macro functional again.

Run a Macro from a Graphical Object

1 Insert or draw a graphical object on the worksheet.

2 Right-click the graphical object.

3 Click Assign Macro.

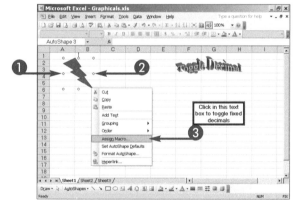

The Assign Macro dialog box appears.

4 Click the macro name.

5 Click OK.

6 Click in the worksheet to deselect the object.

The macro runs when you click the object.

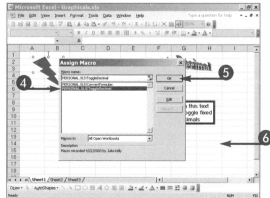

Change a Keyboard Shortcut

Y ou can make a macro easier to run from your keyboard by changing the shortcut key, or by adding a shortcut key, if you did not create one when you recorded the macro.

When you record a macro, the keyboard shortcut is optional; but after you create the macro you may find that either you want to use a shortcut key and did not create one, or the shortcut you created is inconvenient and you want to change it.

Most keyboard shortcuts in Excel, such as Ctrl+C to copy or Ctrl+Z to undo, are already assigned to an action. When you assign a shortcut key that is already in use as a built-in program shortcut key, your new macro shortcut key overrides the built-in shortcut key. It may be difficult to find a convenient shortcut key that you do not already use occasionally; but if you include the Shift key in your shortcut key, many Ctrl+Shift keystrokes are available. To include the Shift key in your keyboard shortcut, press the Shift key while you type the shortcut letter in the Shortcut key box.

Change a Keyboard Shortcut

1 Click Tools.

2 Click Macro.

3 Click Macros.

The Macro dialog box appears.

4 Click the name of the macro.

5 Click Options.

The Macro Options dialog box appears.

6 Click in the Shortcut key field and type the shortcut key.

7 Click OK.

8 Click Cancel in the Macro dialog box.

Pressing the new shortcut key runs the macro.

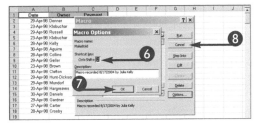

Record a Macro with Relative References

You can record a macro that selects a cell some distance from the active cell — rather than a specific cell — by recording relative references. For example, you can record a macro that writes a formula in the cell below a list. No matter how long the list is, if the last cell is the active cell, the macro selects the cell below it.

A relative reference refers to a cell that is located some rows and columns away from the active cell. When you click the Relative Reference button while recording a macro, the recorder writes any cell selections from that point forward as *relative* to the previous cell.

Relative references use the `Offset` property of the `ActiveCell` object. The arguments for the `Offset` property are (`rows, columns`). Positive numbers refer to the number of rows down or columns to the right of the active cell. Negative numbers refer to the number of rows up or columns to the left of the active cell.

For example, the selection statement `ActiveCell.Offset(-2, 3).Range("A1").Select` selects a cell that is two rows up and three columns right from the active cell.

Record a Macro with Relative References

① Click a cell.

② Right-click the toolbar area and select Visual Basic from the drop-down list.

③ On the Visual Basic toolbar, click the Record Macro button (⊙).

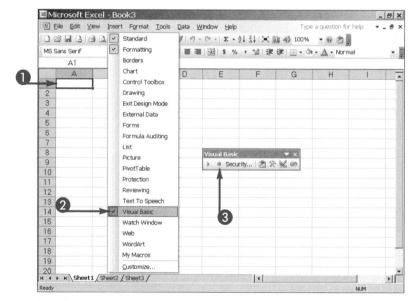

The Record Macro dialog box appears.

④ Click in the Macro name field and type a name for the macro.

⑤ Click in the Shortcut key field and type a character to create a shortcut key.

⑥ In the Store macro in box, click ⊡ and select the notebook where you want to store your macro.

⑦ Click OK.

The Stop Recording toolbar appears.

8 Click the Relative Reference button (▦).

9 Click a cell four columns to the right of the cell you clicked in step **1**.

The recorder writes a relative selection four columns to the right of where you started (in cell A1).

10 Click the Stop Recording button (▣).

11 Select any cell in the worksheet.

12 Run the macro.

● The macro selects the cell four columns right of the active cell you selected in step **11**.

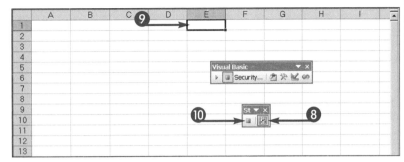

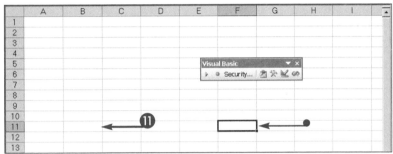

How do I turn relative references off?

▼ To turn relative references off, click the Relative Reference button again. Turning off the Relative Reference button before you click the Stop Recording button is a good practice because if you leave it turned on, the next time you record a macro, the recorder records using relative references until you notice that the button is depressed and turn it off. While you record a macro, you can turn relative references on and off as many times as necessary.

How can I record a macro to choose the last cell in a list that changes length?

▼ You can record a macro that chooses the last cell in a list of any length by changing your selection method. Select a cell in a list and then start the macro recorder. Press Ctrl+Down Arrow. The active cell jumps to the last cell in that column. It does not matter if relative references are on or off because the recorder writes the same code for both. The recorder writes Selection.End(xlDown). Select, and the macro selects the cell at the bottom of the list no matter where the starting point is.

Record a Worksheet Template Macro

You can record a macro to create identical new copies of a worksheet, just as if you opened a worksheet template, but faster and using fewer computer resources. If you repeatedly use new copies of the same worksheet, such as an invoice or a sales list, you can record a macro that enters the worksheet labels, formulas, formatting, and header for you whenever you need a new empty copy of that worksheet. For example, if you keep all invoices in a specific workbook, you can run a macro to prepare a worksheet whenever you want to create a new invoice in your invoice workbook.

If you store the macro in This Workbook, the macro travels with the workbook to other computers, such as a home computer, and you can create a new copy of the worksheet without needing to keep a separate template file in the computer.

If the worksheet is complex, planning and running through creating a copy of the worksheet before you record the macro saves time. If you plan and perform the actions in an orderly manner as you record the macro, the resulting macro is much easier to read and runs faster.

Record a Worksheet Template Macro

① Start the macro recorder.

Note: To start the macro recorder, see Chapter 1.

● The Stop Recording toolbar appears when the macro recorder begins recording.

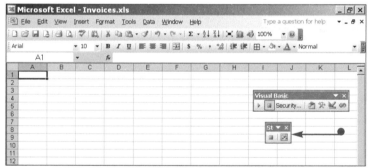

② Set up the worksheet template with all labels, formulas, formatting, headers, and footers.

③ When the worksheet is complete, click 🔲 to stop recording.

The macro is complete.

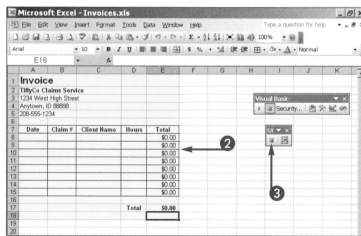

④ Click a Sheet tab to open a blank worksheet in which to run the macro.

⑤ Open the Macro dialog box.

You can press Alt+F8 or click Tools→Macro→ Macros to open the Macro dialog box.

Note: *To run a macro from the Macros dialog box, see the section "Run a Macro" in Chaper 2.*

⑥ Click Run.

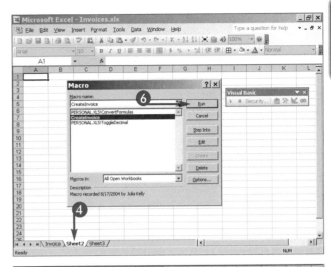

● The macro creates an identical new copy of the worksheet you recorded.

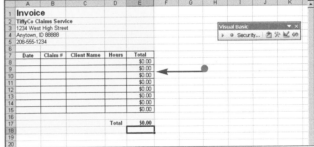

How can I correct a mistake in the macro without recording the whole macro again?

▼ You can edit the macro to correct misspellings, change cell and range selections, change object properties, and change anything else in the procedure. Click Tools, Macro, and then Macros. Select the macro name, click Edit, and make your changes in the code window. For example, if you recorded a misspelled a text entry, you can open the macro in the Visual Basic Editor, find the misspelling, and correct it. Be sure you do not delete the quote marks around the text entry. Finally, save the macro.

How can I protect the original macro before I edit it?

▼ If you test an edited macro before you save it, your changes may result in an endless loop or cause Excel to crash. You can protect the original macro code by copying and pasting the entire procedure to a text file such as Word or Notepad. After that, make your edits in the macro, save the workbook and macro, and test the edited macro. You can also test your edited statements in the Immediate window before you make any edits in the code window.

Convert Formulas to Values

You can reduce the number of steps necessary to convert formulas to constant values by recording the procedure as a macro. Without a macro, you copy the range of formulas, click Edit, Copy, Edit again, Paste Special, select Values in the Paste Special dialog box to convert all the selected formulas to their current values, and then click OK. With a macro, you press a shortcut key or click a button.

For example, if you have a worksheet that uses text formulas such as CONCATENATE to combine the entries in separate cells, such as First Name and Last Name, you need

to convert the formula results to values before you delete the precedent cells — the First Name and Last Name cells that the formulas connect together using the function. If you store the macro in the Personal Macro Workbook, it is available to any workbook.

You can create a range of mock data for testing with the Random function =rand(), which results in random numbers between 0 and 1 that are regenerated every time the workbook is recalculated.

① Click and drag to select the cells containing the formulas you want to convert.

Note: *Select the cells before you record the macro so you do not record cell selection.*

② Start the macro recorder.

Note: *To start the macro recorder, see Chapter 1.*

● The Stop Recording toolbar appears.

③ Click the Copy button (📋).

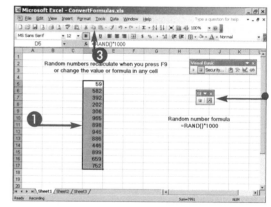

A flashing border appears around the copied selection.

④ Click Edit.

⑤ Click Paste Special.

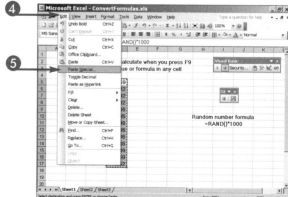

The Paste Special dialog box appears.

6 Click Values (○ changes to ⊙).

7 Click OK.

The formulas convert to values.

8 Press the Escape key.

The flashing border disappears.

9 Click ☐ to stop recording.

The Stop Recording toolbar disappears.

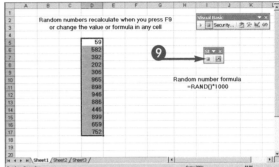

10 Open a worksheet containing formulas.

11 Click and drag to select a range of formulas.

12 Run the macro.

The formulas in the selected range convert to values.

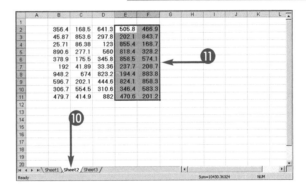

Why did my macro disappear?

▼ If you stored the macro in This Workbook when you recorded it, and then closed the workbook without saving so you could test the new macro on your formulas, you lost the macro you recorded as well as the converted values. If you save the macro in the Personal Macro Workbook, the macro is available even after you close This Workbook without saving. When you store or edit a macro in the Personal Macro Workbook, you are asked to save the Personal Macro Workbook when you close Excel.

Why does my macro only run in specific cells?

▼ If you selected cells after you started the macro recorder, your macro recorded the selection of those specific cells as the first step in the procedure. To fix the macro without rerecording it, open the macro for editing and delete the entire opening selection line — the line that reads `Range("cell address:cell address").Select` — and then run the macro again to test it. Without the selection statement, the macro runs in whatever range is currently selected.

Cut and Paste a Dynamic Range of Cells

Y ou can record a macro that will cut and paste ranges of different sizes, which makes the macro usable on many different datasets. A range that can change in length, such as a daily sales list, is called a *dynamic* range.

To record cutting a dynamic range, record the selection of all the cells below the active cells in a list, and then record pasting the cells to a new location. The recorded macro contains five statements you can reduce to three by editing the macro after you record it. Reducing the number of statements makes the macro run faster and easier to read.

After cutting the cells, record where to paste them. The `Selection.Cut` statement has an optional argument, `Destination`, that enables you to tell the macro where to paste the cut cells immediately, rather than using two more statements to select a paste location and then paste the cells. The Cut method, edited to add the `Destination` argument, reads `Selection.Cut Destination:=Range("cell name")`. Because the macro pastes dynamic ranges, you use a single cell address as the paste range so that it does not matter how large the range is.

Cut and Paste a Dynamic Range of Cells

① Select the cell or cells at the top of a list of entries.

Note: Select the cells before you start recording.

② Start the macro recorder.

Note: To start the macro recorder, see Chapter 1.

③ Press Ctrl+Shift+Down Arrow.

The cells below the active cells are selected.

④ Click the Cut button ([✂]).

● The selected range has a flashing border around it.

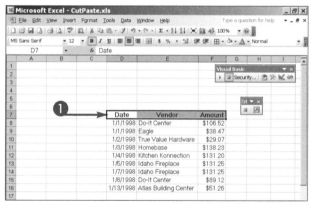

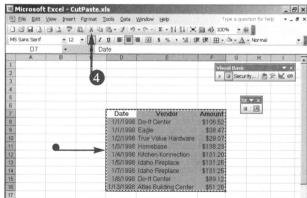

36

⑤ Click in the cell where you want to paste.

⑥ Click the Paste button (🖺).

The cut range is pasted.

⑦ Click 🔲 to stop recording.

⑧ Open the macro in the Visual Basic Editor.

⑨ At the end of the `Selection.Cut` statement, type the argument **destination: =range("cell address")** .

The paste destination in this example is cell A1.

⑩ Select the last two statements and press Delete.

⑪ Click the Close button (🗙) to close the Visual Basic Editor.

⑫ Run the macro.

Run the macro on a different worksheet from where you recorded the macro.

The macro cuts the dynamic range and pastes it to the range you set in the `Destination` argument in step **9**. The range from which the data was cut remains highlighted.

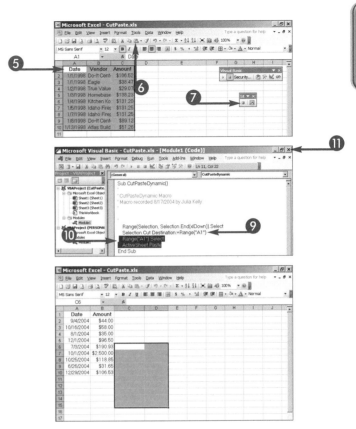

How can I have the macro AutoFit the pasted cell columns?

▼ To best fit the data after the range is pasted, you can use the `AutoFit` method to resize the columns in the destination area. Below the `Selection .Cut Destination:=Range("cell address")` statement in the procedure, type the new statement `Range("column letter:column letter").Columns.AutoFit`. Be sure the AutoFit column range matches the destination cell range. For example, if your destination range is cell A1, the AutoFit range selection should be (A:A). After the range is pasted into your designated paste cell, that entire column is resized to AutoFit all the entries.

How can I paste the range near the cut range without specifying a cell?

▼ You can paste the cut range to an offset range, away from the location of the cut range. For example, to paste the range two cells to the left of the cut range, type this destination argument in the `Selection.Cut` statement: `Destination: =ActiveCell.Offset(0, -2).Range("A1")`. This destination argument pastes the range two columns left of the cut location. If the cut range is located too close to the left edge of the worksheet, you get an error because the range cannot be pasted off the edge of the worksheet.

Sort a List

You can record a macro to sort a list or table and then use that macro alone for repetitive sorting tasks in similar lists, or as a short sub-procedure in a longer VBA procedure. You can record sorting a list using the Sort buttons on the Standard toolbar, or you can record the sorting macro using the Sort dialog box. If you sort by multiple fields, a macro recorded using the Sort dialog box is shorter and more compact than a macro recorded with the toolbar buttons.

If you want to record sorting multiple fields using the toolbar Sort buttons, remember to sort by minor fields first, and then sort by progressively more major sort fields. If you use the Sort dialog box, record sorting by the major field first and then progressively more minor or detailed fields.

The macro recorder records the exact procedure you perform on the worksheet, including specific cell and range selections for the list. Every time you use the recorded macro, the exact same range is selected; in other words, the macro does not work on longer or shorter lists unless you edit the initial range selection statement to select and sort the Current Region.

Sort a List

① Start the macro recorder.

Note: To start the macro recorder, see Chapter 1.

② Select a cell in the column according to which you want to sort the list.

③ On the Standard toolbar, click a Sort button ( ).

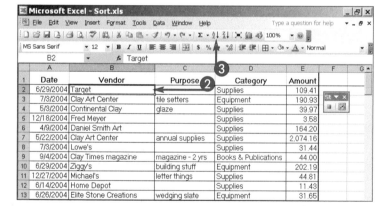

● The list is sorted according to the field you selected in step **2**.

④ Click a cell in a different column to sort the list according to a second field.

⑤ On the Standard toolbar, click .

● The list is sorted according to the second field you selected.

⑥ Click ▣ to stop recording.

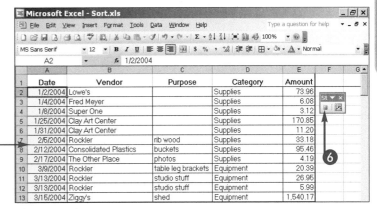

⑦ Resort the list according to a different field so you can test the macro.

⑧ Run the macro.

The macro sorts the list.

How can I edit this macro to sort lists of different lengths?

▼ Edit the range selection statement at the beginning of the macro to select the *current region*, which is the entire list around the active cell. The first line in the recorded macro selects the absolute range of this list. For the macro to work on a list of any length, the macro must always select the current region and then run the sort procedure on that selected range. Edit the macro to replace the initial selection statement `Range("cell").Select` with the statement `Selection.CurrentRegion.Select`. Then edit statements that begin with `Range("cell:cell").Sort Key1:` to read `Selection.Sort Key1:`.

How can I edit this macro to sort by a different order?

▼ You can edit the Order arguments in the macro to use the `xlAscending` or `xlDescending` sort order constants. You enter or change the sort order constant in the `Order` argument that follows the specific `Key` argument that you want to sort. For example, if your recorded macro shows `Sort Key1:=Range("B2"), Order1:=xlAscending` as part of the statement, the macro is sorting column B in ascending order. To change the sort order to descending, replace the `xlAscending` constant with `xlDescending`.

Filter and Subtotal a List

You can record a macro to turn on the AutoFilter in a list and add a SUBTOTAL function below the list. The list is set up for filtering, and when a user selects a different filter criterion, the list is still correctly subtotaled. The SUBTOTAL function calculates only the visible cells in a range, so the formula result always calculates the filtered range.

This macro starts by writing a SUBTOTAL formula at the bottom of a list, and the macro uses relative references so it does not matter how long the list is. You record writing the

SUBTOTAL formula first because you want it placed two cells below the unfiltered list. If the formula is placed in a cell directly below the list, Excel considers the formula part of the list and the formula may be hidden when the list is filtered. You record the placement of the formula with relative references so that the formula is written two cells below the bottom of the list regardless of length.

After writing the formula, the macro turns on the AutoFilter and sets a specific filter criterion. After running the macro, the user can change the filter criteria because the AutoFilter is turned on.

Filter and subtotal a List

① Start the macro recorder.

Note: To start the macro recorder, see Chapter 1.

The Stop Recording toolbar appears.

② Check to make sure the Relative Reference button (▦) is turned off, not depressed or highlighted, so that you begin to record absolute references.

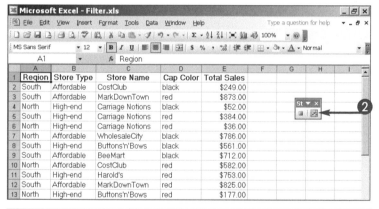

③ Click the cell at the top of the column of which you want to subtotal.

Cell E1, in the Total Sales column, is clicked.

④ Click ▦ to turn the Relative References button on.

You want to record the relative location of the subtotal formula so the macro runs on a list of any length.

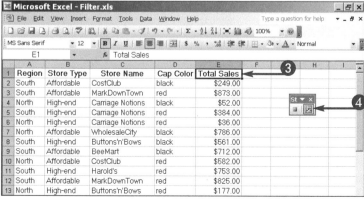

5 Press Ctrl+Down Arrow key.

● The active cell jumps to the last entry in column E.

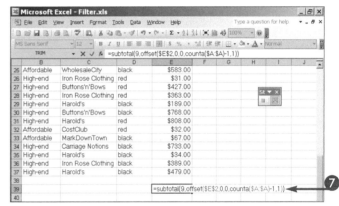

6 Press the Down Arrow key twice.

The active cell moves down two cells.

7 Type the formula **=subtotal(9,(offset($E$2,0,0,counta($A:$A)-1,1))**.

This formula subtotals a dynamic range that includes all the cells in the column.

8 Press Enter.

Why do I get a Circular Reference error when I run this macro?

▼ Because you may have placed the subtotal formula at the bottom of the column in which the formula is counting rows. In this example, the formula counts the entries in column A and uses that number to determine how many rows to include in the subtotal formula. The circular reference tells you that the formula is trying to include the formula itself in the formula. Be sure to write the formula in a cell that is not in the column counted in the COUNTA part of the nested SUBTOTAL formula.

Why am I getting a Circular Reference error even though my formula is in column E?

▼ If you have other entries in column A below the list, the offset function counts those entries when it counts the number of rows to include in the subtotal formula. If you have two or more entries in column A below the list, the formula adds those rows to the COUNTA calculation. That means the formula is including its own row and trying to include itself in its calculation. For this dynamic formula to work, there cannot be any entries in column A other than those in the table.

continued

Filter and Subtotal a List

(Continued)

This macro writes a SUBTOTAL formula with a nested *dynamic* OFFSET function. Dynamic means that the formula adjusts to any length of list that you want to subtotal. The OFFSET function has a nested COUNTA function that counts the number of rows in the table to determine a range, and then provides that number to the SUBTOTAL function for summing.

The nested function OFFSET($E$2,0,0,COUNTA($A:$A) -1,1) tells Excel to set a range beginning in cell E2, count down 0 rows and over 0 columns (so the range begins exactly in E2), and then make the range as many rows deep as there are entries in column A (less one so as not to include the header) and 1 column wide.

Because the nested function COUNTA counts all the entries in column A to determine the number of rows to calculate, there cannot be any entries in column A below the list, nor any blank cells in column A within the list.

The OFFSET function is nested in the SUBTOTAL function as the range argument =SUBTOTAL(9,(OFFSET ($E$2,0,0,COUNTA($A:$A)-1,1)))).

Type all the function names in lowercase. If you misspell one, Excel does not capitalize it, which is how you know if a function is spelled wrong.

Filter and Subtotal a List *(continued)*

⑨ Click 🔲 to turn the Relative References button off.

Note: *From here on you do not want to record relative references.*

⑩ Press Ctrl+Home.

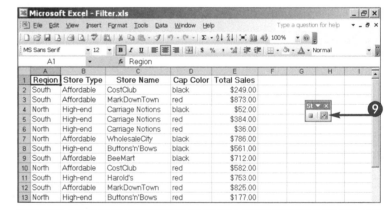

- Cell A1 is selected.

⑪ Click Data.

⑫ Click Filter.

⑬ Click AutoFilter.

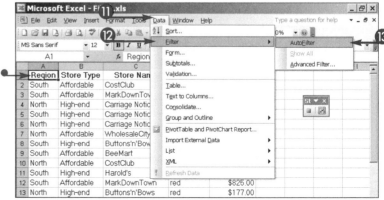

AutoFilter buttons appear on the column headers.

⑭ Click the Filter arrow (▾) in the column you want to filter.

⑮ Click a criterion for the filter.

In this example, the criterion Carriage Notions is selected in the Store Name field.

⑯ Click ▣ to stop recording.

The recorded macro is complete.

⑰ Save the workbook and macro.

⑱ Repeat steps **11** to **13** to remove the AutoFilter.

⑲ Delete the SUBTOTAL formula.

⑳ Add or delete rows of data to test the dynamic formula.

㉑ Run the macro.

The macro filters and subtotals the list.

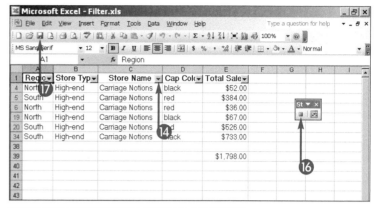

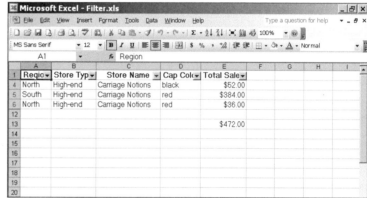

Where can I learn more about the SUBTOTAL and OFFSET functions?

▼ In the Excel help files. The fastest way to get help on a specific function is to click Insert and then click Function. In the Function Wizard, select the function you want help with, and then click the Help On This Function link in the lower-left corner of the dialog box.

Why does the macro use a SUBTOTAL function instead of a SUM function?

▼ Because SUBTOTAL calculates only the visible, filtered cells. When you change the filter criteria, the SUBTOTAL result changes to calculate the new set of filtered cells, whereas the SUM function sums all the cells in the range, even if the range is filtered. The first argument in the SUBTOTAL function, the number 9, tells Excel to SUM the numbers in the range.

Subtotal a List

You can record a timesaving macro to subtotal detailed lists that you need to summarize on a regular basis, such as a list of business expenses. When data is subtotaled, the data is summarized in an outline structure, and the user can then show or hide any level of detail they want.

When you subtotal a list by two or more fields, you must subtotal the major field — the major sort key — first. Then you can add progressively more minor or detailed fields to

subtotal. Remember to clear the Replace current subtotals check box before you add more levels of subtotals, or you lose the previous subtotals.

To make subtotaling effective, you must sort the data before you subtotal it. To make the macro even more efficient, you can first record a macro to sort the data and then record the macro to subtotal the sorted data; after that, either string the macros together or copy and paste the statements from the two macros into a single macro.

Subtotal a List

① Start the macro recorder.

Note: To start the macro recorder, see Chapter 1.

The Stop Recording toolbar appears.

② Click cell A1.

Even if cell A1 is already selected, you need to record the selection of the upper-left corner of the list to start the macro.

This example data is already sorted by Category and then by Vendor.

③ Click Data.

④ Click Subtotals.

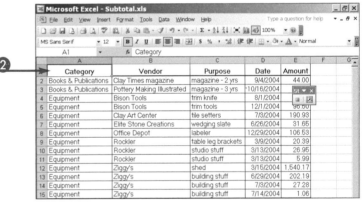

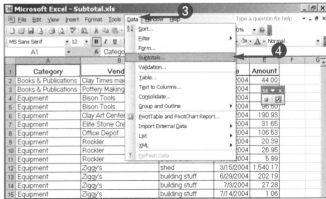

The Subtotals dialog box appears.

5 In the At each change in field, click ⊡ and select the major sort key.

6 In the Use function field, click ⊡ and select a calculation.

In this example the Sum function is selected.

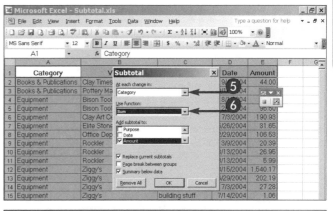

7 Click an option for the numeric field to subtotal, making sure the other options are deselected (☐ changes to ☑).

In this example the Amount field is subtotaled.

8 Click OK.

The list is subtotaled at the first level.

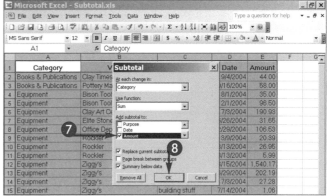

Why do I need to record the selection of cell A1 to start the macro?

▼ The Subtotal procedure selects the current region around the active cell, so the macro places the active cell within the list before running the Subtotal feature. Initially selecting cell A1 also means that the list you want the macro to subtotal must start in cell A1. If you routinely have other worksheet information in the first few rows, you can select a different cell to start the macro, or select the initial cell before starting to record so that the macro runs from the active cell, wherever it is.

Can I use this macro on other kinds of lists?

▼ Yes, as long as the list structure is the same. In the completed macro, the first Selection.subtotal statement selects the entire list around the active cell, regardless of size. Then the macro groups and calculates the columns corresponding to the fields you selected in the macro, regardless of the column headings. The macro records your field selections as Column1, Column5, and so on. You can run this macro on different lists as long the list is organized with columns to be grouped and calculated in the same positions.

continued

Subtotal a List
(Continued)

This macro records subtotaling on two levels and leaves the worksheet ready for quick analysis; but you can record the macro to subtotal as many levels as you want, and leave the list showing whatever level of detail you select as the last step in the macro. The user can change the detail level to whatever level they need after the macro has run.

If you store the macro in This Workbook and then save the workbook when you are finished, the macro remains in the subtotaled workbook even if you close it and reopen it. This is advantageous if you need to send the workbook and macro to someone else.

If you save the macro in the Personal Macro Workbook, you can use it in any workbook you have open, as long as the list you want to subtotal is organized in the same way as the list in which you recorded the macro. If you save the macro in the Personal Macro Workbook and then subtotal a workbook and send the workbook to another user, the macro does not travel with the workbook, but the subtotaling performed by the macro remains intact and functional in the workbook.

Subtotal a List *(continued)*

⑨ Click Data.

⑩ Click Subtotals.

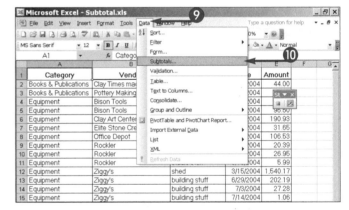

The Subtotals dialog box opens again.

⑪ In the At each change in field, click ⬇ and select the second level subtotal field.

Leave the same selections in the Use function and the Add subtotal to boxes.

⑫ Uncheck the Replace Current Subtotals check box (☑ changes to ☐).

⑬ Click OK.

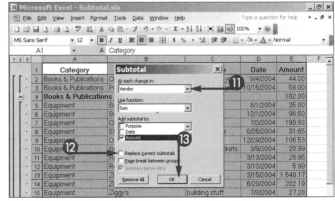

The list is subtotaled on two levels.

⓮ Click a Level button to hide subtotal details.

In this example, the level 3 button is clicked.

⓯ Click ■ to stop recording.

⓰ Click the Save button (■).

The workbook and macro are saved.

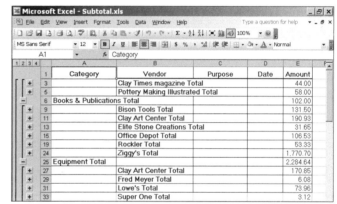

⓱ Open a similarly organized list to subtotal.

You can remove the subtotals in this list by clicking Data and then Subtotals. After that, click the Remove All button in the lower-left corner of the dialog box.

⓲ Run the macro.

The list is subtotaled.

Why do I have subtotals in columns other than the numeric column I set?

▼ Because when you set up the Subtotal dialog box, you had other check boxes marked in the Add Subtotal To list. Subtotals are only of value in columns that list numeric entries, such as sales or quantities, so when you set up a subtotal you need to be sure that only check boxes for fields you want subtotaled are marked.

Why did my second-level subtotals erase the first level of subtotals?

▼ Because in the Subtotal dialog box you left the Replace Current Subtotals check box marked. That check box tells Excel to run an entirely new set of subtotals on the data, which is useful if the data in the list has changed. If you clear the Replace Current Subtotals check box, you can add more levels of subtotals to the existing subtotals.

What are the other options for subtotaling?

▼ You can subtotal the same group with multiple functions, such as SUM and AVERAGE, by adding another subtotal with a different function to the same fields. Remember to clear the Replace current subtotals check box. You can also set up the worksheet to print each subtotal group on a different page if you mark the Page break between groups check box.

Make a Macro Easier to Read

You can make your macro code easier to read by inserting indents and comments. The recorder inserts indents and comments when it records a macro, but when you edit or write your own code, you must insert indents and comments yourself. Even after you have recorded the macro, inserting more comments makes the macro easier to understand.

For example, if you record creating Page Setup entries on a worksheet, the macro writes a With-statement, or *block*. The With block enables you to execute several *statements* (or actions) on an *object* (the active worksheet page setup) without having to repeat the name of the object again. A With block begins with a statement that reads

`With objectname` and ends in the statement `End With`. If the subordinate statements in the block are indented, your eye can find the beginning and end of the With block more easily.

Comments save a great deal of time when you and other people need to understand or edit code you wrote many months ago. Neither indents nor comments are required in a procedure, but they make the procedure easier to understand quickly. Comments start with an apostrophe and can run to the end of the line in the Visual Basic Editor Code window. You can type comments on separate lines or type following a macro statement, as long as they begin with an apostrophe.

Insert comments

① Open the macro in the Visual Basic Editor.

Note: To open a macro in the Visual Basic Editor, see Chapter 1.

In this example macro, there are no comments.

② Click where you want to start the comment, and type an apostrophe (') and then the comment text.

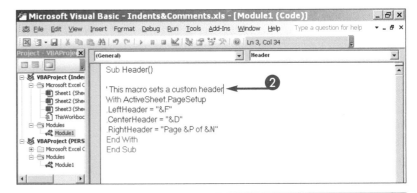

③ Press Enter, or click away from the comment line.

The comment text turns green.

You can enter comments anywhere in the macro as long as the comments begin with an apostrophe (').

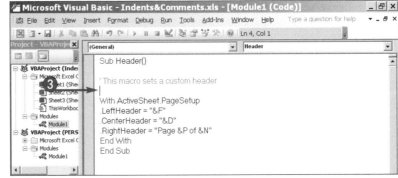

Indent lines

In this example macro, the statements are all left aligned.

1 Click to position the mouse ⬉ to the left of a statement.

2 Press Tab.

The statement is indented.

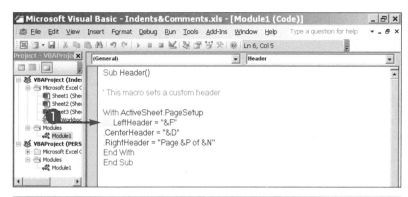

3 Repeat steps **1** and **2** to indent additional statements.

The macro is much easier to read and understand when appropriate statements are indented.

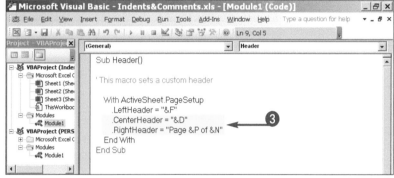

How do comments and indents affect the macro?

▼ Indents and comments have no effect on the macro, other than making the macro easier to read, which is helpful when you need to edit code that you wrote a long time ago. Comments simply remind you of what each statement does and why you included it. Comments are also helpful to other people who need to use or edit procedures you wrote.

Are there any rules for indenting?

▼ No, just use indents to make your code easier to follow visually. Programmers usually indent subordinate statements, such as those that refer to the same object in a With block, or when parsing a long statement into shorter statements. You can indent lines farther by pressing the Tab key again, and you can unindent lines with either Backspace or Shift+Tab.

How else can I use comments in a macro?

▼ You can use comments to disable statements in a macro when you are debugging a macro. If you type an apostrophe to the left of a macro statement in the Code window, the statement becomes a comment and is ignored when the macro runs, which can help you determine if a particular statement is causing an error.

Simplify Macro Statements

You can make your recorded macros easier to read and faster to run by breaking long lines of code into shorter ones and deleting unnecessary lines. When the macro recorder records a very long statement, the statement does not fit on a single line in the code window. A good example of this is the single statement the recorder generates if you record converting formulas to values:

```
Selection.PasteSpecial Paste:=xlValues,
Operation:=xlNone, SkipBlanks:=False,
Transpose:=False
```

The Visual Basic Editor breaks the statement into separate lines with an underscore character (_) at the break point. The underscore tells Excel that the statement continues on the next line, but the broken segments that Excel creates are still too long to read easily. Rather than scrolling back and forth across the code window, you can break the long statement into shorter segments by adding an underscore character at the end of each segment.

You can also delete extra arguments when the recorder writes more code than is necessary. An *argument* is the segment of a statement that tells Excel how to do something. The arguments in a recorded macro always include all the options available in any dialog box. You can delete unnecessary arguments.

Simplify Macro Statements

① Open a macro for editing in the Visual Basic Editor.

The macro shown converts formulas to values.

② Click to position the mouse ▷ where you want to break the line.

The cursor appears at the beginning of the segment that will start the new line.

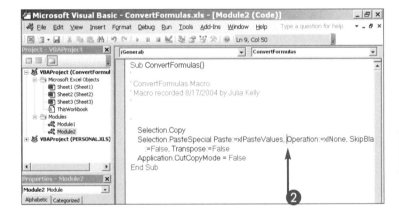

③ Type an underscore character (_).

④ Press Enter.

● The statement breaks to a new line after the underscore.

⑤ Repeat steps **3** and **4** every place you want to break the statement.

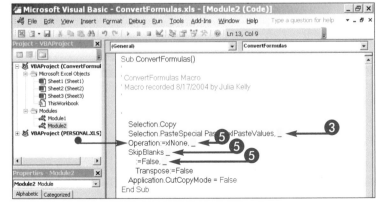

Underscores and line breaks where Excel originally broke the statement are deleted.

In this example, every comma in the original statement is followed by a space and an underscore.

⑥ To delete an unnecessary segment, select the entire segment.

⑦ Press Delete.

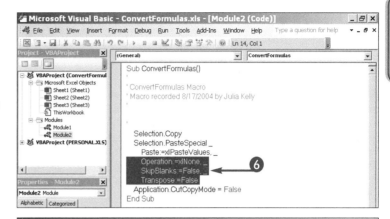

Unnecessary arguments are deleted, and the macro is simplified.

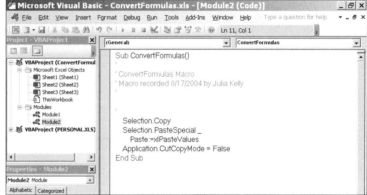

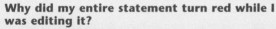

Why did my entire statement turn red while I was editing it?

▼ Because you made a mistake in your edit, or you have not finished your edit. Excel uses the red color to remind you that the statement is not correct yet. Continue editing, and when the statement syntax is correct, the red color disappears. Common syntax errors include extra commas where none are needed, extra underscores or a missing underscore, or a missing space character. To learn the proper syntax, record the macro again and look closely at how Excel writes the code.

Why does my Stop Recording toolbar not appear when I record?

▼ Your Stop Recording toolbar does not appear because you closed it while you were recording a macro. Normally the toolbar appears when you start recording and disappears when you stop recording; to reset the automatic behavior of the toolbar, you need to start recording another macro. When the recorder starts, click View→Toolbars→ Stop Recording to open the Stop Recording toolbar. Click the Stop Recording button on the toolbar and delete the empty macro you recorded.

Rename a Macro

After you create the macro, you can rename it to something more recognizable. If you want to save a test macro that you created, but Excel has given it a generic name like Macro21, you can give the macro a more descriptive name of your own. Alternatively, if you create two macros that are similar and you want them to have names that are easy to differentiate, you can change the name of either macro.

To change a macro name, you must open the macro in the Visual Basic Editor, change the name in the Sub line at the top of the macro code, and then save the macro and

workbook. If a macro has an event associated with it, the macro name is followed by an underscore (_) and then the event name. When you rename the macro, do not delete the underscore or the event name because that removes the launch event from the macro.

If the macro was assigned to a toolbar button, menu command, or graphical object, the object tries to run a macro that no longer exists after you rename it. You need to reassign the renamed macro to the object.

Rename a Macro

① Open the macro in the Visual Basic Editor.

Note: To open a macro for editing, see Chapter 1.

② Select the macro name in the Sub line.

The macro name is the single word to the right of the keyword Sub.

③ Type the new macro name to replace the old name.

Remember to follow macro-naming rules.

④ Click the Save button (🖫) to save the macro and workbook.

The macro is renamed.

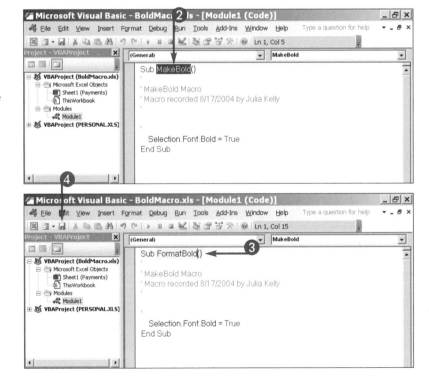

Password-Protect a Macro

Y ou can prevent others from reading, editing, or copying any of the macros in a workbook by locking and password protecting the entire VBA project, which includes all of the VBA code in the workbook. After you lock a project, the project cannot be viewed or edited unless it is unlocked using the password you set.

You set password protection in the Visual Basic Editor's VBAProject Properties dialog box for the project you want to lock. After you lock the project, you must save and close the workbook for the lock to take effect.

When you attempt to open a locked project in the Visual Basic Editor, you are asked for the password before anything in the project opens. Like all passwords in Microsoft programs, you cannot recover lost passwords in Excel.

To remove password protection, open the workbook and the Visual Basic Editor. Use the password to open the project, and then open the VBAProject Properties dialog box. On the Protection tab, clear the Lock project for viewing check box, and then save and close the workbook.

Password-Protect a Macro

① Open the Visual Basic Editor.

② In the Project window, right-click the Project name.

   The Project name is the same as the workbook name.

③ Click VBAProject Properties.

   The Project Properties dialog box appears.

④ Click the Protection tab.

⑤ Click the Lock project for viewing option (☐ changes to ☑).

⑥ Click in the Password field and type a password to view project properties.

⑦ Click in the Confirm password field and retype the same password.

⑧ Click OK.

⑨ Click 🖫 to save the workbook.

⑩ Click the Close button (☒) to close the workbook.

   The project, which contains the VBA code for the workbook, is password protected.

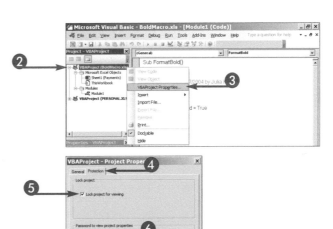

Use Macro Virus Protection

Y ou can protect your computer from macro viruses by setting an appropriate level of macro security. A macro virus is a macro that can do some damage in a workbook — such as overwrite text or delete sections of data — when you perform an action that triggers the macro to run. Most macro viruses also spread to other workbooks on your computer or network.

Because macro viruses are so easy to spread, Excel has protection built in. Even if someone sends you a file without realizing that it is infected with a macro virus, you can be warned that a macro is present before you open the file.

The Excel macro security feature enables you to choose one of four settings: Low, Medium, High, and Very High. Low allows all macros to run with no warnings. Medium warns you when you open a workbook that contains a macro, and gives you the opportunity to enable or disable macros before opening the workbook. High allows only signed macros from trusted sources to run and disables all others. Very High allows only macros in trusted locations to run and disables all others, even if they are signed.

Use Macro Virus Protection

① Click Tools.

② Click Macro.

③ Click Security.

The Security dialog box appears.

④ Click the Security Level tab to display the options.

● You can click the Help button (⁇) to open help files about security and macro viruses.

⑤ Click a security option (◯ changes to ◉).

⑥ Click OK.

Your macro security level is set.

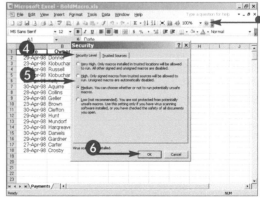

Create a Personal Digital Signature

Y ou can avoid being asked to Enable or Disable Macros every time you open your workbooks that contain macros by creating and using a personal digital signature for your own macros. When you create and use a personal digital signature, Excel opens your signed workbooks without the Medium level security query. When you edit a macro, the signature is discarded and the workbook project must be signed again. Your signature is recognized on the computer on which you create the workbook, but the signature is keyed to that particular computer. Personal digital signatures created on a different computer are not recognized.

To create a personal digital signature, the Digital Certificate for VBA Projects feature must be installed. If you do not have that feature installed, you can install it from your Microsoft Office CD. The Digital Certificate for VBA Projects feature is listed under Office Shared Features.

After you create a signature, add it to each workbook project. See the section "Add Your Digital Signature to a Project." For Excel to recognize that signature when you open a signed workbook, add the signature to your list of trusted sources. See the section "Add a Digital Signature to Your List of Trusted Sources."

Create a Personal Digital Signature

① Click in the Search field and type **selfcert.exe**.

② In the Look in box, click ⊡ and select the drive in which to search for the file.

The file is somewhere in your Microsoft Office folders.

③ Click Search Now.

④ Double-click the file to open it.

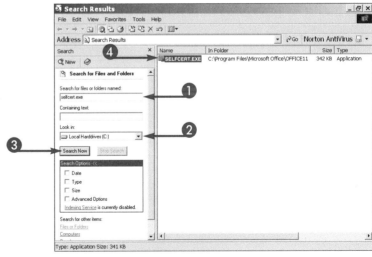

The Create Digital Certificate dialog box opens.

⑤ Click in the Your certificate's name field and type a name for your certificate, which is your personal digital signature.

⑥ Click OK.

Your personal signature is created.

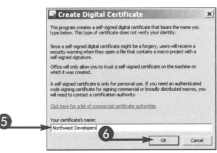

Add Your Digital Signature to a Project

To avoid being asked to Enable or Disable Macros every time you open a workbook that contains your own macros, you can add your personal digital signature to each of your VBA projects. Excel recognizes your personal digital signature and opens your signed workbooks without the Medium level security query.

You sign a VBA project in the Visual Basic Editor's Digital Signature dialog box. For security purposes, your signature is removed when a macro is edited in any way. After you edit a macro, you must add your signature to that

workbook project again. Workbooks that are not signed, especially ones that contain macros that have been edited, display the Medium level security query when you open them.

For macro security to recognize your signature every time you open a signed workbook, you must add your digital signature to your list of trusted sources. To create and use a digital signature, see the section "Create a Personal Digital Signature." To add your digital signature to your list of trusted sources, see the section "Add a Digital Signature to Your List of Trusted Sources."

Add Your Digital Signature to a Project

① Open the Visual Basic Editor in a workbook that contains one of your macros.

② Click Tools.

③ Click Digital Signature.

The Digital Signature dialog box appears.

④ Click Choose.

The Select Certificate dialog box appears.

⑤ Click the signature name.

⑥ Click OK.

⑦ In the Digital Signature dialog box, click OK.

⑧ Save and close the workbook.

Your signature is added to that workbook project.

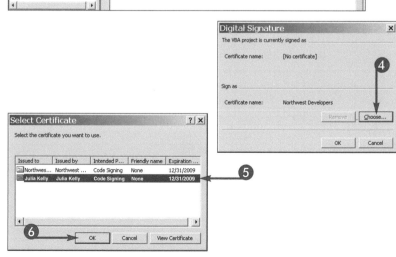

Add a Digital Signature to Your List of Trusted Sources

Y ou can add your personal digital signature to your list of trusted sources so that every signed workbook opens without the Medium-level security query. You can also add other macro developers to your list of trusted sources if their signatures are from an official certificate authority.

To add your digital signature to your list of trusted sources, add your signature to at least one workbook. When you open that workbook under Medium-level security, you get the security query, and then you can add the digital signature to your list of trusted sources.

To send your signed workbooks to other users, you can get an official digital signature, or certificate, from an official certificate authority. To find one, look up digital signature in the Excel help files.

If you get a security warning without an Always trust macros from this publisher check box, the project in the workbook is not digitally signed. You must open a workbook that has a digital signature to add that digital signature to your list of trusted sources.

To remove a name from your list of trusted sources, click Tools, Macro, and Security. On the Trusted Sources tab, click the name and then click Remove.

Add a Digital Signature to Your List of Trusted Sources

① Open a workbook that has macros and a digital signature.

The security warning dialog box appears.

② Click the Always trust macros from this publisher option (☐ changes to ☑).

③ Click Enable Macros.

④ Save and close the workbook.

⑤ Open a workbook signed with the digital signature you added to your list of trusted sources.

The workbook opens with macros enabled.

⑥ Right-click the toolbar area and click Visual Basic to show the Visual Basic toolbar.

⑦ Click Security on the Visual Basic toolbar.

The Security dialog box appears.

⑧ Click the Trusted Sources tab.

The signature is listed in Trusted Sources.

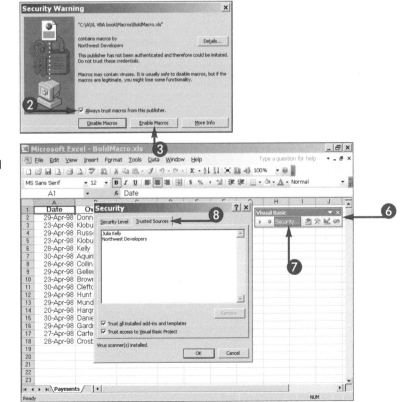

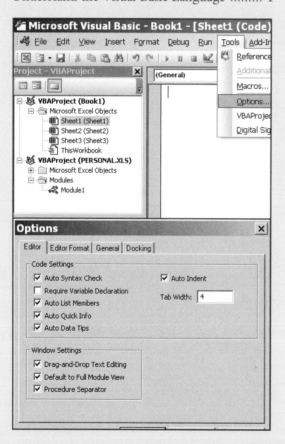

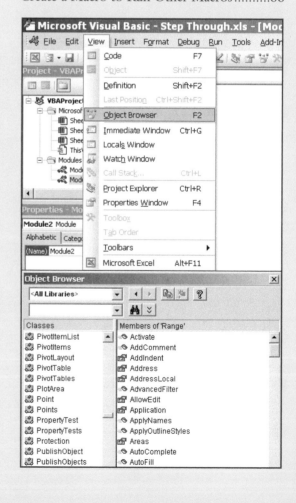

7   Manipulating Modules and Projects

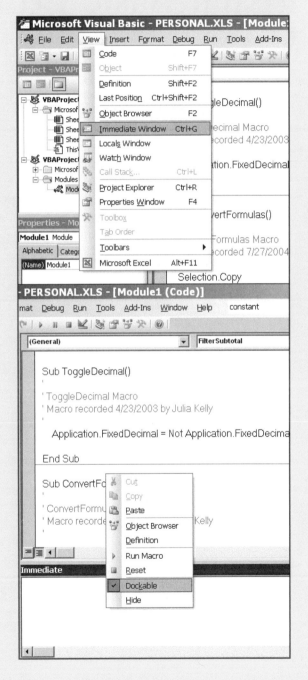

Explore the
Visual Basic Editor

Y ou can write and edit your own procedures, or VBA code, in the Visual Basic Editor when you need a procedure that is more complex than the macro recorder can record. The Visual Basic Editor is arranged in a series of windows that you can move around as needed for a more convenient environment. The Visual Basic Editor

remembers the last window layout you set each time you open it. Not all windows display the first time you open the Visual Basic Editor, but you can select any window you want to open from the View menu. The typical Visual Basic Editor display includes just the Project window, Properties window, and Code window.

The Visual Basic Editor Window

A Project Explorer Window

Displays the list of open projects and their objects, modules, and forms.

B Properties Window

Displays properties for the object currently selected in the Project Explorer window.

C Locals Window

Shows values of local variables during debugging.

D Watches Window

Shows the set watches during debugging.

E Immediate Window

Provides immediate results for statements.

H Object List Box

Lists objects associated with the selected project.

G Procedure List Box

Lists procedures associated with the object currently selected in the Project Explorer window.

F Code Window

Displays the VBA code of the selected module.

The Project Explorer Window

The Project Explorer window, also called the Project window, is structured like the file and folder trees in Windows Explorer. Each entry in the Project window is called a *node*. The top nodes, in bold font, are the open projects. Each Project has the same name as the workbook with which it is associated. The PERSONAL.XLS project holds the VBA code for the Personal Macro Workbook, which always opens when you start Excel. Below each project node are folder nodes for Microsoft Excel Objects, Modules, and Forms. The Modules and Forms folders appear when you create procedures and custom forms in the project.

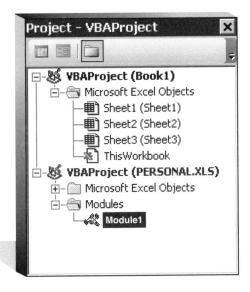

Microsoft Excel Objects

The Microsoft Excel Objects folder contains a node for each sheet in the workbook and a node for the workbook. The sheets can be worksheets or chart sheets. Each sheet object and the workbook object can hold procedures that are triggered by specific worksheet or workbook events, such as worksheet activation or workbook opening. To display the code in an object, double-click the object node.

Modules

The Modules folder lists code modules in the project. Modules contain general procedures, which can be either subroutines or functions. A new module is created each time you open the workbook and record a macro, but additional macros recorded during the same open session are added to the same module. You can add new modules to segregate procedures, or combine procedures into the same module by copying and pasting from one module to another. To display the code in a module, double-click the module node.

Forms

The Forms folder appears when you create a custom form for the project. Each custom form you create in a project has a separate node in the Forms folder. Custom forms are custom dialog boxes you create to allow a user to interact with your procedure. See Chapter 21 for more information about custom forms. To display the code in a form, double-click the form node.

The Properties Window

The Properties window displays the properties for the object selected in the Project window. You can change the properties for the selected object by typing or selecting a different value in the Properties window. For example, you can rename a sheet by changing the Name property for the sheet. To display the properties for an object, click the object in the Project window.

Set Options for the Visual Basic Editor

You can customize the Visual Basic Editor to make your work more comfortable. The customization settings in the Visual Basic Editor are independent of the settings in the Excel window. You can set a variety of options on the Editor tab and Editor Format tab that makes your work more convenient and the text in the Code window easier to read.

Under Code Settings, Auto Syntax Check checks syntax when you type code. Require Variable Declaration forces you to declare the variables in every module. Auto List Members gives you logical information to complete

statements. Auto Quick Info displays function information as you type. Auto Data Tips displays the value of any variable at which you point the mouse while in Break mode.

Window settings include Drag-and-Drop in Text Editing, which allows you to drag text between the Code window and the Immediate and Watch windows. Default to Full Module View places all the procedures of a module in one scrollable list in the Code window; turning it off displays each procedure alone. Procedure Separator places a horizontal line between each macro in a scrollable list of macros.

The Editor Format options control the font of text in the Code window.

Set Options for the Visual Basic Editor

① Open the Visual Basic Editor.

Note: To open the Visual Basic Editor, click Tools, Macro, and Visual Basic Editor.

② Click Tools.

③ Click Options.

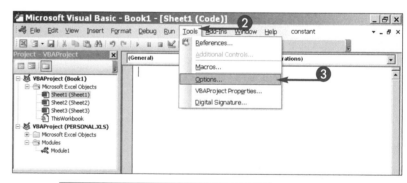

The Options dialog box opens.

④ Click the Editor tab.

⑤ Click the options you want to turn on (☐ changes to ☑).

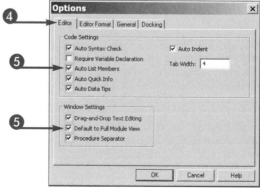

6 Click the Editor Format tab.

7 Select a code text type.

8 Click ⊡ to set the Foreground, Background, and Indicator colors for the text.

The Sample box shows the results of your selections.

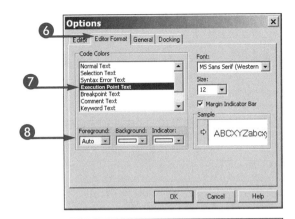

9 Click ⊡ and select a font for all the text in the Code window.

10 Click ⊡ and select a size for all the text in the Code window.

● The Sample box shows the results of your selections.

11 Click OK.

The Visual Basic Editor uses your Editor and Editor Format settings.

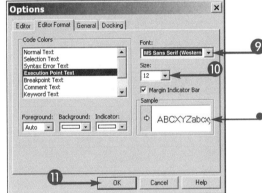

What is in the General tab in the Options dialog box?

▼ The General tab contains grid settings for custom forms and mechanisms for handling errors. It also has choices to show or hide ToolTips, and options to hide windows for a project when you collapse that project in the Project window. You can even tell the Visual Basic Editor when to compile code from the General tab, but the default settings are fine.

What is in the Docking tab in the Options dialog box?

▼ The Docking tab lists the six dockable windows in the editor. If a check box is marked, that window can be docked in the editor program window; and if a check box is cleared, the window opens full-screen on top of the Code window. You should leave all check boxes marked because you can easily dock or undock windows in the editor.

I modified all my colors in the Editor Format tab. How can I get the default color settings back?

▼ Set all colors to Auto for Normal and Selection text. Set Syntax Text to bright red Foreground and Auto Background and Indicator. Set Execution Point Text to Auto Foreground and yellow Background and Indicator. Set Breakpoint Text to white Foreground and brown Background and Indicator. Set Comment Text to Dark Green Foreground and Auto Background and Indicator.

Open and Dock Windows in the Visual Basic Editor

You can open and arrange the windows in the Visual Basic Editor to be convenient for the task, whether you are writing code, testing statements, setting object properties, or debugging code. You can open whatever window you need and then arrange it in the most convenient way by *docking* it (fastening it to the side, top, or bottom of the program window) or *undocking* it (allowing it to float wherever you move it, including outside the Visual Basic Editor window). Other windows cannot cover a docked window.

You can undock windows by dragging them away from the docked position, and you can dock a window by dragging it to the top, bottom, or side of the program window. If you right-click a window and click Dockable from the pop-up menu, you create a *child* window, a window that is maximized inside the editor and hides any floating windows under the child window. The Code window is the only window that is not Dockable.

When you are writing code, you usually need just the code window, the Properties window, and the Project Explorer window. These three windows are open and arranged by default the first time you open the Visual Basic Editor.

Open and Dock Windows in the Visual Basic Editor

Make sure the Code window, Project window, and Properties window are open.

①	Click View.

②	Click Immediate Window.

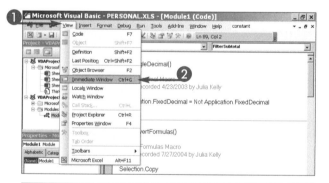

The Immediate window appears docked.

③	Right-click in the Immediate window.

④	Click Dockable.

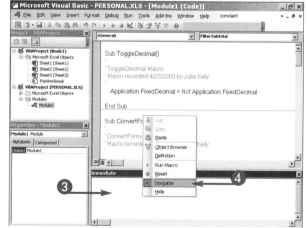

The Immediate window becomes a child window that hides the Code window.

The Immediate label appears in the editor title bar.

⑤ Right-click in the Immediate window.

⑥ Click Dockable.

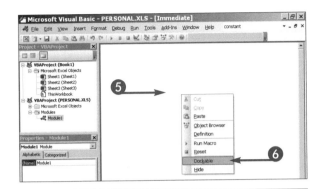

The Immediate window docks again.

⑦ Click the Close button (⊠) in the Immediate window.

You can also right-click in the window and click Hide.

The Immediate window is closed, and the editor is returned to its original layout.

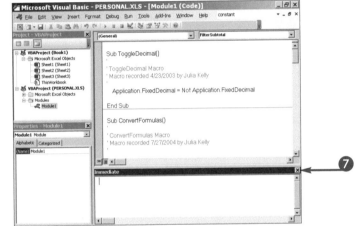

How can I find the code windows hidden by a child window?

▼ Child windows, including the Code window, have the standard Minimize, Restore, and Close buttons in the upper-right corner. You can click the Restore button to resize all the child windows to an intermediate size, and then double-click the title bar for the window you want on top. You can also select a child window from the Window menu.

How can I float and redock a window?

▼ You can double-click the title bar of the docked window, or you can drag the title bar of the docked window to pull it into the center of the editor program window. After the docked window is floated, you can resize it by dragging a side or corner of the window. To redock the window, double-click the title bar.

How can I resize docked windows?

▼ Docked windows have rigid borders around them to separate them; you cannot cover them with other windows, but you can resize docked windows to keep all the windows you need open. The mouse, when pointed at a window border, becomes a two-headed arrow. You can click and drag the border with the two-headed arrow to resize a docked window.

Arrange the Excel and Editor Windows

You can arrange the Excel and Visual Basic Editor windows so that you can write a macro in the editor window and watch the macro run in the Excel window. By arranging the windows this way, you avoid spending extra time and mouse clicks repeatedly switching back and forth between the two windows.

You can arrange the two program windows with the Visual Basic Editor window resized smaller and on top of the Excel window. Then, as you run or step through the statements in the Visual Basic Editor window, you can watch the execution of the code in Excel.

To arrange the windows, leave the Excel window maximized and resize the Visual Basic Editor window on top of the Excel window, dragging the corners and sides to make the editor small enough to see the portion of the Excel window where the code runs. You can also see more of the Code window in the editor by resizing or closing the internal editor windows other than the Code window.

Arrange the Excel and Editor Windows

① In the Visual Basic Editor program window, click the Restore Down button (🗗)

The Restore Down button becomes a Maximize button, and the program window is resizable.

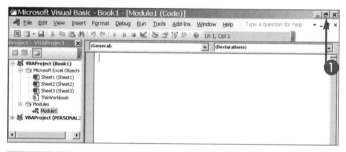

② Click and drag the editor window sides and corners to make it smaller than the Excel window.

Leave the editor window big enough for you to type and read code.

③ Click and drag the border of the internal editor window to reduce the window.

● You can click 🗵 to close unnecessary internal editor windows.

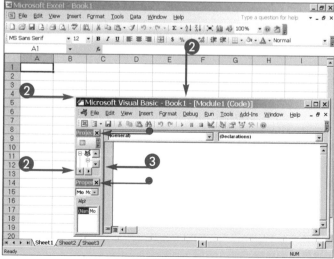

The editor window resizes so you can run or step through a macro while watching the impact of the macro code on the worksheet.

④ Double-click the editor window title bar.

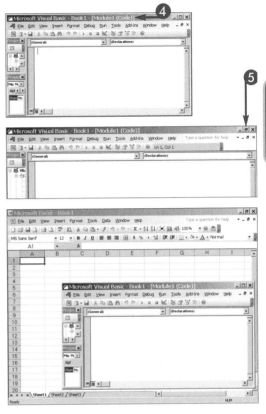

The editor window is maximized.

⑤ Click 🗗 to restore the editor window to its previous size.

The editor window resumes its previous smaller size and shape.

How can I see just the Code and Excel windows?

▼ You can see just the Code window and the Excel window if you close all the internal editor windows except the Code window. To close an internal editor window, click the Close button in the window's upper-right corner. To display an internal window again, click View and then click the name of the window. The window opens in its former position.

How can I work with the Immediate window and Excel?

▼ You can work in the Immediate window alone if you undock it and drag it out of the editor window. You can make the editor window very small, but still keep it open and visible, and work with just the Immediate window on top of the Excel window. For more information about docking windows, see the section "Open and Dock Windows in the Visual Basic Editor."

How can I get the editor window back if I click in the Excel window?

▼ You can get the Visual Basic Editor window back into view in several ways. You can click the Microsoft Visual Basic Editor button in the Windows taskbar at the bottom of the computer screen; you can click the Visual Basic Editor button on the Visual Basic toolbar; you can click Tools→Macro→Visual Basic Editor; or you can press Alt+F11.

Use the Immediate Window

You can use the Immediate window to check the results of a statement or get an answer to a question without writing a whole macro. You can explore and experiment with objects, properties, and methods, and then drag the statement or function into position in the Code window.

You can also use the Immediate window to debug code by running and editing a single statement or set of statements rather than running the entire procedure repeatedly. You can ask a question about a property by typing a question mark in front of the property statement, and the Immediate window returns the current value of the property.

You can use the Immediate window outside of the editor window, on top of the Excel window, so that you can watch the results of a statement appear in the worksheet. Because the Immediate window is a Dockable window, you can undock it, drag it outside the boundary of the editor, and resize the editor window to be very small. You can then type a statement or custom function you want to test in the Immediate window and press Enter. The statement or function takes place immediately in the Excel window.

Use the Immediate Window

① Click View.

② Click Immediate Window.

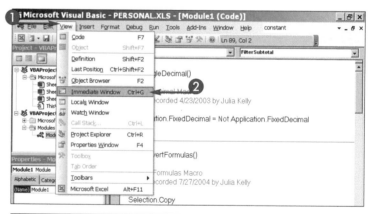

The Immediate window opens.

③ Double-click the Immediate window title bar.

The window is undocked.

④ Click 🗗 to resize in the editor window.

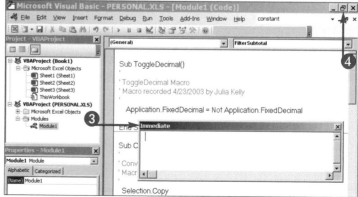

The editor is resized and the Immediate window can float outside the editor.

5 Resize the editor so you can see the Immediate window and the worksheet.

6 In the Immediate window, type a statement to test.

In this example, the statement being tested is **selection.interior.colorindex = 3**.

7 Press Enter.

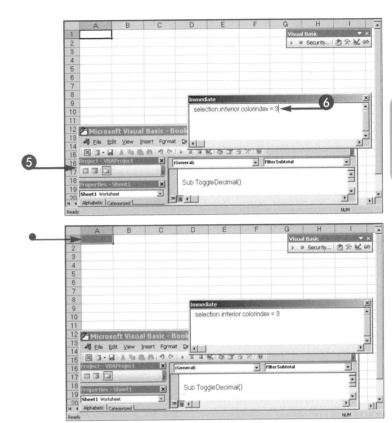

● The results of the statement are visible in the worksheet.

How can I restore the editor windows when I am finished?

▼ Double-click the Immediate window title bar to dock it again, and then double-click the editor window title bar to maximize it. Clicking the Close button in the upper-right corner of the Immediate window returns the editor to its original configuration. When you close any editor window, it reopens in the same size, shape, and configuration the next time you open it.

How can I use the Immediate window to ask a question?

▼ Type a question mark in front of an expression that returns a value and press Enter. For example, type **?worksheets.count** and press Enter. The number of worksheets in the active workbook is returned on the next line. If you type **?activeworkbook.path** and press Enter, Excel returns the path of the active workbook on the next line.

How can I use the Immediate window to test parts of a macro?

▼ Open the macro you want to test, and then select and drag the statements you want to test into the Immediate window. If you press the Ctrl key while you drop the statements into the Immediate window, the statements are copied. Press Enter repeatedly to perform each statement and move to the next statement. You can edit statements to experiment with your macros, such as changing color properties for an object, and see the results immediately.

Save Code from the Immediate Window

After you write successful code fragments or specific VBA statements in the Immediate window, you can save the code by copying it into a procedure or storing it away safely in a text editor. When you close a workbook without saving, any code in the Immediate window is lost.

Building a macro step by step in the Immediate window is easy because you can watch the macro develop statement by statement, experiment with different properties, and catch code errors immediately as you write them. However,

after you write a functional procedure that you want to keep, you must save the code as a macro in the Code window or as lines of code in a text editor such as Notepad or Word.

You can select and drag the entire contents of the Immediate window into the Code window, or select and copy the code in the Immediate window and paste it into a text editor. You can copy procedure code from a text editor and paste into the Code window for a module when you are ready to use the code in a macro.

Save Code in a Module

① Double-click the module name in which you want to save the code.

② Select the code in the Immediate window.

③ Click and drag the selected code into the Code window.

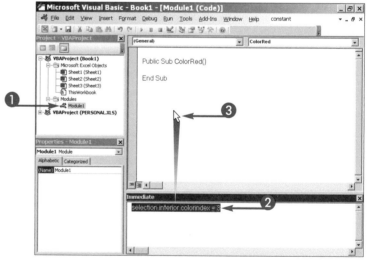

④ Release the mouse button.

⑤ Click the Save button (🖫) to save the project and workbook.

The code is moved into the module and saved.

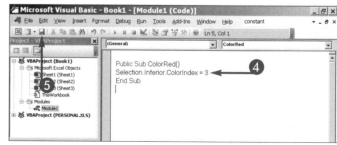

Save Code in a Text Editor

1 Open a text editor such as Notepad.

2 In the Immediate window, select the code.

3 Click the Copy button ().

4 Switch to the text editor.

5 Click Edit.

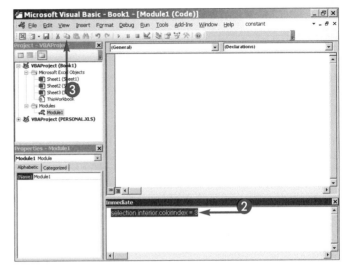

6 Click Paste.

7 Save the text editor file.

The code is saved in the text editor.

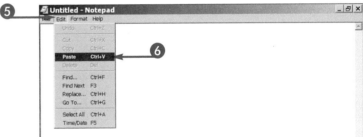

How can I put code saved in a text editor into a macro?

▼ Open both the Visual Basic Editor and the text editor. In the text editor, select the code, click Edit, and then click Copy. Switch to the Visual Basic Editor and open the module in which you want to paste the code. Click in the Code window, click Edit, and then click Paste. The code is pasted into the code window.

Why does the code not run after I copy it into the Code window?

▼ The code in the Immediate window does not require a complete subprocedure construction because each statement runs immediately on its own. But code placed into the code window does not run on its own. Code in the Code window must begin with the Sub line and a name and end with the End Sub line.

I closed the Immediate window before I saved the code. How can I get the code back?

▼ The code in the Immediate window is not lost until you either delete the code or close the workbook. Until then, if you close the Immediate window and then open it again, the code is still there. And if you close the Visual Basic Editor and then open it again, the code is still in the Immediate window.

Locate a Specific Macro

I f you keep many macros in a single module, you can locate a specific macro quickly in a long list of procedure code by selecting the macro name in the Procedure list box.

Keeping all the macros you use often in the Personal Macro Workbook is common; this can lead to a very long list of code in a single module. On the other hand, a module may contain just a few macros, but they are very long and lots of scrolling is needed to find the macro you want. In either case, if you know which module the macro is in, you can select the macro by name in the Procedure list box without leaving the Visual Basic Editor.

If you cannot remember which workbook or module a macro is in, you can still locate the macro quickly by switching to the Excel window and opening the Macro dialog box. In the Macro dialog box, you can select All workbooks, select the macro name, and click Edit. The Visual Basic Editor opens and the macro you selected appears in the Code window.

Locate a Specific Macro

1 Double-click the module name that contains the long list of macros.

2 Click ☑ in the Procedure list box.

3 Select the macro name.

The selected macro appears in the Code window.

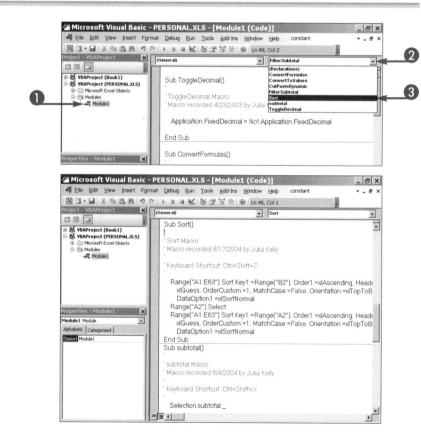

Save Your VBA Work

Saving your work periodically while you write code is a good idea, so that if you have a crash of any kind, you do not lose the code you have already written or recorded. Your VBA code is created in a project, which is the hidden VBA portion of a workbook. When you save a workbook, you automatically save all the VBA code in that workbook's underlying project; and when you save the project in the Visual Basic Editor, you also save the workbook.

The procedure for saving your work from either the Visual Basic Editor window or the workbook window is the same, but the commands are slightly different in the two

windows. In both windows, however, you can click the Save button on the Standard toolbar. Although the labels are slightly different, both Save buttons save both the workbook and the VBA project.

The Personal Macro Workbook is always open but hidden when you work in Excel. If you wrote, recorded, or edited any procedures in the Personal Macro Workbook, both the workbook named PERSONAL.XLS and then Excel ask you to save that hidden workbook when you quit Excel.

Save Your VBA Work

1 In the Visual Basic Editor, click File.

2 Click Save and your *workbook name*.

You can also press Ctrl+S to save the project and workbook.

The workbook and project are saved.

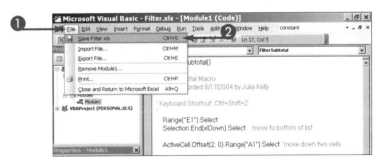

3 In the workbook window, click File.

4 Click Save.

You can also press Ctrl+S to save the project and workbook.

The workbook and project are saved.

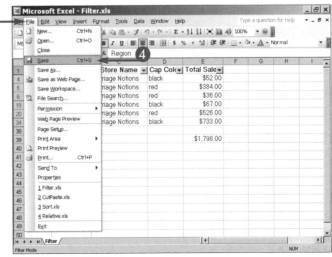

73

Understand the Visual Basic Language

You can write more complex and effective VBA code when you understand the terminology and capabilities of the VBA language. You can also communicate with other developers and read the Visual Basic help files more clearly when you understand the language.

Objects and Collections

Every item in Excel is an object, including Excel itself, which is an application object. Each workbook is an object, as is each worksheet, each chart, each cell, each selection, and so forth. A group of similar objects is a collection. Each object belongs to a collection of those objects, and each object is itself a collection of smaller objects. For example, each workbook is an object that belongs to the workbooks' collection, each workbook contains a collection of worksheets, and each worksheet contains a collection of cells. In your code, you can refer to an individual object or to the entire collection of objects, depending on what you want to accomplish.

Properties and Methods

Objects have properties and methods. A collection object has properties and methods that are different from the properties and methods of the individual objects in the collection. For example, when you add a new worksheet, you add the worksheet to the worksheets collection object, not to an individual worksheet object.

Properties describe or identify an object. For example, a worksheet object has a Name property, and a cell object has Height and Color properties. Properties have values that describe the property. For example, the Color property of a Cell object may have a value of Red.

Methods are activities that objects perform or that are performed on objects. For example, when you add a new worksheet, you execute the Add method on the Worksheets collection object. When you copy a range of cells, you execute the Copy method on the Selection object.

The distinction between properties and methods is not always clear, but Excel provides tools to help you find the methods and properties you need for an object. It does not matter whether you define code as a property or a method as long as you make the procedure do what you want.

Modules, Sub-Procedures, and Functions

A module is the part of a project where macros and procedures are stored. When you open a module (by double-clicking the module node in the Project window), the code stored in that module appears in the Code window.

In the Code window, every macro or procedure begins with the keyword Sub and ends with the keyword End Sub. Sub stands for sub-procedure or subroutine, probably because every procedure or macro can be a sub-procedure in another larger procedure. The word *sub-procedure* is not often used because the shorter words — *macro* and *procedure* — mean the same thing. A procedure is just a block of code that performs specific actions.

Functions in VBA perform calculations that can be used in the macros that call them. A function is created in a module and looks similar to a procedure, but a function does not appear in a list of macros. Functions can only be called, or used, by a macro. In the module, a function begins with the keyword Function and ends with the keyword End Function.

Public and Private refer to the functions in a module. If the word *Public* is entered to the left of the word *Function*, or if no word is entered to the left of the word *Function*, that function is available to all modules in the workbook. If the function begins with the word *Private*, the function is available only to procedures within that module.

```
Sub InsertRandomNumber()
    Range("B3"). Select
    ActiveCell.FormulaR1C1 = MyRandomNumber
    Range("B4").Select
End Sub
```

```
Function MyRandomNumber()
    MyRandomNumber = Rnd
End Function
```

```
Worksheets.Add

Worksheets(1).Name = "Invoice"
```

Data Types

Data types tell VBA how to store data in memory. Data types come in different sizes. You can see the sizes and limits of different data types if you look up "data type summary" in the Visual Basic Editor help files.

Data types include Object, Numeric, Date, Boolean, String, and Variant. When you declare a variable as one of these data types, Excel sets aside the appropriate amount of memory for the data type.

If you do not assign a data type to a variable, VBA assigns the Variant data type by default. However, the Variant data type can hold any type of data and uses the largest amount of memory, so processing these data types can slow down your procedure considerably. For example, you can declare the result of a function procedure as a specific data type to make your function macro run more quickly. Otherwise, the result of the function is a data type of Variant.

Variables

A variable is a named location for storing data during the execution of a procedure. You can declare a variable to be a specific data type, thereby limiting the processing needed and speeding up a complex procedure.

You can introduce a new variable at any point by using it in your procedure, but you normally use a Dim statement to declare variables at the beginning of a procedure. *Dim*, which stands for dimension, enables you to specify a data type. You give the variable a name and a data type, and then you can assign a value to a variable or point the variable to an object using the Set command.

If you use the Option Explicit statement at the beginning of the module, VBA forces you to declare all variables in the module so that you do not misspell them and cause errors.

```
Dim UserName As String
Set UserName = "Julia"
```

Constants

A constant is a named item that retains a constant value throughout the execution of the macro. You can define your own constants and use them anywhere in the procedure in place of values.

If you need to use the same value or string throughout a long procedure, declaring the value or string as a constant can save a lot of time. If the value or string ever needs to be changed, you only need to make the change in the constant declaration at the beginning of the procedure. You declare a constant the same way you declare a variable.

By default a constant is Private and not available outside the module where it is created. To make the constant available in all modules in a workbook, type *Public* to the left of the constant declaration.

```
Const StateTax As Double = "0.65"
```

Syntax

You read VBA statements backwards. For example, the statement `Selection.Font.Bold = True` means turn on the Bold value in the Font property of the Selection. Objects, properties, and methods are separated by periods without spaces. Text strings are always enclosed within quote marks. Arguments for values or functions are always enclosed within parentheses. Spelling counts. If you enter all code in lowercase letters, Excel converts the letters to the proper case when they are recognized. If you spell a word wrong, Excel does not change the case, and that is your indication that the word is misspelled.

Enter
VBA Code

You can make the process of writing your own procedures easier and faster when you type VBA code in the Code window yourself. Code that you type must follow the rules of VBA language, also known as the *syntax* of the language, which defines how you can combine elements of the language into expressions and statements that VBA can execute.

Statement syntax is *object.method* or *object.property = value*. An object can have a child object. For example, in the statement `Selection.Font.Bold = True`, *Font* is a child object of the Selection object, and *Bold* is a method of the Font object. Values entered as text strings must be in quotes.

Start each statement on a new line. You can leave blank lines between sections of related statements and use indents and comments to make code easier to read.

Whenever possible, simplify your statements. For example, the two statements `Range("B5").Select` and `ActiveCell.Value = 0.075` require two lines, but you can accomplish the same results by typing the single statement `Range("B5").Value = 0.075`. If you need to change several properties in a single object, use a With block to simplify your code.

Enter VBA Code

① Start a new line by pressing Enter at the end of the preceding line.

② Type an object name and a period.

③ Type a method, property, or child object name.

This statement selects the range A1 to D4.

④ Press Enter.

A new line is started, and the first line has the proper case.

⑤ Press Tab to create an indent.

⑥ Type **with selection** to start a With block for the selected range.

⑦ Press Enter.

With Selection has the proper case, and the keyword `With` is colored blue.

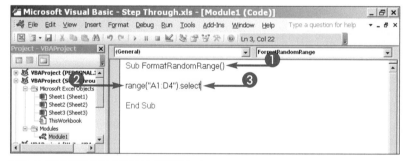

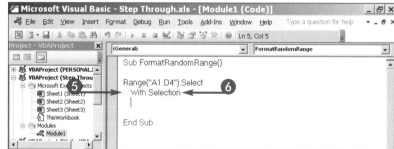

⑧ Press Tab.

A new indented line is started in the With block.

⑨ Type a period and then the rest of the object, method, or property statement for the With block object.

⑩ Press Enter.

The statement has the proper case, and the new line begins with the same indent as the previous line.

⑪ Repeat steps **9** and **10** for the rest of the With block statements.

⑫ Press Backspace to remove the indent from the End With line.

⑬ Type **end with**.

⑭ Press Enter.

A complete and simplified set of VBA statements is entered.

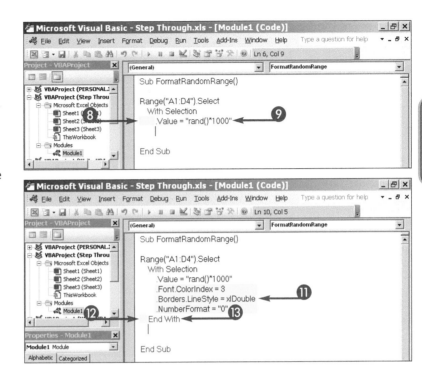

Why did my code turn red while I was typing?

▼ Because you made a mistake in syntax; or you pressed Enter before you finished typing a statement in proper syntax, and the Auto Syntax Check is turned on. To turn Auto Syntax Check on or off, click Tools, Options, and then click the Editor tab. Sometimes the error is as simple as typing a comma instead of a period.

How can I tell if I have spelled words correctly?

▼ Type code in lowercase. The editor recognizes all object, method, and property names. If spelled correctly, the names are made the proper case when you press Enter or click away from the statement. If you use named ranges from the worksheet that are enclosed in quotes in your code, the editor will not pay attention to them. You know the ranges are wrong when you get a worksheet error.

Where can I find a list of objects and their methods and properties?

▼ You can find the complete object library in the Object Browser. The Object Browser lists all Excel objects and their associated properties and methods. It can be helpful when used in association with the VBA help files. To open the Object Browser, click View and then click Object Browser. For more information, see the section "Look Up VBA Words in the Object Browser."

Write a Macro without Recording

I f you write your own macros, you can make Excel do things that you cannot record in the macro recorder, and make a macro more efficient or flexible than the code the recorder writes. When you know how to enter the VBA code yourself, typing your own code is also faster than recording and editing.

Some of the things a macro can only do if you write the code yourself include asking a user for input, making decisions while the macro runs, and calculating with complex custom functions that are part of the macro rather than part of a workbook.

You can start your macro in the Macro dialog box by giving the macro a name and clicking the Create button. VBA sets up the macro for you by entering the Sub and End Sub lines and the macro name in a module, and all you need to do is type your code in between those lines. Every macro must begin with a Sub line, which includes the macro name, and end with an End Sub line that tells Excel where the macro stops.

Write a Macro without Recording

① Click Tools.

② Click Macro.

③ Click Macros.

The Macro dialog box appears.

④ Click in the Macro name field and type a name for the macro.

⑤ Click Create.

The Visual Basic Editor opens with your macro already started.

⑥ Click to position the cursor between the Sub and End Sub lines.

⑦ Type your macro code.

This macro enters a text string and a formula into two cells.

This macro is shorter and more efficient than the recorder can write.

⑧ Click the Save button ().

The macro is written without recording.

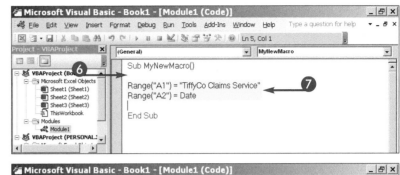

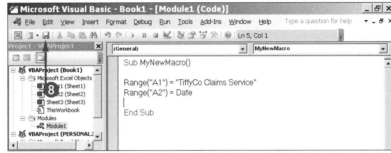

How can I create a shortcut key for a macro I write myself?

▼ When you write a macro yourself, you cannot create a shortcut key in the Visual Basic Editor. If you want to run the macro with a shortcut key, you need to switch to Excel and open the Macro dialog box again. Click the macro name, and then click the Options button. Create a shortcut key in the Options dialog box.

Is there another way to start a new macro?

▼ Yes. If you are already working in the Visual Basic Editor and you need to create a new macro, you can click Insert and then Procedure. In the Add Procedure dialog box, give the macro a name and leave the Sub and Public options selected. Click OK, and the new macro is added to the bottom of the open module.

Is there an even faster way to start a new macro?

▼ Yes. In a new module, or at the end of the module you have open, press Enter after the last End Sub line. Type *sub* and a macro name, and then press Enter. The editor creates a new macro for you, with the cursor in between the Sub and End Sub lines ready for you to begin typing code.

Declare a Variable

You can make your procedures run more efficiently and use fewer resources if you declare your variables. A variable is a temporary storage space in memory for information used in a procedure. When you declare a variable, you name that memory storage space and give it a data type.

You declare a variable at the beginning of your procedure by using a Dim statement. Following the Dim statement, you set the value of the variable.

A variable can be named and used without declaring it with a Dim statement, but if you do not declare the variable, VBA assigns the variant data type to the variable because

VBA does not know what kind of data the variable stores. The variant data type uses the maximum amount of memory storage, which is inefficient because the data type must be determined every time the variable is used. To see the full list of data types, look up *data type summary* in the VBA help files.

To ensure that your variables are always properly declared, use the Option Explicit statement at the beginning of the module. To add Option Explicit to modules automatically, click Tools and then Options. On the Editor tab, select the Require Variable Declaration check box.

Declare a Variable

① Type **Option Explicit** at the top of the module.

② Start a new procedure by typing **sub** and a macro name and pressing Enter.

③ Below the Sub line, type **dim**.

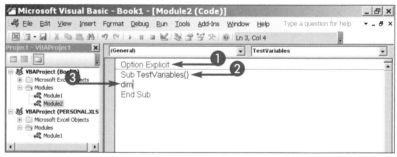

④ Type the name of the variable, followed by **as** and the data type for your variable.

● If an Auto List appears, you can either select a data type from the list or continue typing your data type.

⑤ Press Enter.

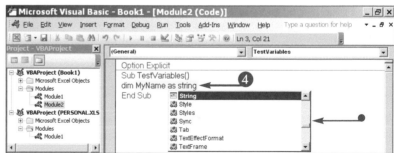

A new line is started.

⑥ Type the variable name, followed by an equal sign (=) and a value for the variable.

⑦ Press Enter.

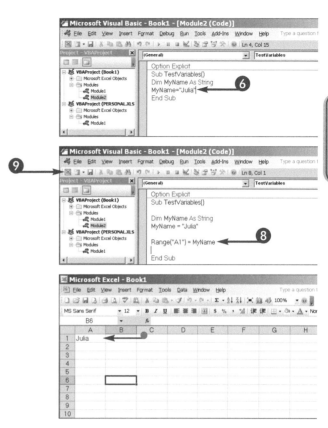

A new line is started.

⑧ Type the rest of your procedure.

This macro enters the variable text string in the cell A1 in the active worksheet.

⑨ Click the View Microsoft Excel button (⊠) to switch to Excel.

⑩ Run the macro.

● The macro enters the declared variable value in cell A1.

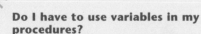

Do I have to use variables in my procedures?

▼ No, and many procedures do not need variables. But if you need to use the same value repeatedly during a procedure, creating a variable and setting the value in the variable makes editing the procedure later easier. You can change the value in the variable rather than replacing the value throughout the procedure.

What are the rules for naming variables?

▼ The rules for variable names are similar to the rules for macro names. Variable names can be up to 255 characters long and must begin with a letter. They cannot contain spaces or periods. They must be unique within the procedure; in other words, no duplicate names can exist within the procedure, although you can have duplicate variable names within the same module.

Do I have to use the Option Explicit statement?

▼ No, but Option Explicit is helpful because it keeps track of the variables you declare. If you misspell a variable name without Option Explicit, the procedure passes by that variable without executing it. But if you misspell a declared variable name with Option Explicit turned on, you see a Variable Not Defined error when the procedure gets to that point.

Use an Auto List

You can write statements more quickly and accurately when you use the Auto List, which is a list of methods and properties appropriate for the object you type in a code statement. The Auto List appears when you type a period following a correctly spelled object name.

The Auto List can help you complete the VBA statement you are typing. You do not need to use the list because if you know what property or method you want, you can just keep typing and the Auto List disappears. However, if you

are typing statements for objects you are unfamiliar with, the list can be very helpful by showing you which properties and methods are available for the object and how they are spelled. You always get Auto Lists for declared variable objects because Excel knows exactly what kind of objects they are. To be sure your initial object is a valid, defined object, you can use Complete Word to start the statement with an Auto List.

You can turn the Auto List on or off by clicking Options under the Tools menu. On the Editor tab, select or deselect the Auto List Members check box.

Use an Auto List

① Click Edit.

② Click Complete Word.

If you already know the correct object name, you can type it without using Complete Word.

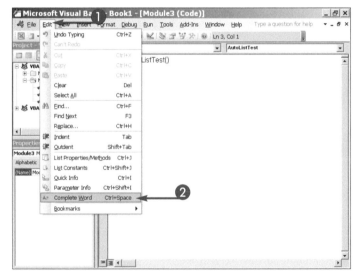

An Auto List of objects appears.

③ Type the first letter of the object you want.

The selection jumps to the first entry beginning with that letter.

④ Double-click the object name you want.

The object is entered in the statement.

5 Type a period.

An Auto List appears for the object.

You can type a letter to jump to that point in the list, or scroll to find the entry you want.

6 Double-click the method or property you want.

The method or property is entered in the statement.

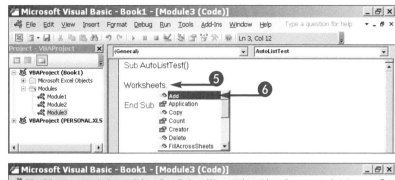

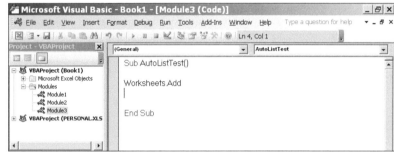

Why is there no Auto List when I type an object name?

▼ Possibly the object name was misspelled, or the object name was too indefinite. For example, *ActiveSheet* could be a worksheet or a chart sheet, and because Excel does not know which you mean, it does not show an Auto List. But if you declare a variable with a statement such as `Dim MySheet As Worksheet`, and set that variable to the active sheet with the statement `Set MySheet = ActiveSheet`, you have a defined object and can get an Auto List when you type the declared object name MySheet.

What is the ScreenTip with parentheses that I sometimes see when I type properties and functions?

▼ That is an Auto Quick Info ScreenTip. It shows you the arguments for the property or function you are typing. For example, if you type `range(` to begin a statement, you see an Auto Quick Info ScreenTip about the Range property when you type the opening parenthesis. The ScreenTip is a reminder about what arguments you need, in this case cell addresses to define the range. If you need help with those arguments, click to position the cursor within the property or function name and press F1 to open a help file.

Step through a Macro

You can watch a macro run by stepping through each macro statement and seeing the results as each statement is performed. Stepping through a macro helps you to locate and fix problems in your code and find ways to edit the code to make it better.

When you step into the current procedure, the editor highlights the Sub line. As you continue to step through the procedure, each preceding statement is performed and the following statement is selected, all the way through the End Sub line, after which the stepping-though process is completed.

You can start the step-through process by pressing F8 in the Excel window, the Macro dialog box, or the Visual Basic Editor. You can copy individual statements into the Immediate window to test other values while you step through the code, and then edit the code based on your Immediate window experiments.

If your code calls another macro or function procedure, that procedure is also opened and stepped through in turn. See the section "Create a Macro That Runs Other Macros" for more information about calling other procedures.

Step through a Macro

① Open the macro in the Visual Basic Editor.

② Arrange the editor window and the Excel window so you can see both.

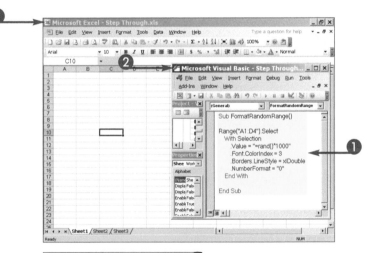

③ Click Debug.

④ Click Step Into.

You can also start the process by pressing F8.

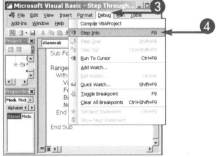

84

- The Sub line highlights.

5 Press F8.

- The first statement in the macro highlights.

6 Press F8 again.

- The first statement is performed in the worksheet and the next statement is highlighted.

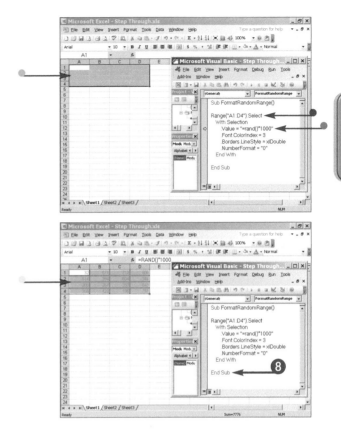

7 Continue to press F8 to step through the entire macro.

- Each step is highlighted and the preceding step is performed in the worksheet as you watch.

8 When the End Sub line is highlighted, press F8 again.

The step-through process is completed.

How can I stop the step-through process and start over?

▼ If you are in the middle of a step-through process and want to edit the code, perhaps to change a value, you can start over stepping through the changed code from the top without stepping all the way through the macro. You can either click Run and then Reset, or click the Reset button on the editor toolbar.

How can I test individual statements without stepping through the entire macro?

▼ To test different values in statements without repeatedly stepping through the macro, open the Immediate window and copy a statement into it. Edit a value, click in the statement, and press Enter to run the statement. To open the Immediate window, click View and then Immediate Window. Close the window by clicking the Close button in the upper-right corner.

How can I arrange my windows to see both the worksheet and the Visual Basic Editor?

▼ In the editor window, click the Restore Window button in the upper-right corner, and then resize the window so it is smaller than the worksheet window and on top of the worksheet. To resize interior windows in the editor, point to the vertical border between the code window and the project window, and drag the two-headed arrow to make the project window narrower.

Look Up VBA Words in the Object Browser

You can find a complete list of all the VBA objects and their methods, properties, events, and constants in the Object Browser. If you need to look up a spelling, get help with an object or method, or just want to know what methods, properties, events, and constants are available for a specific object, the Object Browser is your source.

You open the Object browser from the View menu. When the Object Browser displays, you can look up names of object collections in the Classes list, and all the events, properties, methods, and constants for the selected object are displayed in the Members list.

If you need more information about a specific item in the object browser, click the item and press F1 to open a help file containing detailed information and examples for the selected item.

The object browser items have identifying icons that you may need help understanding. If you type *object browser icons* in the Ask A Question box, and then click the Objects Used in the Object Browser and Code Windows link in the search results list, you see a list of object browser icons and descriptions of what they mean.

① Click View.

② Click Object Browser.

You can also press F2 to open the Object Browser.

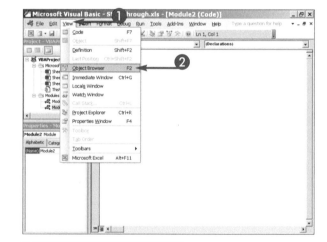

The Object Browser appears.

③ In the Classes list, click any entry.

The browser focus shifts to the Classes list.

④ Type the first letter of the object you want.

In this example, the letter **r** is typed to find the object Range.

● The selection jumps to the first entry that begins with the letter you typed.

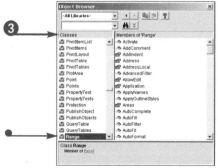

⑤ Scroll down to the object you want.

⑥ Select the member you want in the Members list.

In this example, the Select method is selected.

⑦ Click the Help button (⚙) to get details and examples about the selected member.

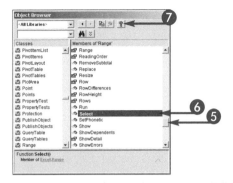

PART II

Help files are displayed for the selected member.

⑧ Click the Close button (⌧) to close the Help window.

⑨ Click ⌧ to close the Object Browser window.

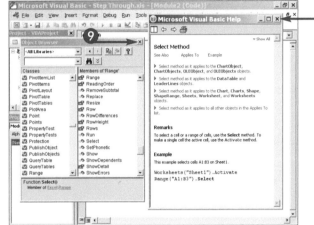

The Object Browser covers up all my other windows. How can I make it smaller?

▼ The Object Browser is a dockable window, and you can use it just like any other dockable window. Double-click the title bar to undock the window and make it float above the other windows, and then drag the window borders to resize and reshape it. Whenever the Object Browser opens, it retains the configuration it had when last closed.

How can I use what I find in the Object Browser?

▼ Select a method or property, and then click the Copy button in the Object Browser window. Right-click in the Immediate window or Code window and click Paste. Type a period following the pasted property to display an Auto List containing all of the available methods and properties for the item. For more information about Auto Lists, see the section "Use an Auto List."

What is the globals class in the Object Browser?

▼ The globals class is a list of all the methods and properties you can use without specifying an object, and all the VBA functions. For example, the Range property is in the globals class. You can assign a value to the range property without specifying an object, as in the statement `Range("A1") = Date`, which places the current date in cell A1 in the active worksheet.

Create a Macro to Run Other Macros

I f you have created an application in short segments by writing or recording separate macros, you can create a macro that runs all those shorter macros one after another in the order you set. The shorter macros become subordinate macros, or *subroutines*, in the combined macro.

The macros can be in different workbooks as long as all the workbooks are open. Macros in the current workbook can be called by their names alone, but macros in other workbooks must be called by the full application statement `Application.Run "workbook.xls!macroname"`.

You can record this macro by recording as you run each subordinate macro in turn from the Macros dialog box; but the resulting recorded macro is wordy, and you must wait for each macro to run even though you record only the name in the combined macro. Writing the combined macro yourself in the Visual Basic Editor is both faster and easier to read.

Each macro starts to run wherever the previous macro left off, so you may have to insert statements at the start or end of some macros to put the active cell in position for the next macro to run.

Create a Macro to Run Other Macros

① Open the Visual Basic Editor.

② Type **Sub** and the macro name, then press Enter to start a new macro.

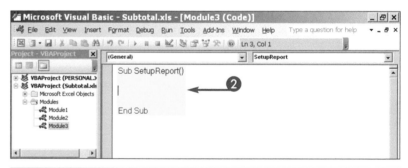

③ Type the first macro name.

④ Press Enter.

If the macro you want to call is in this workbook, type just the macro name.

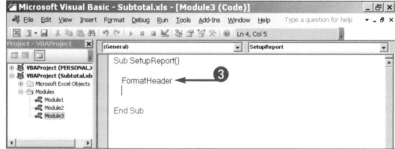

5 Repeat steps **3** and **4** to list all the macros in the order in which you want to run them.

- To run a macro that is in a different workbook, type the statement **Application.Run** *workbookname* **.xls!***macroname*.

This macro runs the ToggleDecimal macro in the Personal Macro Workbook PERSONAL.XLS.

6 Click 🔢 to switch to Excel.

7 Run the macro.

You can press Alt+F8 to open the Macro dialog box.

All the macros run in order.

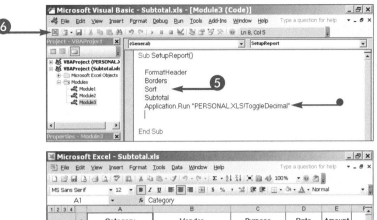

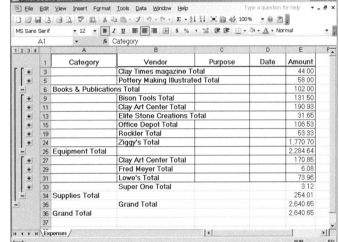

Can I step through this macro?

▼ Yes, but it takes a long time and is very boring because Excel steps through every statement in every macro that the combined macro calls. You can step through all the macros more quickly if you press and hold down the F8 key instead of stepping through one statement at a time. Stepping through the subordinate macros as you create them and then fixing any errors that appear when you run the combined macro is a better idea.

Why do I get an error when I run the combined macro, even if the subordinate macros run with no problems?

▼ Be sure the macro names are spelled correctly. There is no VBA spellchecker to find misspelled macro names. Read the error message and then click the Debug button. The debugger switches to the Visual Basic Editor and highlights the portion of code that is causing a problem. If the error is at the beginning of a macro, the macro may need a range selection statement for a starting point. You can place that range statement at the beginning of the stopped macro or at the end of the preceding macro.

Move and Add Macros to a Module

You can find macros faster if you keep them organized in a single module, or in different modules according to the macro purpose, rather than in many undifferentiated modules. When you record macros in the same Excel session, all the macros are written in the same module. However, when you close and reopen Excel, new macros you record are written to a new module. You end up with several modules in a workbook project, which makes finding the specific macro code you want difficult.

When you write a new macro, the Macro dialog box opens a new module; but you can choose the module in which you want to write the macro. You can also move existing macros into a new module by copying or cutting them from their current module and pasting them into the module you want. You can write a new macro in the module of your choice by opening the module you want and starting the new macro at the bottom of the list.

When you add a new macro with the Add Procedure dialog box, you should leave the default Sub and Public options selected to write a subprocedure that can be used in any open workbook.

Move Existing Macros to a Module

① Double-click the module that has the macro you want to move.

② Select the entire macro.

③ Click the Cut button ( ).

If you want to copy the macro, click the Copy button ( ).

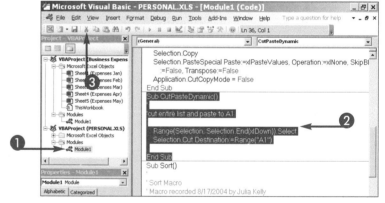

④ Double-click the module into which you want to move the macro.

⑤ Click to position the mouse ⬚ below the last Sub line.

⑥ Click the Paste button ( ).

● The macro is moved into the module.

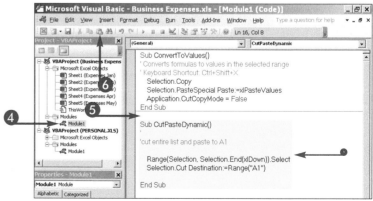

Add New Macros to a Module

① Double-click the module in which you want to write the macro.

② Click Insert.

③ Click Procedure.

The Add Procedure dialog box appears.

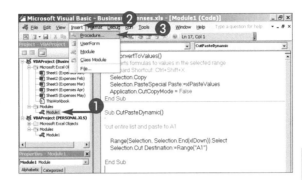

④ Click in the Name field and type a name for the macro.

⑤ Click OK.

● A new macro is started at the bottom of the list.

Another way to start a new macro is to type **sub** and a macro name, and then press Enter.

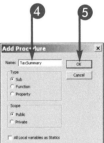

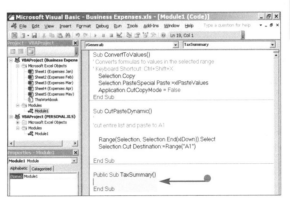

What are the other options in the Add Procedure dialog box?

▼ A Function procedure creates a VBA function that other macros can call, and a Property procedure is a complex way to create a property with arguments that have the variant data type. The Private option means a Function procedure can be only called from a macro in that module. If a Sub or Function line does not begin with Private, it is a public subroutine, with or without the word Public. The All Local variables as Statics check box means all variables retain their values as long as the code is running.

How can I organize macros without keeping them all in the same module?

▼ You can organize your macros by segregating them into specific modules according to type. For example, you can keep all your financial macros in one module, all your template macros in another module, and all your public functions in yet another module. You can keep macros in separate workbook projects, or all in the same workbook project but in separate modules in that project. You can add modules and rename them to identify the types of macros stored in each. For more information, see the section "Add and Rename a Module."

Add and Rename a Module

You can keep your procedures well organized and easy to find by adding and renaming modules in your workbook projects, and then keeping related macros in identifiable modules. When you close and reopen Excel, new macros you record are written to a new module. You can end up with several unidentified modules in a workbook project, with each module containing an assortment of unrelated macros. If you need to find a specific macro, searching each module to find the macro you want is inefficient and time-consuming.

You can add a module into which you want to move existing macros or write new macros. If you already have a disorganized assortment of macros in unidentifiable modules, you can organize the macros by copying or moving them into new modules, and then rename the new modules to reflect their contents.

You can add modules with the Insert menu and rename a module by changing the Name property in the Properties window. After you reorganize modules, you may have modules you no longer need. To delete unneeded modules, see the section "Delete a Module."

Add a Module

① Navigate through the Project window and double-click the project in which you want to create a new module.

② Click Insert.

③ Click Module.

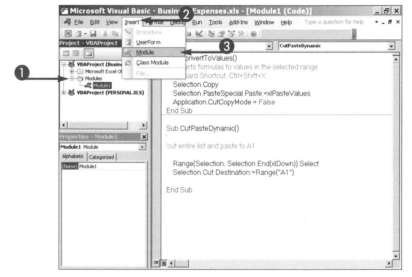

● A new empty module is added to the project.

You can also right-click the module's node in the Project window, and then click Insert and Module.

Rename a Module

① Display the Project and Properties windows.

Note: To display windows, see Chapter 5.

② Click the module you want to rename.

③ In the Properties window, select the name in the Name box.

④ Type a new name.

⑤ Click away from the Name box.

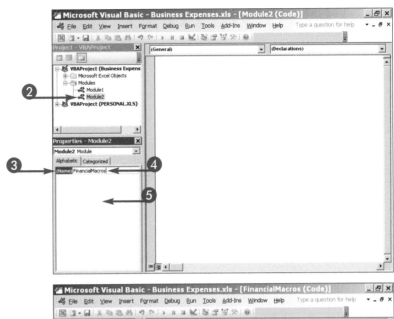

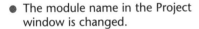

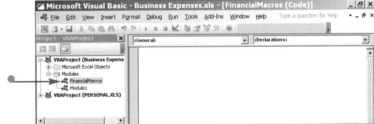

● The module name in the Project window is changed.

What are the rules for module names?

▼ The rules for module names are the same as the rules for all object, procedure, constant, variable, and argument names in a Visual Basic module. A name cannot have more than 255 characters and must begin with a letter. Spaces and most punctuation marks are not allowed. You can use capital letters or underscore characters to separate words in a name, and you can use numbers. Do not create any names that are the same as keywords or function, method, property, or object names in Visual Basic.

How can I print the code in a module?

▼ You cannot quickly print the code for a single module, but you can print all the code in a project. In the Project window, right-click anywhere in the project and click Print. To print a single module, open the module and click the Full Module View button in the lower-left corner of the Code window to display the module code in a single list. Select all the code in the module, copy and paste it into a text editor such as Word or Notepad, and print the text file.

Copy Modules from One Workbook to Another

You can copy your macros from one workbook into another workbook without recreating the macro code. You can do this by copying an entire module from one workbook project to another. You copy a module by dragging it from one project and dropping it in the Project window of another project.

When you copy a module, the module keeps its original name. If you copy a module into a project that already has a module of the same name, VBA adds a number to the end of the copied module name. For example, if you copy

Module1 to a workbook that already has a Module1, the copied module is renamed Module11. Another copied Module1 is renamed Module12, and so on. Of course, you can always change the name of a copied module. For more information, see the section "Add and Rename a Module."

You can create a central storage workbook to keep copies of all the modules in all your workbooks so that you always have a safe backup copy of all your code. Then, when you need to use an existing module in a new workbook, you can quickly copy the stored module into the new workbook.

Copy Modules from One Workbook to Another

① Click the module you want to copy.

② Drag the selected module onto the other project name.

- The plus symbol on the mouse icon means you are copying the module.

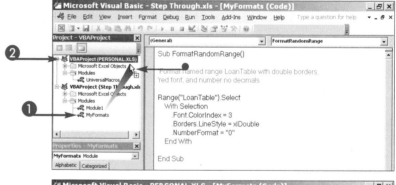

- A copy of the module appears in the modules list for the other workbook project.

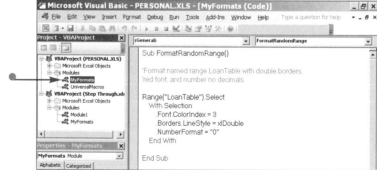

Delete a Module

You can make a project more efficient if you delete modules that you no longer need. If you have reorganized your macros into logical modules, or if you have several modules that either have no macros in them or have unnecessary macros in them, you can delete those modules to make your project organized and easy to work in.

To delete a module, click File and Remove Module. When you delete a module, you have the opportunity to export it to a file outside of Excel. The file can be stored in any folder in your computer, imported back into any

workbook project, or sent to another user who can import the file into their workbook project. For more information on importing an exported file, see the section "Import a Text File" in Chapter 8.

You do not have to export a module when you delete it. If you click No when asked if you want to export the module, the module is deleted and you are finished. You do not have to delete a file to export it. You can export a copy of the file and leave the original in place. For more information, see the section "Share Macros by Exporting a Module" in Chapter 23.

Delete a Module

① In the Project window, click the module you want to delete.

② Click File.

③ Click Remove *modulename*.

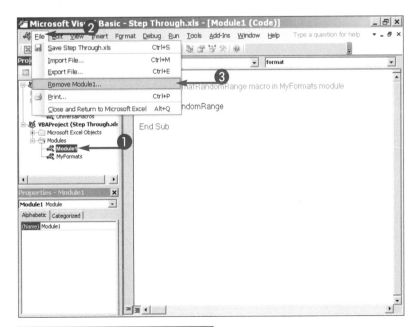

A dialog box appears asking if you want to export the module to a file.

④ Click No.

The module deletes from the project.

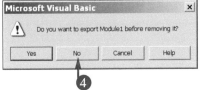

Hide a Macro

Y ou can prevent other users from easily accessing a macro by hiding it so that it does not appear in the Macro dialog box in Excel. When you hide a macro, another user cannot run, delete, or edit it from the Macro dialog box. You cannot run a hidden macro with a shortcut key or call it from a macro in another module; you can only run it from a toolbar button or a menu command.

To hide a macro, open the macro and type the word `Private` on the left end of the Sub line. For example, to hide a macro named `ToggleDecimal`, edit the Sub line to read `Private Sub ToggleDecimal()`.

Hiding a macro from the Macro dialog box does not prevent a knowledgeable user from opening, running, editing, or deleting the macro in the Visual Basic Editor. To keep knowledgeable users from accessing the macro, you must lock the project. Locking a project does not prevent macros from being run from a toolbar button or from being called by another macro; it only prevents access to the macro code. For more information about locking a project, see the section "Password Protect a Macro" in Chapter 4.

Hide a Macro

1 In Excel, click Tools.

2 Click Macro.

3 Click Macros.

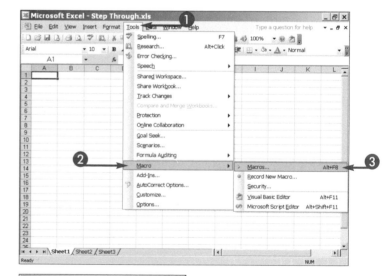

The Macro dialog box lists all the available macros.

4 Click the name of the macro you want to hide.

5 Click Edit.

The macro opens in the Visual Basic Editor.

6 Click at the left end of the Sub line.

7 Type **private**.

8 Click away from the Sub line.

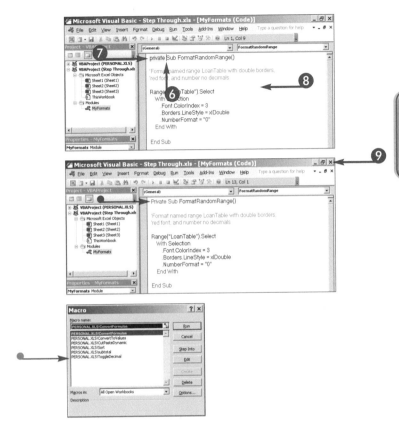

- The keyword Private is capitalized.

9 Click the Close button (⊠) to close the Visual Basic Editor.

10 Repeat steps **1** to **3** to open the Macro dialog box.

You can press Alt+F8 to open the Macro dialog box.

- The hidden macro is not listed.

PART II

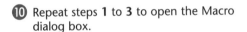

How can I unhide a hidden macro?

▼ You hid the macro by adding the keyword `Private` to the Sub line. To make the macro visible again, open the macro in the Visual Basic Editor and delete the keyword `Private` from the Sub line. The macro is visible in the Macro dialog box again, available to other users, and callable by macros in other modules.

Why does my hidden macro not run when another macro calls it?

▼ If you try to run a hidden macro by calling it from a macro in a different module, even in the same project, you will get an error that reads *Sub or Function not defined*, which means the calling macro cannot find the hidden macro. You can call the hidden macro from another macro in the same module, or unhide the macro.

How can I run a hidden macro?

▼ You can run a hidden macro by assigning it to a menu command, a toolbar button, or a graphical object, or by calling it from another macro within the same module. For more information, see the section "Create a Macro to Run Other Macros" in Chapter 6, and Chapter 2, "Running Macros."

Get VBA Help

You can get instant VBA help when you need to understand more about an item in the VBA code or need examples of how to use specific objects, methods, properties, or functions. Excel and the Visual Basic Editor have different help files, and you find the most help with VBA in the Visual Basic Editor help files. The online help system for VBA contains the entire VBA language reference.

You can access the help files in a couple of ways. You can type a word or phrase in the Ask A Question box and then press Enter. You can click Help and then Microsoft Visual

Basic Help. You can use the Office Assistant if you have this feature enabled in Microsoft Office. On the other hand, you can click to position the mouse cursor in a code word and then press the F1 key for direct help about that word.

If you are not connected to the Internet, you see the help files that were installed with Excel. If you are connected to the Internet, Excel connects to the online help files, which are always up-to-date and provide a wider selection and variety of content.

Get VBA Help

① Open a macro in the Visual Basic Editor.

② Click to position the mouse 👆 within the word for which you are seeking help.

③ Press F1.

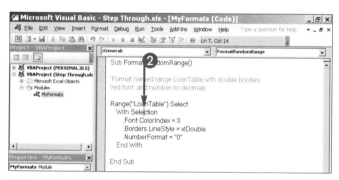

A help window opens with information and examples about the word in which you clicked.

④ Click a highlighted blue word to open another help file.

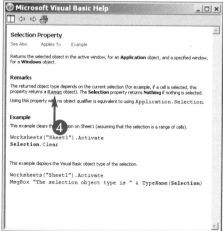

A help file opens about the word you clicked.

5 Click a blue link at the top of the help window.

A list of items opens.

6 Click an item in the list for help on that item.

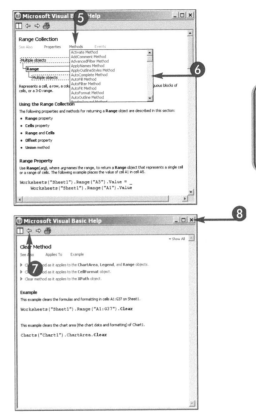

Another help file opens.

7 Click the Back button to go back through help files you have opened.

8 Click ✕ to close the Help window.

How can I find the whole Excel object model?

▼ In the Visual Basic Editor, click Help and then Microsoft Visual Basic Help. In the Visual Basic Help pane, click the Microsoft Excel Visual Basic Reference link. At the top of the table of contents that opens, click the Microsoft Excel Object model. A window opens with a graphical representation of the entire Excel Visual Basic object model.

How can I use what I find in the help files?

▼ When you find a help file example that you want to test in your code, drag to select the example statement in the help file, right-click the selected statement, and click Copy or press Ctrl+C to copy the statement. Next, switch to the Code window or Immediate window, click where you want to paste the statement, and press Ctrl+V.

How can I find the help I need more easily?

▼ You probably need to conduct a better search. Type anything in the Ask A Question box and press Enter. In the Search Results pane that opens, click the Can't find it? link at the bottom, under Search Help. A Help window opens with tips for better search results and advice to make your help search more productive.

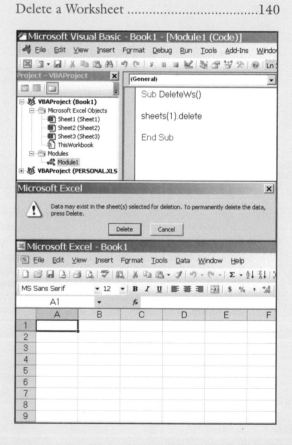

PART III
MANIPULATING WORKBOOKS
AND WORKSHEETS

10   Changing Worksheet Settings

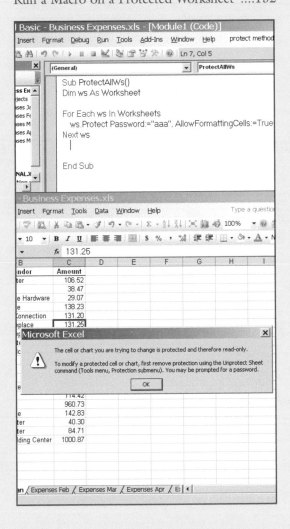

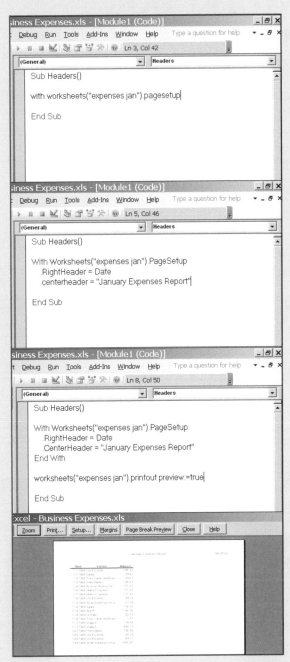

Add a New Workbook

You can write a macro, or a statement in a macro, to create a new, unsaved workbook. For example, if you write or record a macro to set up a new copy of a worksheet that you use often, such as an invoice, you can start the procedure with a statement that opens a new workbook in which to set up the invoice worksheet.

You can create a new, unsaved workbook by using the Workbooks.Add statement, which adds a single new workbook to the Workbooks collection you have open. The new workbook opens unsaved with a consecutively numbered title.

The statement Workbooks.Add opens a new workbook from the general Workbook template in Excel with all of the features that are set under the General tab in the Tools-Options dialog box. The optional `Template` argument enables you to open a copy of a template other than the general workbook template. For example, if you want to open a workbook with a single worksheet, you can use the constant value `xlWBATWorksheet` in the statement, as in `Workbooks.Add (xlWBATWorksheet)`. You can also use any Excel workbook or template file as a template in the `Template` argument.

Add a New Workbook

① Type **Sub** and the macro name, then press Enter to start a new macro in an open module.

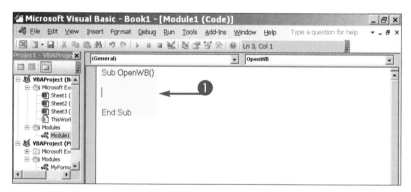

② Type **workbooks** followed by a period.

● The Auto List appears when you type the period.

③ Double-click Add in the Auto List.

④ Press Enter.

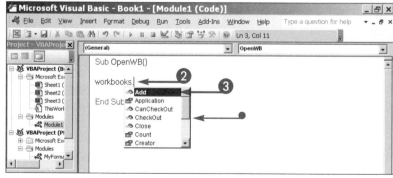

- The statement is complete.

Note: *When typing in the Visual Basic Editor, type in lowercase so you can locate misspellings. The Visual Basic Editor automatically title cases when it is spelled correctly.*

To add additional arguments, repeat steps **2** to **4**.

⑤ Click the Run Sub/UserForm button (▶) to run the macro.

⑥ Click the View Microsoft Excel button (⊠) to switch to Excel.

- A new, unsaved workbook file opens.

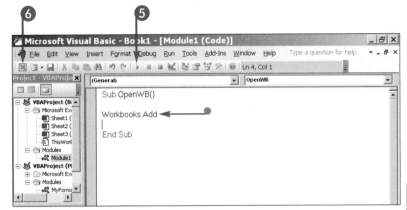

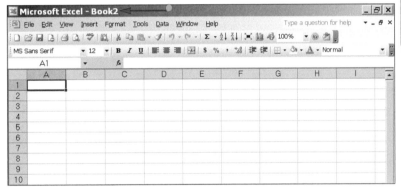

PART III

Why does the Auto List not appear when I type a period?

▼ Check your spelling of the object name. You probably typed *Workbook* instead of *Workbooks*. The singular Workbook is not an object name that the Auto List responds to because VBA does not know which workbook you want. ActiveWorkbook and ThisWorkbook are objects VBA responds to, but they are not collections to which you can add an item. The objects' Auto Lists display their methods and properties. To make sure you start a statement with a viable object name, click Edit→Complete Word and then select the object name from the list.

How can I open a new workbook from a template?

▼ To create a new copy of a workbook or template, add the Template argument to the Workbooks.Add statement. For example, if you have a workbook named Invoice.xls that is empty of data and ready for use, you can type the statement **Workbooks.Add Template:="Invoice.xls"** to open a new, unsaved copy of the workbook named Invoice2. If the workbook you want to use as a template is in a different folder, use the path and file name in quotes, as in Template:="C:\Business\Invoice.xls".

Open a Workbook

Y ou can create a procedure, or a statement within a procedure, to open a specific workbook by using the Open method of the Workbooks collection.

The Open method has several optional arguments, but only the Filename argument is required. The Filename argument is the name of the workbook file you want to open. If the file is in the same folder as the workbook running the macro, you need only type the file name, ending in .xls, between quotes, as in Workbooks.Open Filename:="Invoice.xls". However, if the file is located in a different folder, you need to specify the full path as part

of the file name. For example, Workbooks. Open Filename("C:\Business\Invoice.xls") opens the Invoice.xls file in a folder named Business on the C: drive. If you use the statement in the Personal Macro Workbook, you should always specify the path in the file name.

When you type the Open keyword, a Quick Info screentip displays all the available arguments for the Workbooks. Open method. Always type the required Filename argument first, and then any optional arguments you want separated with commas and spaces.

① Type **Sub** and the macro name, then press Enter to start a new macro.

② Type **workbooks.open**.

③ Type **filename:="***workbookname***"**, replacing *workbookname* with the full path and name of the workbook file.

You can type a comma, a space, and then any optional arguments you want to include.

④ Click 🗷 to switch to Excel.

⑤ Click Tools.

⑥ Click Macro.

⑦ Click Macros.

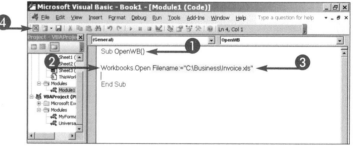

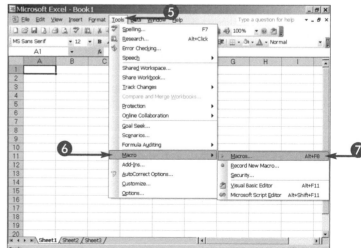

The Macro dialog box appears.

8 Select the macro name.

9 Run the macro.

You can press F5 to run the macro from the Visual Basic Editor.

● The workbook opens as the active workbook.

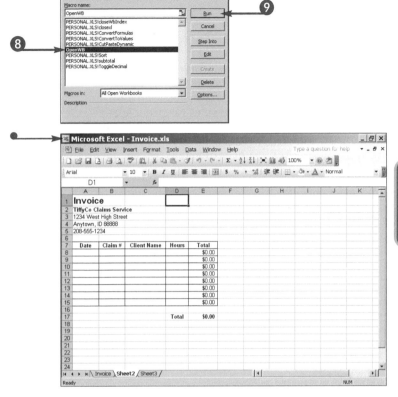

What does the Password argument do in the Workbooks.Open method?

▼ The Password argument is useful if the workbook is password protected against opening. If the workbook requires a password to be opened, the user is prompted for the password when the macro opens the workbook; but if you write the password into the statement, as Password: ="password", the macro enters the password and the file opens.

Why is my password-protected workbook opening with frozen windows?

▼ You probably protected the workbook by clicking Tools→ Protection→Protect Workbook from the menu and selecting the password option, which does not protect against opening the file. To set a password to open the file, click File→Save As. In the Save As dialog box, click the Tools menu button and select General Options. Type a password in the Password field to open box and click OK.

How can I have the workbook open read-only?

▼ If you want the workbook to open read-only, so the user can view the workbook but not save changes, add the argument ReadOnly:= True to your Workbooks.Open statement. Users can make changes to the workbook, but they cannot save the changes unless they create a copy of the workbook. The value False, or leaving the argument out, makes the workbook editable.

Import a Text File

You can import a text file into Excel without going through the Text Import Wizard steps by using the Workbooks.OpenText statement. Receiving a file in text file format is common because you can open it in any spreadsheet program, but opening a text file in Excel starts the Text Import Wizard. A macro can do the job much more quickly, especially if you need to import text files on a regular basis.

You can specify how the text file opens using the OpenText arguments. The only required argument is FileName, but you should use the entire path in the argument to be sure

you open the correct file. For more information on referring to workbook files, see the section "Refer to a Workbook in Macros."

Among the optional arguments are the specific delimiter characters Tab, Semicolon, Comma, or Space, and StartRow, which specifies what row to start the import with if you do not want to start at the first row.

Before you write the macro to import a text file, you need to determine the characteristics of the text files you want to open, including delimiters and the start row you want to use.

Import a Text File

① Type **Sub** and the macro name, then press Enter to start a new macro.

② Type **workbooks.opentext** and a space.

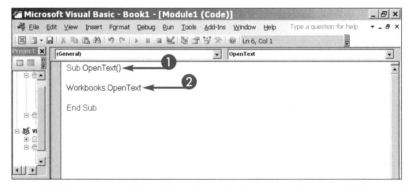

③ Type **filename:=** "*path and filename*".

④ Type a comma, and then **tab:=true**.

If the delimiter is a comma, type **comma:=true** instead.

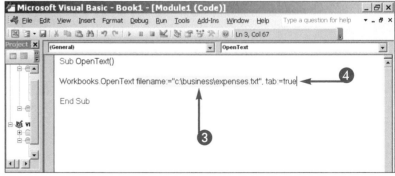

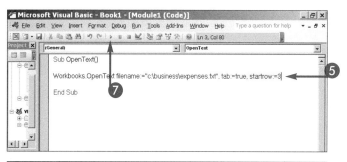

⑤ Type a comma, and then **startrow:** = *startrownumber*, replacing *startrownumber* with the value of the first row you want to import.

This example imports a tab-delimited text file starting with row 3.

⑥ Press Enter.

⑦ Click ▶ to run the macro.

You can press F5 to run the macro from the Visual Basic Editor.

The text file imports into Excel without running the Text Import Wizard.

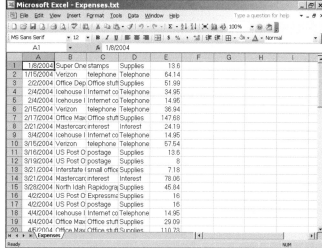

How do I set an Other Character for a delimiter?

▼ If a text file has a delimiter character other than Tab, Semicolon, Comma, or Space, you set the `DataType` argument to the delimited constant value `xlDelimited` and use the `Other` and `OtherChar` arguments. For example, if the delimiter is the pipe symbol (|), you add the three arguments `DataType:= xlDelimited, Other:= True, OtherChar:= "|"` after the `FileName` argument.

How can I set the correct characters for thousands separators and decimals?

▼ You can use the `DecimalSeparator` and `ThousandsSeparator` arguments in the `OpenText` method. Be sure you type the decimal and thousands characters you want to use as strings within quotes. For example, to use a period as a decimal character, type the argument `DecimalSeparator: = "."`. To specify a comma as the thousands separator in numbers, type the argument `ThousandsSeparator:= ","`.

How can I save the imported file as an Excel file?

▼ After you write the `OpenText` method and all the accompanying arguments you want, you can use the `Workbooks.SaveAs` statement with the `FileFormat` argument to save the file as an Excel file type. Type the argument as `ThisWorkbook.SaveAs FileName:= ("filename. xls"), FileType:= xlWorkbookNormal`. For more information, see the section "Save a Workbook with a New Name."

Save a Workbook with a New Name

You can write a statement to save a file, or to save a file with a different name, with no user input. To save a file, you can use either the Save or SaveAs method for the Workbooks object.

You can save a workbook quietly with its current file name by using the Workbooks("*filename*.xls").Save statement. You can save a workbook with a different name by using the Workbooks("*filename*.xls").SaveAs statement with the FileName argument. For example, Workbooks("Invoice.xls").SaveAs FileName: = ("Receipt.xls") creates a copy of Invoice.xls in the current folder and names the file Receipt.xls.

The SaveAs method creates a copy of the file with the new file name, either in the current folder or in the folder you specify in the FileName argument. You can only save files that are open.

You can refer to the workbook by file name, index number, ThisWorkbook, or ActiveWorkbook, whichever is appropriate for your macro. Remember that index numbers can change with each Excel session. For more information about referring to workbooks, see the section "Refer to a Workbook in Macros."

The Save method has no arguments, but the SaveAs method has several. After you type *SaveAs* in the statement, the Quick Info screentip appears with a list of the arguments.

Save a Workbook with a New Name

① Type **Sub** and the macro name, then press Enter to start a new macro.

You can also test your statement in the Immediate window.

② Type **activeworkbook.save**.

③ Click ▶ to run the macro.

You can press F5 to run the macro from the Visual Basic Editor.

● The active workbook is saved with its current name and in the current folder.

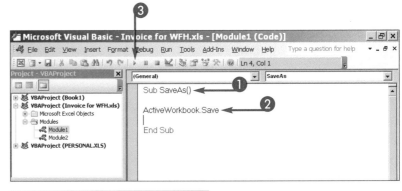

4 Edit the statement to read **activeworkbook.saveas filename:=** "*filename*.xls", replacing *filename* with the file name you want.

5 Click ▶ to run the macro.

You can press F5 to run the macro from the Visual Basic Editor.

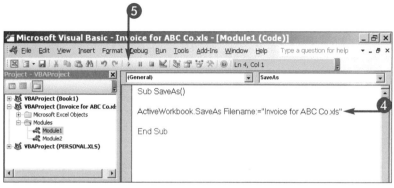

● A copy of the workbook is saved in the current folder with the new file name.

You can save the file in a different folder by typing the new path and file name in the `FileName` argument.

How can I save a workbook with a password?

▼ You can use the `SaveAs` method with the optional `Password` argument. For example, to save a file with its current file name and a password, include the argument `Password:= "password"`. To make this password effective quietly, so the user does not see it run, enter the three statements `Application.DisplayAlerts = False`, `ActiveWorkbook.SaveAs Password:= "password"`, and `Application.DisplayAlerts = True`.

How can I save a file in a different format?

▼ You can use the `FileFormat` argument with an `xlFileFormat` constant as a value. For example, if you want to save the workbook as a text file with a .txt extension, type the argument `FileFormat:= xlCurrentPlatformText`. If the file you want to save is not an Excel file, you can save it as an Excel file with the argument `FileFormat:= xlNormal`.

How can I quickly find out what the current folder is?

▼ You can save a file with the current file name in the `SaveAs Filename` argument, but saving only the file name saves the file in the current folder. If you need to find out what the current folder is, open the Immediate window, type **?CurDir** and press Enter. The current path and folder name appear on the next line.

Refer to a Workbook in Macros

You can refer to any specific workbook in a macro by using the correct reference. When you want to execute any method or property on a specific workbook, such as Activate or Close, you need to tell Excel exactly which workbook you mean.

You can refer to a workbook by pointing to ThisWorkbook or ActiveWorkbook, or you can refer to a workbook more specifically by name. When you refer to a workbook by name, you can be sure you are executing code on the correct workbook. When you use a workbook name, enclose the name or path in quotes, as in the statement

`Workbooks("Invoice.xls").Close`. If the workbook is in the current folder, the file name alone is enough; but if the workbook is in a different folder, you must include the path in the file reference.

You can also refer to a workbook by index number, which indicates the workbook's position in the collection of open workbooks. A specific workbook's index position may change in every Excel session, except for the Personal Macro Workbook, which opens when you start Excel. A reference to Workbooks(1) is typically the Personal Macro Workbook.

Refer to a Workbook in Macros

① Open two workbooks in Excel.

② Arrange your Excel and Visual Basic Editor windows so you can see both.

③ Open and float the Immediate window so you can see it and the Excel window easily.

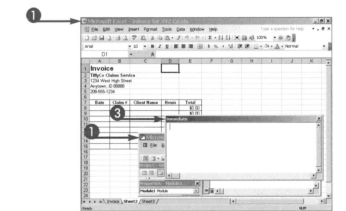

Note: To open and float windows, see the section "Open and Dock Windows" in Chapter 5.

④ In the Immediate window, type **?workbooks(2).name**.

⑤ Press Enter.

● The Immediate window displays the name of the workbook that has index number 2.

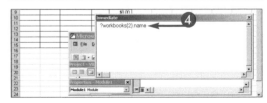

⑥ On a new line in the Immediate window, type **workbooks("*filename*.xls").close**, replacing *filename* with the name of an open workbook.

⑦ Press Enter.

110

The open workbook with the file name you typed closes.

8 In the Immediate window, type **activeworkbook.close** and press Enter.

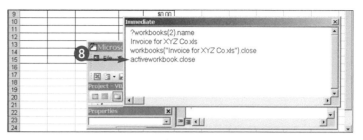

- The active workbook closes. If there was only one workbook still open, Excel remains open but without workbooks showing in the Excel window.

You can refer to workbooks in your code by file name, by index number, or as ActiveWorkbook or ThisWorkbook.

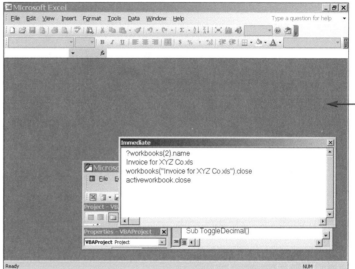

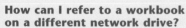

How can I refer to a workbook on a different network drive?

▼ When you refer to a workbook on another drive by file name, include the entire path beginning with the drive letter in the file name. For example, if the workbook named Invoice.xls is in the Business folder on the network drive Q:, refer to the workbook with the string (`"Q:\Business\Invoice.xls"`). Remember that the network drive must be connected and shared.

Why do I get errors when I refer to a workbook by file name?

▼ It is probably a typing error. Common typing errors include neglecting to type the final *s* in Workbooks, misspelling the file name or typing the wrong path, and forgetting to type the closing quote around the file name string. Typing the file name or path in lowercase letters is not a problem. Excel recognizes paths and file names regardless of capitalization.

How can I tell what the index number is for a specific workbook?

▼ Open the Immediate window and ask a series of questions. If you have three workbooks open, type `?workbooks(1).name` and press Enter, `?workbooks(2).name` and press Enter, and then `?workbooks(3).name` and press Enter. Each time you press Enter, the name of the indexed workbook appears on the next line. You can find out how many workbooks are open with the question `?workbooks.count`.

Show a Toolbar in a Specific Workbook

You can write a macro that displays a specific toolbar, custom or built-in, when a particular workbook is opened, and that closes the toolbar when the workbook is closed. The macros that run when a workbook opens and closes respond to Workbook events that trigger the macros to run. The workbook event that displays the toolbar is the Workbook_Open() event. VBA creates this event as a Private subprocedure so it cannot be called from other modules, and runs all the code listed in the event procedure. The workbook event that hides the toolbar is the `Workbook_BeforeClose()` event. VBA also

creates this event as a Private subprocedure so it cannot be called from other modules, and runs all the code listed in the event procedure.

You can type these events yourself, but using the Visual Basic Editor techniques to write them is easier. When you double-click the ThisWorkbook node in the Project window, you can choose Workbook in the Object list and select the event from the Procedure list at the top of the Code window. When you select the event, the Visual Basic Editor inserts the procedure and you write all your statements between the Sub and End Sub lines.

Show a Toolbar in a Specific Workbook

① Open the Microsoft Excel Object node for the project in the Project window.

② Double-click the ThisWorkbook node.

③ Click Workbook in the Object list.

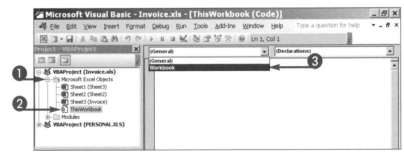

The Visual Basic Editor may insert the Workbook_Open procedure for you.

④ If the Visual Basic Editor did not insert the Workbook_Open procedure, click ⏷ and select Open in the Procedure list.

● Excel starts a Private macro that runs when the workbook opens.

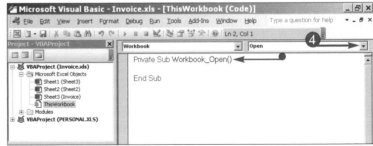

⑤ Type the statement **application. commandbars("*toolbarname*").visible = true**, replacing *toolbarname* with the toolbar name in a string, and press Enter.

⑥ Save and close the workbook.

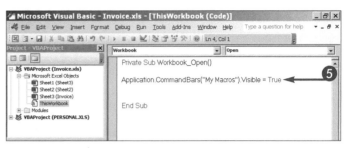

⑦ Open the workbook.

● The toolbar appears when the workbook opens.

The toolbar remains open until you close Excel, unless you create a BeforeClose macro to hide it.

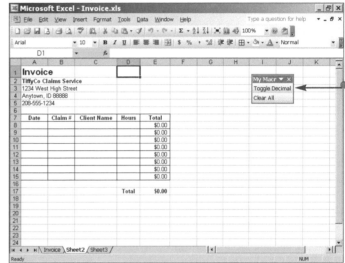

How do I hide the toolbar when the workbook closes?

▼ If you display a toolbar when a specific workbook opens, the toolbar remains open until you close Excel. If you want the toolbar to close when the workbook closes, you can create a Workbook_ BeforeClose macro in the same ThisWorkbook module where you created the Workbook_Open macro. Select `BeforeClose` in the Procedure list. In the `BeforeClose` macro, type the statement `Application.CommandBars("toolbarname"). Visible = False`. Statements in this macro run immediately before the workbook closes. It does not matter if the `Open` procedure is before or after the `BeforeClose` procedure in the Code window.

How can I create a custom toolbar that resides in a workbook but not in Excel?

▼ To create a toolbar that is limited to use within a specific workbook and cannot be opened from the Toolbars list in Excel, you can create a programmatic toolbar that is created when a specific workbook opens and is deleted when that workbook closes. You can create the code for the custom toolbar and buttons and insert that code into a Workbook_Open procedure in the specific workbook. To delete the toolbar, type the statement `Application. CommandBars("toolbarname").Delete` in a Workbook_BeforeClose macro. For more information, see the section "Create a Programmatic Custom Toolbar."

Create a Programmatic Custom Toolbar

Y ou can send a workbook to someone else with a custom toolbar created in the workbook's VBA code. A custom toolbar you create programmatically for that workbook travels with the workbook file, so you do not have to send a separate toolbar add-in along with the workbook.

You create a toolbar by using the statement CommandBars.Add to add a new item to the CommandBars collection. The Add method has several properties and arguments, the most important of which are Temporary, Name, Position, and Visible. If you create the new toolbar with no optional arguments or properties,

a new toolbar named Custom 1 is added to the Toolbars menu and remains hidden until you open it from the Toolbars menu.

The Temporary argument controls whether the toolbar remains available in Excel after you close the program. If the value is True, the toolbar is removed when Excel closes and does not display when you reopen Excel. The toolbar must be launched again from the macro. The Visible property sets the display of the new toolbar, and the Name property names the new toolbar.

This procedure is easier to write and more efficient to run if you declare your toolbar variables.

Create a Programmatic Custom Toolbar

① Type **Sub** and the macro name, then press Enter to start a new macro.

② Type the variable declaration **dim** *variablename* **as commandbar**, replacing *variablename* with your variable name.

This statement declares the variable to be a CommandBar item.

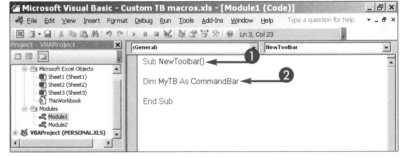

③ Type **set** *variablename* **= commandbars. add(temporary:=true)**, replacing *variablename* with your variable name.

④ Type **with** *variablename*, replacing *variablename* with your variable name.

⑤ Type **.name="***toolbarname***"**, replacing *toolbarname* with your toolbar name.

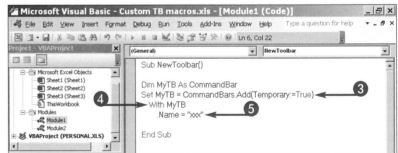

6 Type **.position=msobarfloating**.

This value makes the new toolbar float on the worksheet.

7 Type **.visible=true**.

The Visible property displays rather than hides the created toolbar.

8 Type **end with**.

9 Click ▣ to switch to Excel.

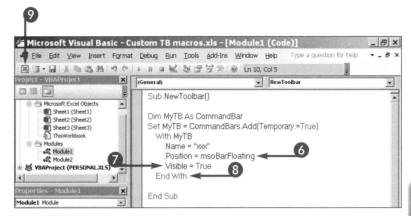

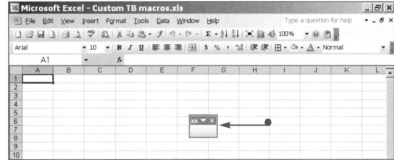

10 Run the macro.

Note: *To run a macro from Excel, see the section "Run a Macro" in Chapter 2.*

● The new empty toolbar is created and displayed floating on the worksheet.

PART III

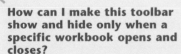

How can I make this toolbar show and hide only when a specific workbook opens and closes?	**How can I add buttons to a programmatically created toolbar?**	**Why do I get an error the second time I run this macro?**
▼ To make a toolbar appear when a workbook opens, you must write the procedure in a macro that is triggered by the Workbook_Open event. To delete a toolbar when the workbook closes, you must write a procedure that is triggered by the Workbook_BeforeClose event. For more information, see the section "Show a Toolbar in a Specific Workbook."	▼ To add buttons to the new toolbar, write statements that add items to the CommandBarControls collection for the CommandBar object. Each button is created with a unique variable and set of properties. Declare the button variables and write the button statements within the macro that creates the toolbar. For more information, see the section "Create Programmatic Toolbar Buttons."	▼ You get an error at the .Name property because the macro already created a toolbar with that name. When the macro tries to create that name again, you get an error. You must delete the new toolbar before you run the macro again. To delete a toolbar when the workbook closes, type the statement `Application. CommandBars("toolbarname"). Delete` in the `Workbook_ BeforeClose` macro.

Create Programmatic Toolbar Buttons

I f you create a programmatically controlled toolbar, you need to programmatically add buttons to the toolbar or the toolbar is empty. You can write a macro to create all the custom toolbar buttons you need for the custom toolbar. You can program the buttons to run macros even in workbooks that are not open.

You can add buttons to a toolbar with the Add method of the Controls property of the CommandBar object, which is the toolbar, as in the statement Set *buttonvariable* = *toolbarvariable*.Controls.Add (Type: =msoConrolButton). You can then add the optional properties.

The most important optional properties include .FaceId, which gives the button an icon, and .OnAction, which assigns a macro to the button.

Using declared variables when you create macros for toolbars and toolbar buttons is important because variables make the procedures run more efficiently, and make the code easier to write and read.

Because a programmatically created toolbar needs programmatically created buttons, you should place the button procedures within the toolbar procedure so the procedures run efficiently one right after the other.

Create Programmatic Toolbar Buttons

① Open a macro that creates a custom toolbar.

Note: To create a custom toolbar, see the section "Create a Programmatic Custom Toolbar."

② Below the With block for the toolbar, type **dim** *variablename* **as commandbarcontrol**, replacing *variablename* with your button variable name.

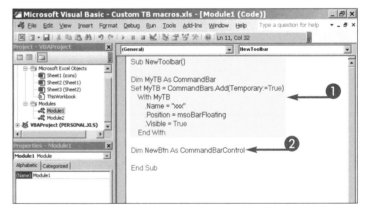

③ Type **set** *variablename* = *toolbarvariable*.**controls.add**.

④ Type the argument (**type: =msocontrolbutton**).

⑤ Type **with** *variablename*.

⑥ Type the property **.faceid = 24**, replacing the value with the value you want.

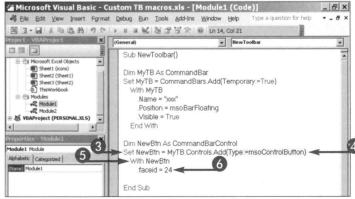

⑦ Type **.onaction = "macroname"**, replacing *macroname* with the macro you want the button to run.

If the macro is in another workbook, use "*workbookname!macroname*" as the value.

⑧ Type **end with**.

⑨ Click ⊠ to switch to Excel.

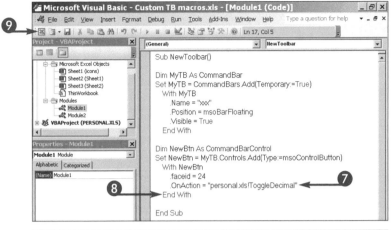

⑩ Run the macro.

Note: *To run a macro from Excel, see the section "Run a Macro" in Chapter 2.*

● The macro creates a new toolbar and adds a new button that runs a macro.

To add more buttons, repeat steps **2** to **8** with a new, unique variable name for each button.

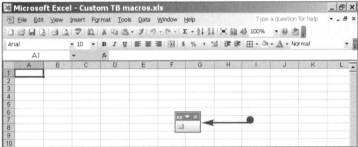

How can I add built-in buttons to my custom toolbar?

▼ In place of the Dim and Set statements, use the statement `Application.CommandBars("xxx").Controls.Add Type:=msoControlButton, ID:=Idcontrolvalue`, replacing *Idcontrolvalue* with the value of the built-in control. You need the ID value of each control, but Microsoft does not provide a list. This macro lists them all:

```
Sub GetControlID()
    Dim RowID As Integer
    Dim Tb As CommandBar
    Dim Btn As CommandBarControl
    RowID = 1
    For Each Tb In CommandBars
    Cells(RowID, 1) = Tb.Name
    For Each Btn In
    CommandBars(Tb.Name).Controls
    Cells(RowID, 2) = Btn.ID
    Cells(RowID, 3) = Btn.Caption
    RowID = RowID + 1
    Next
    Next
End Sub
```

How can I find out which FaceId values I want?

▼ The FaceId property has values from 0 to 3499, but Microsoft does not provide a list in Excel to look up which values give which button faces. The best way to find out is to write the macro and experiment with different FaceId values. Create the macro with several buttons, and change the FaceId values every time you run the macro to see what button faces the numbers create. You need to delete the new toolbar every time you want to run the macro again.

Close a Workbook and Save Changes Quietly

You can close a specific workbook by writing a statement using the `Close` method on a workbook object you designate, and you can make that workbook close quietly, without asking the user to save the file. When you close the workbook quietly, you can tell VBA to save changes or discard changes.

The workbooks collection contains all of the currently open workbooks and assigns them index values that are numbered sequentially in the order in which they were opened. You can identify a particular workbook by index number, file name, or as ActiveWorkbook or ThisWorkbook.

The first workbook you open in an Excel session is identified by index number as `Workbooks(1)`. Because the first workbook Excel always opens is the Personal Macro Workbook, `Workbooks(1)` always refers to the Personal Macro Workbook. To identify a file by file name, enclose the file name in quotes and parentheses, as in `Workbooks ("Invoice.xls")`. The statement to close a workbook named Invoice.xls is `Workbooks("Invoice.xls"). Close`.

Among the optional arguments you can add to the statement are `SaveChanges` and `FileName`. The `SaveChanges` argument closes the workbook without asking about saving changes, and the `Filename` argument saves the workbook with a different name.

Close a Workbook and Save Changes Quietly

① Type **Sub** and the macro name, then press Enter to start a new macro, or start a new statement in an existing macro.

You can also type the statement in the Immediate window, and after you know the statement works, you can copy it into a macro.

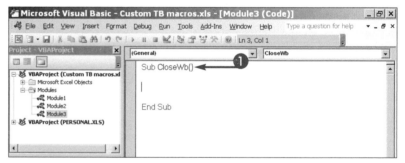

② Type **activeworkbook.close**.

③ Click ▶ to run the macro.

You can press F5 to run the macro from the Visual Basic Editor.

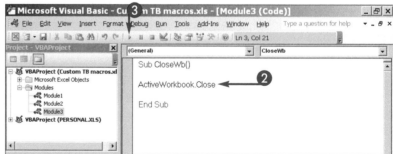

- The macro closes the active workbook and Excel asks if you want to save changes.

④ Click Cancel in the save changes query.

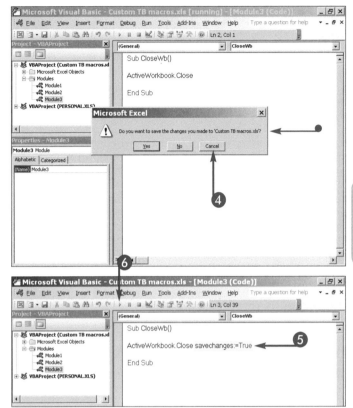

⑤ At the end of the statement, type the argument **savechanges:=true**.

⑥ Click ▶ to run the macro.

The active workbook closes without asking you to save changes. Any changes in the workbook are saved.

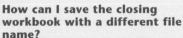

How can I save the closing workbook with a different file name?

▼ Add the argument `Filename:=("filename.xls")` to the statement. If you do not specify the full path with the file name, the workbook saves in the My Documents folder. You must place the `Filename` argument ahead of the `SaveChanges` argument, as in `ActiveWorkbook.Close FileName:= ("Invoice.xls"), SaveChanges:= True,` or the file is saved and closed before the macro gets to the `Filename` argument.

How can I close all of my workbooks at once?

▼ You can type the statement `Workbooks.Close`, which acts on the entire workbooks collection and closes all of the open workbooks. If you do not add the `SaveChanges` argument, Excel checks each open workbook for changes and asks you if you want to save any workbooks with unsaved changes. To close all the workbooks and save all changes quietly, type the statement `Workbooks.Close SaveChanges:=True`.

How can I close Excel completely after I close all the workbooks?

▼ After you close all the workbooks, Excel remains open and running. If you want Excel to close after you close the workbooks, you can use the `Quit` method with the Application object. Type `Application.Quit` at the end of the macro. The `Quit` method has no arguments.

Delete a Workbook

Y ou can quickly clean out old and unnecessary workbook files, or any files in your system, completely and quietly by using the Kill statement.

The Kill statement deletes any file in its path. To delete a workbook file in the current folder, use the statement `Kill "workbookname.xls"`. To delete a workbook file in a different folder, assuming that C: is your hard drive, use the statement `Kill "c:\foldername\workbookname.xls"`. You can use this statement to delete any type of file in the system, and you can use wildcard characters to delete multiple similar files with one statement. There Kill statement has no other arguments.

Before you use this statement in a macro, it is a good idea to test it on empty waste files that you can delete without doing any damage to your data, because when this statement is properly executed, the killed files are gone completely. You can quickly test the statement by creating a waste Excel file and then typing the Kill statement in the Immediate window.

You can only delete closed files. If you try to delete an open file, you see the error *Permission denied*.

Delete a Workbook

① Determine the location of the workbook you want to delete.

② Type **Sub** and the macro name, then press Enter to start a new macro, or start a new line in an existing macro.

③ Type **kill** followed by a space.

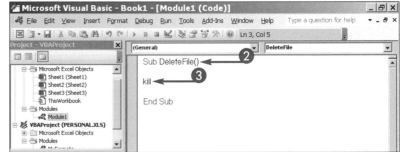

④ Type the file name or path as a string by enclosing the characters in quotes.

This statement deletes the workbook named BadData.xls in the My Documents folder on the C: drive.

⑤ Click ▶ to run the macro.

You can press F5 to run the macro from the Visual Basic Editor.

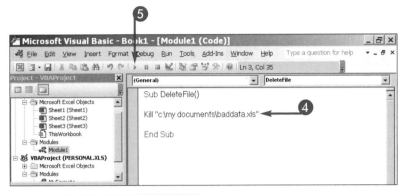

● The workbook is deleted.

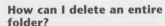

How can I delete an entire folder?

▼ You can delete an entire folder or directory by using the RmDir statement, which has the same syntax as the Kill statement. The syntax is RmDir "C:\ *foldername*". You must remove all files from the folder before you can delete the folder. If you want to delete a folder and its files, run the Kill statement followed by the RmDir statement.

How can I delete multiple files with one statement?

▼ The Kill statement accepts multi-character (*) and single-character (?) wildcards in the Pathname argument. For example, to delete all the Excel workbook files in a folder, use the multi-character wildcard, as in Kill "C:\Business*. xls". If you have sequentially numbered workbooks — for example, workbooks named Invoice1.xls, Invoice2.xls, and so forth — you can delete them with the statement Kill "Invoice?.xls".

How can I recover files I deleted in error?

▼ When you use the Kill statement, the files are removed completely from the drive in your Kill statement path name. You can only recover those files if you use a good backup system regularly and have copies of those deleted files backed up. A backup system enables you to recover the most recent backed-up version of any file.

Refer to a Worksheet

Y ou can refer to any worksheet in a macro by using the correct reference. When you want to execute any method or property on a specific worksheet, such as Activate or Delete, you must tell Excel exactly which worksheet you mean.

You can refer to the active worksheet with the object name ActiveWorksheet, or you can refer to a worksheet object more specifically by sheet name. In the Project window, the sheet name is the name in parentheses. When you use a worksheet name, enclose the name in quotes, as in the statements Sheets(`"sheetname"`) and Worksheets (`"sheetname"`). You can refer to worksheets with either

the Worksheets object or the Sheets object. To refer to a worksheet in a different workbook, you must include the workbook object, as in Workbooks(`"filename.xls"`). Sheets(`"sheetname"`).

You can also refer to a worksheet by index number, which indicates the worksheet's position in the workbook. The worksheets are indexed sequentially from left to right, so a reference to Sheets(1) or Worksheets(1) always refers to the leftmost worksheet in the workbook. A sheet's index position in the workbook may change every time a worksheet is added, deleted, moved, or copied, so referring to a worksheet by name is more specific.

Refer to a Worksheet

- All the sheet names, in parentheses, are listed in the Project window.

1 In a new macro, type **worksheets (*"sheetname"*).delete**, replacing *sheetname* with a worksheet name in the open workbook, and press Enter.

This example refers to and deletes the worksheet named Sheet1.

2 Click the Run Sub/UserForm button (▶) to run the macro.

3 In the deletion message, click Delete.

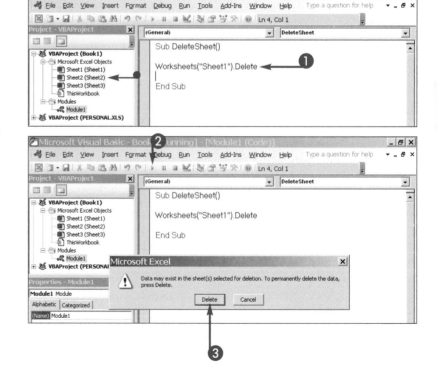

- The worksheet named Sheet1 is deleted.

④ Edit the macro statement to **worksheets(1).delete**.

The index number *1* refers to the leftmost worksheet in the workbook.

⑤ Click View Microsoft Excel () to switch to Excel.

⑥ Run the macro.

Note: To run a macro from Excel, see the section "Run a Macro" in Chapter 2.

⑦ In the deletion message, click Delete.

- The leftmost worksheet, which has VBA index number 1, is deleted.

Why do I see the Macros dialog box when I press F5 to run the macro in the Visual Basic Editor?

▼ The Macros dialog box appears because the insertion point is not within the macro, so Excel does not know which macro you want to run. For example, if the cursor is blinking in the empty line below the End Sub line, the cursor is not within the macro. To run a macro from the Visual Basic Editor, click to place the insertion point within the macro.

What are the different ways in which I can run a macro in the Visual Basic Editor?

▼ You can run a macro from the Visual Basic Editor in four ways. First, click to place the insertion point within the macro you want to run. Then you can either press F5, press F8 to step through the macro, click the Run Sub/UserForm toolbar button, or click Run and then click Run Sub/UserForm.

How can I tell what the index number is for a specific worksheet?

▼ You can open the Immediate window and ask a series of questions. You can find out how many worksheets are in the workbook with the question `?worksheets.count`, which tells you how many index numbers there are. Then type `?worksheets(1).name`. When you press Enter, the name of the indexed worksheet appears on the next line. Repeat the question for each worksheet index number.

Add a New Worksheet

Y ou can add a new worksheet to a workbook using the Add method with a Sheets or Worksheets object. If you use the Sheets object, you can add either a worksheet or a chart sheet. The Sheets.Add statement adds a worksheet by default, but you can add a chart sheet instead by adding the argument Type:=xlChart. If you use the Worksheets object, you can add only a worksheet.

Both Add statements add new sheets to the active workbook, but you can direct Excel to add the new sheet to a specific workbook by referring to the workbook in the Add statement. For example, the statement

`ThisWorkbook.Sheets.Add` adds a new sheet to the workbook in which the macro is stored. The statement `ActiveWorkbook.Sheets.Add` adds a new sheet to the active workbook, regardless of where the macro is stored. The statement `Workbooks("Invoice.xls").Sheets.Add` adds a sheet to the Invoice.xls workbook if it is open.

Both Add statements have four optional arguments, Before, After, Count, and Type. The Before and After arguments position the new worksheet in the workbook, the Count argument tells Excel how many worksheets to add, and the Type argument tells Excel which type of sheet to add.

Add a New Worksheet

① Type **Sub** and the macro name, then press Enter to start a new macro.

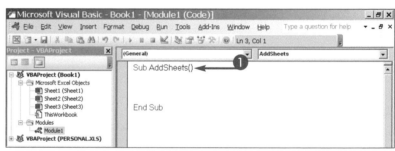

② Type **worksheets.add**.

This statement adds a new worksheet to the active workbook.

③ Press Enter.

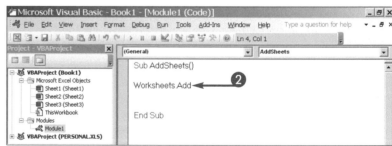

④ Click ▶ to run the macro.

The macro adds a worksheet to the workbook.

⑤ Click ⊠ to switch to Excel.

● A new worksheet is added to the workbook.

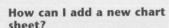

How can I add a new chart sheet?

▼ You can use the Sheets.Add statement to add a new chart sheet. Use the Type argument and the xlChart value, which is a VBA constant. For example, to add a new chart sheet to the active workbook, use the statement ActiveWorkbook.Sheets.Add Type:= xlChart. This statement adds a new chart sheet to the left of the active worksheet.

How can I add the new worksheet in a specific position?

▼ The worksheets are index numbered by VBA from left to right, so the statement ActiveWorkbook.Worksheets.Add Before:= Worksheets(1) positions the new worksheet as the leftmost worksheet in the workbook. The statement ActiveWorkbook.Worksheets.Add After:=Sheets("January") adds a new sheet to the right of the sheet named January. For more information about referring to worksheets, see the section "Refer to a Worksheet."

How can I add several worksheets at once?

▼ Use either the Sheets.Add or Worksheets.Add statement with the Count argument and the number of sheets you want to add as the value. For example, to add four new worksheets to the active workbook, use the statement ActiveWorkbook.Workheets.Add Count:= 4. This statement adds four new worksheets to the left of the active worksheet.

Name a Worksheet

You can rename a worksheet with a macro by changing the Name property of the Sheets or Worksheets object. In the statement, you must identify the worksheet you want to rename by index number, sheet name, or as ActiveSheet. You change a sheet name with the statement `Sheets(sheetidentity).Name = "newname"` or `Worksheets(sheetidentity).Name = "newname"` or `ActiveSheet.Name = "newname"`. The Worksheets object can only rename worksheets, but the Sheets object can rename both worksheets and chart sheets. Remember that an index number is not enclosed in quotes, but a sheet name is a string and must be enclosed in quotes.

Unless you identify the open workbook in which you want to rename a sheet, the rename macro is executed in the active workbook. To be sure you are renaming the correct sheet, use the statement `Workbooks("filename.xls").Sheets("sheetname").Name = "newsheetname"`.

In the project window, Excel keeps track of the sheets in the workbook's Sheets collection. You can see the sheets listed in collection order with sheet names in parentheses. The collection order in the Project window is not the same as the index order in the workbook.

Name a Worksheet

① Type **Sub** and the macro name, then press Enter to start a new macro.

② Type **activesheet.name** = "*newname*", replacing *newname* with your new sheet name.

③ Click ⊠ to switch to Excel.

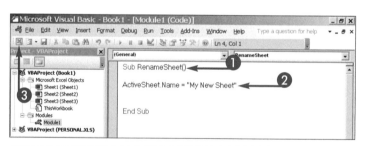

④ Click Tools.

⑤ Click Macro.

⑥ Click Macros.

You can also press Alt+F8 to open the Macro dialog box.

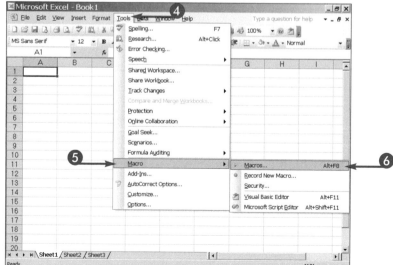

The Macro dialog box appears.

7 Click the macro name in the Macro dialog box.

8 Click Run.

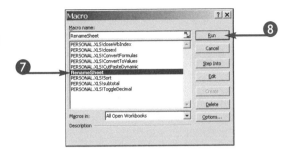

● The active sheet name changes.

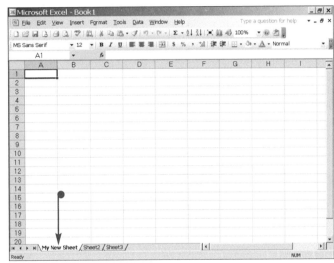

Why does the Auto List not appear when I type the period after `Sheets`?

▼ Because a workbook can contain different kinds of sheets, and VBA does not know what kind you mean. To get the Auto List, declare a variable for the object reference. For example, `Dim Sht as Worksheet`, and then `Set Sht = Worksheets(1)`. The statement `Sht.Name = "newname"` then shows the Auto List. For more information, see the section "Declare a Variable" in Chapter 6.

How can I rename a chart sheet?

▼ You can rename a chart sheet by using the Sheets object. The statement `Sheets (indexnumber).Name = "newname"` renames the first sheet in a workbook, whether the sheet is a worksheet or chart sheet. You can also rename a chart sheet by using the Sheets object and the chart sheet name, as in `Sheets ("chartsheetname").Name = "newname"`.

How can I be sure the macro is renaming the correct sheet?

▼ Because users can easily change the name of a sheet from within Excel, or change a sheet's index positionby moving it, you must be careful when you identify a sheet by name or index number in a macro. To learn how to safely identify sheets by unchanging code names, see the section "Identify Worksheets by Unchanging Code Names."

Identify Worksheets by Unchanging Code Names

If you record a macro that references worksheets, the macro can be destroyed if a user moves a worksheet or changes a worksheet name. You can make the macro invulnerable to changes in worksheet name or position by using unchanging code names as worksheet references.

The Project window lists all the worksheets in a workbook. A code name and a sheet name exist for each sheet icon. The code name is the name outside of the parentheses, and the sheet name is the name within parentheses. Excel keeps track of all sheets by code name, no matter what a sheet's name or position in the workbook is. You can use code

names to reference any kind of sheet because all sheets, whether worksheets or chart sheets, have unique code names.

You can change a code name in the Properties window by clicking the sheet icon in the Project window and then changing the name in the Properties window Name box. You can reference the worksheet by using the code name as the object in the statement. For example, if the code name of a sheet is Sheet1, you can select that sheet with the statement `Sheet1.Select`.

You cannot use a code name to reference a sheet that resides in another workbook.

Identify Worksheets by Unchanging Code Names

① Open a module in the workbook in which you want to use code-name references.

You can double-click a module to open it.

② Type **Sub** and the macro name, then press Enter to start a new macro.

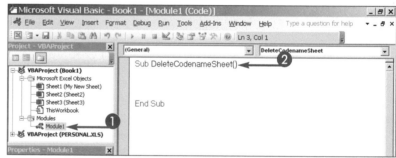

③ Type *codename*, replacing *codename* with the sheet code name, followed by a period.

In this example, the sheet with code name Sheet1 is the object.

An Auto List appears because a code name is a known object.

④ Click a method from the Auto List.

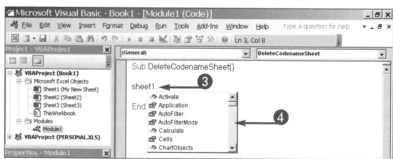

- In this example, the Delete method is selected.

5 Click [▷] to run the macro.

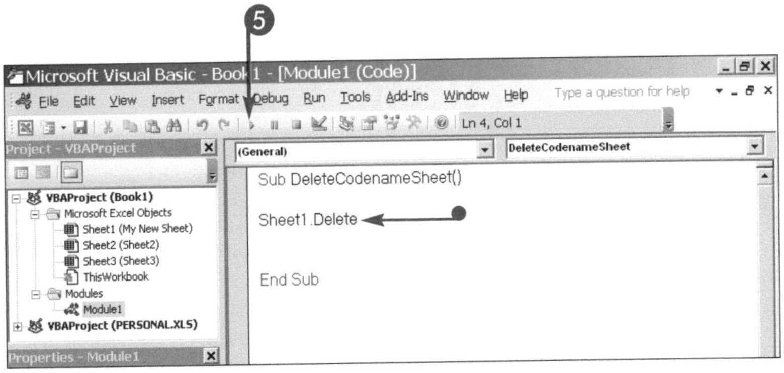

- The method you selected is executed on the code-named sheet. For example, if you selected the Delete method, the sheet with your code name is deleted from the Project window.

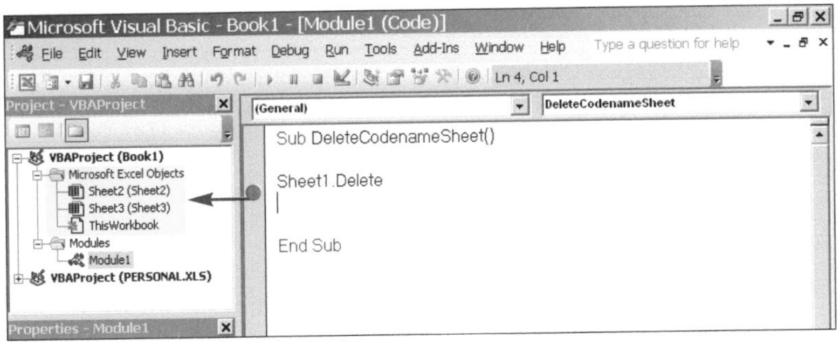

MASTER IT

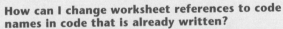

How can I change worksheet references to code names in code that is already written?

▼ You can replace sheet references with code names throughout the workbook project if your workbook is already full of VBA code that references sheet names or locations. Be sure you are in a module in the workbook where you want to replace references. Click in the Code window, click Edit, and then click Replace. In the Replace dialog box, type the worksheet reference to replace in the Find What box, and type the code name in the Replace With box. In the Search area, click the Current Project option and then Replace All.

Why do I get an error when I use a code name reference?

▼ You may get an error if you are creating a macro in a different workbook. Code names can only be used as sheet references in code in the workbook project where the code-named sheets exist. And because VBA recognizes a code name as an object, you may also get an error if the code name is spelled incorrectly. When you create a new code name for a sheet in the Properties window, the code name cannot have spaces or punctuation marks.

Copy or Move a Worksheet

You can copy or move a sheet and paste it in a new location in the same workbook by using the Copy or Move method with the Sheets, Worksheets, and Charts objects. The Move and Copy methods both have two arguments, the Before argument and the After argument. You can use one argument or the other, but not both. Both arguments are optional, but if you do not use one or the other, VBA creates a new workbook containing the one sheet you are copying or moving.

You can use the Before argument to specify the sheet to the left of which you want to place the moved or copied sheet,

as in `Sheets("Invoice").Move Before:= Sheets("Expenses Jan")`. You can use the After argument to specify the sheet to the right of which you want to place the moved or copied sheet, as in `Sheets(1).Copy After:= Sheets(3)`. You can refer to sheets by their sheet names, index numbers, or code names. If you want to be sure the moved or copied sheet goes to the front of the workbook, use the `Before:= Sheets(1)` argument because Sheets(1) is always the leftmost sheet at the front of the workbook.

Copy a Worksheet

① Type **Sub** and the macro name, then press Enter to start a new macro.

② Type **sheets("*sheetname*").copy**, replacing *sheetname* with the name of the sheet to copy.

③ Type a space and **after:=sheets("*sheetname*")**, replacing *sheetname* with the name of the sheet to place the copy after.

This example places a copy of Sheet1 to the right of Sheet3.

④ Click 🗷 to switch to Excel.

⑤ Run the macro.

Note: To run a macro from Excel, see the section "Run a Macro" in Chapter 2.

● The sheet is copied to its new location. The copied sheet name has *(2)* added.

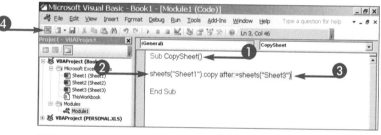

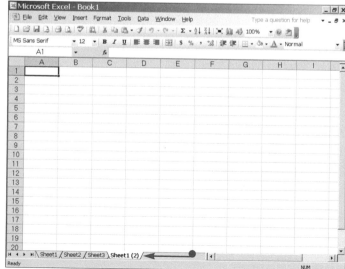

Move a Worksheet

① Type **Sub** and the macro name, then press Enter to start a new macro.

② Type **sheets("*sheetname*").move**, replacing *sheetname* with the name of the sheet to move.

③ Type a space and **before:=sheets(1)**.

This example moves Sheet3 to the first sheet in the workbook.

④ Click ⊠ to switch to Excel.

⑤ Run the macro.

Note: To run a macro from Excel, see the section "Run a Macro" in Chapter 2.

● The sheet is moved to its new location.

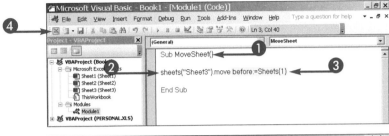

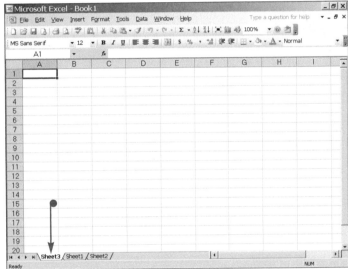

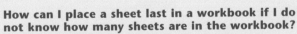

How can I place a sheet last in a workbook if I do not know how many sheets are in the workbook?

▼ You can declare a variable in your macro that counts the number of sheets in the workbook, and use the result as the index number in the argument sheet reference. For example, type `Dim LastSht As Long` and then `LastSht = Sheets.Count`. This variable uses a function that counts the sheets in the workbook. In your statement, type the argument `After:= Sheets(LastSht)`, which uses the number determined by the LastSht variable as an index number to identify the last sheet. For more information about declaring variables, see the section "Declare a Variable" in Chapter 6.

Why do I get a Subscript out of range error?

▼ You may get a Subscript out of range error if either of the sheets you want to reference, as the object or in the argument, are referenced incorrectly. Some common errors include using misspelled or nonexistent sheet names in a reference or forgetting the quotes around a string that is a sheet name. You also get an error if you use a nonexistent sheet index number; for example, referencing Sheets(4) when only three sheets exist in a workbook or using a misspelled or nonexistent code name causes an error.

Hide a Worksheet

You can write code to hide specific sheets in a workbook so that the user does not have access to them. If your workbook application uses ranges of values on a separate sheet to calculate data, restricting access to that sheet may possibly prevent the user from breaking the application. Hiding the worksheet where the ranges of values are located keeps those values safe.

To hide a specific sheet, use the Visible property of the Sheets object, as in `Sheets("Sheet1").Visible = False`. You can use any method to refer to the sheets you want to hide, according to name, index number, or code name. For more information about referring to sheets in code, see the section "Refer to a Worksheet."

A knowledgeable user can unhide a hidden sheet using the Format menu, so if you want to take more permanent measures to make data inaccessible, you should consider protecting the worksheet. For more information, see the section "Protect a Worksheet" in Chapter 10.

Excel requires that a workbook have at least one visible sheet, so you cannot hide all of the sheets in a workbook.

Hide a Worksheet

① Arrange the Excel and Visual Basic Editor windows so you can see both.

Note: To arrange editor windows, see the section "Open and Dock Windows in the Visual Basic Editor" in Chapter 5.

② Type **Sub** and the macro name, then press Enter to start a new macro.

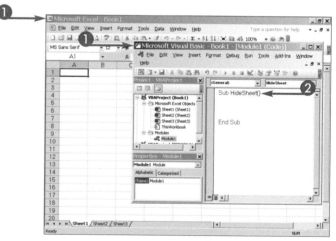

③ Type **sheets(1).visible = false**, replacing the object name *Sheets(1)* with the sheet object reference of your choice.

Sheets(1) refers to the leftmost sheet in the workbook.

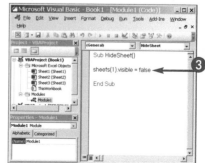

④ Click ▶ to run the macro.

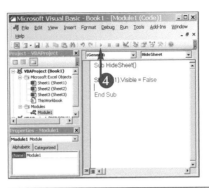

● The leftmost worksheet disappears. The worksheet is not deleted, just hidden.

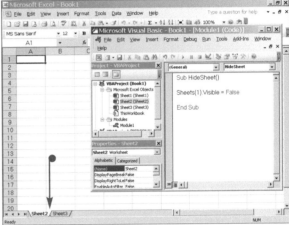

How can I hide several worksheets at once?

▼ You can hide several worksheets with a single statement by using an *array* reference, a reference to several worksheets in the object name. To hide the first three sheets in a workbook, type the statement Sheets(Array (1,2,3)).Visible = False. You can also use a loop to hide several sheets. For more information, see the section "Hide Several Worksheets."

How can I unhide worksheets using a macro?

▼ You can unhide a hidden worksheet by setting the Visible property of the Sheets object to True, as in Sheet1.Visible = True. To make all worksheets visible again, type the three statements For Each sh in Sheets, sh.Visible = True, and Next sh. This For Each loop makes all worksheets visible regardless of current visibility settings.

Why do I get a runtime error when I run the macro?

▼ You may get the runtime error "Unable to set Visible property of the Sheets class" because your macro code is attempting to hide all the sheets in the workbook, which can happen if a user deletes sheets in the workbook before the macro runs. To prevent users from deleting sheets, you can protect the workbook structure using the Protect Workbook command under the Tools menu.

Make a Worksheet Very Hidden

You can prevent even knowledgeable users from opening a worksheet that by making the worksheet very hidden. When you hide a worksheet, either by using Excel procedures or by using the *sheetobject*.Visible = False statement in a macro, a user can unhide the worksheet by clicking Format, Sheet, and Unhide, and then selecting the sheet name from the list of hidden sheets. However, when you make a worksheet very hidden, the worksheet is hidden from view in the workbook and cannot be opened from the Format menu.

You can make a worksheet very hidden by setting the worksheet Visible property to xlSheetVeryHidden in the Properties window in the Visual Basic Editor. You can

also make a worksheet very hidden by using the xlVeryHidden constant value for the sheet object's Visible property in a macro. To make a worksheet very hidden by using a macro, write the statement *sheetobject*.Visible = xlVeryHidden. The worksheet is hidden and the Visible property in the editor Properties window is xlVeryHidden.

A workbook must have at least one visible worksheet, so if your macro attempts to hide the last visible worksheet, you get a runtime error.

Make a Worksheet Very Hidden

① Type **Sub** and the macro name, then press Enter to start a new macro.

② Type *sheetobject* and a period, replacing *sheetobject* with your sheet object reference.

Note: Fore more information about sheets object references, see the section "Refer to a Worksheet."

③ Type **visible = xlVeryHidden**.

④ Click ▶ to run the macro.

You can also press F5 to run the macro in the Visual Basic Editor.

⑤ Click ⊠ to switch to Excel.

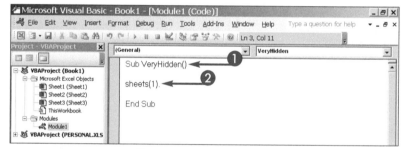

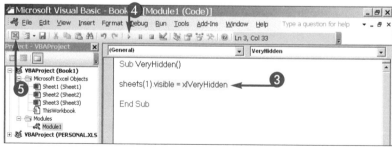

● The sheet is hidden.

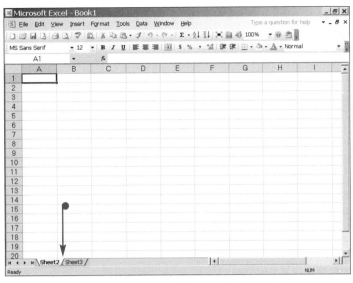

6 Click Format.

7 Click Sheet.

● The Unhide command is unavailable. You cannot unhide very hidden sheets from within Excel.

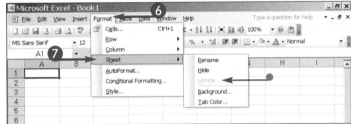

How can I unhide a very hidden worksheet?

▼ You can unhide a very hidden worksheet with a macro by setting the sheet objects's Visible property to True, as in the statement *sheetobject*. Visible = True. You can also make a very hidden worksheet visible by selecting the worksheet name in the Project window, and then select the value xlSheetVisible in the Visible box of the Properties window.

How can I make all my hidden worksheets visible?

▼ You can use a very short For Each block of statements in a macro to make all the worksheets visible. In a new macro, type For Each sh In Sheets on one line, sh.Visible = True on the next line, and type Next sh on the last line. The word *sh* is an undeclared variable name that simplifies this short macro.

How can I keep a knowledgeable user from resetting the Visible setting in the Visual Basic Editor?

▼ You can keep a user from resetting the Visible setting in the Visual Basic Editor by making the workbook project inaccessible. To make the project inaccessible, you can lock the project and set a password so that the workbook project cannot be opened without the password. For more information about locking a project, see the section "Password-Protect a Macro" in Chapter 4.

Hide Several Worksheets

You can hide several worksheets by writing a For Next loop, which leaves the leftmost worksheets visible and hides the worksheets to the right. The worksheets you do not want to hide must be the leftmost sheets in the workbook because the loop uses index numbers to identify the worksheets, and worksheets are indexed by position from left to right.

To hide worksheets, set the value of each worksheet's Visible property to False. A For Next loop sets the value for several worksheets, one at a time. For example, to hide all but the first two sheets in a workbook, use a variable name such as

Lst. Declare the variable `Dim Lst As Long`, and then `Set Lst = Sheets.Count`. Then write the loop statements `For N = 3 To Lst, Sheets(N).Visible = False`, and `Next`.

The variable counts the worksheets in the workbook, regardless of the quantity. The total number of worksheets is also the index number of the last sheet. That variable, the index number of the last sheet, identifies the last sheet in the Sheets object. This example loop starts at Sheets(3) and sets the Visible property for each sheet through the last sheet.

Hide Several Worksheets

① Type **Sub** and the macro name, then press Enter to start a new macro.

② Type **dim** *variablename* **as long**, replacing *variablename* with your variable name, and then press Enter.

Note: For more information about declaring variables, see the section "Declare a Variable" in Chapter 6.

③ Type *variablename* = **sheets.count**, replacing *variablename* with your variable name, and then press Enter.

④ Type **for n = 2 to** *variablename,* replacing *variablename* with your variable name, and then press Enter.

This example hides sheets beginning with index (2).

⑤ Type **sheets(n).visible = false** and then press Enter.

⑥ Type **next** and then press Enter.

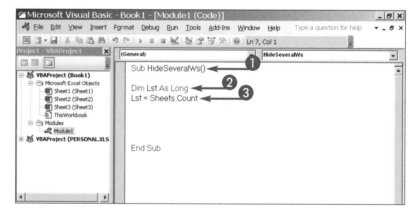

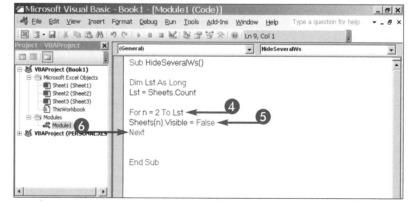

⑦ Click ▶ to run the macro.

⑧ Click 🗵 to switch to Excel.

● All sheets beginning with the index number you typed in step **4** are hidden.

How can I make all the worksheets visible again?

▼ You can make the worksheets visible again by changing the Visible property to = `True` in this macro and then running the macro again. You can also create a new macro by typing the statements `For Each ws in Sheets`, `ws.Visible = True`, and then `Next ws`. This For Each loop makes all worksheets visible regardless of current visibility settings.

What other ways can I hide several worksheets?

▼ You can hide several worksheets with a single statement if you use an *array object reference*, a reference to multiple sheet index numbers. For example, the statement `Sheets(Array (2,3)).Visible = False` hides the sheets with index numbers (2) and (3). Remember that the sheet index numbers can change if a user moves, copies, or deletes sheets in the workbook.

Why do I get an error when I hide worksheets with an array object reference?

▼ When you hide multiple worksheets with a macro, you risk hiding them all, which Excel does not allow you to do. If a user has deleted worksheets so that the array object reference inadvertently tries to hide all remaining worksheets, you get the runtime error that says "Unable to set the Visible property of the Worksheet class."

Print a Worksheet

Y ou can create a macro to print a worksheet to your specifications using the PageSetup and PrintOut methods. If you want to be sure a user prints a worksheet the way you intended it to be printed, you can write a macro that makes all the print decisions, such as determining print area, page range, number of copies, orientation, header and footer, which printer to use, and more.

You can write the *sheetobject*.PageSetup statements first to control the worksheet print settings, and then the *sheetobject*.PrintOut statement to direct the printout. You can use a With block to set the PageSetup arguments efficiently. The arguments for the PageSetup method are too numerous to list, but you can look them up in the Object Browser. You do not have to use the PageSetup method to print a worksheet.

The PrintOut method without the PageSetup method prints the worksheet with the print settings that are already set up in the worksheet. The PrintOut method has several arguments, including Copies to set the number of copies, and ActivePrinter to send the worksheet to a specific printer. Be sure to type a comma and space between the arguments.

① Type **Sub** and the macro name, then press Enter to start a new macro.

② Type *sheetobject*.**pagesetup**, replacing *sheetobject* with the worksheet reference.

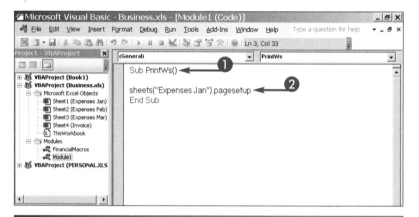

③ Type a period and then **printarea =** "*printrange*", replacing *printrange* with the range to print in the form of absolute references.

④ Press Enter.

Your *printrange* must be in the format "$A$1:$D$4".

⑤ Type *sheetobject*.**printout**, replacing *sheetobject* with the worksheet reference.

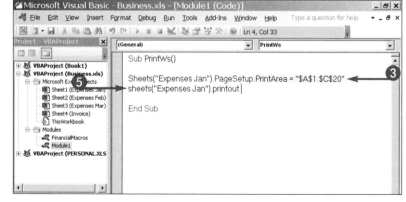

138

6 Type **preview: = true**.

This argument sends the worksheet to Print Preview. You can leave the argument off to send the worksheet directly to the printer.

7 Click ▶ to run the macro.

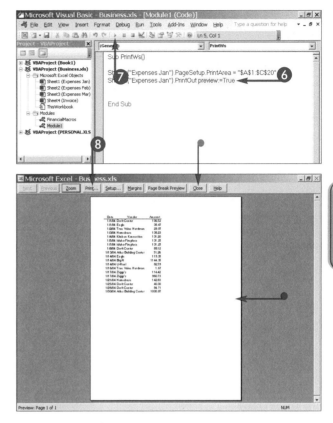

● The worksheet appears in the Print Preview window.

8 Click Print to send the worksheet to the printer.

● You can click Close to close the Print Preview without printing.

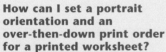

How can I set a portrait orientation and an over-then-down print order for a printed worksheet?

▼ You can use the PageSetup properties to set print orientation and the print order. For efficiency, you can type use a With block. On separate lines, type the statements `With sheetobject.PageSetup`, `.Orientation = xlPortrait`, `.Order = xlOverThenDown`, and then `End With`. When you type the equal sign, the Visual Basic Editor shows the possible values for that property.

How can I use the Object Browser?

▼ You can press F2 to open the Object Browser quickly. In the Classes list, click a class, such as PageSetup, and the Members list displays all the methods and properties for the selected class. Click a method or property you want to know more about, and click the question mark button to open a help file about that item.

How can I set a print area that changes to fit the size of the range in the worksheet?

▼ You can set a print area in the PageSetup.PrintArea property that always selects the current region, the entire range of data surrounding the active cell. To set a current region print area, be sure your macro has placed the active cell within the print range, and use the statement `sheetobject.PageSetup.PrintArea = ActiveCell.CurrentRegion.Address` to set the print area.

Delete a Worksheet

You can write a macro to delete a sheet, either a worksheet or a chart sheet, from a workbook. Use the Delete method on the Sheets object to delete both worksheets and chart sheets, and specify which sheet to delete, as in the statement `Sheets(1).Delete`.

Sheets are indexed with sequential index numbers from left to right, so the statement `Sheets(1).Delete` identifies and deletes the worksheet with index number 1, which is always the leftmost sheet in the workbook. You can also identify sheets as ActiveSheet, or by their sheet names, or by their workbook and sheet names, as in the statement

`Workbooks( "Expenses.xls").Sheets ("January").Delete`. If you do not identify the workbook in your statement, the sheet is deleted from the active workbook. You can identify workbooks as ActiveWorkbook, ThisWorkbook, or by file name.

You can only delete sheets in open workbooks in which the sheets are available to modify. If the workbook is opened read-only, or the workbook is protected, a macro to delete a sheet cannot run.

When you delete a worksheet, all the data in that worksheet is deleted permanently. No Recycle Bin exists for deleted sheets, and you cannot retrieve the deleted data.

Delete a Worksheet

① Type **Sub** and the macro name, then press Enter to start a new macro.

② Type **sheets(1).delete**.

This statement deletes the leftmost sheet in the active workbook, which has index number (1).

③ Click ▣ to switch to Excel.

④ Run the macro.

Note: To run a macro from Excel, see the section "Run a Macro" in Chapter 2.

⑤ In the deletion warning, click Delete.

● The leftmost sheet in the active workbook is deleted.

⑥ Switch to the Visual Basic Editor.

You can press Alt+F11 to switch to the Visual Basic Editor.

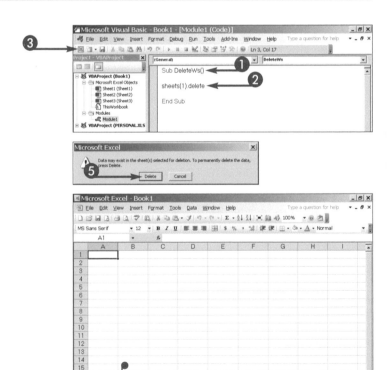

7 Delete the previous statement.

8 Type **sheets("*sheetname*").delete**, replacing *sheetname* with an existing worksheet name.

● You can watch the sheet deletion in the Project window.

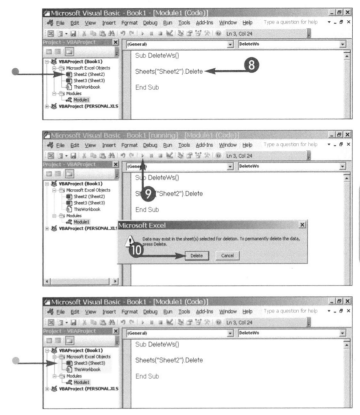

9 Click ▶ to run the macro.

You can also press F5 to run the macro in the editor.

10 In the deletion warning, click Delete.

● In the Project window, the named worksheet in the active workbook is deleted.

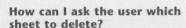

How can I ask the user which sheet to delete?

▼ You can write a short macro that uses an input box to ask the user for the sheet name. Type the statements `Dim variablename As String, variablename = InputBox("Which sheet?")`, and then `Sheets (variablename).Delete`. The macro places an input box on the worksheet, the user types the sheet name and clicks OK, and the sheet is deleted.

How can I delete several worksheets at one time from a workbook?

▼ You can use an array to select several worksheets by their index numbers, and execute the Delete method on all of them with a single statement. For example, if you want to delete the first and fourth worksheets, use the statement `Worksheets (Array(1,4)).Delete`. The worksheets with index numbers 1 and 4, the first and fourth worksheets from the left, are deleted.

How can I delete chart sheets?

▼ You can use the Delete method on the Sheets object, and specify the chart name in the statement, as in `Sheets("2004 Sales Chart").Delete`, or you can use the Delete method on the Charts object, as in the statement `Charts(1).Delete`, which deletes the first chart in the workbook. The Charts collection contains all the chart sheets in the workbook.

Build a Worksheet Header

You can write macro statements to print out a worksheet that displays automated page header entries. The entry may include the user name entered in the General tab under the Excel program's Tools menu. You can also create automated page header entries such as the current date, file name, full path, and worksheet name, or create fixed-name header entries such as a standardized report title.

All header properties, including LeftHeader, CenterHeader, and RightHeader, are properties of the PageSetup object, written as `Worksheets("sheetname").PageSetup. property = value`.

The text you want a header to display is written in the macro as the value for that header property. For example, to use the current date in a center header, use the VBA value Date and write the statement `Worksheets ("sheetname").PageSetup.CenterHeader = Date`. To display the Excel user name, write `Worksheets ("sheetname").PageSetup.CenterHeader = Application.UserName`. To display a fixed entry, write the header property value in quotes, as in `"your text string"`.

You can write multiple properties most efficiently if you write them in a With block, as in `With Worksheets("sheetname").PageSetup`, followed by `.property = value` on a succeeding line, and ending with the line `End With`.

Build a Worksheet Header

① Type **Sub** and the macro name, then press Enter to start a new macro.

② Type **with worksheets("*sheetname*") .pagesetup**, replacing *sheetname* with the worksheet name.

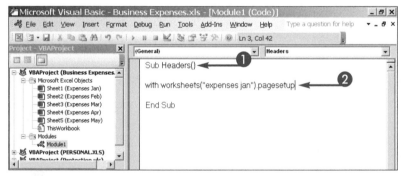

③ Type **.rightheader** = *property*, replacing *property* with your property.

In this example, the current date is in the right-hand header.

④ Type **.centerheader = "*textstring*"**, replacing *textstring* with a fixed-text header entry.

In this example, the center header displays a report title.

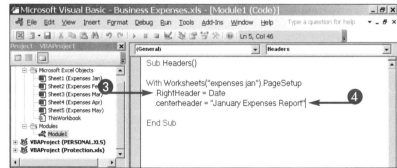

5 Type **end with**.

6 Type **worksheets("*sheetname*").printout preview: = true**, replacing *sheetname* with the worksheet name.

The Printout method with the Preview property displays the printed pages in Print Preview.

7 Click the Run Sub/UserForm button (▶) to run the macro.

The macro runs.

● The printed page appears in Print Preview with all your Page Setup settings.

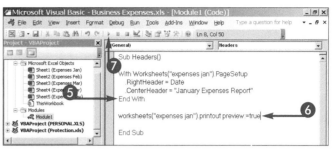

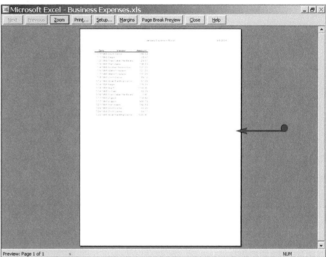

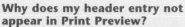

Why does my header entry not appear in Print Preview?

▼ You can make sure every header entry appears if you remember to type the period at the beginning of the property statement in the With block. In a With block, if you do not type the period to begin a property statement, the macro does not give an error when it runs; it merely ignores the property statement.

How can I create a header entry that shows the worksheet name?

▼ You can create a header entry that shows the worksheet name by using the property value ActiveSheet.Name in the header property, as in the statement `Worksheets("sheetname")` `.PageSetup.CenterHeader =` `ActiveSheet.Name`. You can also use the property code `"&A"`, as in the statement `Worksheets("sheetname")` `.PageSetup.CenterHeader =` `"&A"`. To find property codes, look up Formatting Codes for Headers and Footers in the VBA help files.

How can I create a header entry that shows the full path and file name of the workbook?

▼ You can create a header entry that shows the full path and file name of the workbook by using the property value ActiveWorkbook.FullName in the header property, as in the statement `Worksheets("sheetname")` `.PageSetup.CenterHeader =` `ActiveWorkbook.FullName`. You can also show just the workbook file name by using the property value ActiveWorkbook.Name or `"&F"`.

Create a Worksheet Footer

You can create a macro to print a worksheet that displays page footer entries. The entry can include the user name entered in the General tab under the Excel program's Tools menu. You can also create page footer entries that include page numbers, file name, full path and file name, and worksheet name.

All footer properties, including LeftFooter, CenterFooter, and RightFooter, are properties of the PageSetup object, written as `Worksheets("`*`sheetname`*`").PageSetup.` *`property = value`*.

The text you want a footer to display is written as the value for that footer property. For example, to use the current date in a center footer, use the VBA value Date and write

the statement `Worksheets("`*`sheetname`*`").PageSetup. CenterFooter = Date`. To use the Excel user name, write `Worksheets("`*`sheetname`*`").PageSetup.CenterFooter = Application.UserName`. To use a fixed entry, write `Worksheets("`*`sheetname`*`").PageSetup.CenterFooter = "`*`textstring`*`"`.

You can use property codes to set many automatic values for footer or header properties, such as &P to print the page number and &N to print the total number of pages. To find a list of property codes you can use in property values, look up Formatting Codes for Headers and Footers in the VBA Help files.

Create a Worksheet Footer

① Type **Sub** and the macro name, then press Enter to start a new macro.

② Type **with worksheets("**_sheetname_**") .pagesetup**, replacing _sheetname_ with the worksheet name.

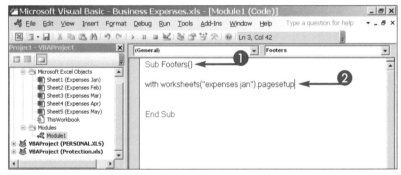

③ Type **.leftfooter** = _property_, replacing _property_ with your property.

In this example, the current date is in the left-hand footer.

④ Type **.centerfooter** = _property_, replacing _property_ with your property.

In this example, the center footer uses codes and text to display the page number and total pages.

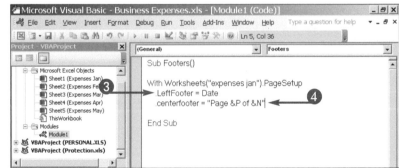

5 Type **end with**.

6 Type **worksheets("***sheetname***").printout preview: = true**, replacing *sheetname* with the worksheet name.

The Printout method with the Preview property displays the printed pages in Print Preview.

7 Click ▶ to run the macro.

The macro runs.

● The printed page appears in Print Preview with all your Page Setup settings.

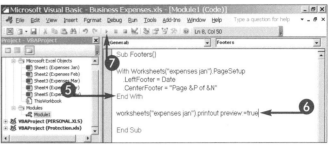

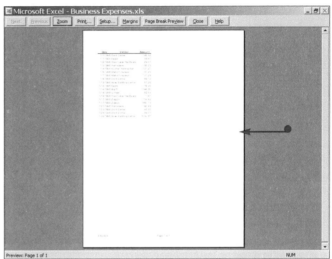

Why does my footer entry not appear in Print Preview?

▼ You can make sure every footer entry appears if you remember to type the period at the beginning of the property statement in the With block. In a With block, if you do not type the period to begin a property statement, the macro does not give an error when it runs; it merely ignores the property statement.

How can I create a footer entry that is formatted in bold?

▼ You can create a footer entry that is formatted bold by including the formatting code &B in the quotes for the footer property code. For example, the statement Worksheets ("*sheetname*").PageSetup. Centerfooter = "&B&A" shows the worksheet name formatted bold in the center footer. To find a list of formatting codes, look up Formatting Codes for Headers and Footers in the VBA Help files.

How can I include an ampersand (&) in a text string and format the string in italics?

▼ You can create a text string entry that includes an ampersand by typing the ampersand twice. For example, to create the text string entry "Dogs & Cats, Inc", type the value "Dogs && Cats, Inc.". You can display the text in italics by including the formatting code &I in the text string ahead of the text string characters, as in "&IDogs && Cats, Inc."

Specify Page Setup Settings

You can write statements in a macro that define all the page setup settings for a printed page before the page goes to the printer. The page setup settings control every aspect of the layout of data on the printed page.

The page setup settings are properties of the PageSetup object, which itself is a property of the Worksheets object, as in `Worksheets("sheetname").PageSetup.property = value`. You can write multiple properties most efficiently if you use a With block.

Among the important PageSetup properties are PrintArea, which designates the print area of the worksheet, CenterHorizontally, which centers the printed data horizontally on the page, and PrintTitleRows, which prints identifying column titles at the top of each page of a multipage list.

You can find a list of the many PageSetup properties and examples in the VBA Help files. In the Ask A Question box, type Page Setup Object. Click the PageSetup Object link in the Search Results pane, and then click the Properties link at the top of the Help window that appears. In the list of properties, click the property for which you want to see an example.

Specify Page Setup Settings

① Type **Sub** and the macro name, then press Enter to start a new macro.

② Type **with worksheets("*sheetname*").pagesetup**, replacing *sheetname* with the worksheet name, and press Enter.

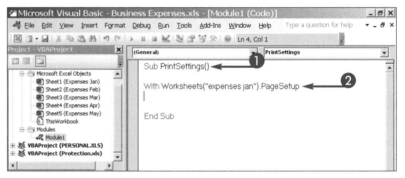

③ Press Tab and type **.printarea = activecell.currentregion.address**, and then press Enter.

This statement selects the entire region around the active cell.

④ Type **.centerhorizontally = true** and press Enter.

⑤ Press Backspace, type **end with**, and press Enter.

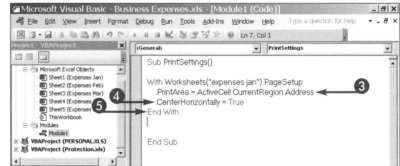

146

6 Type **worksheets("*sheetname*").printout preview:=true**, replacing *sheetname* with the worksheet name.

This statement displays the printed pages in Print Preview.

7 Click ▶ to run the macro.

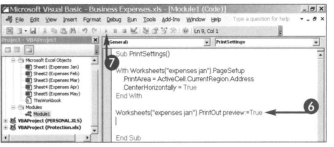

The macro runs.

● The printed page appears in Print Preview with all your Page Setup settings.

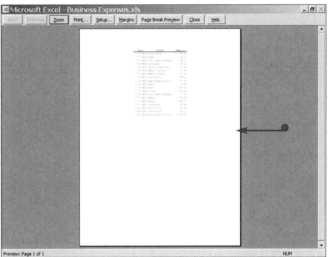

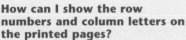

How can I show the row numbers and column letters on the printed pages?

▼ You can show the worksheet row numbers and column letters on the printed pages with the PrintHeadings property. In a With block for the PageSetup object, type `PrintHeadings = True`. You can also show the gridlines on the printed page with the PrintGridlines property. In a With block for the PageSetup object, type `PrintGridlines = True`.

How can I fit the printed data to a specific number of pages tall or wide?

▼ You can fit the printed data to a specific number of pages wide by using the FitToPagesWide property. In a With block for the PageSetup object, type `FitToPagesWide = x`, replacing *x* with the number of pages wide. You can use the `FitToPagesTall = x` property to fit the printed data onto a limited number of pages tall.

How can I print the column headings on each page to identify the columns in a long list?

▼ You can identify the columns in a multipage list with the PrintTitleRows property. In a With block for the PageSetup object, type the statement `.PrintTitleRows = ActiveSheet.Rows(1).Address`, replacing (1) with the row number of the row containing your column headings. You can also use the PrintTitleColumns property to print the column of row labels on each page of a wide table.

Protect a Worksheet

You can protect a worksheet so that users can make only certain types of modifications or no modifications at all. To protect a worksheet, use the Protect method for the Sheets or Worksheets object, as in the example `Sheets("Invoice").Protect`.

If you protect a worksheet with the `sheetobject.Protect` statement and use no optional arguments, everything in the worksheet is protected from changes. You can use optional arguments to allow specific changes, such as `Allow FormattingCells = True` to allow a user to format cells.

Sixteen optional arguments appear in the Quick Info for the method. They correspond to the options in the Protect Sheet dialog box under the Tools, Protection menu. You can use the optional Password argument to set a password without which a user cannot unlock the worksheet.

The cells in a worksheet are locked by default and protection makes their contents uneditable. You can make specific cells editable in a protected worksheet by unlocking those cells before you protect the worksheet. After the worksheet is protected, the unlocked cells are editable but the remaining locked cells are not.

Protect a Worksheet

① Type **Sub** and the macro name, then press Enter to start a new macro.

② Type *sheetobject*.**protect**, replacing *sheetobject* with the worksheet object reference.

Note: For more information about worksheet object references, see the section "Refer to a Worksheet" in Chapter 9.

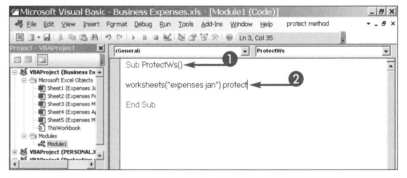

③ Type **password:="***password***"**, replacing *password* with your password.

The password argument is optional. Without it the worksheet is easily unprotected.

④ Type optional arguments, separated by commas, with values set to True to allow users to change those items.

In this example, the optional arguments allow cell formatting and row insertion.

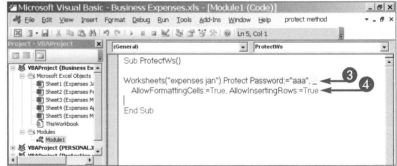

5 Click ⏵ to run the macro.

6 Click the View Microsoft Excel button (⊠) to switch to Excel.

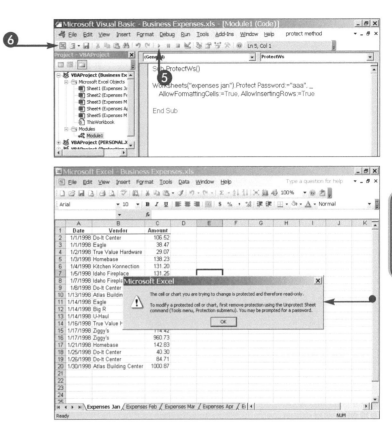

7 Type any character in a cell on the protected worksheet.

- A message appears stating the worksheet is protected and cannot be modified except for those actions you allow in the Protect method arguments.

How can I unlock specific cells for editing before I protect the worksheet?

▼ You can unlock specific cells that need user input before you protect the worksheet. Select the cells or ranges and then click Format and Cells. In the Format Cells dialog box, click the Protection tab. Clear the Locked check box and click OK. After you protect the worksheet, cells that are still locked are uneditable, but unlocked cells can be edited.

How can I unprotect a password-protected worksheet?

▼ You can unprotect a password-protected worksheet from within the workbook if you know the password. Click Tools, Protection, and Unprotect Sheet. In the Unprotect Sheet dialog box, type the password and click OK. You can unprotect a sheet in a macro with the statement *sheetobject*. Unprotect Password:= "password". The Unprotect method has no other arguments.

How can I protect a chart?

▼ You can protect a chart in the same way you protect a worksheet, by using the Protect method with the Charts object, as in *chartsobject*.Protect. The Protect method for Charts objects has only five arguments, including the Password argument. After you type the method Protect, the Quick Info shows the arguments for the method.

Protect All Worksheets at Once

You can protect all the worksheets in a workbook at once without having to protect each sheet individually, and because you use a single password to protect all the worksheets, you can unprotect all the worksheets quickly with a macro if you need to make changes in the workbook.

You can protect each worksheet in a workbook individually by writing separate macro statements for each worksheet, but this is inefficient if you want to protect all the worksheets in a workbook. Even though you can protect all the worksheets at once with a macro, you can still use your

protection password to unprotect individual worksheets from within Excel by using the Protect Sheet option under the Tools menu.

To protect all worksheets at once, you can write a For Each loop macro that uses a declared variable. First, declare a variable as a worksheet. Write the statements `For Each variablename in Worksheets` and `variablename.Protect Password:="password"` as well as any optional protection arguments, and then `Next variablename`. The macro loops through all the worksheets and sets identical protection and passwords for each.

Protect All Worksheets at Once

① Type **Sub** and the macro name, then press Enter to start a new macro.

② Type **dim** *variable* **as worksheet**, replacing *variable* with your variable name.

③ Type **for each** *variable* **in worksheets**, replacing *variable* with your variable name.

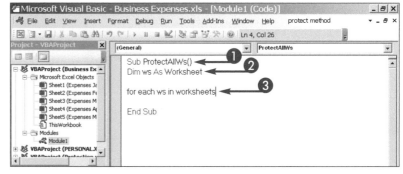

④ Type *variable*.**protect password:=** "*password*", replacing *variable* with your variable name and *password* with your password.

● You can add optional protection arguments separated by commas. In this example, the optional argument allows cell formatting.

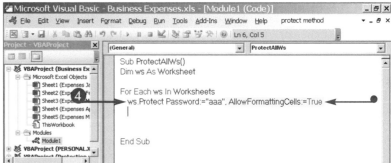

⑤ Type **next** *variable*, replacing *variable* with your variable name.

⑥ Click ▶ to run the macro.

⑦ Click ⊠ to switch to Excel.

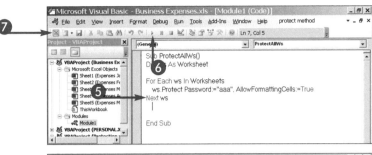

⑧ Type any character in any cell in any worksheet.

● A message appears stating all worksheets in the workbook are protected.

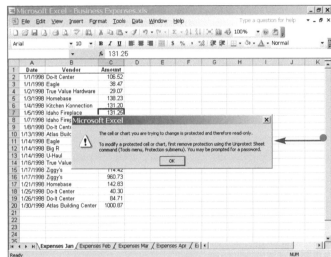

How can I unprotect all the worksheets at once?

▼ You can unprotect all the worksheets at once by writing a similar For Each loop macro, but substituting the method .Unprotect for the method .Protect. You must use the password argument, as in `.Unprotect Password:= "password"`, and use the same password with which you protected the worksheets. The Unprotect method has no arguments other than the Password argument.

Why is my password not unprotecting a worksheet from within Excel?

▼ You may have misspelled the password in your macro. Open the macro and check the password spelling, and then use the misspelled password to unprotect all worksheets and reprotect the worksheets with the correct password. Alternatively, a user may have unprotected a worksheet in Excel using your password, and then reprotected the worksheet with a different password.

How can I protect the worksheets without setting a password?

▼ You can protect a single worksheet, or all worksheets at once, without setting a password by simply not using the optional `Password:="password"` argument. If you do not use a password when you protect a worksheet, the worksheet can be quickly and easily unprotected by choosing Tools→Protection→ Unprotect Sheet, after which you are not asked for a password.

Run a Macro on a Protected Worksheet

I f you run a macro on a fully protected worksheet, the macro may not run because worksheet protection prevents changes to the worksheet. You can avoid errors from running a macro on a protected worksheet by writing statements that protect only the user interface rather than the entire worksheet. Protecting only the user interface prevents users from making changes, but does not prevent the worksheet from running your macros.

When you save and close a protected workbook, all protected worksheets are fully protected. When you reopen the workbook, the protection must be set to User Interface

Only again to allow macros to run. You can make sure a workbook always opens with just the user interface protected by running the worksheet protection macro with the `Workbook_Open()` event every time the workbook opens. For more information about events, see Chapter 22.

You can write a For Each protection loop that starts with the line `Private Sub Workbook_Open()`, and that includes the Password and UserInterfaceOnly arguments and any optional arguments, to set protection for every worksheet in the workbook. For more information about protecting all worksheets at once, see the section "Protect All Worksheets at Once."

Run a Macro on a Protected Worksheet

① In the Properties Window, double-click ThisWorkbook.

② In the Object box, click 🔽.

③ In the Object list, select Workbook.

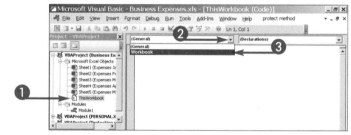

● A new macro is created containing the Workbook_Open event in the Sub line.

④ Type **dim** *variable* **as worksheet**, replacing *variable* with your variable name.

⑤ Type **for each** *variable* **in worksheets**, replacing *variable* with your variable name.

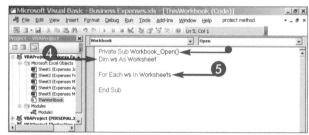

⑥ Type *variable*.**protect**, replacing *variable* with your variable name.

⑦ Type **password:="***password***"**, replacing *password* with your password.

⑧ Type a comma and a space, and then **userinterfaceonly:=true**.

● Type optional arguments, separated by commas.

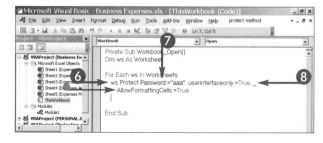

⑨ Type **next** *variable*, replacing *variable* with your variable name.

⑩ Click 🖫 to save as *workbook*.xls.

⑪ Click ⊠ to close the Visual Basic Editor and the workbook.

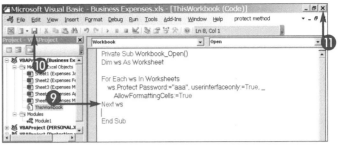

⑫ Open the workbook.

⑬ Type any character in any cell in any worksheet.

● All worksheets in the workbook are protected from user changes — except for changes you allow in the Protect method arguments — but your macros run because only the user interface is protected.

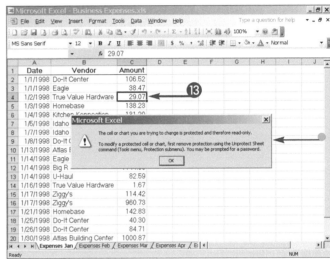

How can I unprotect a single worksheet to make changes in a workbook that opens fully protected?

▼ You can unprotect individual worksheets in the Excel window by choosing Tools→Protection→ Unprotect Sheet. You must supply the password you set in the macro. When you close and reopen the workbook, the Workbook_Open() macro reprotects the worksheets. Do not reprotect an individual worksheet with a different password because the different password generates an error the next time the workbook opens and attempts to run the Workbook_Open() macro. If you need to unprotect a worksheet while working in Excel, leave the worksheet unprotected and close the workbook so the opening macro reprotects the worksheets.

How can I find out what the other Protect arguments are?

▼ You can find out what the optional Protect method arguments are by using Quick Info or VBA Help. If the Quick Info does not appear when you type a statement that uses the Protect method, right-click the word Protect and click Quick Info. You can also type *protect method* in the Ask A Question box and click the Protect Method link in the Search Results pane. In the Help window that appears, click the Protect method as it applies to the Worksheet object link. The Help window lists the arguments and explanations.

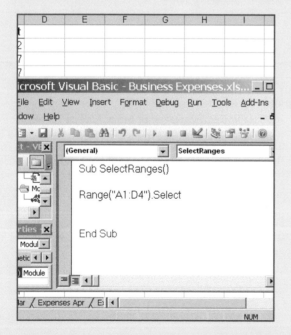

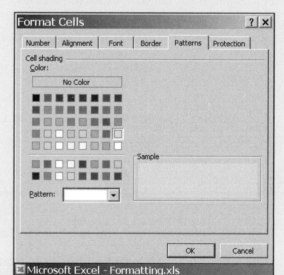

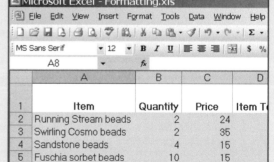

13   Entering Data and Formulas

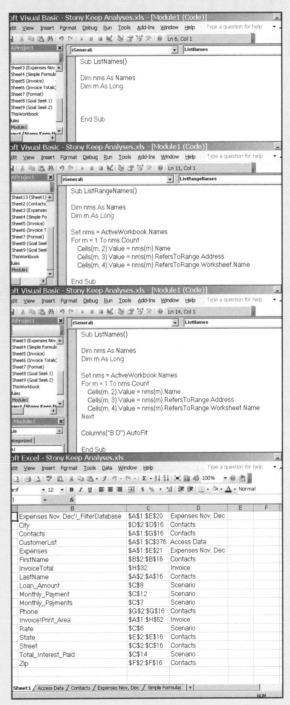

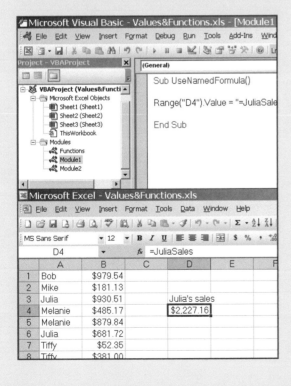

Write a Range Reference to Specific Cells

Y ou can write macros that execute on any kind of range when you understand how to write range references. The Range object enables you to specify the address of any range you want, whether to select the range, enter values, apply formatting, copy or cut, or more.

When you write the Range object, enclose the range of cells you are referring to in quotes and parentheses, as in *sheetobject*.Range("A1:D4"), which refers to the range A1:D4 on the specified worksheet. If you do not specify a worksheet object, the Range object is

executed on the active worksheet. You can refer to a single cell, as in Range("C3"), or you can refer to the entire contiguous region of data around the active cell, as in ActiveCell.CurrentRegion, or the entire contiguous region of data around a specific cell no matter where the active cell is, as in Range("*celladdress*").CurrentRegion.

The Range object has no arguments, but because VBA recognizes the Range object, you get an Auto List when you type the period, and the Auto List shows all the methods and properties you can select for execution on the Range object.

Write a Range Reference to Specific Cells

① Arrange your editor and Excel windows so you can see both windows.

Note: To arrange the Excel and editor windows, see the section "Arrange the Excel and Editor Windows" in Chapter 5.

② Type **Sub** and the macro name, then press Enter to start a new macro.

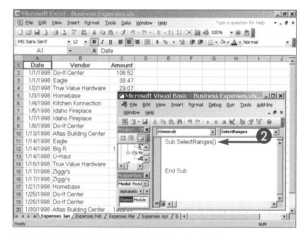

③ Type **range("*A1:D4*").select**, replacing *A1:D4* with your range address.

④ Click the Run Sub/UserForm button (▶) to run the macro.

The macro runs.

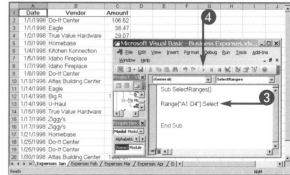

156

● The specified range is selected.

⑤ Edit the statement to **activecell.currentregion.select**.

⑥ Click ▶ to run the macro.

The macro runs.

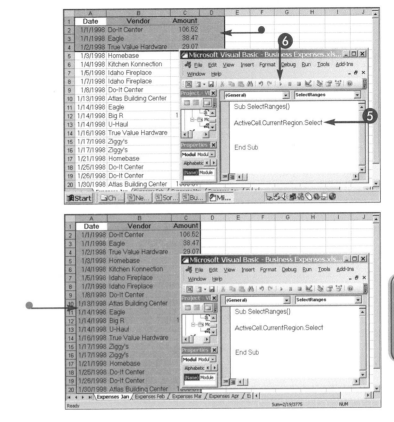

● The entire table is selected.

If the active cell is not in a table, only the active cell is selected.

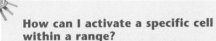

How can I activate a specific cell within a range?

▼ You can activate a specific cell within a range by using the Activate method. First, select the range by whatever means is most convenient for the macro you are writing. Following that statement, write the statement `Range("celladdress").Activate`, replacing *celladdress* with the address of the specific cell you want to activate.

How can I refer to part of a table?

▼ You can use the Offset and Resize properties to refer to part of a table, such as the first five rows of a table below the header row. Declare a variable for the table range, and then write the statement `variablename.Offset(1).Resize(5).` followed by the method you want to execute. For more information, see the section "Build an Offset Range Reference."

How can I refer to a named range?

▼ You can refer to a named range by using the range name as a text string in the range reference, as in `Range("rangename")`. Referring to a named range works the same way for both a name that was created in the workbook or a range name created in the macro. For more information, see the section "Name a Range."

Create a Range Reference to Rows or Columns

You can write statements in a macro that refer to rows or columns so that you can perform operations such as deleting, inserting, copying, moving, or formatting on those referenced rows or columns.

When you refer to a Rows or Columns object, you must refer to single or contiguous rows or columns. You can refer to single rows or columns by name or index number. For example, `Columns(3)` and `Columns("C")` both refer to the third column from the left, column C. `Rows(2)` and `Rows("2")` both refer to row 2. You can refer to multiple

contiguous rows or columns by name, as in `Rows("2:4")` or `Columns("B:G")`. References by name must always be enclosed in quotes.

If you use the Rows or Columns object without a worksheet reference, VBA executes the statement on the active worksheet, as if the statement is written `ActiveSheet.Rows` or `ActiveSheet.Columns`. To make sure the reference is on the correct worksheet, write the statement with a worksheet reference. For example, `Worksheets("Sheet3").Columns(3)` refers to column C on the worksheet named Sheet3. To learn more about worksheet references, see the section "Refer to a Worksheet" in Chapter 9.

Create a Range Reference to Rows or Columns

① Arrange your editor and Excel windows so you can see both windows.

Note: To arrange the Excel and editor windows, see the section "Arrange the Excel and Editor Windows" in Chapter 5.

② Type **Sub** and the macro name, then press Enter to start a new macro.

③ Type **columns(3).select**, replacing the index number *3* with your column index number.

④ Click ▶ to run the macro.

The macro runs.

● The entire column is selected.

⑤ Edit the statement to **columns("A:D").select**, replacing the column letters *A:D* with your column letters.

⑥ Click ▶ to run the macro.

The macro runs.

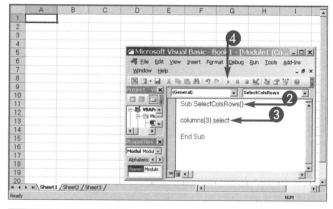

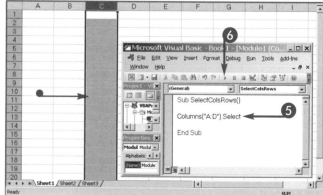

● The columns in which you typed the
  statement are selected.

7 Edit the statement to **rows("2:4").select**,
replacing the row numbers *2:4* with your row
numbers.

8 Click 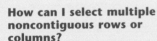 to run the macro.

The macro runs.

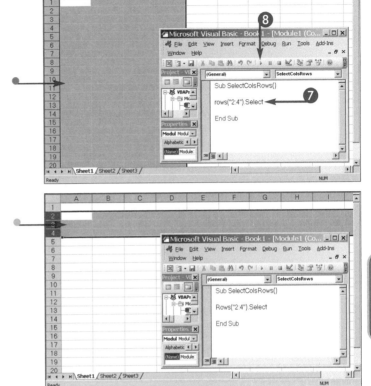

● The rows in which you typed the
  statement are selected.

How can I select multiple noncontiguous rows or columns?

▼ You can select multiple noncontiguous rows or columns by using the Range object instead of the Rows or Columns object. In the Range object, you use the row or column names, in quotes and separated by commas, that refer to entire rows or columns, as in the reference `Range("A:A","D:D")`, which references columns A and D.

How can I select rows or columns within a specific range?

▼ You can select rows or columns within a specific range by selecting the specific range, and then selecting the Rows or Columns object within the Selection object. For example, you can select the table around the active cell with the statement `ActiveCell.CurrentRegion.Select`, and then select the second row in that table with the statement `Selection.Rows(2).Select`.

How can I select the entire row or column around the active cell?

▼ You can select the entire column around the active cell by writing the statement `ActiveCell.EntireColumn.Select`. You can select the entire row around the active cell by writing the statement `ActiveCell.EntireRow.Select`. You can type in place of the Select method any method you want to perform on the entire row or column, such as Delete or Clear.

Refer to Ranges within the Current Region

You can work with the headers of a table separately from the body, or the body separately from the headers, by referring to miniranges within the table. For example, you can format the header row of a table regardless of the size of the table if you can designate a specific cell as the starting point for a current region.

You can manipulate miniranges within a table, regardless of the size of the table, by declaring a variable as a range and setting the variable equal to the current region of the table, as in the variable declaration `Dim mrg as Range` and `Set`

`mrg = Range("E6").CurrentRegion`. In this example, cell E6 is a cell within the table, and the statement sets the variable named mrg equal to the current region surrounding cell E6.

VBA treats the declared variable as a Range object, and you can execute any Range methods and properties on it, including selecting and formatting rows and columns within the range. You specify a row or column by index number within the table region, not within the worksheet, so row and column index numbers may not be the same as worksheet index numbers.

Refer to Ranges within the Current Region

① Arrange your editor and Excel windows so you can see both windows.

Note: To arrange the Excel and editor windows, see the section "Arrange the Excel and Editor Windows" in Chapter 5.

② Type **Sub** and the macro name, then press Enter to start a new macro.

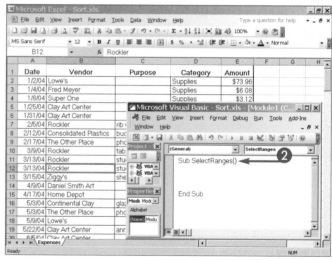

③ Type **dim** *MyRange* **as range**, replacing *MyRange* with your variable name.

④ Type **set** *MyRange* = **range("C4").currentregion**, replacing *MyRange* with your variable name and *C4* with a cell address within the table.

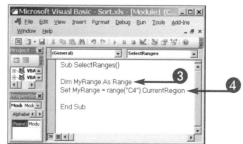

⑤ Type *MyRange*.rows(*1*).select, replacing *MyRange* with your variable name and the row index number *1* with the row index number you want.

⑥ Click ▶ to run the macro.

The macro runs.

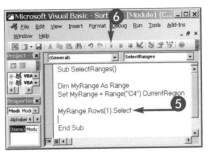

● The row index number you specified is selected in the table.

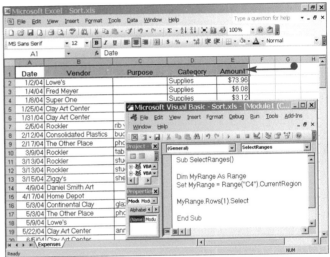

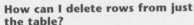

How can I delete rows from just the table?

▼ You can delete rows from just the table by declaring a variable and setting it equal to the current region of the table, and then use the statement *variablename.*`Rows(`*indexnumber*`).Delete`. The row referenced by the index number is deleted from the table without affecting the remainder of the worksheet, except for the specific worksheet cells that shift when you delete that row.

How can I format just the header row in bold font?

▼ You can format just the header row by declaring a variable and setting it equal to the current region of the table, and then using the statement `variablename.Rows(1).Font.Bold = True`. This statement selects the first row in the table, the header row, and applies bold font formatting. You can use any formatting properties you want in this statement.

How can I format just the table body?

▼ You can format the table body by declaring a variable and setting it equal to the current region of the table, and then using the statement `variablename.Offset(1).Resize(`*variablename*`.Rows.Count - 1).Select` to select the body of the table regardless of length. You can use formatting properties in place of the Select method. For more information, see the section "Build an Offset Range Reference."

Build an Offset Range Reference

You can use the Offset property to write a range reference that is shifted up, down, left, or right from a starting selection, and you can use the Resize property to change the size of the shifted range. By combining these two Range object properties, you can define a new range relative to a starting point and then select, format, or execute other procedures on that new range.

To build an offset range reference, declare a variable and set it equal to a specific cell or range. For example, you can set the variable equal to a specific cell, as in `Set variablename = Range("celladdress")`. You can then

use the Offset and Resize properties to shift and resize the variable range. For example, the statement `variablename .Offset(3,4).Resize(5,2)` defines a new range that is offset down three rows and right four columns from the variable range, and is resized to five rows tall and two columns wide.

The Offset property is written as `Offset(NumberOfRows, NumberOfColumns)`. Positive numbers designate rows down or columns to the right, and negative numbers designate rows up and columns to the left. The Resize property is written as `Resize(NumberOfRows, NumberOfColumns)`, and the arguments specify number of rows tall and number of columns wide.

Build an Offset Range Reference

① Arrange your editor and Excel windows so you can see both windows.

Note: To arrange the Excel and editor windows, see the section "Arrange the Excel and Editor Windows" in Chapter 5.

② Type **Sub** and the macro name, then press Enter to start a new macro.

③ Type **dim** *variable* **as range**, replacing *variable* with your variable name.

④ Type **set** *variable* **= range("***celladdress***")**, replacing *variable* with your variable name and *celladdress* with a cell address.

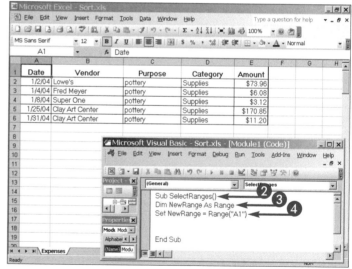

⑤ Type *variable*.**offset(***1,2***).select**, replacing *variable* with your variable name and *1,2* with your row and column offset arguments.

⑥ Click ▶ to run the macro.

The macro runs.

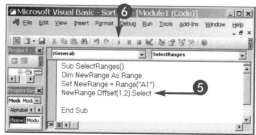

● A new range, offset by your Offset arguments from the variable range, is selected.

⑦ Edit the statement to **variable.offset(1,2).resize(5,3).select**, replacing *variable* with your variable name, *1,2* with your row and column offset arguments, and *5,3* with your resize arguments.

⑧ Click ▶ to run the macro.

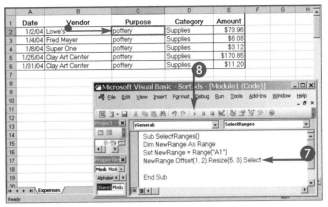

● A new range is selected that is offset from the variable range by your Offset arguments and sized according to your Resize arguments.

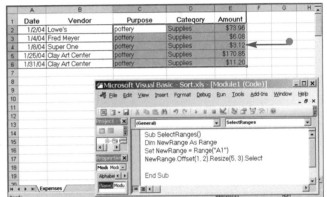

How can I select the row below a table?

▼ You can select the row immediately below the table by declaring a variable that is set to the current region around a cell in the table, and then using the Offset and Resize properties to refer to the row below the table. Declare the variable with `Dim variable As Range` and `Set variable = Range("celladdress").CurrentRegion`. Then write the statement `variable.Offset(variable.Rows.Count).Resize(1).Select`. This statement counts the rows in the table, uses that number in the Offset NumberOfRows argument, and then resizes the offset range to one row tall. There are no NumberOfColumns arguments for either property.

How can I format the header row in a table?

▼ You can execute formatting methods on the header row in a table by declaring a variable that is set to the current region around a cell in the table, and then using the Resize property to refer to the first row in the table. Declare the variable with `Dim variable As Range` and `Set variable = Range("celladdress").CurrentRegion`. Then write the statement `variable.Resize(1).` to refer to the first row in the current region and add formatting properties. No Offset property is necessary because you are not shifting the range, just resizing it to one row tall.

Ask a User for a Range

You can ask a user to enter a range with an input box, then use that range in the macro. The range the user types becomes the Range object. The user can type a cell range, as in A1:D4, or an existing named range in the workbook or macro.

The Input Box function has seven arguments, but only the first, Prompt, is required. The Prompt argument is the text the user sees in the input box. The optional Title argument is the title on the input box. If you do not use the optional Title argument, the input box has the default title "Microsoft Excel."

Declare a variable as a range and set the variable equal to the input box function, as in *variable* = InputBox (*"prompttext"*, *"titletext"*). Then type the range selection statement Range(*variable*).Select. When the macro runs, the user types a range or range name and clicks OK. Users who click Cancel get an error, so you must include If Then statements to handle the potential error. Type If *variable* <> "" Then, the range selection statement, and then End If. The input box closes quietly if the user clicks Cancel.

You should include an error handler in case a user enters an invalid range. For more information, see Chapter 16.

Ask a User for a Range

① Type **Sub** and the macro name, then press Enter to start a new macro.

② Type **dim** *variable* **as string**, replacing *variable* with your variable name.

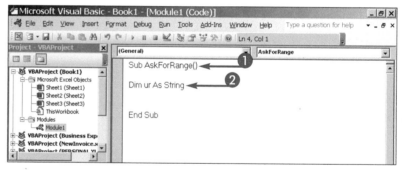

③ Type *variable* = **inputbox("***prompttext***", ***titletext***")**, replacing *variable* with your variable name, *titletext* with your title text, and *prompttext* with your prompt text.

④ Type **if** *variable* <> "" **then**, replacing *variable* with your variable name.

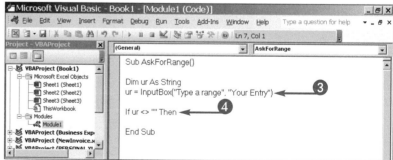

⑤ Type **range(*variable*).select**, replacing *variable* with your variable name.

⑥ Type **end if**.

⑦ Click the View Microsoft Excel button (◻) to switch to Excel.

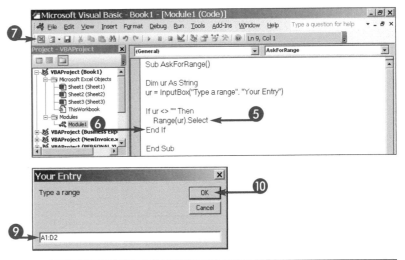

⑧ Run the macro.

Note: To run a macro, see Chapter 2.

The input box appears.

⑨ Type a range or range name in the input box.

⑩ Click OK.

● The input box disappears and the range is selected.

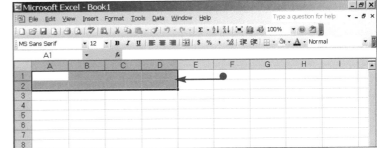

How can I set a default range entry in the Input Box?

▼ You can set a default range or range name entry in the Default argument in the InputBox function. The Default argument displays a default range that can be used by clicking OK when the input box appears. To enter a default range, type the input box function as *variable* = InputBox ("*prompttext*",*titletext*","*defaultrange*"). The default range, like the user-entered range, can be a range address such as A1:E15, or it can be a range name, such as January Sales. The range name must already exist in the workbook or the macro.

How can I show the user name in the Input Box?

▼ You can personalize the Input Box with the Excel user name by declaring a *username* variable for the Application.UserName object and using that variable in the InputBox *Prompt* argument. For example, type Dim *username* As String and then *username* = Application.UserName. Then type the input box variable as *variable* = InputBox("Type a range, " & *username*). In this example, the input box opens with the prompt Type a range, *username*. The user name is the name entered in the User name box under the Tools→ Options→General tab.

Insert Columns

You can write statements in a macro to insert a column or multiple columns in a specific location in a worksheet. Columns are inserted using the Columns object and the Insert method. You must specify the location to insert the columns as a column number or letter reference in parentheses in the Columns object.

To insert a single column, write *sheetobject*.Columns(*columnref*).Insert. The new column is inserted at the position of the *columnref* reference. To insert multiple columns, write *sheetobject*.Columns ("*columnref:columnref*").Insert. The new columns

are inserted at the position of the *columnref* references, which must be enclosed in quotes. If you do not specify the worksheet, the columns are inserted on the active worksheet. For more information about referring to columns, see the section "Create a Range Reference to Rows or Columns." For more information about referring to worksheets, see the section "Refer to a Worksheet" in Chapter 9.

The Insert method has no arguments when it applies to the Columns object. Columns are inserted to the left of the reference specified in the Columns object, and the existing worksheet columns shift right.

Insert Columns

1 Arrange your editor and Excel windows so you can see both windows.

Note: To arrange the Excel and editor windows, see the section "Arrange the Excel and Editor Windows" in Chapter 5.

2 Type **Sub** and the macro name, then press Enter to start a new macro.

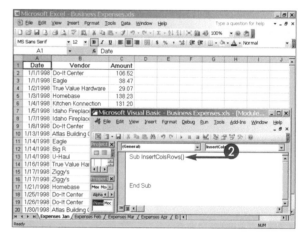

3 Type *sheetobject*.**Columns(3).Insert**, replacing *sheetobject* with your worksheet reference and the column number *3* with the column index number where you want to insert the new column.

You can replace the index number with a column letter if you enclose the column letter in quotes.

4 Click ▶ to run the macro.

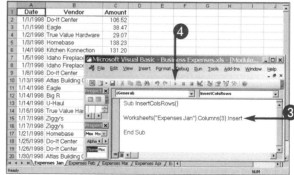

The macro runs.

● Excel inserts a new column.

⑤ Edit the statement to *sheetobject.***Columns("***B:D***").Insert**, replacing *sheetobject* with your worksheet reference and the column letters *B:D* with the column letters where you want to insert the new columns.

⑥ Click ▶ to run the macro.

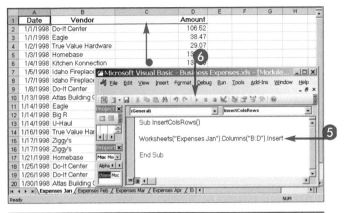

The macro runs.

● Excel inserts new columns in the position you specified.

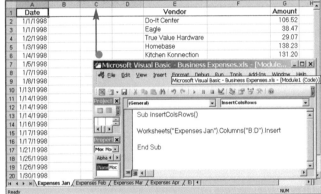

How can I insert columns on a protected worksheet?

▼ You can insert columns on a protected worksheet if you first unprotect the worksheet from within Excel by using the Tools→Protection→Unprotect Sheet menu, or if you originally set up your programmatic worksheet protection by using the UserInterfaceOnly = True argument in the Protect method. The UserInterfaceOnly = True argument allows macros to run and make changes in a worksheet while protecting the worksheet from user changes. For more information, see the sections "Protect a Worksheet" and "Run a Macro On a Protected Worksheet" in Chapter 10.

How can I insert columns in a single table rather than the entire worksheet?

▼ You can limit the column insertion to a single list or table, without affecting the the worksheet below the table, if you write a macro to select the list range first and then insert columns within the selected range. Declare a variable as a range and set it equal to the table range. Then use the variable as the first object in the statement, as in `variablename.Columns("columnref").Insert`. For more information, see the sections "Declare a Variable" in Chapter 6 and "Refer to Ranges within the Current Region."

Delete Columns

You can write statements in a macro to delete a single column or multiple columns from a specific location in a worksheet. Columns are deleted using the Columns object and the Delete method. You must specify the columns to delete with column index numbers or letters in parentheses in the Columns object.

To delete a single column, write the statement `sheetobject.Columns(columnref).Delete`. To delete multiple columns, write the statement `sheetobject.Columns("columnref:columnref").Delete`. If you do not specify the worksheet, the columns

are deleted from the active worksheet. You can refer to a single column with either an index number or with the column letter enclosed in quotes, but you can only refer to multiple columns by using column letters enclosed in quotes. For more information about referring to columns, see the section "Create a Range Reference to Rows or Columns." For more information about referring to worksheets, see the section "Refer to a Worksheet" in Chapter 9.

There Delete method has no arguments when it applies to the Columns object. When columns are deleted, the existing worksheet columns shift left.

Delete Columns

① Arrange your editor and Excel windows so you can see both windows.

Note: To arrange the Excel and editor windows, see the section "Arrange the Excel and Editor Windows" in Chapter 5.

② Type **Sub** and the macro name, then press Enter to start a new macro.

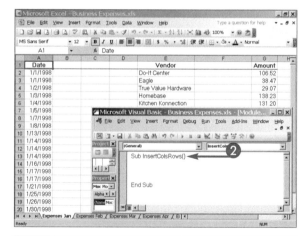

③ Type *sheetobject*.**columns(6).delete**, replacing *sheetobject* with your worksheet reference and the column number 6 with the index number for the column you want to delete.

You can replace the index number with a column letter if you enclose the column letter in quotes.

④ Click ▶ to run the macro.

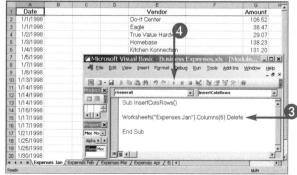

The macro runs.

- Excel deletes the column and shifts the remaining columns left.

⑤ Edit the statement to *sheetobject*.**columns("*B:D*").delete**, replacing *sheetobject* with your worksheet reference and the column letters *B:D* with the letters for the columns you want to delete.

⑥ Click ▶ to run the macro.

The macro runs.

- Excel deletes the columns and shifts the remaining columns left.

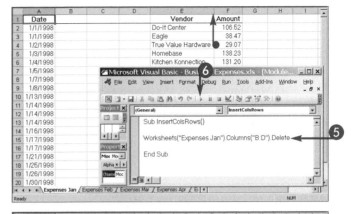

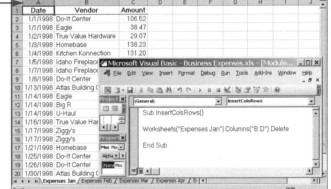

How can I delete columns on a protected worksheet?

▼ You can delete columns on a protected worksheet if you first unprotect the worksheet from within Excel by using the Tools→Protection→Unprotect Sheet menu, or if you originally set up your programmatic worksheet protection by using the UserInterfaceOnly = True argument in the Protect method. The UserInterfaceOnly = True argument allows macros to run and make changes in a worksheet while protecting the worksheet from user changes. For more information, see the sections "Protect a Worksheet" and "Run a Macro On a Protected Worksheet" in Chapter 10.

How can I delete columns in a single table rather than the entire worksheet?

▼ You can limit the column deletion to a single list or table, without affecting the the worksheet below the table, if you write a macro to select the list range first and then delete columns within the selected range. Declare a variable as a range and set it equal to the table range. Then use the variable as the first object in the statement, as in `variablename.Columns("columnref").Delete`. For more information, see the sections "Declare a Variable" in Chapter 6 and "Refer to Ranges within the Current Region."

PART IV

Insert Rows

You can write statements in a macro to insert a row or multiple rows in a specific location in a worksheet. Rows are inserted using the Rows object and the Insert method. You must specify the location to insert the rows as a row number reference in parentheses in the Rows object.

To insert a single row, write `sheetobject.Rows(rownumber).Insert`. The new row is inserted at the position of the *rownumber* reference. To insert multiple rows, write `sheetobject.Rows("rownumberrange").Insert`. The new rows are inserted at the position of the

rownumberrange reference, which must be enclosed in quotes. If you do not specify the worksheet, the rows are inserted on the active worksheet. For more information about referring to rows, see the section "Create a Range Reference to Rows or Columns." For more information about referring to worksheets, see the section "Refer to a Worksheet" in Chapter 9.

The Insert method has no arguments when it applies to the Rows object. Rows are inserted above the reference specified in the Rows object, and the existing worksheet rows shift down.

For more information about referring to rows, see the section "Create a Range Reference to Rows or Columns." For more information about referring to worksheets, see the section "Refer to a Worksheet" in Chapter 9.

Insert Rows

① Arrange your editor and Excel windows so you can see both windows.

Note: *To arrange the Excel and editor windows, see the section "Arrange the Excel and Editor Windows" in Chapter 5.*

② Type **Sub** and the macro name, then press Enter to start a new macro.

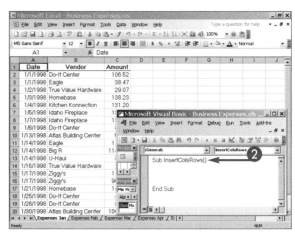

③ Type *sheetobject*.**Rows(3).Insert**, replacing *sheetobject* with your worksheet reference and the row number 3 with the row number where you want to insert the new row.

④ Click ▶ to run the macro.

The macro runs.

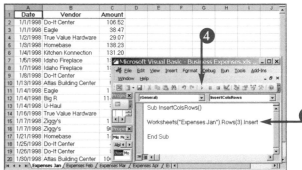

- Excel inserts a new row in the position you specified.

5 Edit the statement to read *sheetobject*.**Rows("8:10").Insert**, replacing *sheetobject* with your worksheet reference and the row numbers *8:10* with the row numbers where you want to insert the new rows.

6 Click ▶ to run the macro.

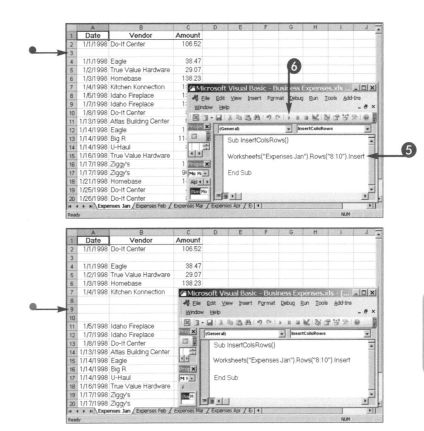

The macro runs.

- Excel inserts the new rows in the position you specified.

PART IV

How can I insert rows on a protected worksheet?

▼ You can insert rows on a protected worksheet if you first unprotect the worksheet from within Excel by using the Tools➔Protection➔Unprotect Sheet menu, or if you originally set up your programmatic worksheet protection by using the UserInterfaceOnly = True argument in the Protect method. The UserInterfaceOnly = True argument allows macros to run and make changes in a worksheet while protecting the worksheet from user changes. For more information, see the sections "Protect a Worksheet" and "Run a Macro On a Protected Worksheet" in Chapter 10.

How can I insert rows in a single table rather than the entire worksheet?

▼ You can limit the row insertion to a single list or table, without affecting the rest of the worksheet, if you write a macro to select the list range first and then insert rows within the selected range. Declare a variable as a range and set it equal to the table range. Then use the variable as the first object in the statement, as in *variablename*.Rows ("*rowref*").Insert. For more information, see the sections "Declare a Variable" in Chapter 6 and "Refer to Ranges within the Current Region."

Delete Rows

Y ou can write statements in a macro to delete a specific row or multiple rows in a worksheet. Rows are deleted using the Rows object and the Delete method. You must specify the rows to delete as a row number reference in parentheses in the Rows object.

To delete a single row, write `sheetobject.Rows (rownumber).Delete`. The new row is deleted at the position of the *rownumber* reference. To delete multiple rows, write `sheetobject.Rows("rownumber:rownumber"). Delete`. The referenced rows, which must be enclosed in

quotes, are deleted. If you do not specify the worksheet, the rows are deleted from the active worksheet. For more information about referring to rows, see the section "Create a Range Reference to Rows or Columns." For more information about referring to worksheets, see the section "Refer to a Worksheet" in Chapter 9.

The Delete method has no arguments when it applies to the Rows object. When rows are deleted, the existing worksheet rows shift up. You cannot delete noncontiguous rows in a single statement because Excel only allows deletion of multiple rows if they are in a contiguous region.

Delete Rows

① Arrange your editor and Excel windows so you can see both windows.

Note: *To arrange the Excel and editor windows, see the section "Arrange the Excel and Editor Windows" in Chapter 5.*

② Type **Sub** and the macro name, then press Enter to start a new macro.

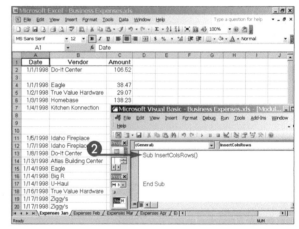

③ Type *sheetobject*.**rows(3).delete**, replacing *sheetobject* with your worksheet reference and the row number 3 with the number of the row you want to delete.

④ Click ▶ to run the macro.

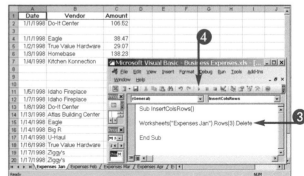

The macro runs.

● Excel deletes the row and shifts the remaining rows up.

5 Edit the statement to *sheetobject*.**rows("*7:9*").delete**, replacing *sheetobject* with your worksheet reference and the row numbers *7:9* with the numbers of the rows you want to delete.

6 Click ▶ to run the macro.

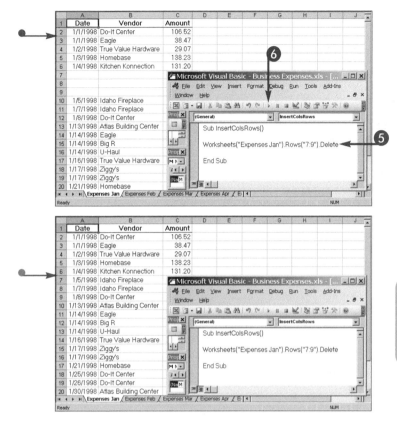

The macro runs.

● Excel deletes the rows and shifts the remaining rows up.

How can I delete rows on a protected worksheet?

▼ You can delete rows on a protected worksheet if you first unprotect the worksheet from within Excel by using the Tools→Protection→Unprotect Sheet menu, or if you originally set up your programmatic worksheet protection by using the UserInterfaceOnly = True argument in the Protect method. The UserInterfaceOnly = True argument allows macros to run and make changes in a worksheet while protecting the worksheet from user changes. For more information, see the sections "Protect a Worksheet" and "Run a Macro On a Protected Worksheet" in Chapter 10.

How can I delete rows in a single table rather than the entire worksheet?

▼ You can limit the row deletion to a single list or table, without affecting the the worksheet to the left or right of the table, if you write a macro to select the list range first and then delete rows within the selected range. Declare a variable as a range and set it equal to the table range. Then use the variable as the first object in the statement, as in `variablename.Rows("rowref").Delete`. For more information, see the sections "Declare a Variable" in Chapter 6 and "Refer to Ranges within the Current Region."

Insert Cells

You can write statements in a macro to insert cells in a specific location in a worksheet. Cells are inserted using the Range object and the Insert method. You must specify the location to insert the cells as a range reference in parentheses in the Range object.

To insert cells, write `sheetobject.Range("celladdress: celladdress").Insert`. The new cells are inserted at the position of the range reference, which must be enclosed in quotes. If you do not specify the worksheet with a *sheetobject* reference, the cells are inserted on the active worksheet. For more information about referring to cells

and ranges, see the section "Write a Range Reference to Specific Cells." For more information about referring to worksheets, see the section "Refer to a Worksheet" in Chapter 9.

The Insert method has two optional arguments when it applies to the Range object. When cells are inserted, the existing worksheet cells shift to the right or down. If you do not specify the shift direction, Excel chooses the shift direction based on the shape of the current region. To shift the cells in the direction you want, add the optional argument `Shift:=xlShiftDown` or `Shift:=xlShiftToRight`.

Insert Cells

① Arrange your editor and Excel windows so you can see both windows.

Note: To arrange the Excel and editor windows, see the section "Arrange the Excel and Editor Windows" in Chapter 5.

② Type **Sub** and the macro name, then press Enter to start a new macro.

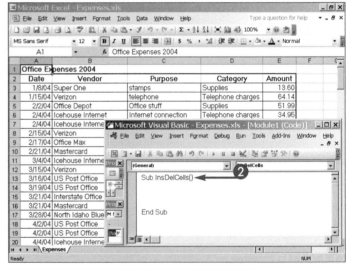

③ Type *sheetobject*.**Range("A3:A5").Insert**, replacing *sheetobject* with your worksheet reference and the range reference *A3:A5* with the range where you want to insert the new cells.

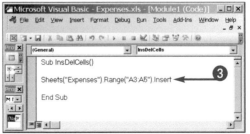

④ Type **shift:=xlshiftdown**, replacing the constant *xlShiftDown* with *xlShiftToRight* if you want to shift the cells to the right instead of down.

⑤ Click ▶ to run the macro.

The macro runs.

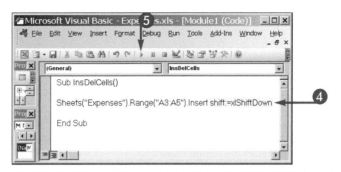

● Excel inserts cells in the range you specified, and shifts the surrounding cells in the direction you set.

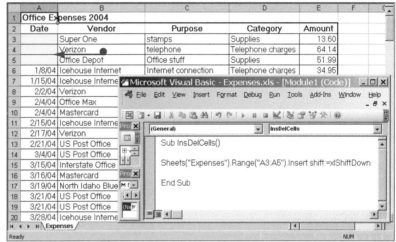

PART IV

How can I format the newly inserted cells?

▼ You can format newly inserted cells by writing statements immediately following the Insert statement that format the inserted range, as in `Range (celladdress:celladdress). Interior.colorIndex = 3`. When cells are inserted into a range, they automatically acquire the same formatting as the cells they shift; but if you want to format the inserted cells differently, use the same Range object to format them.

How can I insert an entire row into an existing table?

▼ You can insert an entire row into an existing table by declaring a variable as a range and setting it equal to the table range. Use that variable as the first object in a row-insert statement, as in `variablename.Rows ("rowref").Insert`. For more information, see the sections "Declare a Variable" in Chapter 6 and "Refer to Ranges within the Current Region."

How can I enter a value into an inserted cell?

▼ You can enter a value into a newly inserted cell by typing the statement `Range(cell address) = "textstring"`, replacing *celladdress* with the address of the cell, and replacing *textstring* with the value or text or formula you want to enter in the cell. If you reference multiple cells in the Range object, the same value is entered in all the cells.

Delete Cells

You can write statements in a macro to delete a specific range of cells in a worksheet. Cells are deleted using the Range object and the Delete method. You must specify the range of cells to delete as a range reference in parentheses in the Range object.

To delete cells, write the statement *sheetobject.* `Range("celladdress:celladdress").Delete`. The cells are deleted according to the range reference, which must be enclosed in quotes. If you do not specify the worksheet with a *sheetobject* reference, the cells are deleted from the active worksheet. For more information about referring to

cells, see the section "Write a Range Reference to Specific Cells." For more information about referring to worksheets, see the section "Refer to a Worksheet" in Chapter 9.

The Delete method has two optional arguments when it applies to the Range object. When cells are deleted, the existing worksheet cells are shifted to the left or up. If you do not specify the shift direction, Excel chooses the shift direction based on the shape of the current region. To shift the cells in the direction you want, add the optional argument `Shift:=xlShiftUp` or `Shift:=xlShiftToLeft`.

Delete Cells

① Arrange your editor and Excel windows so you can see both windows.

Note: To arrange the Excel and editor windows, see the section "Arrange the Excel and Editor Windows" in Chapter 5.

② Type **Sub** and the macro name, then press Enter to start a new macro.

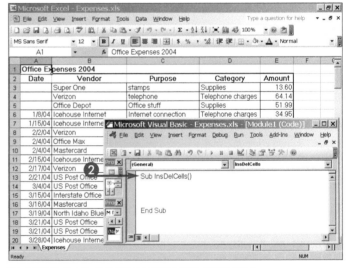

③ Type *Sheetobject.***Range("***A3:A5***").Delete***, replacing *Sheetobject* with your worksheet reference and the range reference *A3:A5* with the range you want to delete.

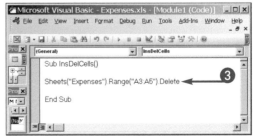

④ Type **shift:=xlshiftup**, replacing the constant `xlShiftUp` with `xlShiftToLeft` if you want to shift the cells to the left instead of up.

⑤ Click ▶ to run the macro.

The macro runs.

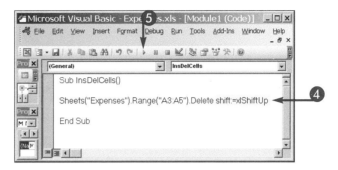

● Excel deletes the range of cells you specified and shifts the surrounding cells in the direction you set.

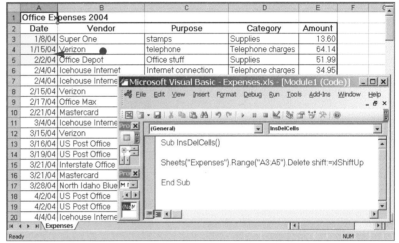

How can I delete cells on a protected worksheet?

▼ You can delete cells on a protected worksheet if you first unprotect the worksheet from within Excel by using the Tools→Protection→Unprotect Sheet menu, or if you originally set up your programmatic worksheet protection by using the `UserInterfaceOnly = True` argument in the Protect method. The `UserInterfaceOnly = True` argument allows macros to run and make changes in a worksheet while protecting the worksheet from user changes. For more information, see the sections "Protect a Worksheet" and "Run a Macro On a Protected Worksheet" in Chapter 10.

How can I undo the deleted cells after the macro runs?

▼ You can undo a programmatic cell deletion only by closing the workbook without saving changes, so the workbook loses the changes the macro made. When a macro makes changes in a workbook, the Undo button on the Standard toolbar is unavailable because a user cannot undo programmatic changes from the Excel user interface. If the macro is programmed to save changes quietly, without asking the user, you cannot undo any of the changes the macro makes.

Name a Range

You can assign a name to a specific range of cells programmatically with the Name property of the Range object. When you assign a name to a range, you can reference the range name instead of a specific range address in your macros. For example, you can create an invoice with the sales tax rate in cell G2 and name that cell SalesTaxRate. You can then refer to the cell named SalesTaxRate in your code instead of remembering the address G2.

Range names you assign become part of the worksheet and are usable in the worksheet even if you delete the macro that created the names. Range names are unique and

worksheet-specific, and you cannot create the same name on more than one worksheet. You can, however, create the same name on multiple worksheets if you incorporate the worksheet name in the range name, as in Sheet3!Sales and Sheet4!Sales. Assigned range names are selectable in the Excel Name box and usable in worksheet formulas.

Range names must be one word and are always referenced in code as strings enclosed in quotes. You can create names using underscore characters or capital letters, as in Tax_Rate or TaxRate.

1 Type **Sub** and the macro name, then press Enter to start a new macro.

2 Type **range("*celladdress*:*celladdress*")**, replacing *celladdress:celladdress* with the range address.

3 Type **.name** = "*rangename*", replacing *rangename* with your range name.

4 Click ▶ to run the macro.

The macro runs.

5 Click ▣ to switch to Excel.

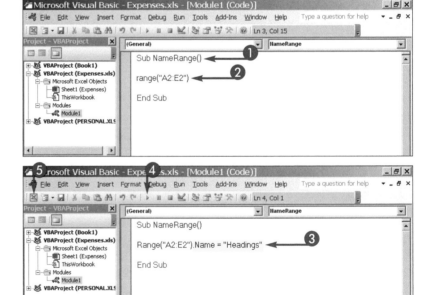

6 Click the Name box ▼.

7 Click the range name.

● Excel selects the named range.

You can reference this range name in your macros as Range("*rangename*").

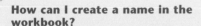

How can I create a name in the workbook?

▼ You can create a name in a workbook by selecting the range, typing the name in the Name box, and then pressing Enter. Whether you create a name in a macro or in the Name box, you can use the name in both macros and worksheet formulas. Names are enclosed in quotes in macros but not in worksheet formulas.

Why do I get an error when I run a macro that references a name?

▼ Running a macro on a worksheet that does not contain the range name generates an error. You must activate the worksheet in which the range name exists before you run a macro that references the range name. Another possible reason for errors is a misspelled range name. Unlike a declared variable, VBA cannot tell you if a range name is misspelled.

How can I create the same name on multiple worksheets?

▼ You can create the same name on multiple worksheets if you incorporate the worksheet name in the range name. For example, to name a range Sales on worksheets named January and February, type the statements Worksheets("January").Range("*cell:cell*").Name = "January!Sales" and Worksheets("February").Range("*cell:cell* ").Name = "February!Sales". Running the two statements in one macro creates both names.

List All Names in a Workbook

You can write a macro that lists all the named ranges in the active workbook, along with the cell range and worksheet location for each named range. The following code uses For Next loop to create the list on the active worksheet. Replace the variable nms with your own variable for the workbook names, and replace the variable n with your own variable for row numbers.

```
Sub ListNames()
Dim nms As Names
Dim n As Long
```

```
Set nms = ActiveWorkbook.Names
For n = 1 To nms.Count
Cells(n, 2).Value = nms(n).Name
Cells(n, 3).Value =
nms(n).RefersToRange.Address
Cells(n, 4).Value =
nms(n).RefersToRange.Worksheet.Name
Next
 End Sub
```

Add the final statement Columns("B:D").AutoFit to fit the columns to the entries.

List All Names in a Workbook

1 Type **Sub** and the macro name, then press Enter to start a new macro.

2 Type **dim** *variable* **as names**, replacing *variable* with your names variable.

3 Type **dim** *rownum* **as long**, replacing *rownum* with your row number variable.

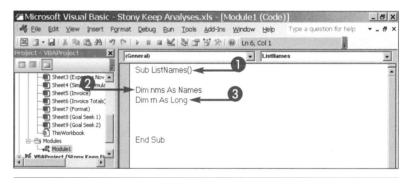

Replace *variable* with your names variable and *rownum* with your row number variable throughout this code.

4 Type **set** *variable* **= activeworkbook .names**.

5 Type **for** *rownum* **= 1 to** *variable***.count**.

6 Type **cells(***rownum***, 2).value =** *variable* **(***rownum***).name**.

7 Type **cells(***rownum***, 3).value =** *variable* **(***rownum***).referstorange.address**.

8 Type **cells(***rownum***, 4).value =** *variable* **(***rownum***).referstorange.worksheet.name**.

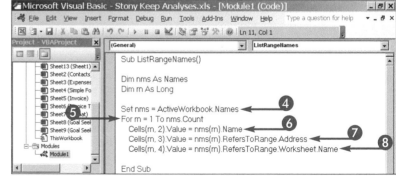

9 Type **next**.

10 Type **columns("B:D").autofit**.

11 Click ▶ to run the macro.

12 Click ▣ to switch to Excel.

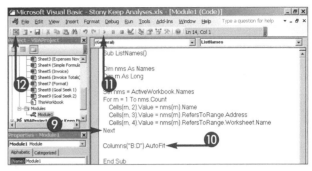

● The macro lists all range names and their locations in the active worksheet.

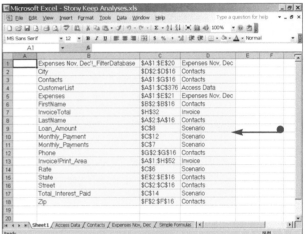

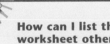

How can I list the ranges on a worksheet other than the active worksheet?

▼ You can list the ranges on any worksheet if you precede the Cells and Columns objects with the worksheet reference where you want the macro to place the list. For example, the `Cells (n, 2).Value = nms(n). Name` statement is written *sheetobject*`.Cells(n, 2). Value = nms(n).Name`, and the `Columns("B:D").AutoFit` statement is written *sheetobject*`.Columns ("B:D").AutoFit`.

How can I remove names from a workbook?

▼ You can remove names from a workbook from within Excel rather than programmatically. Click Insert→Name→Define to open the Define Names dialog box. Click the range name, Delete, and then click OK when you finish deleting names. Names that include the worksheet name only appear in the Define Names dialog box when the worksheet in the name is the active worksheet.

How can I rename a range?

▼ You can rename a range using the `Range("rangeaddress"). Name = "newname"` statement. If you rename an existing named range, the range has both names. Existing range names are not deleted when you rename a range. If you use an existing name to name a range on a different worksheet, the range name moves to the new worksheet.

Hide a Range

Y ou can hide a range of cells that you do not want users to access by using the Hidden property of the Range object. For example, you can hide portions of a worksheet that have values the worksheet uses in calculations, such as a lookup table.

You can only hide entire rows or columns of a worksheet. When rows or columns are hidden, the values and formulas in those ranges are still completely functional. The width of the columns or height of the rows is set to zero so the columns and rows are not visible but remain unlocked. The

column letters and row numbers of hidden ranges are also hidden, and they can be easily unhidden from the user interface unless the worksheet is protected. For more information about worksheet protection, see the section "Protect a Worksheet" in Chapter 10.

To hide rows or columns, use the range references for the rows or columns you want to hide and the Hidden property with the value True, as in *sheetobject*.Columns(*index*). Hidden = True. For more information on column and row references, see the section "Create a Range Reference to Rows or Columns."

Hide a Range

① Arrange your editor and Excel windows so you can see both windows.

Note: To arrange the Excel and editor windows, see the section "Arrange the Excel and Editor Windows" in Chapter 5.

② Type **Sub** and the macro name, then press Enter to start a new macro.

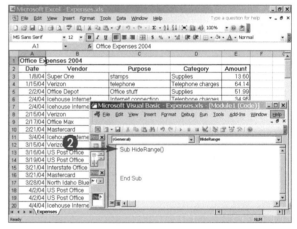

③ Type **columns("***columnletter:columnletter***").** **hidden = true**, replacing *columnletter* with the beginning and ending column letters you want to hide.

④ Click ▶ to run the macro.

The macro runs.

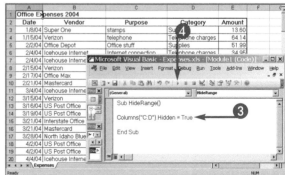

- The columns are hidden, as evidenced by the hidden column letters.

5 Edit the statement to read **rows("***rownumber***:***rownumber***").hidden = true**, replacing *rownumber* with the beginning and ending row numbers you want to hide.

6 Click ▶ to run the macro.

The macro runs.

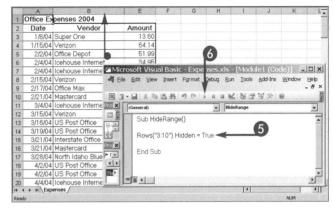

- Excel hides the rows, as evidenced by the hidden row numbers.

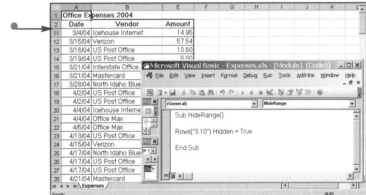

Why did my entire worksheet go blank?

▼ Your entire worksheet goes blank if you hide all the rows or columns. For example, typing `Columns.Hidden = True` with no index numbers or letters specified hides all columns in the worksheet. Change the Hidden value to False and run the macro again to unhide the columns, and then rewrite the macro to specify which columns to hide.

How can I unhide rows or columns?

▼ You can unhide all hidden columns in a worksheet with the statement `Columns.Hidden = False`, and rows with `Rows.Hidden = False`. You can unhide specific rows or columns by writing the statement specifying which rows or columns to unhide, and setting the Hidden value to False. When you unhide specific rows or columns the remaining hidden rows and columns are still hidden.

How can I hide noncontiguous rows or columns?

▼ You can write multiple statements to hide noncontiguous rows or columns. For example, to hide rows 4, 5, 6, and 10, write the statements `Rows("4:6").Hidden = True` and `Rows (10).Hidden = True`. Because row numbers are the same as row index numbers, you can specify a single row with or without quotes, but multiple rows must be enclosed in quotes.

PART IV

Parse a Column into Multiple Columns

You can parse, or separate, a column of text into multiple columns by using the TextToColumns method. For example, if you want to use a column of names containing both first and last names in a mail-merge procedure, or want to sort the list by last name, you can parse that column into a column of first names and a column of last names.

You use the TextToColumns method with the Range object that contains the column to parse. This method has several optional arguments, the most important of which are the Destination and delimiter arguments.

The Destination argument specifies the range where the parsed columns should be placed. You only need to specify the cell in the upper-left corner of that range. The delimiter arguments Tab, Semicolon, Comma, Space, and Other specify the character that breaks delimited data into segments.

To create a macro to parse a column, write the statement Range("*rangeaddress*").TextToColumns and add the optional arguments separated by commas and spaces. You can specify the delimiter character as *delimiter*: = True.

Parse a Column into Multiple Columns

① Type **Sub** and the macro name, then press Enter to start a new macro.

② Type **range("*rangeaddress*")** **.texttocolumns**, replacing *rangeaddress* with the range of the column to parse.

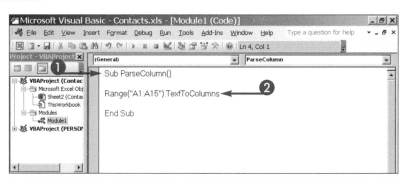

③ Type a comma and a space, and then **destination:=range("*celladdress*")**, replacing *celladdress* with the cell in the upper-left corner of the destination range.

④ Type a comma and a space, then *delimiter*:=**true**, replacing *delimiter* with the name of the delimiter character.

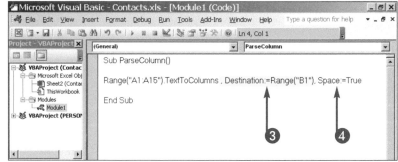

⑤ Click ▶ to run the macro.

The macro runs.

⑥ Click ☒ to switch to Excel.

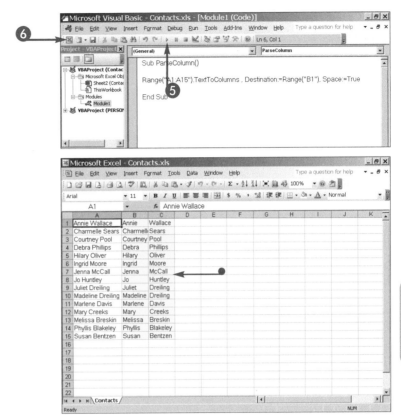

● Excel parses the column into separate columns.

How can I select the whole column if I do not know how long the column is?

▼ You can select the entire column, regardless of how long it is, by selecting the current region around the active cell and then selecting the specific column within the current region. Type the statement `ActiveCell.CurrentRegion.Columns(1)` to select the entire single column, replacing the column index number with your column index number, and follow the statement with the `TextToColumns` method and optional arguments. For more information about referring to columns, see the section "Create a Range Reference to Rows or Columns."

Why do I get a name parsed over three cells in my destination range?

▼ You may get a name parsed over three cells in the destination range if you have multiple consecutive delimiters in your original column. For example, having two spaces inadvertently typed between a first and last name in a column of names is not unusual. When you parse that column, each space character creates a new column for that entry. You can prevent this by typing a Replace statement that runs before the TextToColumns statement in the macro. Type *rangeobject*. `Replace What:=" ", Replacement:=" "`, and replace two space characters with one space character.

Set Cell Formatting

You can set the entire cell formatting for a specific range in a worksheet by using a Range object and the property settings. There are many formatting properties you can set for a range, including font properties such as bold, italic, color, and the font name and size. You can also change the cell color and shrink to fit the entry in the cell.

You can set several properties for the same range most efficiently by using a With block. A With block enables you to combine all the formatting properties for a range into one simple, easy-to-read set of statements.

To see all the properties for the Range object, type a range object and a period in a macro, and then scroll through the Auto List for all the available range properties and methods. To see all the properties and settings for the Font property, type a range object and a period in a macro, then `Font` and a period, and scroll through the Auto List for all the available font properties.

Set Cell Formatting

① Type **Sub** and the macro name, then press Enter to start a new macro.

② Type **with range("*rangeref*")**, replacing *rangeref* with your range reference.

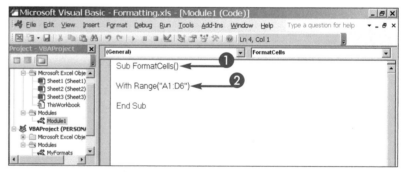

③ Type a period, then a property you want to apply, then = and a value for the property.

④ Repeat step **3** for all the properties you want to apply to the range.

⑤ Type **end with**.

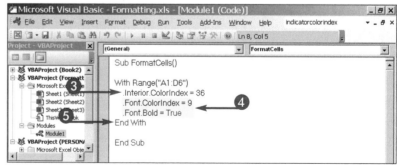

⑥ Click the Run Sub/UserForm button (▷) to run the macro.

⑦ Click the View Microsoft Excel button (▣) to switch to Excel.

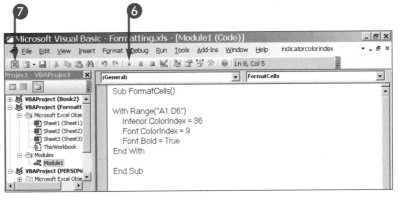

● The range is formatted.

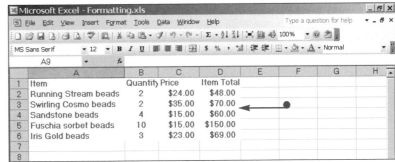

How can I find the ColorIndex value I want?

▼ You can find the ColorIndex values by looking up IndicatorColorIndex in the Visual Basic Help files. The palette of ColorIndex colors and their values is difficult to find unless you search specifically for IndicatorColorIndex.

How can I hide the worksheet formulas?

▼ You can hide worksheet formulas, so that a user cannot see the formula in the Formula Bar, by using the `Range("rangeref").` `FormulaHidden =` `True` statement. The formulas are hidden after you protect the worksheet. To protect a worksheet, see Chapter 10.

How can I refer to the range I want?

▼ You can refer to a range in the Range("*rangeref*") object by replacing *rangeref* with a cell address range or a range name, or with the objects ActiveCell. CurrentRegion or *sheetobject*.UsedRange. You can also use offset range references; for more information about range references, see Chapter 11.

Set Row Height

Y ou can write statements in a macro that set the row height for specific rows in a worksheet, so that the finished worksheet rows are appropriately sized for the data you want to enter. You set row heights by using the RowHeight property for a Rows object.

Excel sets a default row height to accommodate the default font size in new workbooks. You can see or change the default font and font size for new workbooks in the Standard font and Size boxes located under the Tools, Option menu. The default row height depends on the size of the default font. Like font size, row height is measured in points, with 72 points in an inch.

You can set the height of a row or rows by assigning a numeric value to the RowHeight property for the Rows object that specifies the rows. For example, to change the height of row 5 to 36 points, you can write the statement Rows(5).RowHeight = 36. If you do not precede a Rows object with a worksheet reference, the code is executed on the active worksheet.

For more information about referring to rows, see the section "Create a Range Reference to Rows or Columns" in Chapter 11.

Set Row Height

① Type **Sub** and the macro name, then press Enter to start a new macro.

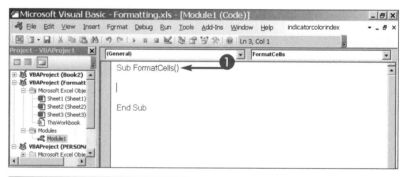

② Type **rows(*rownumber*).rowheight = *height***, replacing *rownumber* with the row number and *height* with the row height in points.

You can resize multiple rows by typing a row number range, as in Rows("1:5") for a Rows object.

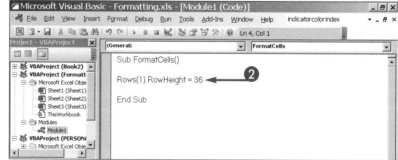

③ Click 🕨 to run the macro.

④ Click 🗷 to switch to Excel.

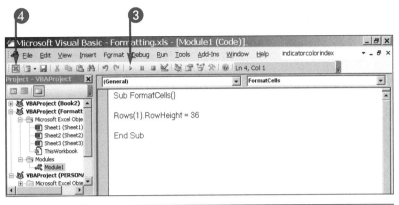

● The rows you specified are resized to the specified height.

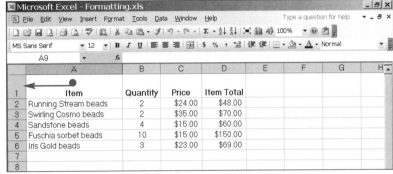

How can I resize all the rows in a list?

▼ You can resize all the rows in a list of any length, even if you do not know the length, by using the CurrentRegion property of the Rows object. If the active cell is within the list you want to resize, type the statement Rows. CurrentRegion.RowHeight = *rowheight*. All the rows in the current region surrounding the active cell are resized.

How can I rezize the rows in just the body of a table?

▼ You can resize the rows in just the body of a table, without knowing the length of the table, by using an offset range reference to select the body. Declare a variable with Dim variable As Range and Set variable = Range ("celladdress").Current Region. The *celladdress* should be a cell within the table. Then write the statement variable. Offset(1).Resize(variable. Rows.Count-1).RowHeight = rowheight.

How can I resize multiple rows?

▼ You can resize multiple contiguous rows by enclosing the row number range in quotes, as in Rows("10:15"), which resizes rows 10 through 15. You can resize multiple noncontiguous rows by writing separate statements for each set of contiguous rows, as in Rows ("2:4").RowHeight = 15 followed by Rows("10:15"). RowHeight = 24. These two statements resize rows 2:4 and rows 10:15 separately.

Set Column Width

You can write statements in a macro that set the column width for specific columns in a worksheet, so that the finished worksheet columns are appropriately sized to display the data. You set column widths by using the ColumnWidth property for a Columns object.

Excel sets a default column width to accommodate the default font size in new workbooks. The default column width is 8.43 characters, which is based on how many zeroes in the default font fit into a column. You can see or change the default font and font size for new workbooks in the Standard font and Size boxes located under the Tools, Option menu.

You can set the width of a column or columns by assigning a numeric value to the ColumnWidth property for the Columns object that specifies the columns. For example, to change the width of column D to 20 characters, you can write the statement `Columns("D").ColumnWidth = 20`. If you do not precede a Columns object with a worksheet reference, the code is executed on the active worksheet.

For more information about referring to columns, see the section "Create a Range Reference to Rows or Columns" in Chapter 11.

---

❶ Type **Sub** and the macro name, then press Enter to start a new macro.

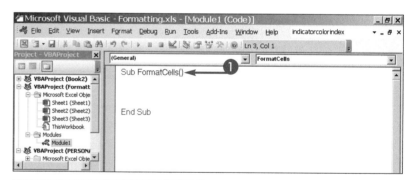

❷ Type **columns("*columnletter*"). columnwidth** = *width*, replacing *columnletter* with the column letter and *width* with the column width.

You can resize multiple columns by typing a column letter range, as in `Columns("B:E")` for a Columns object.

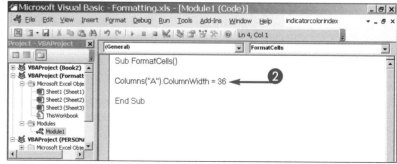

③ Click ▶ to run the macro.

④ Click ⊠ to switch to Excel.

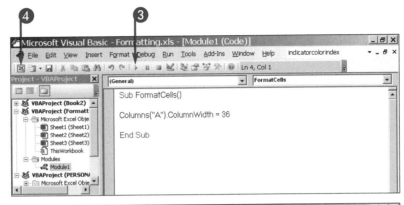

● The columns you specified are resized to the specified width.

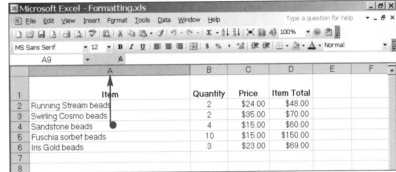

How can I resize all the columns in a table?

▼ You can resize all the columns in a table of any width, even if you do not know the width, by using the CurrentRegion property of the Columns object. If the active cell is within the list you want to resize, type the statement `Columns.Current Region.ColumnWidth = columnwidth`. All the columns in the current region surrounding the active cell are resized.

How can I resize the leftmost column in a table if I do not know the letter of the column?

▼ You can resize the leftmost column of a table if you use the CurrentRegion property of the Columns object. Make sure the active cell is located within the table, and write the statement `Columns.CurrentRegion. Columns(1).ColumnWidth = columnwidth`. The CurrentRegion property selects the table, and the index number (1) selects the leftmost column. For more information on selecting ranges, see Chapter 11.

How can I resize multiple noncontiguous columns?

▼ You can resize multiple noncontiguous columns by writing a separate statement for each set of contiguous columns, as in `Columns("A"). ColumnWidth = 6` followed by `Columns("D:F").Column Width = 20`. These two statements resize column A and columns D:F separately.

Wrap Text and AutoFit a Range

When you import or move or copy data into a new range, often the data does not fit into the new cells. You can solve that problem by writing a macro to AutoFit and wrap text in the new range.

When you AutoFit a column, the column width changes to fit the widest entry in the column, so that each entry is fully displayed but the column is not any wider than it needs to be.

When you wrap text in a cell, long entries wrap at the width of the column and continue on a new line in the same cell. The row height needs to increase to accommodate multiline cells, but columns can be any width you set, and the wrapped text lines break to fit the column width. After you wrap text, you need to AutoFit the rows to accommodate the new cell heights.

You can AutoFit ranges by using the AutoFit method with the Rows or Columns object. You can wrap text in cells with the statement `Range("rangeref").WrapText = True`. If you do not like where the wrapped text breaks, you can add statements to resize specific columns and then AutoFit the rows.

Wrap Text and AutoFit a Range

① Arrange your editor and Excel windows so you can see both windows.

Note: To arrange the Excel and editor windows, see Chapter 5.

② Type **Sub** and the macro name, then press Enter to start a new macro.

③ Type **range("*rangeref*").wraptext = true**, replacing *rangeref* with your range.

④ Type **range("*rangeref* ").columns.autofit**, replacing *rangeref* with your range.

⑤ Click ▶ to run the macro.

● Long cell entries are wrapped, and the columns in the range are AutoFit.

You can widen columns that are too narrow and then AutoFit the rows.

⑥ Type **range("*rangeref* ").columns ("*columnref*").columnwidth = *columnwidth***, replacing *rangeref* with your range, *columnref* with the column to resize, and *columnwidth* with the new column width.

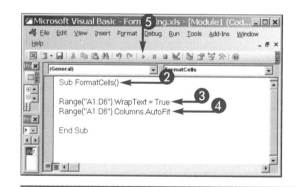

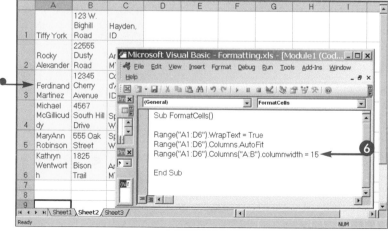

⑦ Type **range("*rangeref*").rows.autofit**, replacing *rangeref* with your range.

⑧ Click ▶ to run the macro.

⑨ Click ☒ to switch to Excel.

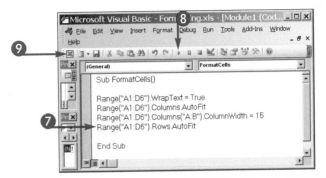

```
Sub FormatCells()

    Range("A1:D6").WrapText = True
    Range("A1:D6").Columns.AutoFit
    Range("A1:D6").Columns("A:B").ColumnWidth = 15
    Range("A1:D6").Rows.AutoFit

End Sub
```

● The specified columns are resized and the rows Autofit to fit the wrapped text in the resized columns.

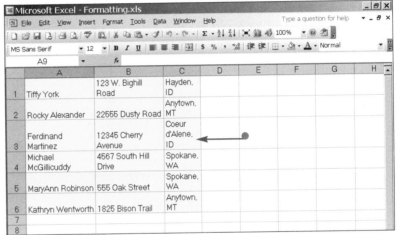

Why is my AutoFit column very wide?

▼ Your AutoFit column is very wide because there is at least one entry in the column that is very long. You can set a specific column width for that column by using a `Columns ("columnref").ColumnWidth = columnwidth` statement. When a specific column width is set, the long entry spills over into the cell to its right unless you set `WrapText`.

Why did my AutoFit row with wrapped text leave a big empty space at the top of the cell?

▼ If you run the statements in the wrong order, you do not get the results you expect. Make sure the statement order in the macro is to set AutoFit on the rows only after the macro sets the column width and wraps the text in the cells.

When I set WrapText and AutoFit for a specific row in a range, the row did not change. What went wrong?

▼ When you set properties for a specific row within a range, the row reference is relative to the range, not the worksheet. For example, in the statement `Range("A2:B3").Rows(2)`, the referenced row is row 2 in the range, but it is row 3 in the worksheet. You can test this by typing `Range("A2:B3").Rows(2).Select` in the Immediate window and pressing Enter.

Add Borders to a Range

Y ou can write macro statements to add borders to a range of cells so that data in the worksheet stands out and is easier to read. For example, when a range of data contains cells with totals, those cells are commonly bordered to make them easy to find.

You can place a border around an entire range or a single cell using the BorderAround method, which has optional arguments to set color, line style, and weight.

The LineStyle argument specifies the style of the border line. For example, the value xlContinuous creates a continuous border line, and is the default if you do not

specify a LineStyle argument. The xlDash argument draws a dashed border line, and the xlDouble argument draws a continuous double line around the range.

The ColorIndex argument allows you to set a ColorIndex value for the border color. If you do not use the argument, the default is black. You can look up the ColorIndex values in the VBA Help files under IndicatorColorIndex.

The Weight argument sets the border line weight and uses constants that you can select when you type the argument. If you do not use the argument, the default is xlThin.

Add Borders to a Range

① Type **Sub** and the macro name, then press Enter to start a new macro.

② Type **range("*rangeref*").borderaround**, replacing *rangeref* with your range.

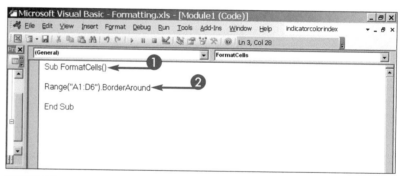

③ Type **linestyle:=xldouble**, replacing the xlDouble constant with your LineStyle constant.

④ Type a comma and **colorindex:=7**, replacing the value 7 with your ColorIndex value.

⑤ Type a comma and **weight:=xlthick**, replacing the xlThick constant with your constant.

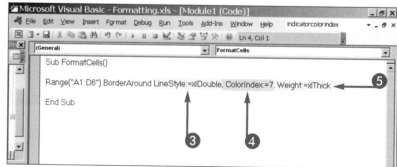

6 Click ▶ to run the macro.

7 Click ⊠ to switch to Excel.

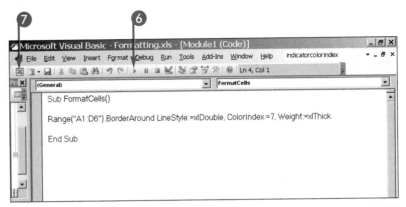

● The specified range has a border around it.

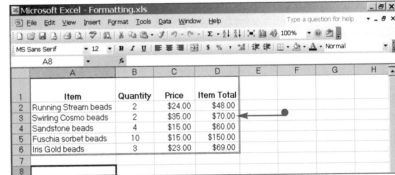

PART IV

How can I apply interior borders to a range?

▼ You can add interior borders within a range by writing a With block for each of the interior borders: the top, bottom, right, left, interior vertical, and interior horizontal. A macro for formatting interior borders is extensive and lengthy to write, and is a good candidate for recording with the macro recorder. When you record a macro to apply interior borders to a range, you can copy and paste that macro into any procedure that requires interior border formatting. For more information about recording a macro, see Chapter 1.

What are all the LineStyle and Weight constants?

▼ The LineStyle constants are xlContinuous, which draws a continuous line and is the default; xlDash, a dashed line; xlDashDot, a broken line of dots and dashes; xlDashDotDot, a broken line of dashes followed by two dots; xlDot, a dotted line; xlDouble, a continuous double line; and xlSlantDashDot, a broken line using a slanted-dash pattern. The Weight constants are xlHairline, xlThin, xlMedium, and xlThick, which are progressively thicker line weights.

Color a Range

You can write a macro to color a range of cells by selecting the specific range, which can be rows or columns or cells, and then setting the color of the cells in that range. You can specify the color of a range by using the Range.Interior.ColorIndex property, which uses one of the 56 preset workbook colors as a property value; or you can color a range by setting the Range.Interior.Color statement, which uses RGB values to create a new color instead of using a predefined ColorIndex value.

The Color property defines a color by setting RGB values, which are the red, green, and blue components of a color. The values for each component range from 0 to 255, and

the lower the value, the darker the color. For example, the `Range.Interior.Color = RGB(0,0,0)` statement colors the range of cells black and the `Range.Interior.Color = RGB(256,256,256)` statement colors the range of cells white.

You can use the same techniques to set the font color in a range, using the Range.Font.Color or Range.Font.ColorIndex properties.

Color a Range

① Type **Sub** and the macro name, then press Enter to start a new macro.

② Type **range(*rangeref*).interior.color**, replacing *rangeref* with your range reference.

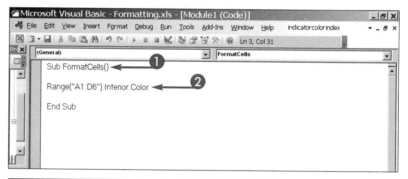

③ Type **= rgb(*redvalue,greenvalue, bluevalue*)**, replacing *redvalue* with your red value, *greenvalue* with your green value, and *bluevalue* with your blue value.

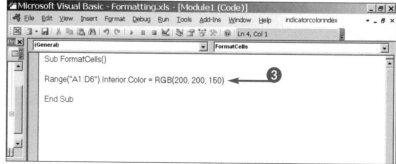

④ Click ▶ to run the macro.

⑤ Click ⊠ to switch to Excel.

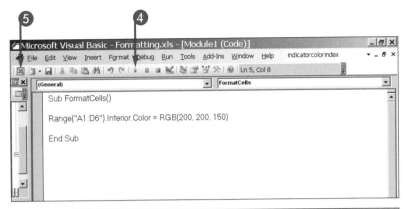

● The referenced range is colored with your new color.

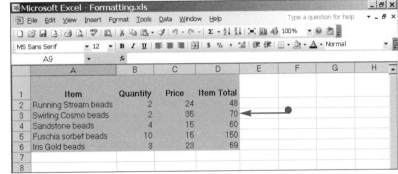

How can I test different RGB values without creating and running a macro?

▼ You can test different RBG values in the Immediate window. Arrange the editor and Excel windows so you can see the results of Immediate window statements without switching windows. Type the statement in the Immediate window and press Enter. The statement is executed in Excel. Change the RGB values and press Enter to execute the changes.

How can I change the color of a preset ColorIndex value?

▼ You can change the color of a preset ColorIndex value in the active workbook by creating a macro that executes the statement `ActiveWorkbook. Colors(colorindex) = RGB(redvalue, greenvalue, bluevalue)`. For more information, see the section "Change the Colors Available in a Workbook." The ColorIndex value is changed for the entire workbook.

How can I color the entire used range in a worksheet?

▼ You can color the entire used range in a worksheet by using the `Range.UsedRange` object as the range object in the statement. You can also use any other range object you want, such as the current region around a specific cell, or an offset range reference. For more information about referring to ranges, see Chapter 11.

Change the Colors Available in a Workbook

You can change the colors available in a workbook if the 56 standard colors are not enough to suit your needs. For example, the lightest standard gray color, when applied to the interior of a cell, is still dark enough to make the font hard to read.

You can change the colors in the palette to any color you want and even lighten the shades of gray. You change a color value by setting the red, green, and blue components of a standard color to new values in the Colors collection of the workbook object.

You can create the new color by using the statement `ActiveWorkbook.Colors(colorindex) = RGB(redvalue,greenvalue,bluevalue)`.

Each red, green, or blue color component is a value between 0 and 255. Higher red, green, and blue components, called RGB values, make lighter colors. You create gray by setting the RGB values to equal values. The lightest gray color in the ColorIndex palette is index number 15. If you set each of the RGB values to 220, the standard light gray is rendered even lighter. Changing a color value affects only the active workbook.

Change the Colors Available in a Workbook

① Type **Sub** and the macro name, then press Enter to start a new macro.

② Type **activeworkbook.colors(*colorindex*)**, replacing *colorindex* with the color index you want to change.

③ Type = **rgb(*redvalue, greenvalue, bluevalue*)**, replacing *redvalue* with your red value, *greenvalue* with your green value, and *bluevalue* with your blue value.

④ Click ▶ to run the macro.

⑤ Click ☒ to switch to Excel.

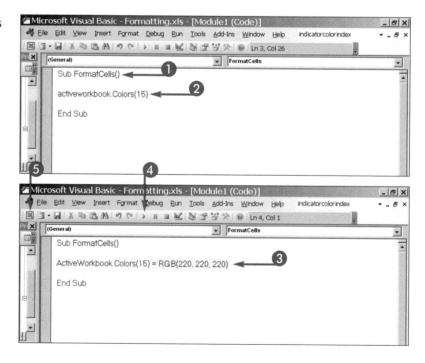

⑥ Select cells to which you want to apply the new color.

⑦ Click Format.

⑧ Click Cells.

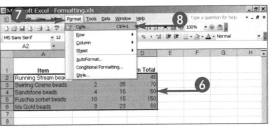

The Format Cells dialog box appears.

⑨ Click the Patterns tab.

⑩ Click the color for which you changed the RGB value.

⑪ Click OK.

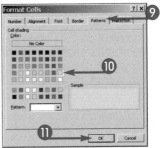

● The changed color is applied to the selected cells.

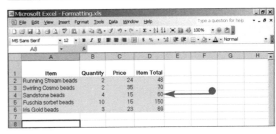

How can I change the colors back to their original values?

▼ You can change the colors back to their original values by resetting all the workbook default color values. Create a new macro with the statement `ActiveWorkbook.ResetColors` and run the macro. All the colors in the workbook are reset to their default values.

How can I use my new colors in another workbook?

▼ You can use the changed colors in another workbook by running the macro in the other workbook. This macro is executed in the active workbook, so if you have both workbooks open, you can activate the workbook where you want the new colors and run the macro from the Macro dialog box. For more information, see Chapter 2.

Where can I find a list of the ColorIndex values?

▼ You can find a list of the ColorIndex values by looking up IndicatorColorIndex Property in the VBA Help files. The Help files have a complete palette of the standard Excel colors and their associated index values. You can change any index value to a different color by using the `ActiveWorkbook.Colors` statement.

Color Unlocked Cells

You can write a macro that applies color to unlocked cells so that when you are developing a worksheet, you can quickly find and lock cells you do not want a user to make entries in, or unlock cells in which a user needs to make entries on a protected worksheet.

All cells in a worksheet are locked by default, and when the worksheet is protected, a user cannot make entries into locked cells. When you develop a worksheet, it is not obvious which cells are locked and which are unlocked, but you can run a macro to color the unlocked cells and make the worksheet preparation much easier.

The macro uses an If – ElseIf conditional statement nested in a For Each loop that looks at each cell in the worksheet's used range and colors the cell according to its locked property. Looping through the used range means the macro does not have to search the entire worksheet. Locked cells are formatted with the ColorIndex property, and unlocked cells are formatted with the ColorIndex set to xlAutomatic. You can declare two variables to make the macro more efficient: one for the cell with the locked property, and one to move the loop to the next cell.

Color Unlocked Cells

① Type **Sub** and the macro name, then press Enter to start a new macro.

② Type **dim cll as range, CellNum as integer**.

Replace *cll* with your range variable and *CellNum* with your counter variable throughout the macro.

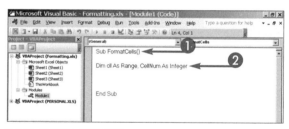

③ Type *CellNum* = 0.

④ Type **for each** *cll* **in activesheet.usedrange**.

⑤ Type **if** *cll*.**locked = false then**.

⑥ Type *cll*.**interior.colorindex = 6**.

The ColorIndex value 6 is yellow.

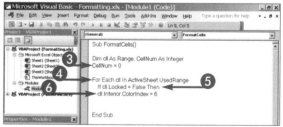

⑦ Type *CellNum* = *CellNum* + 1.

⑧ Type **elseif** *cll*.**locked = true then**.

⑨ Type *cll*.**interior.colorindex = xlautomatic**.

⑩ Type **end if**.

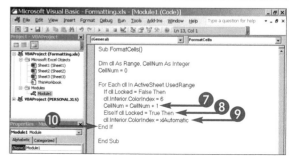

⑪ Type **next**.

⑫ Click ▶ to run the macro.

⑬ Click ✕ to switch to Excel.

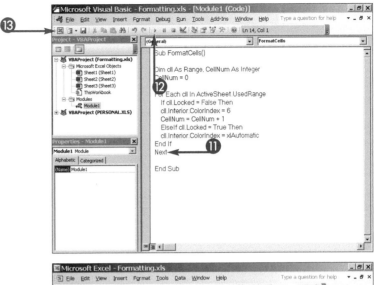

● The unlocked cells are colored.

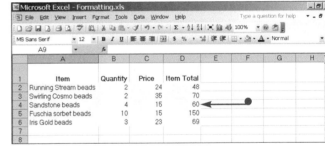

How can I show a message when the macro is finished running?

▼ You can show a message box to indicate the macro is finished by adding a message box statement such as `MsgBox "Unlocked cells are colored"` to the end of the macro, just above the End Sub line. The default message box has an OK button. You can also add a title to the message box as a second argument in the statement. To add a title, type a comma and a space, then `Title:= "your message box title"`. Click the OK button in the message box after the macro runs.

How can I run this macro on a protected worksheet?

▼ You can run the macro on a protected worksheet by adding the statement `ActiveSheet.Unprotect` above the `For Each` statement to unprotect the worksheet before the macro starts, and the statement `ActiveSheet.Protect` below the `Next` statement to reprotect the worksheet when the macro is finished. If the worksheet is protected with a password, make sure you include the password in both protection statements. For more information about protecting worksheets, see Chapter 10.

Set Conditional Formatting

Y ou can write a macro to color a range of cells according to their values, so that specific values stand out to the reader's eye. In Excel, this is called *conditional formatting*. For example, you can color a range of sales data so that numbers below a specific low threshold are colored red, and numbers above a specific high threshold are colored blue.

To make the macro check each cell value and color the cell accordingly, you can use a For Each loop to loop through the cells one at a time, and an If Else conditional block

within the loop to set the color in each cell. You can set a variable for the cells with the `Dim variable As Range` statement to make the macro more efficient; and you can limit either the macro search range to a named range in the worksheet or the used range, so the macro loops through a specific limited range rather than through every cell in the worksheet.

For more information about variables, see Chapter 6. For more information about loops and variables, see Chapters 14 and 15.

For more information about variables, see Chapter 6. For more information about loops and variables, see Chapters 14 and 15.

Set Conditional Formatting

① Type **Sub** and the macro name, then press Enter to start a new macro.

② Type **dim C as range**, replacing C with your variable name.

Note: *Replace C with your variable name throughout this macro.*

③ Type **for each C in range("*range*")**, replacing *range* with a range or a range name.

④ Type **if C.value > 800 then**.

⑤ Type **C.font.colorindex = 5**.

ColorIndex 5 is blue.

⑥ Type **elseif C.value < 500 then**.

⑦ Type **C.font.colorindex = 3**

ColorIndex 3 is red.

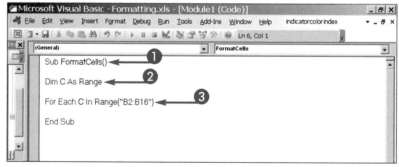

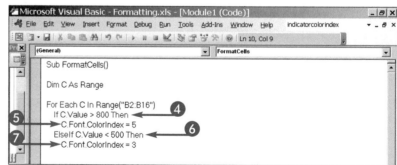

⑧ Type **end if**.

⑨ Type **next**.

⑩ Click ▶ to run the macro.

⑪ Click ⊠ to switch to Excel.

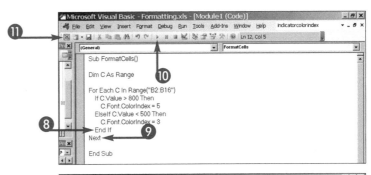

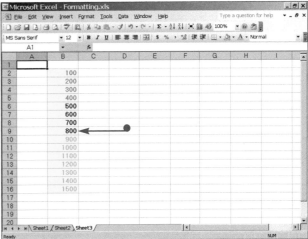

● The range is conditionally formatted based on the values in the cells.

How can I find out what the ColorIndex color values are?

▼ You can find out what the ColorIndex color values are by looking up IndicatorColorIndex Property in the Visual Basic Help files. The Help files display a palette of ColorIndex colors and the associated number values.

How can I make the colored fonts bold?

▼ You can format the colored fonts bold, making them stand out from the worksheet even more, by typing the statement `variable.Font.Bold = True` after the `variable.Font.ColorIndex` statement. Include the Bold statement after the ColorIndex statement for all conditional values you want to format bold.

How can I limit the macro range to the used range in the worksheet?

▼ You can limit the macro range to the used range in the worksheet by using the statement `For Each variable in Active Sheet.UsedRange` at the beginning of the macro. When you specify a range or a range name, the macro only runs in that range. The UsedRange property allows the macro to run in all the used cells in the worksheet.

Create and Apply a Custom Style

You can use a custom style to apply several property settings to a range of cells at one time, whether you are working in a workbook or writing a macro. Custom styles are efficient timesavers if you need to set the same cell formatting repeatedly.

If the custom style already exists in a workbook, you can use that style name in the macro statement. You can apply a custom style to a selected range with a macro by writing the statement `Range("rangeref").Style = "stylename"`.

If the style does not yet exist in a workbook, you can create the custom style by writing the statement `With ActiveWorkbook.Styles.Add(Name:="stylename")` and then listing the style's property settings in the With block. When you run the macro, the style name is created and added to the list of custom styles in the workbook, available to macros and in the workbook. For more information about listing properties in a With block, see the section "Set Cell Formatting."

Create and Apply a Custom Style

① Type **Sub** and the macro name, then press Enter to start a new macro that creates a custom style.

② Type **with activeworkbook.styles.add (name:="***stylename***")**, replacing *stylename* with your custom style name.

③ Type the list of properties to include in the custom style.

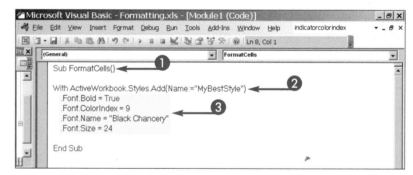

④ Type **end with**.

⑤ Click ▶ to run the macro that creates the custom style.

The macro runs and the custom style is added to the workbook styles.

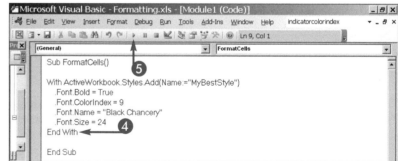

⑥ Type **Sub** and the macro name, then press Enter to start a new macro that applies a custom style.

⑦ Type **range("*rangeref*").style = "*stylename*"**, replacing *rangeref* with your range reference and *stylename* with your custom style name.

⑧ Click ▶ to run the macro that applies the custom style to a range.

⑨ Click ▣ to switch to Excel.

● The custom style is applied to the referenced range.

The style only needs to be created in the workbook one time. When you want to use the style, just run the Range("*rangeref*").Style = "*stylename*" macro.

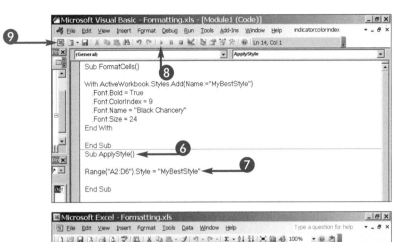

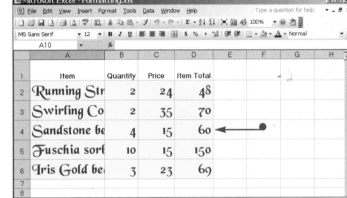

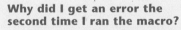

Why did I get an error the second time I ran the macro?

▼ You get an error the second time you run the macro because the style name, created after the macro ran the first time, already exists. You can tell the macro to ignore that error by typing `On Error Resume Next` above the With block that adds the style name.

How can I create a list of the workbook's style names?

▼ You can create a list of a workbook's style names on the leftmost worksheet in the workbook by using this short macro. You can replace the variable *nm* with any variable name. Write the statements `For nm = 1 To ActiveWorkbook.Styles.Count`, `Worksheets(1).Cells(nm, 1) = ActiveWorkbook.Styles(nm).Name`, and `Next`.

How can I change an existing style?

▼ You can change elements of an existing style by using the ActiveWorkbook.Styles ("*stylename*") method and a list of the new or changed properties. For example, you can write the statement `Active Workbook.Styles("Normal").Font.Bold = True` to change the font formatting of the Normal style to Bold.

Enter Values into a Range

You can write statements in a macro to enter numeric values into specific cells or ranges of cells. To enter numeric values into cells, you use the Value property of the Range object and set the value equal to the numeric value you want to enter.

You can enter values into any range object, including `ActiveCell`, `Range("celladdress:celladdress")`, `ActiveCell.Offset(numberrows,numbercolumns)`,

`CurrentRegion.Columns`, and `CurrentRegion.Rows`. For more information about referring to ranges, see Chapter 11.

In addition to entering values into cells and ranges, you can write statements that enter formulas into ranges. For more information about entering formulas, see the section "Enter Formulas into a Range."

Enter Values into a Range

① Type **Sub** and the macro name, then press Enter to start a new macro.

② Type **range("*celladdress*").value =** *value*, replacing *value* with your value and *celladdress* with your cell address.

③ Click the Run Sub/UserForm button (▶) to run the macro.

④ Click the View Microsoft Excel button (▣) to switch to Excel.

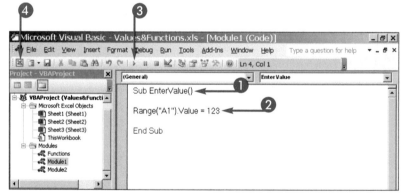

● Your numeric value is entered in the specified cell or range.

When a macro enters values in cells, the location of the active cell is not changed.

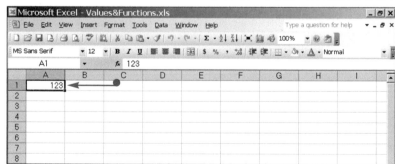

Enter a Named Formula into a Range

You can write a statement in a macro that uses a named formula that exists in the workbook or that is created by a macro. For example, the statement `Range("D4").Value = "=MyFunction"` enters the named formula MyFunction into cell D4.

When you have a lengthy or complex formula, you can name that formula in Excel using the Define Name dialog box. When you need to use that formula in a worksheet, you can use the formula name rather than the entire written-out formula, whether you are working in Excel or writing a macro.

You can also create a named formula with a macro. For more information, see the section "Name a Complex Formula."

To name a complex formula in Excel, click Insert, Name, and then Define. Type a name in the workbook box labeled "Names in," type the formula in the box labeled "Refers to" — beginning with an equal sign — and then click OK. The formula name does not appear in the Formula bar's Name box, but in the Define Name dialog box, and the name can be entered in a cell by typing =**FormulaName**.

Enter a Named Formula into a Range

① Type **Sub** and the macro name, then press Enter to start a new macro.

② Type **range("*celladdress*").value = "=*formulaname*"**, replacing *formulaname* with your formula name and *celladdress* with your cell address.

③ Click ▶ to run the macro.

④ Click ⊠ to switch to Excel.

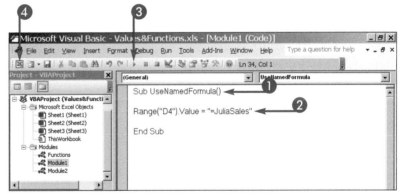

● Your named formula is entered in the specified cell or range.

The cell shows the result of the formula.

● When the cell is selected, the formula bar shows the name of the formula.

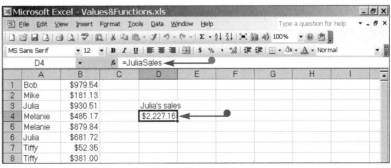

Enter Formulas into a Range

You can write a statement in a macro that enters a formula in a cell just as if a user had typed the formula in the cell. For example, you can write a statement that enters a SUM formula in the cell below a list by using the Range object and entering the formula as a text string in the Value property. For more information about referring to ranges, see Chapter 11.

You can write a formula to calculate specific cells or relative cell references. When you write a relative-reference formula in a macro, you use the R1C1 reference style,

which refers to a cell's relative location as $R[rowsaway]$ $C[columnsaway]$. For example, the formula =SUM(R$[-10]$C:R$[-1]$C sums the cells from 10 rows above the formula to 1 row above the formula. If the C notation has no value, as in this example, the cells calculated are in the same column as the formula cell. Negative values in the R and C notation mean rows above and columns to the left. Positive values in the R and C notation mean rows below and columns to the right.

To write a formula that calculates specific cells, use the cell address in the formula, as in =SUM("A1:A10").

Enter Formulas into a Range

① Type **Sub** and the macro name, then press Enter to start a new macro.

② Type **range("*celladdress*").value = "=*formula*"**, replacing *celladdress* with your cell reference, and *formula* with your formula.

In this example, the formula sums the entries in cells A1 through A5.

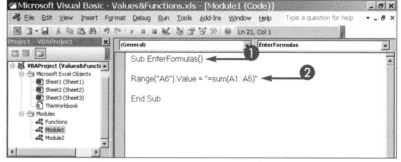

③ Type **range("*celladdress*").value = "=*formula*"**, replacing *celladdress* with your cell reference, and *formula* with your formula.

In this example, the formula sums the entries in the cells above the formula.

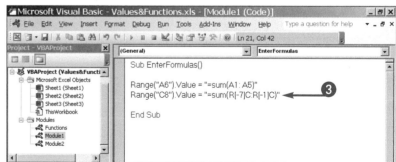

④ Click ▶ to run the macro.

⑤ Click ⊠ to switch to Excel.

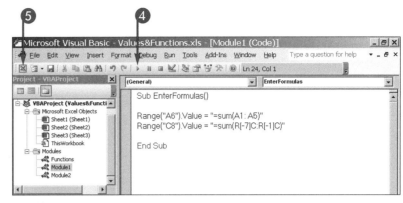

● Your formulas are entered in the specified Range cells.

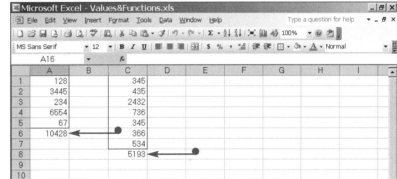

Why does the formula and not the result appear in the cell?

▼ The formula appears in the cell because you did not type the equal sign at the beginning of the formula. The statement syntax includes two equal signs, as in `Range("celladdress").Value = "=formula"`. The first equal sign sets the value for the cell, and the second equal sign begins the formula that is entered in the cell.

Why do both fixed and relative formulas appear in the Formula bar as relative references after the macro runs?

▼ Both types of formulas appear in the worksheet in A1 reference style, without dollar signs in the cell addresses. The difference is that the macro formula with the fixed cell addresses calculates the cells you specify no matter where you write the formula, but the macro formula with the R1C1 style calculates cells that are relative to the cell where you write the formula.

How can I write a formula that creates absolute cell references in the worksheet?

▼ You can write a macro formula that creates absolute cell references, which have dollar signs in the cell addresses, by typing the dollar signs in the cell addresses in the formula. For example, `Range("celladdress").Value = "=sum($A$1:$A$5)"` writes a formula that calculates the cells $A$1:$A$5 as absolute cell references.

PART IV

Name a Complex Formula

I f you have a complex or lengthy formula that you need to use repeatedly, you can write a macro that gives the formula a name you can reference instead of writing out the entire lengthy formula every time you need to use it.

To name a formula by using a macro, you use the Add property of the ActiveWorkbook.Names object, and then add the arguments Name and RefersTo.

The Name argument sets the name of the formula as a string, as in `Name:="NewName"`. The RefersTo argument sets the formula that the name refers to, in A1-style notation, as

in `RefersTo:="=sum(A1:D5)"`. If you want to refer to a relative-reference formula using R1C1-style notation, use the RefersToR1C1 argument instead of the RefersTo argument to set the formula.

When you name a formula by using a macro, the name appears in the Define Name dialog box just as if you had created the name in the dialog box without using a macro. For more information about using named formulas in macros, see the section "Enter a Named Formula into a Range."

Name a Complex Formula

1. Type **Sub** and the macro name, then press Enter to start a new macro.

2. Type **activeworkbook.names.add**.

3. Type **name:="***newname***"**, replacing *newname* with your formula name.

4. Type a comma and **RefersToR1C1: ="***formula***"**, replacing *formula* with your formula.

   Begin the formula with an equal sign, and enclose strings in pairs of two quotes.

5. Click ▶ to run the macro.

6. Click ▣ to switch to Excel.

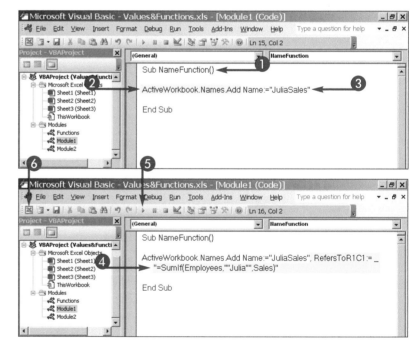

7 Click Insert.

8 Click Name.

9 Click Define.

The Define Name dialog box appears.

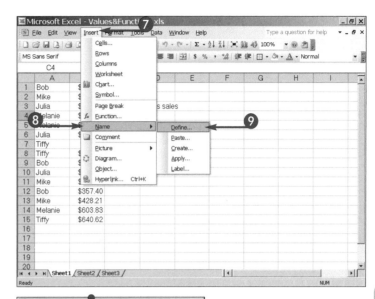

- The new formula name is in the Names in workbook list.

10 Click the new formula name.

- The named formula appears in the Refers to box.

You can use the named formula in macros or when writing formulas in Excel.

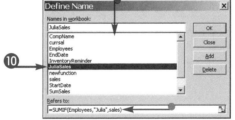

How can I hide a named formula from users?

▼ You can hide the formula from users by using the optional Visible:=False argument in the Add property. When the Visible argument is False, the name does not appear in Excel's Define Name, Paste Name, or Go To dialog boxes. The name appears in any cells that show the formula, but users cannot see the formula defined by the name.

What are the rules for naming formulas?

▼ Formula names can have both letters and numbers and up to 255 characters, but the name must be one word, and the first character must be a letter or an underscore character. You can use capital letters or underscore characters to separate words in a single-word name. Names cannot be cell references, such as FY2004 or R1C1.

How can I use this name in other workbooks?

▼ A named formula is only available in the workbook in which it is created. To create a named formula that you can use in any workbook, you can create a function procedure that is similar to a normal macro but can only be called from another macro. For more information, see the section "Write a Function Procedure."

Write a Function Procedure

You can create a custom function to automate the process of entering a complex calculation that you use frequently in Excel. You write a custom function as a *function procedure*, which is similar to a macro or subprocedure except that it does not appear in the Macro dialog box and cannot be run on its own. It must be *called*, or run from, another macro.

A function procedure returns a value that you can place in a cell or use in a macro calculation. For example, you can assign the function name as a value in a `Range("range").Value = function` statement to place the function result in a range, or use can use the function result in a macro

calculation such as `Range("range").Value = function*3`, which multiplies the function value by 3 and places that result in the specified range.

If your function has arguments — values that need to be supplied to the calculation — type those argument names between the parentheses in the opening procedure line, as in `Function FunctionName(arg1,arg2)`. In the procedure statement, type `FunctionName =` followed by all the calculations the function performs and the arguments where needed.

Write a Function Procedure

① Start a new macro with your function name in the sub line.

② Replace the word *Sub* with the word *Function*.

③ Click away from the opening line.

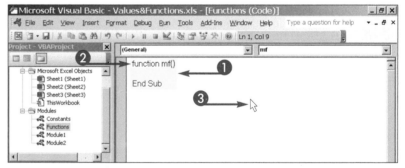

④ Type as *datatype*, replacing *datatype* with the data type your function returns.

When you click away, the closing line End Sub changes to End Function.

⑤ Between the parentheses, type any argument names your function needs.

In this example, the function does not need any arguments.

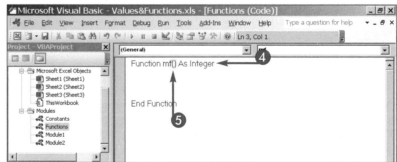

6 Type the function name followed by an equal sign.

7 Type the calculations the function performs.

In this example, the function calculates the number of days between the current date and the date 1/1/1988.

8 Start a new macro that calls the function procedure.

9 Type a statement to call the function procedure.

In this example, the macro enters the function procedure value into a cell.

10 Click ▶ to run the macro that calls the function procedure.

11 Click ⊠ to switch to Excel.

● The macro called the function procedure and entered the function value into the specified range.

How can I use a custom function directly in Excel?

▼ You can use a custom function directly in Excel by creating the custom function in the Personal Macro Workbook. You can click Insert and then Function to open the Insert Function dialog box. Because the Personal Macro Workbook is always open, the custom function, if not marked `Private` in the opening line, appears in the User Defined category.

Why does my function procedure not work when a macro calls it?

▼ If the function procedure is marked `Private` in the first line of the procedure, it can only be called by a macro in the same module. If the function is not marked `Private`, it is a public function and can be called by any macro. You can either make the function public or place the private function and the macro that calls it in the same module.

How can I find a custom function when I write a macro?

▼ You can find a custom function by selecting it from an Auto List of global methods and properties. For example, you can type a statement that begins with `Range("celladdress")`. `Value =`, type a space, then press Ctrl+Spacebar to show the Auto List. Your custom function is listed in the Auto List and can be applied to the object like any other method.

Add a Single Character to Multiple Cells

You can write a macro that adds a single character to every cell in a range without otherwise changing the text in the cell. This is useful if you have a range full of numbers that should be text, such as phone numbers or social security numbers that have no letters or punctuation marks to signify them as text.

To convert a number to a non-calculable text entry, all you need to do is type an apostrophe at the beginning of the number. The apostrophe does not appear in the cell, but it appears in the Formula bar. In a worksheet with a large number of numeric entries that should be text, a macro to convert all the numbers is a great timesaver.

The macro uses an If Else loop nested in a For Each loop to check and change every entry in the range object you select. For example, you can use the statements `If Len(X) > 0 Then` and `X.FormulaR1C1 = Chr(39) & X.Text` to add the character if there is an entry in the cell, and the statements `Else` and `X.FormulaR1C1 = ""` to leave empty cells alone. The X is a variable for the cell address and Chr(39) is the apostrophe character.

① Type **Sub** and the macro name, then press Enter to start a new macro.

② Type **dim *Cel* as variant, *Itm* as variant**, replacing *Cel* and *Itm* with your variable names.

Replace *Cel* and *Itm* with your variable names throughout this macro.

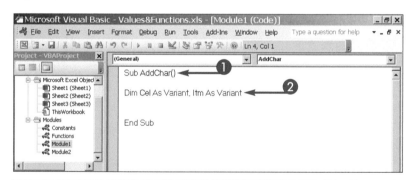

③ Type **activesheet.*rangeobject*.select**, replacing *rangeobject* with your range object.

④ Type **Cel = Selection.Address**.

⑤ Type **for each *Itm* in activesheet.range(*Cel*)**.

⑥ Type **if Len(*Itm*) > 0 then**.

The Len function counts the characters in the variable *Itm*.

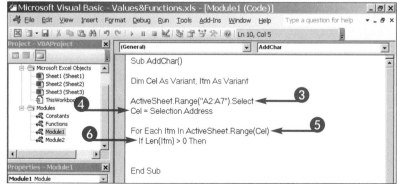

214

⑦ Type *Itm*.**formulaR1C1** = **Chr(39)** & *Itm*.**text**.

If there are characters, an apostrophe is placed at the beginning of the entry.

⑧ Type **Else**.

⑨ Type *Itm*.**FormulaR1C1** = **""**.

If there are no characters, nothing is placed in the cell.

⑩ Type **End If**.

⑪ Type **Next**.

⑫ Click ▶ to run the macro.

⑬ Click ✕ to switch to Excel.

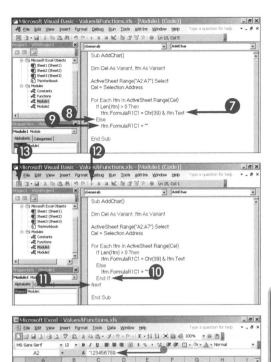

● The numbers are converted to text entries. They are left aligned and not calculable.

● An apostrophe appears at the beginning of the entry in the Formula bar.

How can I add characters other than an apostrophe to several cells at once?

▼ You can add any characters you want to by using this macro. You can replace Chr(39) with your characters in quotes. For example, to place the letters *xx* at the beginning of every cell, you can replace Chr(39) with "xx" and run the macro. Chr(39) is the VBA Chr function. The code number 39 is the argument that represents a specific character — the apostrophe — in the ANSI character set. You can find more information about the Chr function by looking up "Chr Function" in the VBA Help files.

How can I run this macro in specific cells instead of a large range?

▼ You can run this macro in any range you want, including named ranges. You can name a range of noncontiguous cells by pressing and holding the Ctrl key while you click the cells, and then typing a name for the range in the workbook Name box and pressing Enter. The group of selected cells is named as a range, and you can use that range name as the *rangeobject* in this macro. For more information about referring to ranges, see Chapter 11.

Move a Minus Sign from Right to Left

You can write a short macro that converts negative numbers that have a minus sign on the right to negative numbers that have the minus sign on the left. Excel does not recognize numbers with a minus sign on the right as being numbers. Instead, Excel considers those values text, and they cannot be calculated. Data is often imported from a different program that places the minus sign on the right of each negative number, and each value must be converted for the data to be calculable in Excel.

Your macro loops through every cell in a range you specify and moves the minus sign to the left, converting the value to a calculable negative number but leaving positive values untouched. The macro uses a For Each loop to look at every cell in the range. In each cell, the macro uses the conditional statements `If Right(Cel.Text, 1) = "-" Then` to check whether there is a minus sign at the right end of the value, and `Cel.Value = Cel.Value * 1` to convert the value if there is a right-end minus sign.

Move a Minus Sign from Right to Left

① Type **Sub** and the macro name, then press Enter to start a new macro.

② Type **dim** *variable* **as range**, replacing *variable* with your variable name.

Replace *variable* with your variable name throughout this macro.

③ Type *rangeobject*.**select**, replacing *rangeobject* with your range.

Note: For more information about range references, see Chapter 11.

④ Type **for each** *variable* **in selection.cells**.

⑤ Type **if right(***variable*.**text, 1) = "-" then**.

⑥ Type *variable*.**value = ***variable*.**value * 1**.

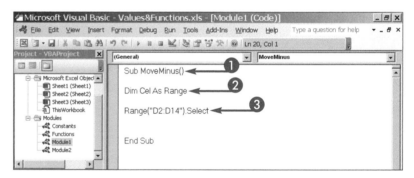

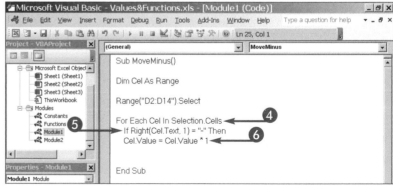

⑦ Type **end if**.

⑧ Type **next**.

⑨ Click ▶ to run the macro.

⑩ Click ⊠ to switch to Excel.

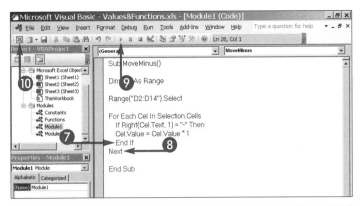

● The values in the range are converted from text to negative numbers.

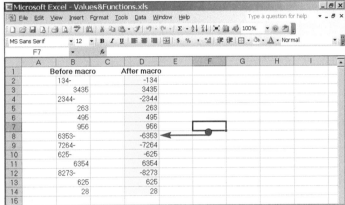

MASTER IT

How can I set the range I want if I do not know the length of the list?

▼ You can set any range by using the appropriate range reference. To set the entire current region around the active cell, use the range reference `ActiveCell.CurrentRegion.Select`. If there is more than one range to convert in the worksheet, you can use the range reference `ActiveSheet.UsedRange.Select` to select the entire used area of the worksheet, without looping through the millions of unused cells in the worksheet. You can select specific columns with column range references. For more information about range references, see Chapter 11.

How can I set the number format I want in the converted range of values?

▼ You can set the number format you want by writing the statement `rangeobject.NumberFormat = "yourformat"` after the Next statement that closes the loop. Replace *yourformat* with one of Excel's custom number format strings, such as `#,##0_);(#,##0)`, which formats negative numbers in parentheses, or `$#,##0_);[Red]($#,##0)`, which formats all numbers with dollar signs and negative numbers in red and parentheses. To find more number formats, open Excel, click Format, and then click Cells. Select the Custom category on the Number tab, and then scroll through the list of formats in the Type box.

Change Debit/Credit Values to Plus/Minus Values

You can write a short macro to convert number values that are identified as negative or positive by the letters *D* and *C* — for "debit" and "credit" — in a different column. Some accounting programs export data as numeric values that are identified as positive or negative by the letters in a different column, rather than in the value itself, and when you import that data into Excel, all the values are positive.

Your macro loops through every cell in a column, and if the cell contains the letter *D*, the value in the corresponding cell to the left is converted to a negative number. The

macro uses a For Each loop to loop through the range. In each cell, the macro uses the conditional statements `If Cel.Value = "D" Then` to check whether there is a *D* in the cell, and `Cel.Offset(0, -1).Value = Cel.Offset(0, -1).Value * -1` to convert the value in the cell to the left if there is a *D*.

You can write your range object to specify the column in which the D and C values are located, and then write the conditional statements to use the appropriate Offset arguments for your data. The Offset arguments are Offset(*rows,columns*).

Change Debit/Credit Values to Plus/Minus Values

① Type **Sub** and the macro name, then press Enter to start a new macro.

② Type **dim** *variable* **as range**, replacing *variable* with your variable name.

Replace *variable* with your variable name throughout this macro.

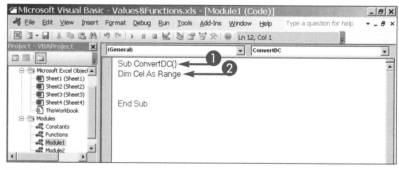

③ Type *rangeobject*.**columns(***columnindex***).select**, replacing *rangeobject* with your range reference and *columnindex* with the index number of the column that contains the D and C values.

Note: For more information about referring to columns and ranges, see Chapter 11.

④ Type **for each** *variable* **in selection.cells**.

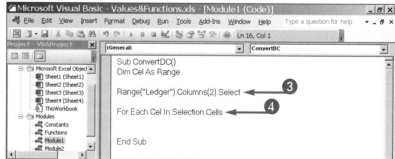

⑤ Type **if** *variable*.**value = "D" then**.

⑥ Type *variable*.**offset(0, -1).value = *variable*.offset(0, -1).value * -1**.

This example assumes the values are one column left of the column with the D and C values. If your data is arranged differently, adjust the Offset arguments.

⑦ Type **end if**.

⑧ Type **next**.

⑨ Click ▶ to run the macro.

⑩ Click 📊 to switch to Excel.

● The values identified with the letter *D* are converted to negative values.

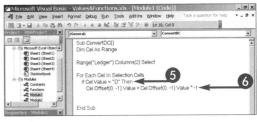

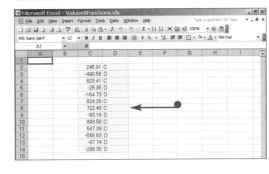

PART IV

Append a List to Another List

You can write a macro to append, or copy and paste, a list in one workbook to the end of a list in another workbook. For example, if you have a list of orders that must be added daily to the end of a monthly or annual list of orders, you can write a macro to perform that task quickly.

The macro selects the current region in the list to append and copies it. Then the macro opens the workbook that contains the main list, activates the correct worksheet, selects the cell just below the bottom of the main list, and

pastes the copied smaller list. Finally, the macro closes the workbook that contains the main list and saves changes quietly, without asking you to save.

This macro begins in the active worksheet that contains the list you want to append, so make sure that the list you want to append is in the active worksheet when you run the macro.

For more information about selecting ranges, see Chapter 11. For more information about opening and closing workbooks, see Chapter 8. For more information about working with worksheets, see Chapter 9.

Append a List to Another List

① Type **Sub** and the macro name, then press Enter to start a new macro.

② Type **activesheet.range("A1").select**.

Make sure the list to append is in the active worksheet.

③ Type **activecell.currentregion.select**.

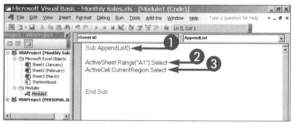

④ Type **selection.copy**.

⑤ Type **workbooks.open filename:="*filename*"**, replacing *filename* with the workbook file name — and path if necessary — that contains the main list to which you want to append the smaller list.

⑥ Type **worksheets("*sheetname*").activate**, replacing *sheetname* with the name of the worksheet where the main list is located.

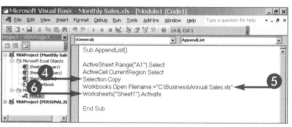

⑦ Type **range("A1").select**.

⑧ Type **selection.end(xldown).select**.

⑨ Type **activecell.offset(1, 0).select**.

⑩ Type **activesheet.paste**.

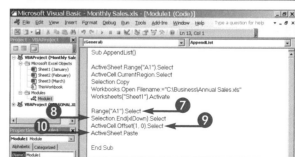

⑪ Type **application.cutcopymode = false**.

⑫ Type **activeworkbook.close savechanges:=true**.

⑬ Click ▶ to run the macro.

⑭ Click ⊠ to switch to Excel.

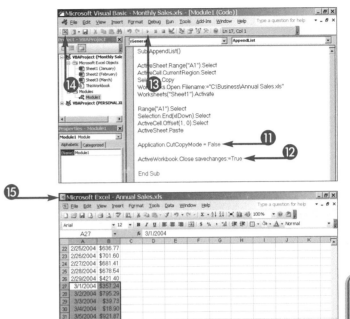

⑮ Open the workbook to which you appended the list.

● The list is appended.

How can I append a list without its header row?

▼ You can append a list without its header row by using an offset range reference such as `ActiveCell.CurrentRegion.Select` to select the entire list, followed by `Selection.Offset(1).Resize(Selection.Rows.Count-1).Select` to select the same region without its header row. The Offset method offsets, or moves, the selected region down one row, and the Resize method resizes the selection to the number of rows in the original table, less one row. When you append a list of data to a larger list, leaving the header rows out is important because interspersed header rows make the data lose integrity.

How can I use range names to make this macro more efficient?

▼ You can use range names to make the macro more efficient by using the range name of the longer list, rather than a specific worksheet and cell. After the statement that opens the workbook file, replace the `Worksheets.Activate` and `Range("A1").Select` statements with the single statement `Range("rangename").Select`. At the end of the macro, before the `Workbook.Close` statement, rename the expanded range with the statement `ActiveCell.CurrentRegion.Name = "rangename"`. The macro does not work until you initially name the range, but after that the macro finds the range, appends the list, and renames the expanded range.

Declare a Constant

You can create *constants*, or named constant values, that refer to a value or string that never changes, and then use that constant in a macro. For example, you can declare a constant with a value of your company name, and refer to the constant every place that the macro needs to enter the company name in a worksheet. Or you can declare a constant named TaxRate with the current sales tax rate, and then have your macro use the constant instead of the actual value. When the sales tax rate changes, you only need to change the value of the constant, rather than changing the tax rate value in each calculation in your macro.

You can declare a constant anywhere in a macro, but for efficiency you should declare it at the beginning of the macro. By default, constant values are private, and only available for use within a single macro. To make a constant available in other macros within the same module, you can declare them in the module declarations. You can make a constant available to other macros in the same workbook project by typing the word *Public* at the beginning of the Const declaration statement.

Declare a Constant

① Type **Sub** and the macro name, then press Enter to start a new macro.

② Type **const** *constantname* as *datatype*, replacing *constantname* with your constant name and *datatype* with the data type for the constant.

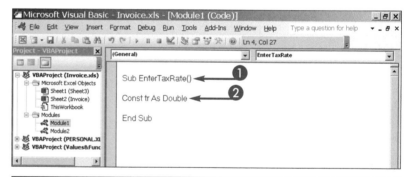

③ Type = *constantvalue*, replacing *constantvalue* with the value of your constant.

If the constant is a string, remember to enclose it in quotes.

④ Type a statement that uses the constant.

This example enters the constant tr as the value in a cell named TaxRate.

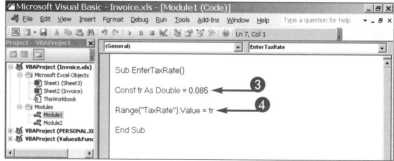

⑤ Click ▶ to run the macro.

The macro runs.

⑥ Click ⊠ to switch to Excel.

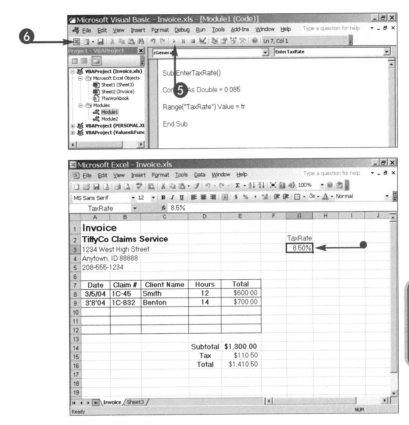

● The statement enters the constant value in the specified cell.

PART IV

What are the rules for naming constants?

▼ The rules for naming constants are the same as the rules for naming macros. You can use up to 255 characters, in any combination of numbers or letters, but the name must begin with a letter. You cannot use spaces or most punctuation marks, and the name cannot be the same as a VBA keyword. If you use all-uppercase characters, constants stand out in your code.

How can I declare a constant in the module declarations?

▼ You can declare a module-level constant by selecting (Declarations) in the Procedure box list, located in the upper-right corner of the Code window. The Declarations area is at the top of the Code window, and appears when you select (Declarations). Type the declaration `Const constantname As datatype = value` in the Declarations area.

Why did my numeric constant appear in the wrong format?

▼ When your macro places the constant value into a cell, the cell formatting does not change. To control the value format, write the statement `Range.NumberFormat = "formatcode"`, replacing *Range* with the range object in the macro and *formatcode* with the code for your format. You can learn codes quickly by recording macros to format cells and then reading the recorded macro.

Ask a User for an Entry

Y ou can ask a user to enter information such as a company name with an input box, then use a macro to enter that information in a worksheet. An input box is a convenient way to interact with a user when a macro is running.

The Input Box function has seven arguments, but only the first, Prompt, is required. The Prompt argument is the text that requests information. The optional Title argument is the input box title. If you do not use the Title argument, the input box is titled Microsoft Excel.

You can declare a variable as `String` and set the variable equal to the input box function, as in `variable = InputBox ("prompttext", "titletext")`, and then write a statement that uses the variable as a value. When the macro runs, the user types the requested information, clicks OK, and the macro uses the entered information.

If the user clicks Cancel they get an error, so you must include If Then statements to handle the potential error. Type `If variable <> ""  Then` above the statement that uses the variable, and `End If` after the statement. That way the input box closes quietly if the user clicks Cancel.

Ask a User for an Entry

① Type **Sub** and the macro name, then press Enter to start a new macro.

② Type **dim** *variable* **as string**, replacing *variable* with your variable name.

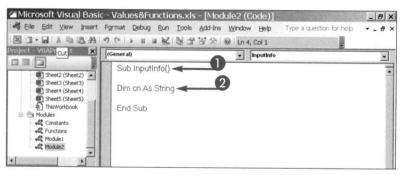

③ Type *variable* = **inputbox("***prompttext***",** "***titletext***")**, replacing *variable* with your variable name, *titletext* with your title text, and *prompttext* with your prompt text.

④ Type **if** *variable* <> "" **then**, replacing *variable* with your variable name.

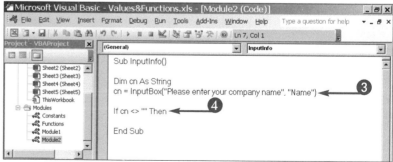

5 Type **range(*rangeobject*).value = *variable***, replacing *rangeobject* with your specified range or cell address and *variable* with your variable name.

Note: For more information about referring to ranges, see Chapter 11.

6 Type **end if**.

7 Click to switch to Excel.

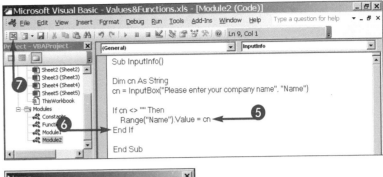

8 Run the macro.

You can also press Alt+F8 to open the Macro dialog box and run the macro.

The input box appears.

9 Type a range or range name in the input box.

10 Click OK.

- The text typed in the input box is entered in the specified cell.

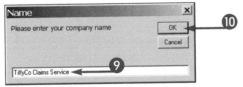

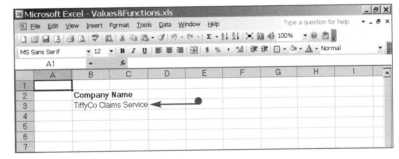

How can I ask the user to enter a number?

▼ You can use the same input box with the Dim *variable* As String statement. Numbers the user types are entered in the cell as calculable numbers, and if the user types a formula beginning with an equal sign, the formula is entered in the specified cell as if the user had typed the formula directly in the cell.

How can I use an InputBox entry in a calculation?

▼ You can use the input box entry in calculations by typing the variable name in your VBA calculation statements. For example, if the user types a number in the input box, you can multiply that number by 2 with the statement `Range ("celladdress").Value = variable*2`. An error occurs if the user entry is invalid for the statement. For more information about errors, see Chapter 16.

How can I set an input box to open with a default value in place?

▼ You can set a default value in an input box by using the optional Default argument. For example, if the user most often types a specific entry in the input box, such as 60000, type the argument `Default:=60000` in the statement along with the `Prompt` and `Title` arguments. If the default entry is a text string, enclose it in quotes.

Add a Comment to a Cell

Y ou can add comments to cells by writing the `Range("celladdress").AddComment "commenttext"` statement in a macro. Comments add considerable value to a worksheet when users are unfamiliar with the workbook, if they need to be reminded about what a cell's data refers to, or if they need to add review notes for the next user.

Comments added from the Excel user interface always begin with the Excel user name and a colon, in bold text. But comments added with a macro only have comment text in the comment, with no user name added.

You can only add a single comment to a cell, but you can add the same comment to several different cells if that is required. An error occurs if a cell already has a comment and your macro attempts to add a comment. You can avoid the error by using the If Then conditional statement `If Range("celladdress").Comment Is Nothing Then` to determine whether the cell already has a comment, and if it does not, to add the comment.

Add a Comment to a Cell

① Type **Sub** and the macro name, then press Enter to start a new macro.

② Type **if range("*celladdress*").comment is nothing then,** replacing *celladdress* with your specified cell.

Note: For more information about referring to ranges, see Chapter 11.

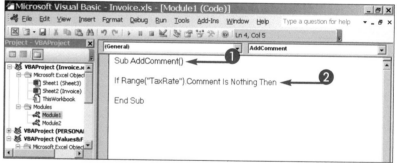

③ Type **range("*celladdress*").add comment,** replacing *celladdress* with your specified cell.

④ Type a space and then your comment text, enclosed in quotes.

⑤ Type **end if**.

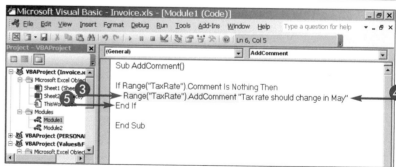

⑥ Click ▶ to run the macro.

⑦ Click 🔣 to switch to Excel.

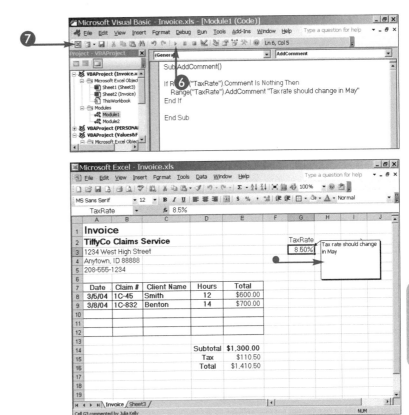

● The specified cell has your comment added.

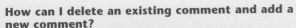

PART IV

How can I delete an existing comment and add a new comment?

▼ If a cell has an existing comment and you want to replace that comment with a new comment, you can use a different If Then conditional statement. Declare a variable as the range in which you want to enter the comment and then type the statements If Not *variable*.Comment Is Nothing Then, *variable*.ClearComments, End If, and *variable*.AddComment "*commenttext*". This set of statements determines whether there is a comment in the variable range, and if there is, the existing comment is deleted. The new comment is then added.

How can I include the current date in a comment?

▼ You can add the current date to a comment by including the VBA function Date in the comment text. For example, the statement ActiveCell. AddComment "Reviewed on " & Date creates a comment in the active cell that reads "Reviewed on" and the date on which the macro runs. You can also use declared constants and variables in comment text, including text entered by the user in an input box. For more information about using input boxes, see the section "Ask a User for an Entry."

List the Comments in a Worksheet

Y ou can write a macro statement to list all the comments in a worksheet as the last page in a printed worksheet. Cell comments can be scattered throughout a worksheet, so a list of cell comments and their locations makes worksheet review more efficient.

PrintComments is property of the PageSetup method of the Worksheets object. The PrintComments property uses the VBA constant xlPrintSheetEnd to print comments at the end of the worksheet.

To list the cell comments in a worksheet, write the statement *sheetobject*.PageSetup.PrintComments = xlPrintSheetEnd. A new final page is added to the worksheet printed pages, and the cell comments and their cell addresses are listed on that page. This statement only sets comment printing for the single worksheet you specify as the *sheetobject*, and you can see the listed comments on the final page when you view the worksheet in Print Preview.

① Type **Sub** and the macro name, then press Enter to start a new macro.

② Type *sheetobject*.**pagesetup.print comments**, replacing *sheetobject* with your sheet reference.

Note: *For more information about referring to worksheets, see Chapter 9.*

③ Type = **xlprintsheetend**.

④ Click ▶ to run the macro.

⑤ Click ▣ to switch to Excel.

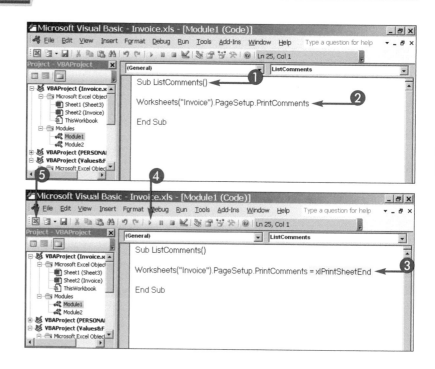

⑥ Click the sheet that you referenced in the macro.

⑦ Click the Print Preview button (🔍).

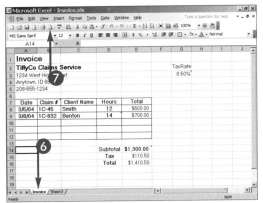

⑧ Click Next until you see the last sheet.

● The worksheet comments are listed.

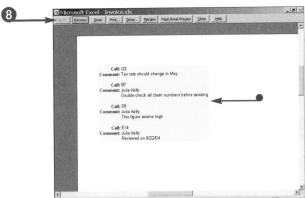

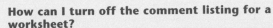

How can I turn off the comment listing for a worksheet?

▼ You can turn off the comment listing for a worksheet by using the xlPrintNoComments property constant in the same macro that is described in this task. Type the statement *sheetobject*.PageSetup. PrintComments = xlPrintNoComments and run the macro. The macro changes the Comments setting for the worksheet, which you can also change in the Excel user interface by clicking File→Page Setup and selecting a setting in the Comments box on the Sheet tab.

How can I list comments on every worksheet in a workbook?

▼ You can list comments on every worksheet in a workbook if you use a For Each loop to change the setting on each worksheet in the workbook. To write the For Each loop, type the statements Dim *variable* As Worksheet, For Each *variable* In ActiveWorkbook.Worksheets, *variable*. PageSetup.PrintComments = xlPrintSheetEnd, and Next. This macro tells VBA that your *variable* is a worksheet, and to set the PrintComments property for every worksheet in the active workbook's worksheets collection. For more information about loops, see Chapter 15.

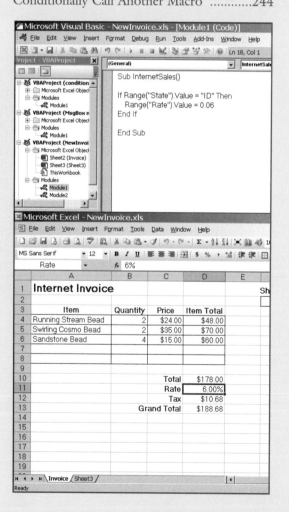

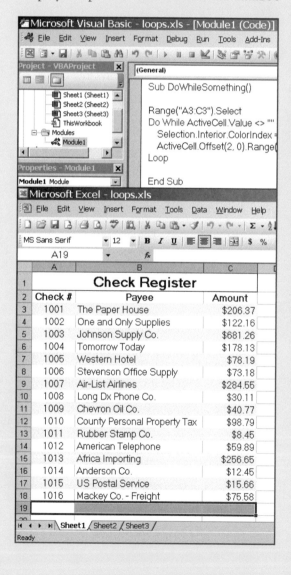

16   Fixing Errors

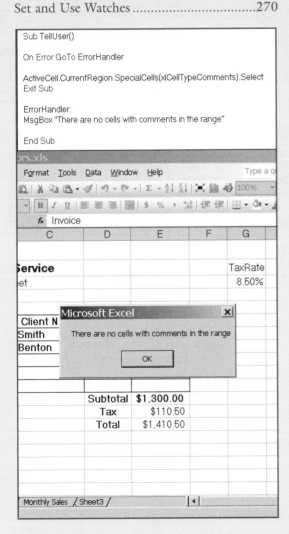

```
Sub TellUser()

On Error GoTo ErrorHandler

ActiveCell.CurrentRegion.SpecialCells(xlCellTypeComments).Select
Exit Sub

ErrorHandler:
MsgBox "There are no cells with comments in the range"

End Sub
```

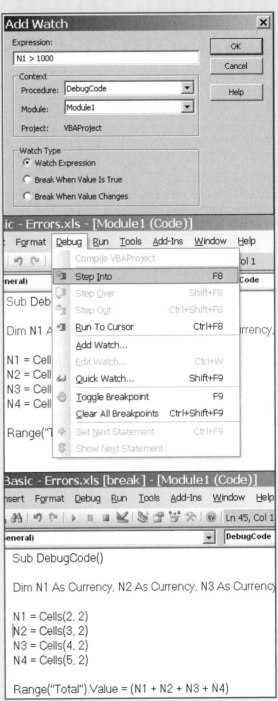

Introduction to Loops and Conditions

Y ou can make long or repetitive tasks much more efficient by writing a macro that combines the separate steps into a single click or keystroke. But if you need to run the macro over and over to accomplish your task, then the act of repeatedly performing the click or keystroke becomes just as inefficient and boring.

That is where loops add tremendous efficiency to your macros. A loop executes a macro repeatedly for as long as you tell the loop to run, and often a long loop runs nearly as quickly as the single macro. You can create loops that run a specific number of times, until a condition is met, or until the macro has been executed on all the objects in a collection.

Another problem with macros is that they perform the statements you write, but they cannot adjust behavior to different circumstances or make decisions about whether a macro should be performed on a specific object. You must check each object or circumstance yourself and decide whether to run the macro. However, you can use conditional statements to add decision-making ability to a macro so that it adjusts to different circumstances or runs only on the objects that meet your requirements.

For Each and For Next Loops

You can create a variety of loops depending on how you need the macro to repeat. For example, you can set a macro to execute in every worksheet in a workbook by using a For Each loop that runs the macro on every worksheet in the workbook's worksheets collection. You can also create a loop that runs a macro a specific number of times by using the more general For Next loop.

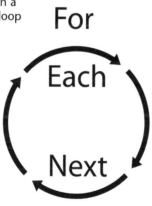

Do Loop

Another category of loops is the Do loops. A Do loop executes a block of statements repeatedly until a condition is true or while a condition remains true. A Do While loop repeats as long as the condition remains true, but does not execute if the condition is initially false. A Do Until loop repeats until the condition becomes true, but does not execute if the condition is initially true. A Loop While loop executes once and then repeats as long as the condition remains true. A Loop Until loop executes once and then repeats until the condition becomes true.

Infinite Loop

If a loop macro takes a long time to execute, you can show the loop's progress to reassure yourself that the loop is running normally. Occasionally, a loop with an error in the code can become an *infinite* loop, which repeats without ending. To stop an infinite loop, press Ctrl+Alt+Delete and then click the Task Manager button. In the Task Manager dialog box, click the Applications tab. Select Microsoft Visual Basic, and click the End Task button. The loop stops and any unsaved changes are lost. For more information about loops, see Chapter 15.

Setting Conditions

You can write a macro that behaves differently in different circumstances by using conditional statements. In a conditional statement, you add a decision-making capability to the macro. The conditional statements include the If Then statement that makes a single decision, the If Then Else statement that makes double decisions, the If Then ElseIf statement that makes multiple decisions, the Select Case statement that works like a simplified If Then ElseIf statement, and message boxes that ask a user to answer questions.

If Then Statement

The If Then statement executes the macro if the condition you set is true. The If Then Else statement executes one set of statements if the condition you set is true, and another set of statements if the condition you set is not true. The If Then Else statement can be expanded to an If Then ElseIf statement to include several levels of conditions and statements to execute if the condition for that level is true.

Select Case Statement

The Select Case statement lets the macro choose which statements to execute based on the value of an object or expression. The Select Case statement bases its decision on an object's value rather a true or false condition.

Conditions Set by Message Boxes

Message boxes ask for an answer from a user — usually Yes, No, or Cancel — and use the answer as the condition to evaluate in an If Then statement. All the conditional statements allow the macro to make decisions while it runs, and therefore do more of your work for you.

Make a Decision with an If Then Macro

You can write a macro that makes a decision to execute the macro statements based on whether conditions you set for an object or property are true.

The `If Then` conditional statement has three parts: The `If` keyword initiates the statement, followed by the condition to evaluate. The keyword `Then` is followed by the statements to execute if the condition is true. The final keyword `End If` closes the conditional statement, and the macro moves on to the next statement in the code.

The macro executes the statements that follow the keyword `Then` only if the condition is true. If the condition is not true, the statements to execute are ignored. The statements to execute can be a block of multiple statements. If there is only one statement to execute, the `If Then` statement can be written on a single line, as in `If condition Then statement`.

You can nest an `If Then` statement in a loop so that the macro executes the conditional statement on repeated objects, as dictated by the loop. For more information about loops, see Chapter 15.

Make a Decision with an If Then Macro

① Type **Sub** and the macro name, then press Enter to start a new macro.

② Type **if** *condition* **Then**.

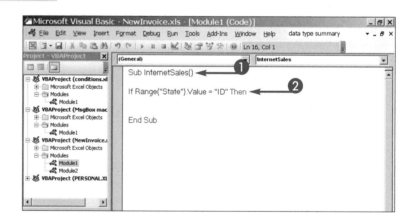

③ Type the statements to execute if the *condition* is true.

④ Type **end if**.

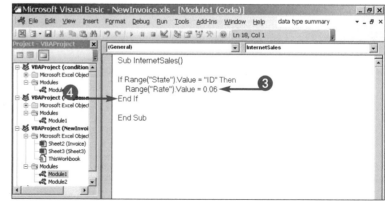

⑤ Click the Run Sub/UserForm button (▶) to run the macro.

⑥ Click the View Microsoft Excel button (▨) to switch to Excel.

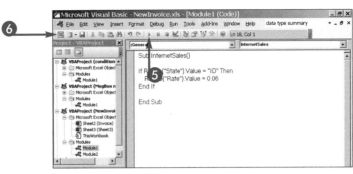

● If the *condition* is true, the macro executes statements.

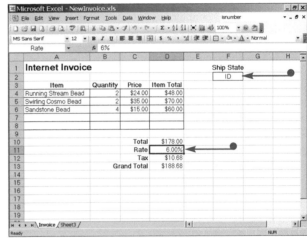

How can I set up an If Then statement to check multiple conditions?

▼ You can set up an If Then statement to check multiple conditions by nesting a second If Then statement inside the first. For example, the block

```
If IsNumeric(Range("A1")) Then
    If Range("A1").Value > 10 Then
        Range("B1").Value = "Good!"
    End If
End If
```

checks whether a cell value is numeric, and if it is, checks whether the value is greater than 10. If both conditions are true, the statement is executed. If the first condition is not true, the macro never looks at the second condition.

How can I make an If Then block easy to read?

▼ You can make an If Then block easy to read by indenting the statements in a logical manner, pressing the Tab key to indent subordinate lines — such as all the statements between related If and End If lines — and keeping the related If and End If lines on the same level of indentation. You can also use comments to make the block easy to understand. Comments remind you of what specific statements in the If Then block do for the macro. For more information about indents and comments, see Chapter 4.

Make a Double Decision with an If Then Else Macro

You can write a macro to execute either of two different sets of statements, based on whether conditions you set for an object or property are true, by using an `If Then Else` conditional statement block. The `If Then Else` block is a variation on the `If Then` conditional statement block.

The `If Then Else` conditional statement has at least four parts: The `If` keyword initiates the statement, followed by the condition to evaluate. The keyword `Then` is followed by the statements to execute if the condition is true. The keyword `Else` is followed by statements to execute if the condition is false. The final keyword `End If` closes the conditional statement, and the macro moves on to the next statement in the code.

One more variation on the `If Then Else` conditional statement block involves checking multiple conditions by using the keyword `ElseIf`. Each `ElseIf` keyword is followed by another condition to evaluate and the keyword `Then`, followed by statements to execute if the `ElseIf` condition is true. The last statement is always `Else`, followed by the statements to execute if all the `If` and `ElseIf` conditions are false.

Make a Double Decision with an If Then Else Macro

① Type **Sub** and the macro name, then press Enter to start a new macro.

② Type **if** *condition* **Then**.

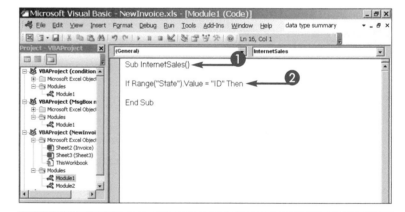

③ Type the statements to execute if the *condition* is true.

④ Type **else**.

⑤ Type the statements to execute if the *condition* is false.

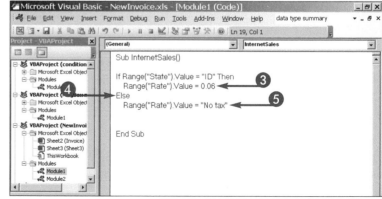

6 Type **end if**.

7 Click ▶ to run the macro.

8 Click ⊠ to switch to Excel.

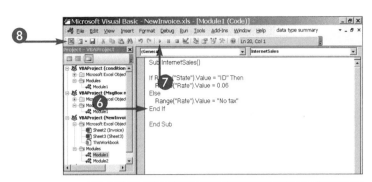

If the *condition* is true, the macro executes the statements.

● If the *condition* is false, the macro executes the Else statements.

How can I write an If Then ElseIf statement block for mutiple conditions?

▼ You can write an If Then ElseIf statement block for multiple conditions by writing the keyword ElseIf in place of the keyword Else, then the ElseIf condition, the keyword Then, and the statements to execute if the ElseIf condition is true. You can use as many ElseIf conditions and statements as you need. For example, the following block uses two conditions and executable statements:

```
If Range("A1").Value > 10 Then
        Range("B1").Value = "Good!"
ElseIf Range("A1").Value > 1000 Then
        Range("B1").Value = "Bonus!"
Else
        Range("B1").Value = "Try harder"
End If
```

What are the functions that give the same result as an If Then Else block?

▼ The functions that give the same result as an If Then Else bock are the IIf function in VBA and the If worksheet function. Although the functions have different names in VBA code and in a worksheet, both functions test a condition. If the condition is true, the functions return one result, and if the condition is false, they return another result. For example, the IIf function in VBA is written =IIf(*condition, result if true, result if false*). The worksheet function is identical, but the worksheet function name is If.

Ask a Question with a Message Box

You can use a message box to ask a user a question while a macro is running. The `MsgBox` function displays a message to the user, and returns a value to the macro depending on the button the user clicks.

You declare a message box variable as an integer because the message box buttons return specific integer values between 1 and 7. Then you set the variable equal to the `MsgBox` function, and create the message box you want with the function arguments. You can use the value returned by the button click in the macro to execute statements according to the user's answer.

The `MsgBox` function has five arguments, but only the first, Prompt, is required. The `Prompt` argument is the question or text the message box displays to the user. The `Buttons` argument specifies the buttons that appear on the message box. If you do not specify buttons, only the OK button appears.

The `Title` argument is the text in the title bar of the message box. The `Helpfile` and `Context` arguments add help to the message box, and they work together to specify the name of the Help file and the context ID of the Help topic.

Ask a Question with a Message Box

① Type **Sub** and the macro name, then press Enter to start a new macro.

② Type **dim** *variable* **as integer**, replacing *variable* with your variable.

③ Type *variable* = MsgBox, replacing *variable* with your variable.

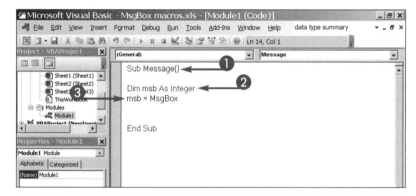

④ Type (**"*prompttext*"**, replacing *prompttext* with your text for the user.

⑤ Type a comma, and click a button constant in the list that appears.

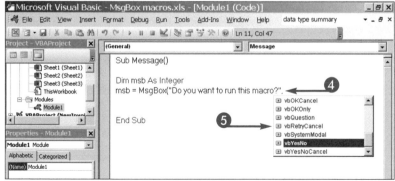

6 Type a comma, then **"*titletext*")**,replacing *titletext* with the message box title.

7 Type **if *variable* = 6**, replacing *variable* with your variable.

The Yes button returns the value 6. You can type the constant *vbYes* instead of 6 to make the macro easy to read.

8 Type **then**.

9 Type a statement that runs if the user clicks Yes.

10 Type **end if**.

11 Click to switch to Excel.

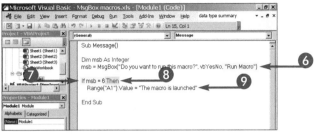

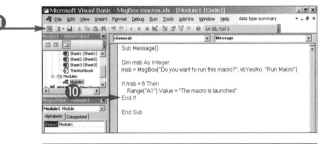

12 Run the macro.

Note: To run a macro, see Chapter 2.

- The message box appears.

- Click Yes to execute the If Then statements.

What are the values returned by the button clicks?

▼ The values returned by the button clicks are 1 for vbOK, 2 for vbCancel, 3 for vbAbort, 4 for vbRetry, 5 for vbIgnore, 6 for vbYes, and 7 for vbNo. You can also use the name of the button constant in the If Then statement instead of the value. For example, instead of writing If *variable* = 6 Then, you can write If *variable* = vbYes Then. The integer values make the code shorter, but the button constant names make the code easier to read.

How can I use more buttons?

▼ You can use more buttons by selecting a different button constant in the buttons argument. You can only use the buttons available in the button constants. In the list of button constants there are several other items which are not buttons but are either icons for the message box or control the behavior of the buttons. You can include these other constants in your buttons arguments by typing a plus symbol between each constant, as in vbYesNo+vbDefaultButton2, which makes the No button, the second button, the default.

Validate Data

If you ask a user for input with an input box, there is a risk that the user may enter invalid data, such as a text entry in an input box that requires a numeric entry. You can write a macro that tests the entry for validity and that uses a message box to inform the user about the problem.

You can test an input box macro with a valid entry, an invalid entry, and the Cancel button, to make sure that all possible actions are handled by the macro without errors. To handle the possibilities of an invalid entry and the Cancel button, you can use a nested `If Then Else` block

of statements. The first `If Then` level, `If inputboxvariable <> ""` Then, tests for the Cancel button by checking for an entry in the input box, closing the macro quietly if the Cancel button is clicked. The nested `If Then Else` block, `If valid(inputboxvariable)` Then, checks for a valid entry, executes the statements if true, and returns an informative message box if false.

For more information about input boxes, see Chapter 13. For more information about If Then Else conditional statements, see "Make a Double Decision with an If Then Else Macro."

Validate Data

① Type **Sub** and the macro name, then press Enter to start a new macro.

② Type **dim** *variable* **as string**, replacing *variable* with your input box variable.

③ Type *variable* = **InputBox("***prompttext***")**, replacing *variable* with your input box variable and *prompttext* with your prompt text.

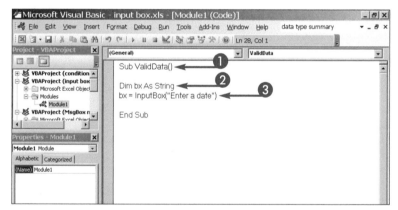

④ Type **if** *variable* **<> "" then**, replacing *variable* with your input box variable.

⑤ Type **if** *validationtest* **then**, replacing *validationtest* with a validation text for your data.

⑥ Type the statements to execute if the *condition* is true.

⑦ Type **else**.

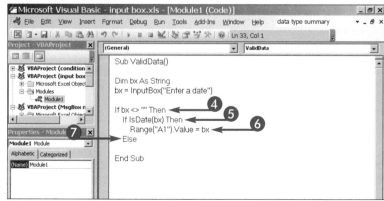

⑧ Type **MsgBox** *"text"*, replacing *text* with informative text.

⑨ Type **end if**.

⑩ Type **end if**.

⑪ Click ⊠ to switch to Excel.

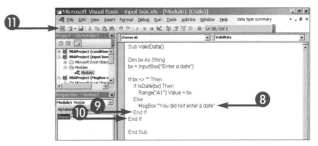

⑫ Run the macro.

Note: To run a macro, see Chapter 2.

● The input box appears.

⑬ Type an invalid entry.

⑭ Click OK.

A message box informs you that the entry is invalid.

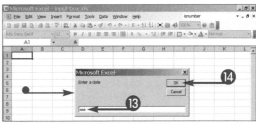

What validation tests can I use?

▼ You can use the VBA Is functions `IsDate` and `IsNumeric`. The `IsDate` function determines whether an expression can be converted to a date, and only returns True or False. The `IsNumeric` formula determines whether an expression can be evaluated as a number and therefore calculated, and only returns True or False.

What are other ways I can validate data?

▼ You can validate entries with any conditional statement that can be evaluated as true or false. For example, the statement `If inputboxvariable > 100 Then` tests for a value that is greater than 100. The statement `If Len(bx) = 16 Then` tests for a string length of exactly 16 characters, which is the length of a credit card number.

How can I set a default value in the input box?

▼ You can set a default value in an input box by using the optional Default argument. For example, if the user most often types a specific entry in the input box, such as Accounting Department, type the string `"Accounting Department"` as the Default argument in the InputBox arguments. For more information about input boxes, see Chapter 13.

Choose a Condition with a Select Case Statement

Y ou can write a macro to execute different statements based on different values of a single object or expression by using a `Select Case` statement. For example, you can use a `Select Case` statement to determine the appropriate sales tax for a sales invoice based on the state in which a customer lives.

The `Select Case` statement is most useful when you need to check a single object or expression for different values, and execute different statements for each of those different values. A single `Select Case` statement does the work of multiple `If Then` statements.

The `Select Case` statement has four parts, which include the object or expression you want to check, the value of that object or expression, the statements to execute for each value, and the `End Select` statement that closes the `Select Case` statement. You can also add a `Case Else` statement that executes if none of the `Case` statements is valid.

If you need to run the `Select Case` statement in multiple cells, you can nest it in a `Do While` loop. For more information about loops, see Chapter 15.

Choose a Condition with a Select Case Statement

① Type **Sub** and the macro name, then press Enter to start a new macro.

② Type **select case** *object*, replacing *object* with the object or expression to evaluate.

③ Type **case** *value*, replacing *value* with the value for this Case statement.

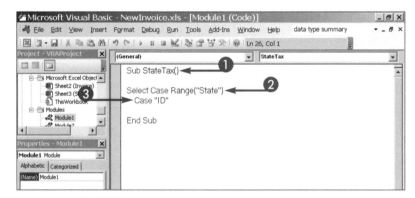

④ Type the statements to execute if the Select Case *object* meets this Case *value*.

⑤ Repeat steps **3** to **4** to add more Case statements and executable statements.

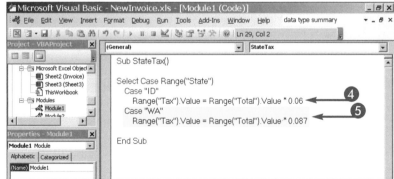

6 Type **case else** and statements to execute if the Select Case *object* does not meet any of the preceding Case *values*.

The `Case Else` statement is optional, but responds to invalid entries.

7 Type **end select**.

8 Click 🗐 to switch to Excel.

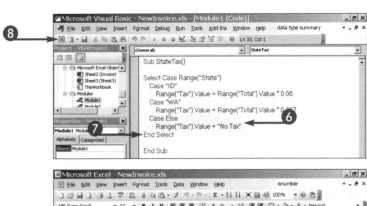

9 Run the macro.

Note: To run a macro, see Chapter 2.

● The macro executes the `Case` statements corresponding to the Select Case *object* value.

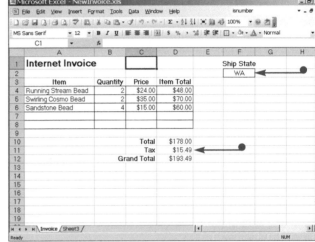

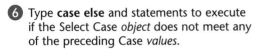

How can I use a Select Case statement for user input?

▼ You can use a `Select Case` statement for user input by creating an input box and using the value entered in the box as the Select Case *object*. For example, declare a variable as `String`, then set the `variable = InputBox(arguments)`. Use the variable as the `Select Case` *object*. For more information about input boxes, see Chapter 13.

Why do the Case Else statements execute when there is a valid entry in the range object?

▼ If the `Case` statement looks for a string, the string must match the string in the object, including capitalization. For example, if you create a `Select Case` statement that looks for states to set sales tax, and the `Case` statement looks for "ID", the Case executables do not execute for "id" or "Idaho", only for "ID".

How can I use variables to make the macro more efficient?

▼ You can make the macro more efficient by declaring variables for all of the objects and expressions in the macro. For example, in the example macro, variables could be declared for the `Range("State")`, `Range("Tax")`, and `Range("Subtotal")`. Each of these objects could be declared with a short variable name and the data type `Range`.

Conditionally Call Another Macro

You can *call*, or run, a different macro at any point in a running macro based on a conditional statement. You do this by using a conditional statement such as an `If Then` statement to set the condition, and combining it with a `Call` statement to call the other macro if the condition is true.

The `If Then` statement checks the value of the condition and passes control to the other macro if the condition is true. After the called macro is completed, control returns to the original macro. If you need to run this macro repeatedly, you can nest it in a loop. For more information about loops, see Chapter 15.

The advantage of calling another macro is that you do not have to type the called macro statements in the original macro code. You create the called macro and then call it from other macros whenever the condition warrants.

You can only call another macro if the macro exists in the same workbook project. If you want to call a macro that exists in a different workbook project, you can copy the module that contains the macro into the current workbook. For more information about copying modules, see Chapter 7.

Conditionally Call Another Macro

① Type **Sub** and the macro name, then press Enter to start a new macro.

② Type **if** *condition* **then**, replacing *condition* with the condition to evaluate.

③ Type **call** *macroname*, replacing *macroname* with the name of the macro to call if the *condition* is true.

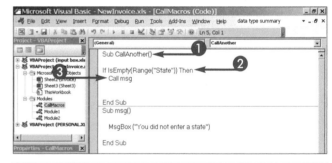

④ Type **else**.

⑤ Type the statements to run if the condition is not true.

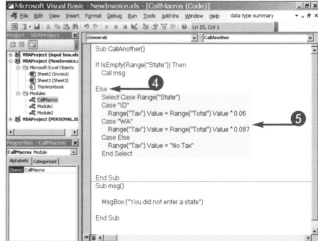

6 Type **end if**.

7 Click 🗶 to switch to Excel.

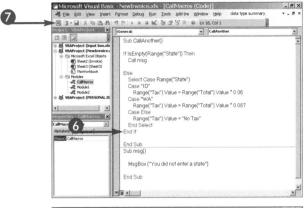

8 Run the macro.

Note: To run a macro, see Chapter 2.

The macro runs.

● If the condition is true, the called macro runs.

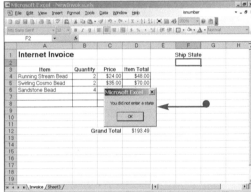

How can I simplify this macro?

▼ You can sometimes simplify this macro by reducing the If Then statement. In an If Then statement, if the executable statement that runs when the condition is true is a single statement, you can combine the If and Then statements on a single line and leave the End If line out. For example, the statements

```
If IsEmpty(Range("State")) Then
    Call msg
End If
```

can be combined into

```
If IsEmpty(Range("State")) Then Call msg
```

which is an easy-to-read space saver in a macro.

How can I end the original macro after the called macro runs?

▼ If you do not want the original macro to continue running after the called macro is complete, write an End Sub statement immediately after the Call statement in the original macro. Then, if the condition is not met, the original macro runs to completion without calling the other macro or encountering the internal End Sub line. If the condition is met, however, the other macro is called; and when control returns to the original macro, the End Sub line after the Call line ends the original macro.

Loop a Specific Number of Times

You can execute a macro a specific number of times by using a For Next loop. For example, if you want a set of statements to run exactly six times, you can use a For Next loop to do that for you. A For Next loop uses a counter variable for which you set the value, and the loop cycles, or reiterates, until the counter reaches the maximum value in the counter variable.

The For Next loop consists of four parts: The For statement initiates the loop. The counter variable gives the loop an initial value and a maximum value, as in *variable*

= 1 To 20. The body of the loop contains the statements that are executed repeatedly until the counter reaches its maximum value. The final part of the loop is the Next statement.

When a For Next loop starts, or starts over again, it checks the counter variable. If the counter variable is less than or equal to the maximum value, the statements inside the loop are executed again. The counter variable increments by one each time the loop runs. When the counter variable exceeds its maximum value, the loop stops and the macro moves on to the next statements after the loop.

① Type **Sub** and the macro name, then press Enter to start a new macro.

② Type **dim** *variable* **as integer**, replacing *variable* with your variable.

③ Type **for** *variable* **= 1 to 10**, replacing *variable* with your variable and *1* and *10* with your counters.

This example loop runs 10 times.

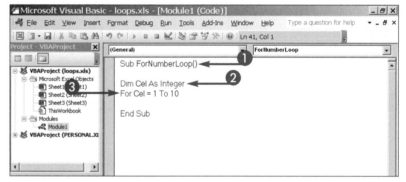

④ Type **activecell.interior.colorindex = *indexnumber***, replacing *indexnumber* with your color index number.

This example colors the active cell. You can replace this statement with your executable statements.

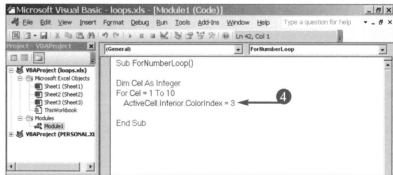

⑤ Type **activecell.offset(1, 0).select**.

ActiveCell.Offset(1.0) moves the active cell down one row.

⑥ Type **next**.

⑦ Click the View Microsoft Excel button (⊠) to switch to Excel.

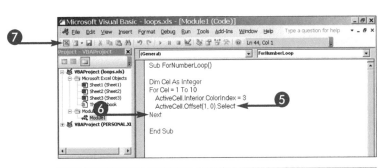

⑧ Run the macro.

Note: *To run a macro, see Chapter 2.*

● The loop executed the macro the number of times you specified in step **3**.

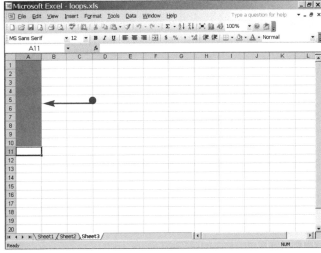

How can I increment a loop by a different number?

▼ You can increment a loop by a different number by using a `Step` statement to set the increment you want in the counter variable. By default the loop counter increments by one with each iteration of the loop, but you can write a `Step` statement to increment the loop by a different value. For example, to increment the counter by two, add the `Step` statement to the counter statement, as in `For variable 1 To 10 Step 2`. The increment must be appropriate for the variable's declared data type.

How can I make a runaway loop stop executing?

▼ You can make a runaway loop, called an *infinite* loop, stop quickly by pressing the Ctrl+Break keys. You can also stop a loop by using the Task Manager, but Ctrl+Break is faster. For example, if you write a `Step` statement in the counter statement for this example macro and make the step 0.5, the loop runs indefinitely because the variable in this example is set as an Integer data type, and the value 0.5 is not an integer. You can stop the execution of the code only by pressing Ctrl+Break.

Loop through a Collection

Y ou can use a `For Each` loop to repeatedly execute statements in every object of a collection or group of objects. For example, you can execute the same statements on every worksheet in a workbook or every cell in a range. The loop ends after executing the statements in the last element of the collection, and the macro moves on to the next statement after the loop.

The `For Each` loop consists of four parts: The `For Each` keyword initiates the loop. The *element* `In range` portion of the `For Each` statement specifies the objects on

which to execute the statements and the collection or group of objects in which the loop runs, as in *variable* `In` *range*. The body of the loop contains the statements that are executed on all the objects in the group. The final part of the loop is the `Next` statement.

At the beginning of the loop, a variable is declared for the objects on which the statements are executed. That variable, which must be declared with the correct data type for the objects in the collection, is used in the *variable* `In` *range* portion of the `For Each` statement.

Loop through a Collection

① Type **Sub** and the macro name, then press Enter to start a new macro.

② Type **dim** *variable* **as** *range*, replacing *variable* with your variable and *range* with your data type.

③ Type **for each** *variable* **in** *collection*, replacing *variable* with your variable and *collection* with your object collection.

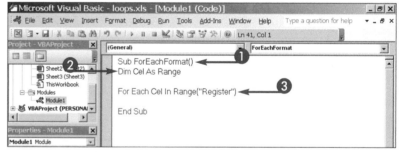

④ Type your executable statements.

This example colors each of the *variable* objects in the range named Register. ColorIndex 3 is red.

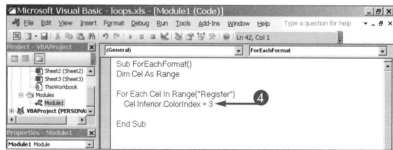

5 Type **next**.

6 Click 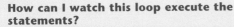 to switch to Excel.

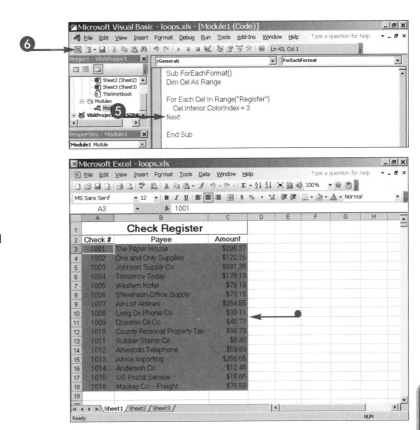

7 Run the macro.

Note: To run a macro, see Chapter 2.

● The statements are executed on all the objects in the collection. In this example, all the cells in the specified range are colored.

How can I watch this loop execute the statements?

▼ You can watch a For Each loop execute its statements by arranging the Excel and Visual Basic Editor windows so that you can see both windows, and then pressing the F8 key repeatedly to step through the loop over and over. As you step through the loop, you see the macro statements executed in the Excel window until you loop completely through the collection. To arrange the Excel and Visual Basic Editor windows, see the section "Arrange the Excel and Editor windows" in Chapter 5.

How can I nest one loop inside another loop?

▼ You can nest one For Each loop inside another by writing a complete interior For Each loop between the outer For Each and Next statements. For example, you can run a loop to color a range of cells on every worksheet in a workbook by writing the statements

```
Dim Cel As Range
Dim ws As Worksheet
For Each ws In Worksheets
ws.Select
    For Each Cel In
ActiveSheet.Range("A1:C10")
        Cel.Interior.ColorIndex = 3
    Next
Next ws
```

In this example, the outer For Each loop selects a new worksheet with each iteration.

Perform Tasks with a Do Until Loop

You can use a `Do Until` loop to execute macro statements until a specific condition is met. For example, you can apply changes to a series of cells until you encounter an empty cell, or you can add values to cells until a formula reaches a specific value.

When you run a `Do Until` loop, the statements you specify between the `Do Until` and `Loop` statements repeat until the condition you specify is met. When the loop determines that the condition you specify is true, the loop closes and the macro moves on to the next statement.

The `Do Until` loop has four parts: The loop initiates with the `Do` statement. The `Until` condition specifies the point at which the loop stops. The body of the loop contains the statements to repeat, and the `Loop` statement closes the loop.

The `Do Until` loop is similar to the `Do While` loop. The `Do Until` loop repeats until a condition is true, and the `Do While` loop repeats as long as a condition remains true. In most circumstances the two loop structures are interchangeable. For more information about the `Do While` loop, see the section "Execute a Task with a Do While Loop."

① Type **Sub** and the macro name, then press Enter to start a new macro.

② Type a starting point for the loop.

In this example, the loop enters values in succeeding cells, beginning with the starting point cell.

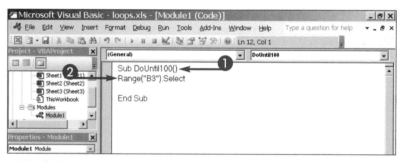

③ Type **do until**.

④ Type an `Until` condition.

In this example, the entered values are summed in a SUM formula in the cell named Sum. The loop runs until the value in the Sum cell is 100.

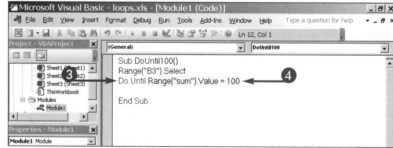

⑤ Type the statements you want the loop to execute.

In this example, the loop enters 20 in the selected cell and then moves down one row in each cycle.

⑥ Type **loop**.

⑦ Click 🔀 to switch to Excel.

⑧ Run the macro.

Note: To run a macro, see Chapter 2.

● The macro repeats until the specified condition is true.

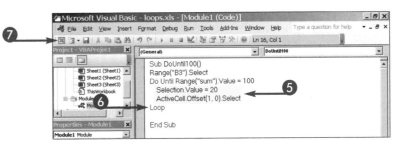

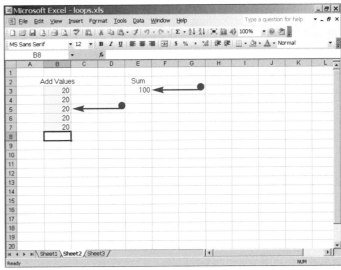

How can I use this loop with a macro formula instead of a worksheet formula?

▼ You can write the formula in the macro before the loop begins so that the macro enters the formula in the cell. The rest of the macro remains the same. You reference the formula cell in the Until condition, then write the macro to enter the values in the cells that are summed by the worksheet formula.

Why does my macro run in an infinite loop?

▼ An infinite loop occurs when the loop cannot meet a condition or find an end point. For example, if you do not create a formula cell or reference the wrong cell in the Until condition, the loop continues to add values to cells and the formula cell never meets the condition. To stop an infinite loop, press Ctrl+Break.

How can I use a Do Until loop to find a specific value?

▼ You can use a Do Until loop to move through cells until the loop finds a cell that meets your condition. For example, the following loop moves down a column of cells until it finds a cell that has the value 52 or is empty. The Exit Do statement stops the loop.

```
Do Until ActiveCell.Value = ""
If ActiveCell.Value = 52 Then
    ActiveCell.Select
    Exit Do
ElseIf ActiveCell.Value <> 52 Then
    ActiveCell.Offset(1, 0).Select
End If
Loop
```

Execute a Task with a Do While Loop

You can use a Do While loop to execute macro statements while a specific condition remains true. For example, you can execute statements on each cell in a table while there are entries in the cells, and the loop stops when it encounters an empty cell.

When you run a Do While loop, the statements you specify between the Do While and Loop statements repeat as long as the condition you specify is true. When the loop determines that the condition you specify is false, the loop exits and the macro moves on to the next statement.

The Do While loop has four parts: The loop initiates with the Do statement. The While condition specifies the condition that must remain true for the loop to continue repeating. The body of the loop contains the statements to repeat, and the Loop statement closes the loop.

The Do While loop is similar to the Do Until loop. The Do Until loop repeats until a condition is true, and the Do While loop repeats as long as a condition remains true. In most circumstances the two loop structures are interchangeable. For more information about the Do Until loop, see the section "Perform Tasks with a Do Until Loop."

Execute a Task with a Do While Loop

① Type **Sub** and the macro name, then press Enter to start a new macro.

② Type a starting point statement for the loop.

This example starts the loop in cells A3:C3.

③ Type **do while**.

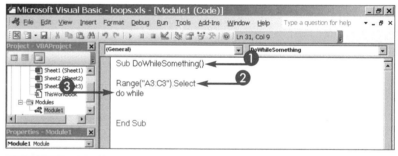

④ Type the While condition that must remain true.

In this example, the loop repeats while the active cell contains entries.

⑤ Type the statements to execute in each cycle of the loop.

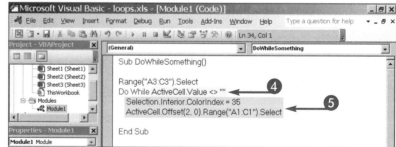

6 Type **loop** to end the loop.

7 Click 🔀 to switch to Excel.

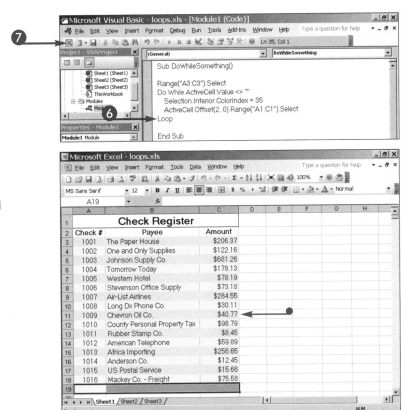

8 Run the macro.

Note: To run a macro, see Chapter 2.

● The macro repeats while the specified condition remains true.

Why does my loop not run?

▼ One reason your loop may not run is because it does not have an appropriate starting point preceding the loop. For example, if your loop refers to the active cell and the active cell is not in an appropriate worksheet location for the loop to run, the loop does not run. Another reason the loop may not run is that the `While` condition is false when the loop starts. The `While` condition must be true before the loop starts or the loop does not run.

How can I run a Do While loop a specific number of times?

▼ You can run a `Do While` loop a specific number of times if you use a counter variable in the loop to count cycles. For example, to write a loop that cycles five times, write `Dim J As Integer` to declare the variable `J`, write `J = 1` to set an initial value for `J`, and then write the loop

```
Do While J < 5
Your statements
J = J + 1
Loop
```

The loop cycles until the counter variable `J` equals 5, at which point the condition is not true and the loop ends.

Show a Loop's Progress

A macro looping through a very long list of data can take a long time to execute. You can show the progress of a loop to reassure yourself that the loop is still working.

You can show the progress of a loop by writing a statement immediately following the loop's start statement. The statement refers to the `Application.StatusBar` object, gives control of the Excel Status bar to the macro, and shows the value of the variable in the loop as the value changes.

Showing a loop's progress is easiest in a `For Next` or `For Each` loop because these loops usually have variable values that change as the loop progresses, and the Status bar statement shows these changing variable values. For example, the statement `Application.StatusBar = "Processing " & variable` shows the word *Processing* and the value of the variable in the Status bar as the loop progresses.

After the closing line of the loop, you return control of the Status bar to Excel with the statement `Application.StatusBar = False`.

① Type **Sub** and the macro name, then press Enter to start a new macro.

② Declare your variables.

This example macro is a `For Next` loop that uses a counter variable to tell the macro how many times to loop.

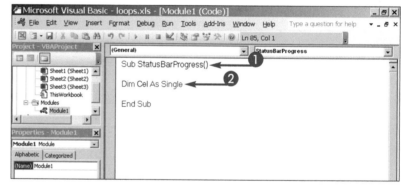

③ Type the opening line of your loop.

④ Type **application.statusbar** = *"text "* & *variable*, replacing *text* with your text and *variable* with the declared variable name.

⑤ Type the rest of your loop.

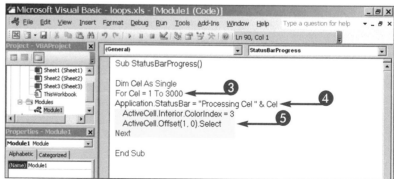

6 Type **application.statusbar = false**.

7 Click ⊠ to switch to Excel.

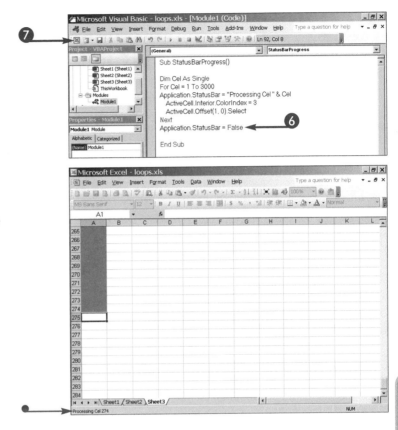

8 Run the macro.

Note: To run a macro, see Chapter 2.

● The status bar shows the progress of the loop while it runs.

If the loop is quick, the status bar flashes briefly, but if the loop is lengthy, the progress is more visible.

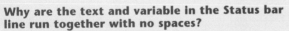

Why are the text and variable in the Status bar line run together with no spaces?

▼ The text and variable in the Status bar line run together with no spaces because you did not type a space between the `text` string and the closing quote in the `Application.StatusBar` statement. The space is a text character that must be included as part of the text string in the statement.

Why does my Excel Status bar not return to normal after I run the macro?

▼ The status bar does not return to normal because you forgot to type the `Application.StatusBar = False` statement after the last line of the loop. When you change the status of any application object, the status remains changed for the entire Excel application until you change it back to normal.

How can I show the progress of a Do While loop?

▼ You can show the progress of a `Do While` or `Do Until` loop if you can identify an object or variable that changes with each cycle of the loop. For example, in a loop such as

```
Do While ActiveCell.Value <> ""
    Selection.Interior.ColorIndex = 35
      ActiveCell.Offset(2, 0).
    Range("A1:C1").Select
Loop
```

the statement `Application.StatusBar = ActiveCell` shows in the status bar the value of the active cell.

Simplify Loops with a With Block

You can make your loops easier to read, faster to write, and more efficient to execute by combining repetitive statements into a `With` block. A `With` block enables you to execute several actions on the same object without having to repeat the name of the object over and over. This means you do less typing, and the statements execute more quickly because the macro does not have to repeatedly select the same object.

To combine a set of statements into a `With` block, write the keyword `With` followed by the object and, if the property is also duplicated, the object property. For example, to combine two statements that format cell font, write `With Selection.Font`. Below that line, write the property value statements, each beginning with a period. An `End With` statement closes the `With` block.

A `With` block is easier to read if the subordinate statements in the block are indented. Indenting the statements enables you to visually locate the beginning and end of a With block easily. For more information on indenting statements, see Chapter 4.

Simplify Loops with a With Block

① Type **Sub** and the macro name, then press Enter to start a new macro.

② Type the beginning of your loop.

③ Type **with** to begin the `With` block in the loop.

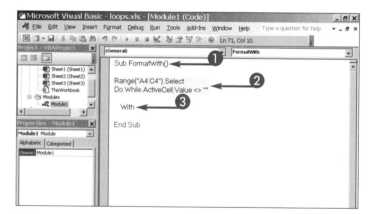

④ Type the object name.

⑤ Type the property statements for the object, each beginning with a period.

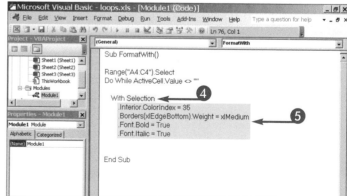

6 Type **end with**.

7 Type the end of your loop.

8 Click ⊠ to switch to Excel.

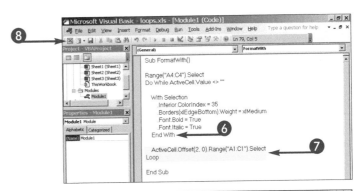

9 Run the macro.

Note: *To run a macro, see Chapter 2.*

● The With block statements are executed in the loop.

The loop runs more quickly because the macro does not reselect the object for every statement in every cycle of the loop.

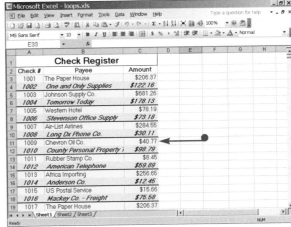

How can I nest a With block inside another With block?

▼ You can nest one With block inside another by typing the entire internal With block, including the End With statement, in between the external, higher-level With and End With statements. For example, in a With block to format cells, you can nest an internal With block that formats just the font, as in the following code:

```
With Selection
.Interior.ColorIndex = 35
    .Borders(xlEdgeBottom).Weight = xlMedium
With .Font
    .Bold = True
    .Italic = True
End With
End With
```

How can I use a With block to add the same range names to three worksheets?

▼ You can use a With block to add the same range names to three worksheets by nesting a With block in a Do While loop. For example, the following code sets the same three range names in the first three worksheets of the active workbook. The *countervariable* determines the worksheet index number.

```
Dim countervariable As Integer
countervariable = 1
Do While countervariable < 4
Worksheets(countervariable).Select
With Worksheets(countervariable).Names
.Add Name:=name1, RefersTo:=range1
.Add Name:=name2, RefersTo:=range2
.Add Name:=name3, RefersTo:=range3 End
With
countervariable = countervariable + 1
Loop
```

Understand Errors

A macro error, called a *runtime* error, is an error that occurs while the macro is running and stops the macro execution. There are other errors, called syntax errors, compile errors, and logical errors, that can also stop your macro from running or give incorrect results.

Syntax Error

Mistyping code statements when you write a macro causes a syntax error. For example, if you forget to type a closing parenthesis or a closing quote in an argument, you get a syntax error. If you use the Visual Basic Editor code settings, the editor tells you when you make a syntax mistake while typing the code, enabling you to correct your mistakes immediately. To turn on the syntax checker in the Visual Basic Editor, click Options under the Tools menu. In the Editor tab, select the Auto Syntax Check check box.

Compile Error

A *compile* error occurs when the VBA code is being compiled, or translated into machine language that your computer understands. In VBA, the code is compiled every time the macro runs; if there is a compile error, you see a message and Excel highlights the location of the error in the editor's Code window. You can check for compile errors before you run the macro by clicking Debug and then Compile from the menu. For more information about compiling macros, see the section "Compile a Macro."

Logical Errors

A *logical* error returns unexpected results because of a mistyped statement. In other words, the code does what you tell it to do but not what you want it to do. For example, if a statement calculates a 7 percent sales tax but you type `Range("Tax").value = 0.7` instead of `Range("Tax").value = 0.07`, the statement runs without errors but calculates a 70 percent sales tax because of the mistyped value.

Logical errors are not obvious and can be difficult to locate in the code. To help you find the source of a logical error, you can step through a procedure and use the Watch window to monitor the changing values of variables in the procedure. For more information about stepping through a macro and using the Watch window, see the sections "Debug a Macro with Break Points" and "Set and Use Watches."

Do While
ActiveCell.Value
<> "" With
Selection.
Interior.
ColorIndex = 35

1011001010101000111001011

Runtime Errors

A *runtime* error occurs as the code executes, at which time a message displays showing a description of the error. Runtime errors often occur because a variable tries to use data of the wrong data type — such as a string entry when the variable is declared as an integer — or tries to execute a statement on an object that does not exist — such as opening a file that does not exist because the file name is misspelled.

To avoid a macro stopping because of a runtime error, you can write different kinds of On Error statements that tell the code what to do if there is an error. An On Error statement tells the code to either ignore the error and continue running the macro, or go to a different macro to handle the error. For more information about On Error statements, see the sections "Ignore an Error and Continue the Macro," "Tell a User What the Error Is," and "Trap an Error with an Error Handler."

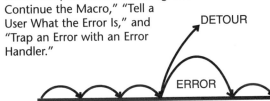

Preventing Errors

Some good programming practices can help prevent errors in your code. One good practice is to use the Option Explicit statement in the General Declarations area at the top of the module. The Option Explicit statement requires that all variables be declared, and keeps track of the variable names so that you cannot misspell them. To automatically set Option Explicit for all new modules, click Options under the Tools menu. On the Editor tab, mark the Require Variable Declaration check box.

Another good practice is to use capital letters in your variable name declarations, and enter your code in all lowercase letters. The editor changes the lowercase variable names to the declared, capitalized format if the variable name is spelled correctly, but any misspelled variable names are not capitalized.

Yet, another good practice is to validate user-entered data, such as data entered in an input box. For more information about validating user-entered data, see the section "Validate Data" in Chapter 14.

Ignore an Error and Continue the Macro

You can tell a macro to ignore any errors and move on to the next statement in the macro by using the On Error Resume Next statement. With this statement in place, VBA skips over any runtime errors during macro execution and continues to run the macro.

You can place the On Error Resume Next statement at the top of the macro, just below the Sub line, so that the macro is not halted by any encountered errors. If an error is encountered, the macro continues but does not correct the

error, which means the results of the macro may not be what you intended. However, in some circumstances the error does not affect the macro results, such as when a macro attempts to delete a file on the hard drive but the file no longer exists.

You should be careful not to ignore errors that need to be handled or corrected in some way. For more information about on handling errors, see the sections "Tell a User What the Error Is" and "Trap an Error With an Error Handler."

Ignore an Error and Continue the Macro

① Type **Sub** and the macro name, then press Enter to start a new macro.

② Type your macro code.

This macro attempts to delete a nonexistent file.

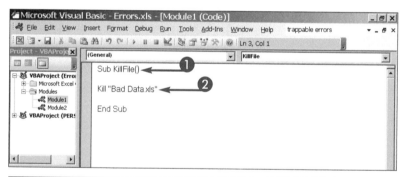

③ Click the Run Sub/UserForm button (▶) to run the macro.

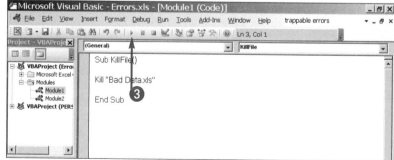

● An error message appears.

④ Click End.

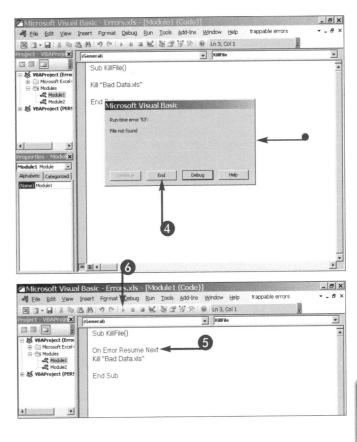

The error message disappears.

⑤ Type **on error resume next** below the Sub line.

⑥ Click ▶ to run the macro.

The macro runs without error messages.

How can I ignore the errors I know about but not ignore all possible errors?

▼ You can ignore or handle the errors you are aware of by either writing a conditional statement in your code or by writing an error handler. A conditional statement allows the macro to determine whether a condition is true before the statements are executed, avoiding an error if the condition is not true. For more information about conditional statements, see Chapter 14. For more information about error handlers, see the sections "Tell a User What the Error Is" and "Trap an Error with an Error Handler."

How can I handle errors caused by user entries?

▼ You can handle errors caused by user entries by validating the entries. User entries are typically made in an input box, and you can validate input box entries by declaring an appropriate data type for the input box variable. For example, if the input box entry should be a number, you can declare the input box variable as `Integer`, `Long`, `Single`, `Double`, or `Currency`. If the entry should be a date, you can declare the variable as a `Date` data type. For more information about validating input box entries, see Chapter 14.

Tell a User What the Error Is

When a macro encounters an error that you expect, you can tell a user what the error is by writing an error handler that displays a message box. For example, if a macro selects all the cells that contain comments in a range, you can expect that sometimes the macro finds no cells with comments and therefore generates an error. You can add an error handler to the end of the macro to tell the user exactly what the problem is when there are no cells with comments in the range.

At the beginning of the macro where the error is likely to occur, write the statement On Error Goto ErrorHandler. At the end of the macro, write the line Exit Sub to stop the macro before it runs the error handler code, then write the error handler code just above the End Sub line within the macro. A macro encountering an error jumps to the error handler code, but a macro executes normally if there is no error.

Tell a User What the Error Is

① Type **Sub** and the macro name, then press Enter to start a new macro.

② Type **on error goto ErrorHandler**.

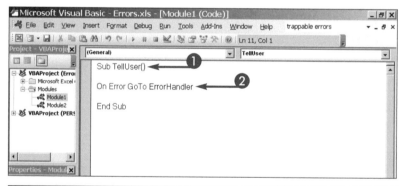

③ Type your macro statements.

This example macro selects cells that contain comments within the current region around the active cell.

④ Type **exit sub**.

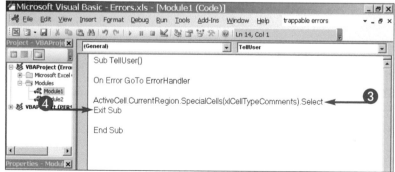

⑤ Type **ErrorHandler:**.

⑥ Type **msgbox "*text*"**, replacing *text* with your message box text.

⑦ Click the View Microsoft Excel button ( ) to switch to Excel.

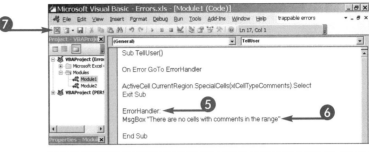

⑧ Run the macro.

Note: To run a macro, see Chapter 2.

● The message box appears if an error occurs when the macro runs.

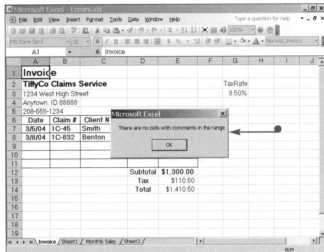

Can I use a different name for the error handler?

▼ Yes, you can use a different name for the error handler. The name *ErrorHandler* is a typical label for an error handler code segment, but you can replace it with any label you want. When an error is generated in the section of code below the `On Error Goto label` statement, the macro jumps to the label. Make sure you spell the error-handler label identically in both the `On Error Goto label` statement and the `label:` statement.

How can I continue running the macro after the error is handled?

▼ You can continue running the macro after the error is handled by adding the line `Resume Next` at the end of the error handler code. The `Resume Next` line sends the macro back to the line following the error location, so the remainder of the macro continues to run. The macro, while running to completion, may not produce the expected results if the error is one that needs to be handled rather than ignored.

Trap an Error with an Error Handler

Y ou can *trap*, or catch and identify, a VBA error using the Err object. The Err object has some useful properties, including Number, which identifies the error, and Description, which describes the error. Because the description's terms are not always meaningful to a user, you can make a trapped error message more useful by adding your own wording to the message.

When an error occurs unexpectedly, you need to know what the error is so that you can edit the macro code to handle or prevent the error. By adding the `Err.Number` and `Err.Description` properties to your error handler

message box, you can track down the source of the error more easily. You can add a message that includes your contact information so users can give you the error number and description.

You can determine the nature of the problem when you know the error number. You can find a list of trappable errors, their numbers and messages, and specific sources and solutions for each error in the VBA Help files. Type trappable errors in the Ask A Question box and press Enter. In the Search Results pane, click the Trappable Errors (Visual Basic for Applications) link.

Trap an Error with an Error Handler

① Type **Sub** and the macro name, then press Enter to start a new macro.

② Type **on error goto ErrorHandler**.

You can replace ErrorHandler with your own label, but make sure you use the same label in the error handler label.

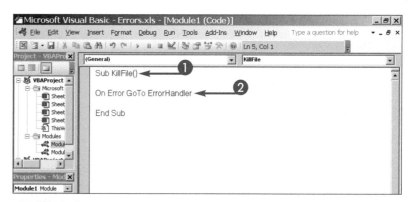

③ Type your macro code.

④ Type **exit sub** at the end of the macro, above the `End Sub` statement.

⑤ Type **ErrorHandler:**.

If you typed a different label in step **2**, use the same label here.

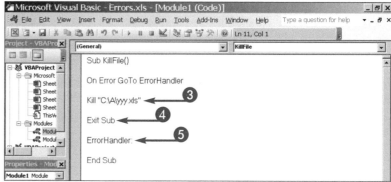

⑥ Type **msgbox** *"text"*, replacing *text* with your message to the user.

⑦ Type **& err.number & " " & err.description**.

Make sure you type a space between the empty quotes.

⑧ Click ▶ to run the macro.

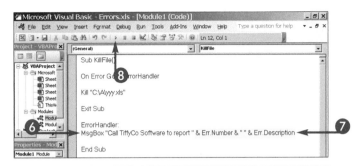

● If the macro encounters an error, the error handler message appears.

The message tells you what the error number and description are so you can locate and solve the problem in the code.

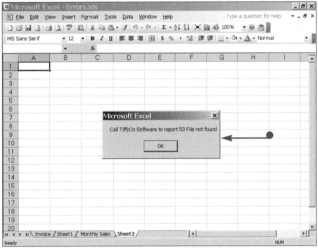

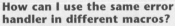

How can I use the same error handler in different macros?

▼ You can use the same error handler in many different macros by copying and pasting the entire error handler sequence into the macro where you want to use it. To make the process of reusing error handlers in multiple macros easier, you can use the same error handler label in all your macros. The label ErrorHandler is typical for that reason.

How can I break text into separate lines in a message?

▼ You can break text into separate lines in a message by using the Visual Basic constant vbCrLf, which means Carriage Return/ Line Feed. It inserts a line break in the message. For example, if you write MsgBox "Error number " &Err.Number & vbCrLf & Err.Description, the message box displays the text and error number on one line and the error description on a second line.

How can I return control to the macro after the error handler runs?

▼ You can return control to the macro from the error handler by typing Resume to return to the statement where the error occurred, or Resume Next to return to the statement following the statement where the error occurred. Be cautious with the Resume statement because if the error is not handled in some way, the error just repeats.

Debug a Macro with Break Points

Y ou can quickly *debug* a macro, correcting logic and runtime errors, by setting *break points* that allow the macro to run to a specific point and then stop. You can set break points at specific lines of code that you think may be generating the error, and then check the values of the macro variables in the Locals window. If a variable does not have an appropriate value when the macro stops at a break point, you know that the error occurred in the code before the break point. Setting break points helps you narrow the location of an error in a long macro. You can continue executing the macro after each break-point stop, and the macro runs up to the next break point.

You can set a break point by clicking in the gray margin of the Code window to the left of the statement where you want the macro to stop. To remove a break point, click the break-point icon in the margin.

You can run the macro up to the first break point by clicking the Run Sub/UserForm button, then continue to run the macro to the next break point by clicking the button again. To end the debugging procedure, click the Reset button.

Debug a Macro

① In the Visual Basic Editor, open the macro you want to debug.

② Click View.

③ Click Locals Window.

Note: For more information about editor windows, see the section "Open and Dock Windows in the Visual Basic Editor" in Chapter 5.

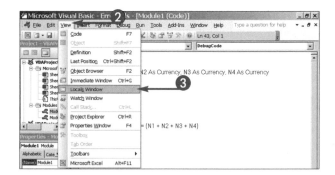

● The Locals window displays in the last displayed location.

④ Click in the margin next to the line where you want to set a break point.

● A break point icon appears in the margin and the line is highlighted.

You can repeat step **4** to add additional break points.

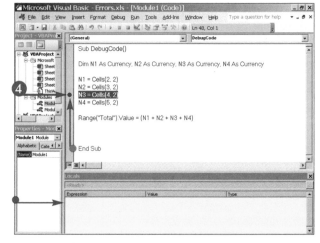

5 Click to run the macro.

● The macro runs to the first break point.

● The values of the declared variables display in the Locals window.

If there are more break points, you can click ▶ to run the macro to the next break point.

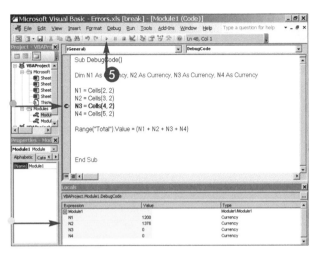

6 Click the Reset button (■) to end the debug procedure.

7 Click each break point icon to remove it.

Break points that you do not remove are removed when you close the workbook.

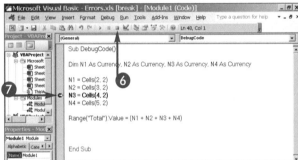

MASTER IT

How can I change the colors for the break point icon and code highlighting?

▼ You can change the colors for the break point icon and code highlighting in the Options dialog box. In the Visual Basic Editor, click Options under the Tools menu. On the Editor Format tab, in the Code Colors list, click Breakpoint Text. Click the colors you want in the boxes below the Code Colors list, and look at the Sample box to see the results of your selections. For more information about Visual Basic Editor options, see Chapter 5.

How can I step through the macro without using break points?

▼ You can step through the macro one line at a time without using break points if you click in the macro, click Debug, and then click Step Into. The Sub line for the macro is highlighted. You can click Debug and Step Into repeatedly to step through the macro. However, pressing F8 repeatedly to step into and then step through the macro is much faster. Each time you press F8, the highlighted line is executed and the next line is highlighted.

Compile a Macro

You can check a macro for syntax errors by using the VBA compiler. *Compiling* is translation of your VBA code into machine language that your computer understands.

In VBA, the code is compiled every time the macro runs, and if there is a compile — or syntax — error, the user sees an error message. You can check for compile errors before you run the macro by clicking Debug and then Compile. If the compiler finds an error, you see a message and the line containing the error is highlighted. After you find and correct an error, you must run the compiler again until all errors are found and corrected.

If you have Auto Syntax Check turned on in the Visual Basic Editor, the code is checked for single-line errors as you write it. However, some syntax errors can occur across multiple lines of code, such as long loop or conditional statements without ending statements. In addition, if you have Auto Syntax Check turned off so that you can write code without being constantly bothered by the syntax checker, none of your syntax errors is caught before you run the macro.

① Type **Sub** and the macro name, then press Enter to start a new macro.

② Type your macro code.

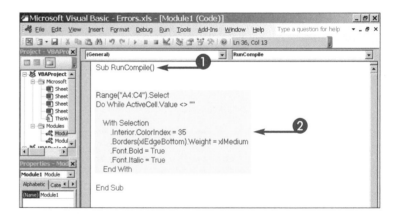

③ Click Debug.

④ Click Compile VBA Project.

● An error message appears.

● The location of the error is highlighted in the Code window.

5 Click OK.

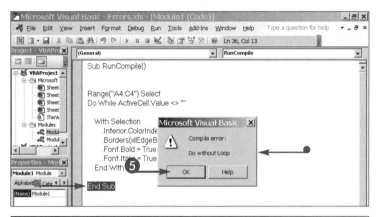

6 Correct the code error.

7 Repeat steps **3** to **4** to compile the project again until no errors occur.

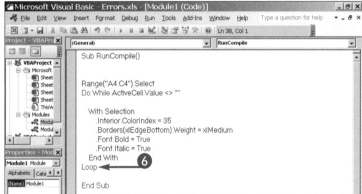

How can I turn Auto Syntax Check on or off?

▼ To turn Auto Syntax Check on or off, click Options under the Tools menu. On the General tab, mark or clear the Auto Syntax Check check box. Auto Syntax Check is sometimes annoying when you write code because it catches every mistake it sees, even when you are not finished typing a statement. If you turn Auto Syntax Check off, make sure you compile your project before you send it to a user, so that any errors are caught and corrected before they cause problems for the user.

Why does the compiler find errors in a different module?

▼ The compiler compiles all the code in the workbook project, so it looks through every macro in every module in the project and stops at every mistake it finds. To compile just a specific macro, you can click in the macro code, click Debug, and then click Step Into. In VBA, the compiler runs on every macro before the macro runs. You can also click in the macro code and press F8 to step into and through a macro.

Set and Use Watches

Y ou can monitor the values of specific expressions or variables as you step through a macro by using *watches*. A watch enables you to monitor the value of a variable or expression as code is executed to help you locate the source of a logical error.

You can set and use watches in the Watches window, which lists the active watches and the current value of the expression or variable being watched.

You can set a watch expression using the Add Watch dialog box. Type the expression you want to watch in the Expression box. Typically, an expression checks for the value of a watched variable to meet a condition, such as `variable > 100`.

After setting the expression, specify the type of watch to perform in the Watch Type options. The Watch Expression option shows the value `True` or `False` according to whether or not the variable meets the expression condition. The Break When Value Is True option stops the macro when the condition becomes true, and the Break When Value Changes option stops the macro when the value changes between true and false. To delete a watch from the Watches window, right-click the watch and click Delete.

Set and Use Watches

① In the Visual Basic Editor, open the macro you want to debug.

② Click View.

③ Click Watch window.

Note: For more information about editor windows, see the section "Open and Dock Windows in the Visual Basic Editor" in Chapter 5.

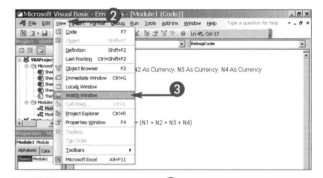

● The Watches window appears in the last displayed location.

④ Click Debug.

⑤ Click Add Watch.

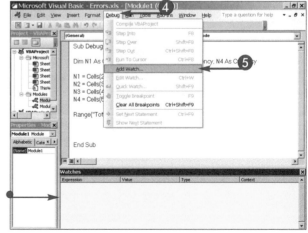

The Add Watch dialog box appears.

6 Type an expression to watch in the Expression box.

7 Click an option for the type of watch (○ changes to ⊙).

8 Click OK.

9 Click Debug and then Step Into from the menu to step through the macro.

You can also press F8 to step through the macro.

● The value of the watch expression displays in the Watches window.

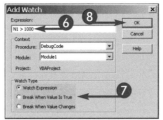

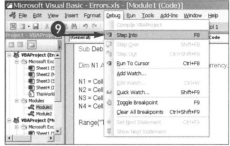

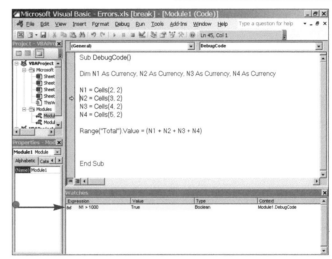

How can I set a watch on the value of a variable in the macro?

▼ You can set watches on the values of variables by using the Quick Watch dialog box. To use Quick Watch, click next to the variable name anywhere in the macro and press Shift+F9. The Quick Watch dialog box appears. Click Add to add the variable to the Watches window. When you step through the macro, the value of the variable displays.

How can I set a watch on an expression in my macro code?

▼ You can set watches on the expressions in the code that have a value of true or false by using the Quick Watch dialog box. Drag to select the entire expression and then press Shift+F9. The Quick Watch dialog box appears. Click Add to add the expression to the Watches window. When you step through the macro, the value of the expression displays.

Why does a watched expression have the value <Out of context>?

▼ A watched expression has the value <Out of context> in the Watches window when the macro is not running or is in break mode. When you step through the macro, the values of the expressions and variables are active and display in the Watches window.

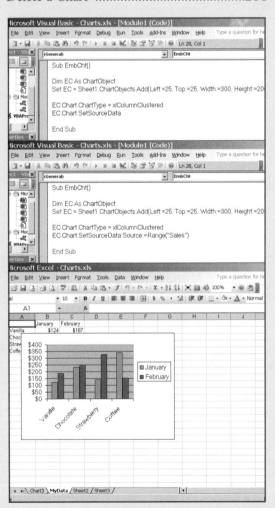

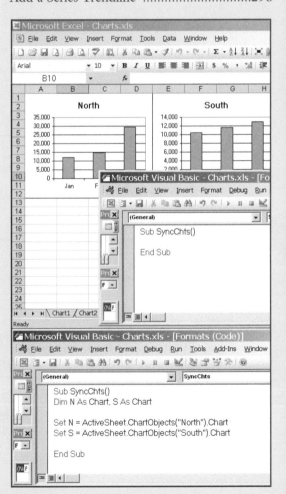

19   Writing PivotTable Macros

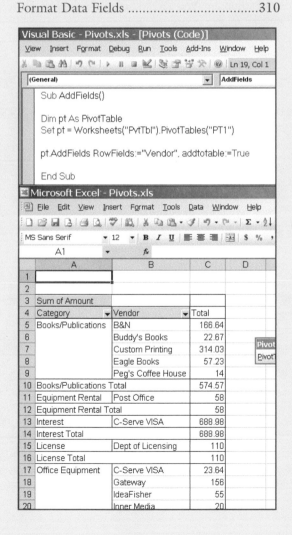

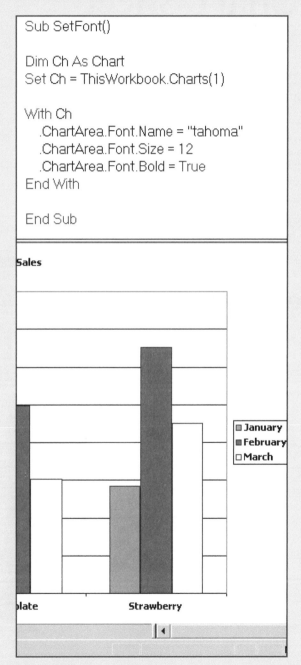

```
Sub SetFont()

Dim Ch As Chart
Set Ch = ThisWorkbook.Charts(1)

With Ch
    .ChartArea.Font.Name = "tahoma"
    .ChartArea.Font.Size = 12
    .ChartArea.Font.Bold = True
End With

End Sub
```

Create a Chart Sheet

You can write a macro to add a new chart sheet to a workbook. When you create a chart, you use the Add method with the Charts object. VBA creates a new Chart object with default settings for child objects such as legend, axes, and titles.

A chart sheet is created on a separate sheet in the workbook rather than on a worksheet. Nothing appears on a chart sheet but the chart. When you add a new chart sheet, you use the SetSourceData property to specify the data displayed in the chart, and the ChartType property to specify the chart type.

The Charts.Add method has three optional arguments. By using the Before argument, you can specify the sheet before which you want to position the new chart sheet. By using the After argument, you can specify the sheet after which you want to position the new chart sheet. By using the Count argument, you can add multiple chart sheets to a workbook.

Create a Chart Sheet

① Type **Sub** and the macro name, then press Enter to start a new macro.

② Type **charts.add**.

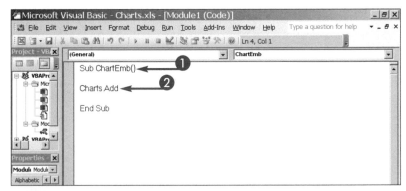

③ Type **activechart. charttype =**.

④ Double-click a chart type in the Auto List.

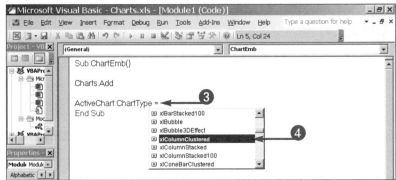

⑤ Type **activechart.setsourcedata**.

⑥ Type **source**:= *sheetobject*.
rangeobject, replacing *sheetobject* with
the worksheet object where the data is
located, and *rangeobject* with the range
object where the data is located.

⑦ Click the View Microsoft Excel button (⊠)
to switch to Excel.

⑧ Run the macro.

Note: To run a macro, see Chapter 2.

● A new chart sheet is created with the
specified data and chart type.

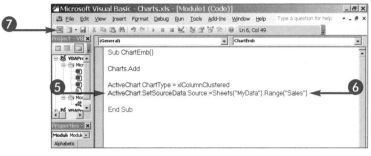

```
Sub ChartEmb()

Charts.Add

ActiveChart.ChartType = xlColumnClustered
ActiveChart.SetSourceData Source:=Sheets("MyData").Range("Sales")

End Sub
```

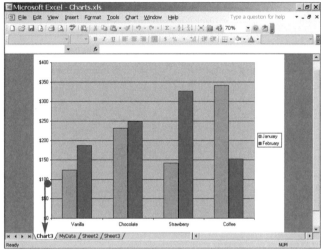

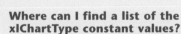

Where can I find a list of the xlChartType constant values?

▼ You can find a complete list of
xlChartType constants in the
VBA Help files. Type **ChartType
Property** in the Ask A Question
box, and then click the
ChartType Property link in the
Search Results pane. In the
ChartType Property help
window, click the blue
xlChartType link near the top of
the window. A long list of all
possible xhChartType constants
appears.

How can I change the chart sheet name?

▼ You can change the chart sheet
name by writing the statement
chartvariable.Name =
"*chartsheetname*", replacing
chartvariable with the declared
variable that represents the chart
object and *chartsheetname* with
the new chart sheet name. For
more information about
declaring variables, see the
section "Declare Variables" in
Chapter 6.

How can I simplify this macro?

▼ You can simplify this macro by
using a `With` block to combine
all the methods and properties
for the chart object. Type **With
*chartvariable***, and then type
each property or method
statement on a new line,
beginning with a period. For
more information about `With`
blocks, see the section "Simplify
Statements with a With Block"
in Chapter 15.

Create an Embedded Chart

You can write a macro to create an *embedded* chart, a chart that is displayed on a worksheet, by using the Add method for the Sheets(*sheetobject*).ChartObjects object. The VBA difference between a chart sheet and an embedded chart is that the Chart object for an embedded chart is a part of the ChartObjects collection of the worksheet, and the Chart object for a chart sheet is part of the Sheets collection in the workbook.

You can simplify your macro by declaring a variable for the object. For more information about declaring variables, see the section "Declare a Variable" in Chapter 6.

You use the SetSourceData method to specify the source data range, and the ChartType method to set the chart type.

The Add method for an embedded chart has four optional arguments that enable you to specify the size and location of the chart on the worksheet. The Left and Top arguments specify the distance in points from the left edge of column A and the top of row 1. The Width and Height arguments specify the width and height of the chart in points. There are 72 points in an inch.

Create an Embedded Chart

① Type **Sub** and the macro name, then press Enter to start a new macro.

② Type **dim** *variable* **as chartobject**, replacing *variable* with your chart object variable.

Replace *variable* with your chart object variable throughout this macro.

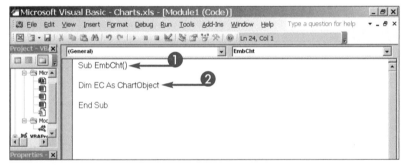

③ Type **set** *variable* = *sheetobject* **.chartobjects.add()**, replacing *sheetobject* with your worksheet reference.

Note: For more information about worksheet references, see Chapter 9.

④ Within the Add method parentheses, type **left:=***points*, **top:=***points*, **width:=***points*, **height:=***points*, replacing *points* with your measurements in points.

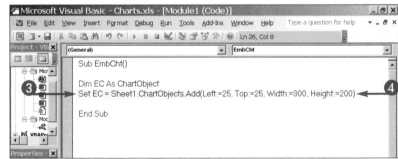

5 Type *variable*.**chart.charttype** = *charttype*, replacing *charttype* with your xlChartType constant value.

6 Type *variable*.**chart.setsourcedata**.

7 Type **source:=** *rangeobject*, replacing *rangeobject* with the range object where the data is located.

8 Click 🖾 to switch to Excel.

9 Run the macro.

Note: To run a macro, see Chapter 2.

● Excel creates on the worksheet a new embedded chart of the size and position you specified.

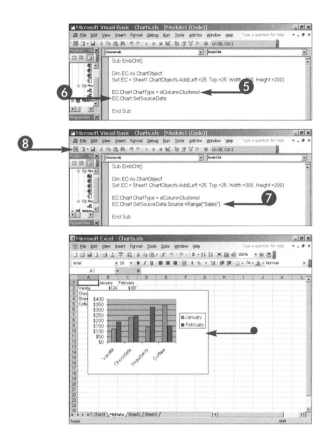

Where can I find a list of the xlChartType constant values?

▼ You can find a complete list of xlChartType constants in the VBA Help files. Type **ChartType Property** in the Ask A Question box, and then click the ChartType Property link in the Search Results pane. In the ChartType Property help window, click the blue xlChartType link near the top of the window. A long list of all possible xhChartType constants appears.

How can I write this macro more easily?

▼ You can write a shorter macro for a default embedded chart by writing the same Charts.Add macro as for a chart sheet, but adding the Location property, as in `ActiveChart.Location Where:=xlLocationAsObject, Name:="worksheetname"`. For more information about chart sheets, see the section "Create a Chart Sheet."

How can I simplify this macro?

▼ You can simplify this macro by using a `With` block to combine all the methods and properties for the chart object. Type **With** *chartvariable*.**Chart**, and then type each property or method statement on a new line, beginning with a period. For more information about `With` blocks, see the section "Simplify Statements With a With Block" in Chapter 15.

Refer to an Embedded Chart

You can refer to charts in your macros when you need to execute statements on an existing chart, such as changing the data source or the formatting of the chart. When you refer to a chart sheet, all you need to know is the sheet name, and you can refer to the chart sheet using the `Sheets("sheetname")` object or the `Charts("sheetname")` object. But when you need to refer to an embedded chart, you refer to an object on a worksheet and you need to know the name of the object.

Every chart on a worksheet has a ChartObjects(*index*) index number and a name. You can use the Immediate window to learn the name of the chart object on a worksheet by typing `?sheetobject.ChartObjects(index).Name` and pressing Enter. The chart object name is displayed on the next line in the Immediate window.

You can refer to a chart object by its name with the statement `sheetobject.ChartObjects(objectname)` or the statement `sheetobject.ChartObjects(indexnumber)`.

Refer To an Embedded Chart

1 Arrange your editor and Excel windows so you can see both windows.

Note: To arrange the Excel and editor windows, see the section "Arrange the Excel and Editor Windows" in Chapter 5.

2 Open the Immediate window.

Note: To display the Immediate window, see the section "Open and Dock Windows in the Visual Basic Editor" in Chapter 5.

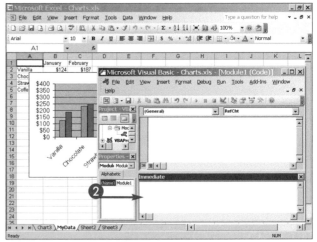

3 Type **?activesheet.chartobjects(1).name**.

This statement selects the first chart object on the worksheet.

4 Press Enter.

● The chart object name is displayed.

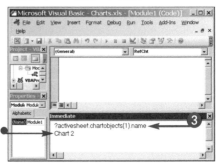

⑤ In the Code window, Type **Sub** and the macro name, then press Enter to start a new macro.

⑥ Type **activesheet.chartobjects** (*"objectname"*).**activate**, replacing *objectname* with your chart object name.

⑦ Click ▶ to run the macro.

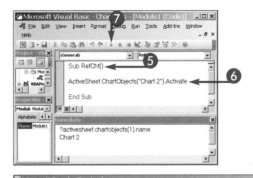

● The chart object is activated, as shown by the black handles around the chart border.

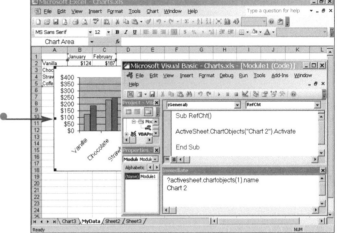

How can I give a chart object a more recognizable name?

▼ When you create a chart, you can give it a more recognizable name by using a statement to name the chart. Start your macro by declaring a variable for the chart, as in `Dim variable As ChartObject`, followed by `Set variable = sheetobject .ChartObjects().Add`. Then use the variable name in the statement `variable.Name = "chartname"`. You can use that chart name in the remainder of your code or in other macros that refer to that chart object.

How can I refer to a chart object on a different worksheet?

▼ You can refer to a chart object on a different worksheet by using the `sheetobject .ChartObjects("chartname")` statement. The `sheetobject` can be a reference to a worksheet name, index number, or codename. The `chartname` can be the original chart name or your own recognizable chart name. The easiest way to refer to a chart object in your code is to declare a variable for `sheetobject.ChartObjects ("chartname").Chart`, and use the variable name in your code. For more information about worksheet references, see Chapter 9.

Use the ChartWizard Method

You can use the `ChartWizard` method to quickly format a chart sheet, much like the ChartWizard does, without the need to set each individual formatting property for the chart. You can use the `ChartWizard` method for a specific `Chart` object. There are eleven optional arguments for the `ChartWizard` method, including Source, Gallery, Format, PlotBy, CategoryLabels, SeriesLabels, HasLegend, Title, CategoryTitle, ValueTitle, and ExtraTitle. Any additional properties you want to apply must be set in separate statements.

You can use the `Source` argument to specify the source data range for the chart. Because you use the `ChartWizard` method on a chart sheet, you must include the worksheet object in the source data range reference. For more information about referring to ranges, see Chapter 11.

The `Gallery` argument specifies an `xlChartType` constant value, and the Format argument specifies one of ten built-in value formats for the specified chart type.

Use the ChartWizard Method

① Type **Sub** and the macro name, then press Enter to start a new macro.

② Type **dim** *variable* **as chart**, replacing *variable* with your variable.

Replace *variable* with your variable throughout this macro.

③ Type **set** *variable* = **thisworkbook.charts.add**.

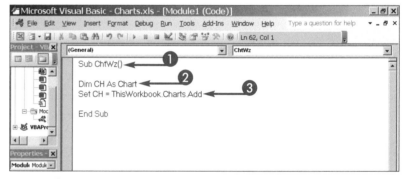

④ Type *variable* **.chartwizard**.

⑤ Type **source:=** *worksheet.range*, replacing *worksheet* with your worksheet reference and *range* with your source range.

⑥ Type **gallery:=** *xlcharttype*, replacing *xlcharttype* with your xlChartType constant.

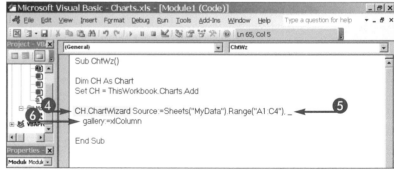

⑦ Type **format:=** *formatnumber*, replacing *formatnumber* with a format value between 1 and 10.

⑧ Type any additional ChartWizard values you want.

Any optional arguments you leave out are given a default value.

⑨ Click ▶ to run the macro.

⑩ Click ▣ to switch to Excel.

● Excel creates the chart sheet using your specified values.

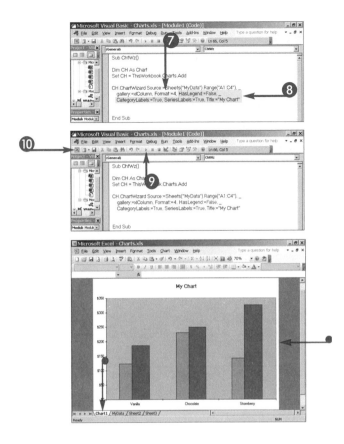

M

Where can I find a list of the xlChartType constant values?

▼ You can find a complete list of xlChartType constants in the VBA Help files. Type **ChartType Property** in the Ask A Question box, and then click the ChartType Property link in the Search Results pane. In the ChartType Property help window, click the blue xlChartType link near the top of the window. A long list of all possible xhChartType constants appears.

Where can I find an explanation of the Format argument values?

▼ There is no list of the Format argument values in the VBA Help files. The values represent the chart subtypes you find in the Excel ChartWizard. You can determine which value you want to use by recording a macro in which you create a chart with the ChartWizard and select the chart type and subtype you want, or by running the macro repeatedly using different argument values each time to see the results.

What values do the other ChartWizard arguments require?

▼ The PlotBy argument takes a value of either xlRows or xlColumns to decide whether the data series are in rows or columns. The Title arguments take strings as the different titles in the chart. The HasLegend argument defaults to True, but you can set it to False if you do not want a legend. The CategoryLabels and SeriesLabels arguments take values of True or False to display the labels in your data range.

Print a Chart

You can write a macro that uses the PrintOut method to print charts. The PrintOut method prints objects to which it is applied, including the Chart object, the Worksheet object, the ActiveSheet object, or the Charts collection in a workbook or worksheet.

You can print a single embedded chart or chart sheet by using the chartobject.PrintOut statement. You can print all the embedded charts on a worksheet, along with all the worksheet data, by using the sheetobject .PrintOut or ActiveSheet.PrintOut statements. You can print all the chart sheets in a workbook by using the workbookobject.Charts.PrintOut statement.

When using the workbookobject.Charts.PrintOut statement to print all the chart sheets in a workbook, eight optional arguments enable you to specify the range of chart sheets to print, From and To, the number of Copies, and whether to send the printout to Print Preview before printing.

The PrintOut method for other objects has no arguments. Printing individual embedded charts automatically scales them to fill the printed page.

Print a Chart

① Type **Sub** and the macro name, then press Enter to start a new macro.

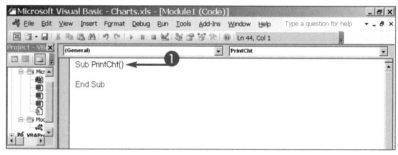

② Type **activeworkbook.charts.printout**.

This statement prints all the chart sheets in the active workbook.

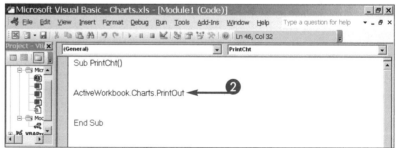

3️⃣ Type **preview:= true**.

4️⃣ Click ▶ to run the macro.

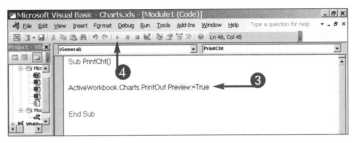

● The chart sheets in the active workbook appear in the Print Preview window.

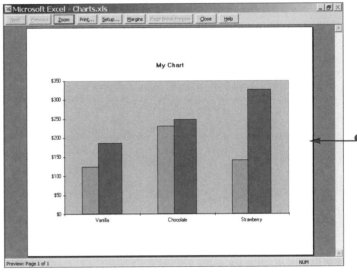

How can I print the embedded charts on a worksheet without the worksheet data?

▼ You can print the embedded charts on a worksheet without the worksheet data by writing a `For Each` loop to print the individual chart objects. Write the following macro:

```
Dim variable As ChartObject
For Each variable In
worksheetobject.ChartObjects
variable.Chart.PrintOut
Next.
```

This macro does not send the charts to print preview; it sends all the embedded charts on the worksheet to the printer.

Why do I get an error when the macro runs?

▼ You may get an error when the macro runs if there are no chart sheets in the active workbook. To avoid showing this error, you can handle the error with the statement `On Error Resume Next` or with an `ErrorHandler` that displays a message saying there are no chart sheets to print. For more information about on handling errors, see Chapter 16.

Delete a Chart

You can write a macro to delete a chart, either an embedded chart or a chart sheet, from a workbook. You use the Delete method on the Sheets or Charts object to delete chart sheets, and on the ChartObjects object to delete embedded charts.

Sheets are indexed with sequential index numbers from left to right; so the statement Sheets(1).Delete identifies and deletes the sheet with index number 1, which is always the leftmost sheet in the workbook, whether it is a chart sheet or a worksheet. The statement Charts(1).Delete deletes the leftmost chart sheet in the workbook.

You can also identify chart sheets by their names, as in the statements Sheets("January").Delete and Charts("January").Delete, and you can identify chart sheets as ActiveChart. If you do not identify the workbook in your statement, the chart sheet is deleted from the active workbook. You can identify workbooks as ActiveWorkbook, ThisWorkbook, or by file name.

You can delete an embedded chart by identifying the worksheet and chart object, as in *sheetobject* .ChartObjects(1).Delete. You can also identify a chart object by name, as in *sheetobject*.ChartObjects ("*chartname*").Delete.

Delete a Chart

① Arrange your editor and Excel windows so you can see both windows.

Note: To arrange the Excel and editor windows, see Chapter 5.

② Type **Sub** and the macro name, then press Enter to start a new macro.

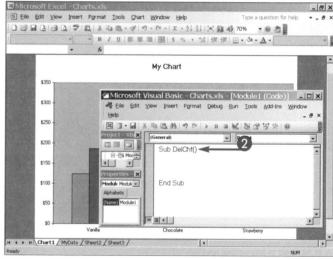

③ Type **charts(***index***).delete**, replacing *index* with your index number.

④ Click ▶ to run the macro.

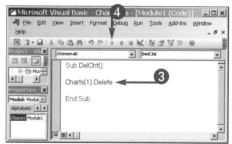

● A deletion warning appears.

5 In the deletion warning, click Delete.

● Excel deletes the chart sheet referenced by your index number.

6 Type **Sub** and the macro name, then press Enter to start a new macro.

7 Type *sheetobject*.**chartobjects**(*index*) .**delete**, replacing *sheetobject* with your worksheet reference and *index* with your chart object index number.

8 Click ▶ to run the macro.

● Excel deletes the embedded chart.

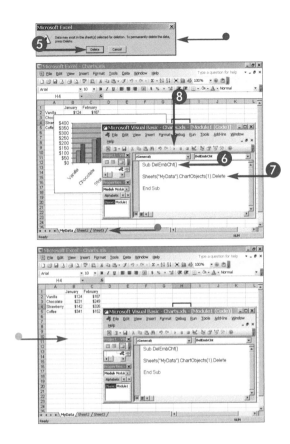

How can I ask the user which chart sheet to delete?

▼ You can write a macro that asks the user for the sheet name with an input box. Type the following statements:

```
Dim variable As String
variable = Input Box("Which chart
sheet?")
Charts(variable).Delete.
```

The macro places an input box on the worksheet, the user types the chart sheet name of the chart sheet to delete and clicks OK, and the chart sheet is deleted. For more information about input boxes, see the section "Request Input with an Input Box" in Chapter 14.

How can I lock a chart so a user cannot change it?

▼ You can lock an embedded chart to protect it from being deleted by a user if you write the *chartobject*.ProtectChartObject = True statement. The locked chart cannot be moved or deleted, but the user can change chart formatting and the chart source data. You can protect a chart sheet from any user changes whatsoever with the statement *chartsheetobject*.Protect (*password*). The *password* argument is optional and case sensitive. Without a password, a user can unlock a chart sheet with the Tools→Protection→ Unprotect Sheet menu.

Change a Chart Data Range

You can change the worksheet data range a chart uses after you create the chart. Changing a chart's data range is often necessary as new series of data are added. For example, a chart of monthly sales needs to change when the next month's data is added.

A *data series* is a group of values that are displayed on the chart. For example, data for sales in three cities for each of three years is grouped by city and by year. The labels for the cities and the years are displayed along the left column and top row of the worksheet data range. When you create

a chart, you decide which groups of values, rows, or columns are the series. The other labels in the data range are the categories.

The data series values are charted along the X-axis, or horizontal axis, of the chart, and the category labels are displayed along the Y-axis, or vertical axis, of the chart. You can add new series to a chart's data range by adding a new Series object to the SeriesCollection collection, as in `chartobject.SeriesCollection.Add Source: =sheetobject.range`.

Change a Chart Data Range

① Type **Sub** and the macro name, then press Enter to start a new macro.

② Type **dim** *variable* **as chart**, replacing *variable* with your variable.

Replace *variable* with your variable throughout this macro.

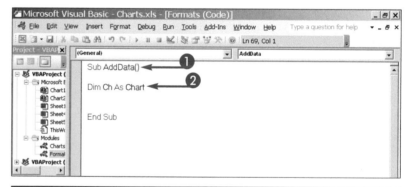

③ Type **set** *variable* = *workbook*.**chart**, replacing *workbook* with your workbook reference and *chart* with your chart reference.

The chart reference can be an index number or a chart sheet name. For more information about workbook references, see Chapter 8.

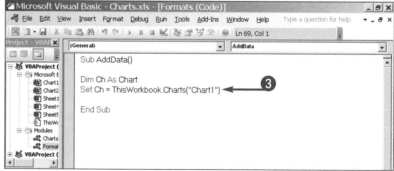

④ Type *variable*.**seriescollection.add**.

⑤ Type **source:=** *worksheet.range*,
replacing *worksheet* and *range* with
the worksheet and range reference
for the new data series.

⑥ Click the View Microsoft Excel button
(⊠) to switch to Excel.

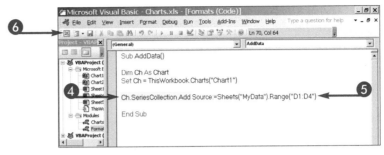

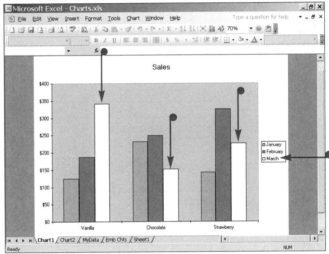

⑦ Run the macro.

Note: *To run a macro, see Chapter 2.*

● The new data series is added to the
chart.

Why does my new data plot incorrectly on the chart?

▼ Your new data series may plot
incorrectly if the data you add is
not a series. For example, if the
chart source data is in series by
columns, and you add a row,
the new row of data is not a
series. To see how series are
plotted, display the chart.
Right-click the chart area and
click Data Source. The Data
Range tab tells you whether the
series are in rows or columns.

How can I delete a series from a chart?

▼ You can delete a series or
category from a chart by using
the Delete method for the
`SeriesCollection` object. You
need to specify the index
number or label of the series to
be deleted. You can delete a
series according to index
number with the statement
workbookobject.chartobject.
seriescollection(index).
`Delete`. You can delete a series
according to series label with the
statement *workbookobject.*
chartobject.series
collection("serieslabel").
`Delete`.

How can I change the series axis?

▼ You can change the axis on
which the series are plotted by
changing the `PlotBy` argument
for the `SetSourceData`
property. Series can be plotted
according to either rows or
columns, and the values for the
`PlotBy` argument are `xlRows`
and `xlColumns`. For example,
to change the axis of a data
series to rows, you can write the
statement *chartobject.*
`SetSourceData Source:`
=sheetobject.datarange,
`PlotBy:=xlRows`.

Change a Chart Type

Y ou can change the chart type for an existing chart by writing a macro that sets the `ChartType` property, using any of the built-in constant values for chart types. You can also use the `PlotBy` property to change how chart series are plotted.

Chart type can have a big impact on the message the audience receives. Charts are a good way to distill data into pictures that an audience can understand quickly, but only if a chart is of a type that your audience understands. For example, only certain audiences can interpret radar charts;

and a bubble chart often needs interpretation, which reduces the value of the chart for sharing information quickly. Column charts are common and easily understood, but to display changes in values over time, a line chart is often a better choice. Also important is the axis on which the data series are plotted.

You can change a chart's type with the statement `chartobject.ChartType = charttypeconstant`. You can change the axis on which data series are plotted with the statement `chartobject. PlotBy = plotbyconstant`.

Change a Chart Type

① Type **Sub** and the macro name, then press Enter to start a new macro.

② Type **dim** *variable* **as chart**, replacing *variable* with your variable.

③ Type **set** *variable* **=** *chartobject*, replacing *variable* with your variable and *chartobject* with your chart object.

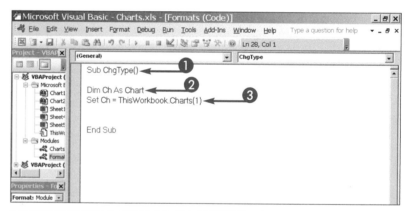

④ Type *variable*.**charttype** =, replacing *variable* with your variable.

An Auto List appears.

⑤ In the Auto List, double-click a ChartType constant.

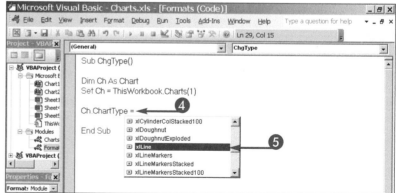

6 Type *variable.* **PlotBy** =, replacing *variable* with your variable.

7 In the Auto List that appears, double-click a PlotBy constant.

8 Click the Run Sub/UserForm button (▶) to run the macro.

9 Click ⊠ to switch to Excel.

● Excel displays the chart with the specified ChartType and PlotBy properties.

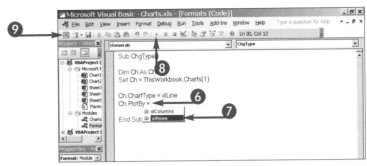
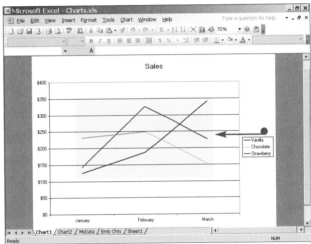

The lines in my line chart are very faint. How can I make the lines heavier?

▼ You can format the weight of a series line in a line chart by writing the statement `chartobject.SeriesCollection(seriesindex.Border.Weight = lineweightconstant`. You can identify and format individual series lines by their index numbers. The line weight constants are xlHairline, xlThin, xlMedium, and xlThick. You can also change the line colors with the `Border` property, as in the statement `chartobject.SeriesCollection(seriesindex).Border.ColorIndex = 3`, which makes the line for the indexed series red.

Why do I not get an Auto List when I type an equal sign in a statement?

▼ One reason why you may not get an Auto List is that Auto List Members is not turned on. In the Visual Basic Editor, click Tools→Options, then click the Editor tab and make sure the Auto List Members check box is marked (☐ changes to ☑). Another reason why you may not get an Auto List is that the editor does not know what kind of object you are referring to. If you declare and use variables in your code, you are more likely to get Auto Lists.

Modify Chart Fonts

You can write macro statements to set or change the font of any text object in a chart. Every object that has associated text, including the chart title, axis titles, legend, and data labels, has a `Font` object that you can format.

The `Font` object enables you to set the font properties for all text items. By setting the `Font` properties in your macro code, you can ensure that all your chart text is uniform. You can set the font properties for the entire chart by setting the font for the `ChartArea` object. All the objects in the

chart use all the ChartArea font settings unless you change the font properties for specific objects. For example, you can set the font properties uniformly for every object in the chart with the statement `chartobject.ChartArea.Font.properties`. Then you can set the chart title font to be different with the statement `chartobject.ChartTitle.Font.properties`.

You can make a macro more efficient and easier to read and write if you use `With` blocks in your code for all the font formatting for a specific chart item. For more information about With blocks, see Chapter 15.

Modify Chart Fonts

① Type **Sub** and the macro name, then press Enter to start a new macro.

② Type **dim** *variable* **as chart**, replacing *variable* with your variable.

③ Type **set** *variable* = *chartobject*, replacing *variable* with your variable and *chartobject* with your chart object.

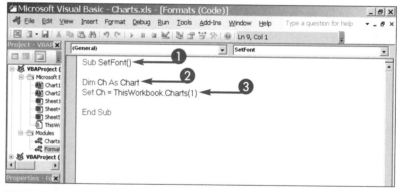

④ Type **with variable**, replacing *variable* with your variable.

⑤ Type **.ChartArea.Font.Name = "fontname"**, replacing *fontname* with your font name.

⑥ Type more font property statements for specific chart objects.

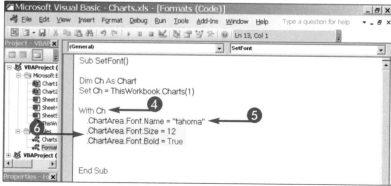

⑦ Type **end with**.

⑧ Click ▶ to run the macro.

⑨ Click 🔳 to switch to Excel.

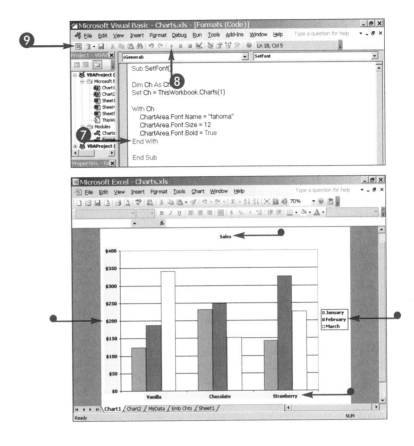

● Excel formats the specified object fonts.

Why does my chart font size change when the chart size changes?

▼ Most text objects in a chart have an `AutoScaleFont` property which by default is set to True. The `AutoScaleFont` property changes the size of the font automatically when the size of the chart changes. To prevent the change in font size when the chart size changes, you can set the `AutoScaleFont` property to False.

Why do I get an error when I set font formatting for a chart title?

▼ If the chart already has a title, you need only write the statements to format the existing title. But if the chart does not have a title, you get an error because there is no title object to format. If the chart does not have a title, you can create one with the statements `chartobject.HasTitle = True` and `ChartTitle.Text = "titletext"`, and then format the title.

How can I nest With blocks to make the macro more efficient?

▼ You can nest `With` blocks by writing an internal `With` block for every set of statements that share the same object. For example, you can write a `With` block to set `ChartArea` font properties, and nest an internal `With` block for all the font properties for the ChartTitle. Make sure you write an `End With` statement to close every `With` block.

Add a Data Table to a Chart

You can add a data table to a chart to display the table of values that are plotted on the chart. Data values plotted on a chart can come from different ranges of data in a worksheet, and a data table displays all the data concisely in a single table regardless of where charted data sources are.

A DataTable object stores the data that is charted in a chart. The Chart object has a HasDataTable property that you can set to either True or False. To display a data table attached to the bottom border of a chart, write the statement chartobject.HasDataTable = True.

After you set the data table to display with the chart, you can format the data table using its own properties. For example, the DataTable object has a Font property, which has its own properties such as Name, Size, Bold, and so forth. The DataTable object also has a Border property with all the Border properties such as ColorIndex, Weight, and LineStyle. When you set several properties for a single object such as Font or Border, you can make the macro more efficient and easier to read by using a With block.

Add a Data Table to a Chart

① Type **Sub** and the macro name, then press Enter to start a new macro.

② Type **dim** *variable* **as chart**, replacing *variable* with your variable.

Replace *variable* with your variable throughout this macro.

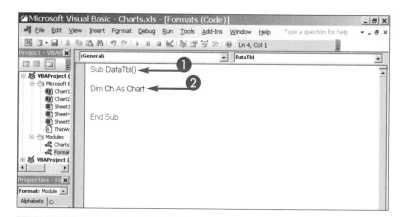

③ Type **set** *variable* = *chartobject*, replacing *chartobject* with your workbook and chart object reference.

④ Type *variable*.**hasdatatable = true**.

⑤ Type **with** *variable*.**datatable**.

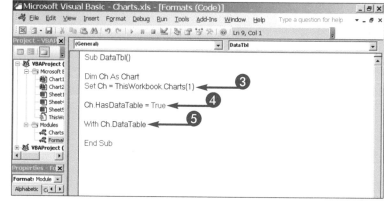

⑥ Type data table formatting statements, beginning each with a period.

⑦ Type **end with**.

⑧ Click ▶ to run the macro.

⑨ Click ⊠ to switch to Excel.

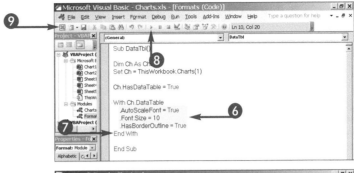

● Excel adds a formatted data table to the chart.

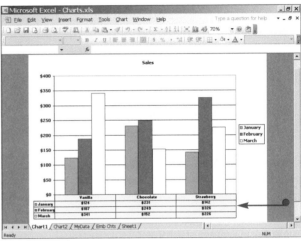

How can I chart separated ranges of data?

▼ You can chart separated ranges of data — which is to say, data series that are not contiguous ranges on the worksheet — by referencing separate series ranges in the chart's SetSourceData method. For example, if you want to chart data series that are on rows 1 and 4 in a worksheet, you can set the chart's source data with the statement *chartobject.* SetSourceData Source:= *worksheet.*Range ("A1:D1, A4:D4"). This example statement charts the data in cells A1:D1 and cells A4:D4 in the same chart, as if they were contiguous data ranges.

How can I show a data table without the chart legend attached?

▼ You can show a data table without the chart legend attached by setting the data table's ShowLegendKey method to False, as in the statement *chartobject.*ShowLegendKey = False. The default setting for the method is True, and a chart only needs one legend; so if you want to show the legend in the data table and not in the chart, you can hide the chart legend with the statement *chartobject.*HasLegend = False.

Customize a Chart Axis

You can customize an axis in a chart by using the various properties of the `Axis` object, which is part of the Axes collection for a chart. The chart axes in a two-dimensional chart consist of the category axis, which is the X-axis or horizontal axis in a column chart, and the values axis, which is the Y-axis or vertical axis in a column chart. In a 3-D chart, there is a third series axis.

You can identify the axes in your code as the xlValue axis, which is the values axis, and the xlCategory axis, which is the categories axis. In a 3-D chart, the third axis is identified by the constant xlSeriesAxis.

You can customize each axis using the `AxisTitle`, `Border`, `Gridlines`, `DisplayUnitLabel`, and `TickLables` objects, each of which has its own set of formatting properties.

You can make a macro more efficient by using a `With` block to set several properties of the same axis. Use a different `With` block for each axis. For more information about `With` blocks, see Chapter 15.

Customize a Chart Axis

① Type **Sub** and the macro name, then press Enter to start a new macro.

② Type **dim** *variable* **as chart**, replacing *variable* with your variable.

③ Type **set** *variable* = *chartobject*, replacing *variable* with your variable and *chartobject* with your workbook and chart object reference.

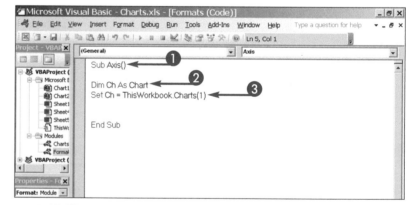

④ Type **with** *variable*.**axes(***axis***)**, replacing *variable* with your variable and *axis* with your axis constant.

⑤ Type **.hastitle = true**.

⑥ Type **.axistitle.text = "***titletext***"**, replacing *titletext* with your title text.

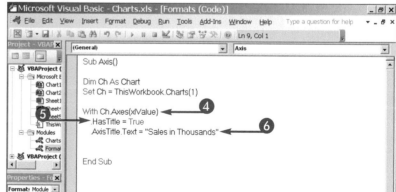

7 Type other formatting statements for the axis referenced in the `With` block.

8 Type **end with**.

9 Click ▶ to run the macro.

10 Click ⊠ to switch to Excel.

● Excel formats the specified axis.

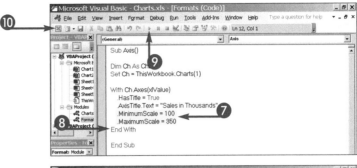

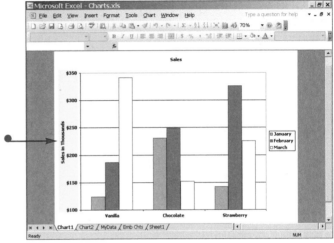

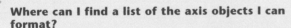

Where can I find a list of the axis objects I can format?

▼ You can find a list of all the axis objects in the Object Browser. To open the Object Browser in the Visual Basic Editor, click View→Object Browser. You can also press F2 to open the Object Browser. In the Classes list, click Axis. All the Axis child objects, methods, and properties are listed in the Members of Axis list in the right-hand pane. To close the Object Browser, click ⊠ in the upper-right corner of the browser window.

How can I add a secondary axis to a chart?

▼ You can add a secondary axis, an axis on the right-hand side of a chart, by adding an AxisGroup to the chart's SeriesCollection. A secondary axis is very useful for displaying related data that has very different values — for example, a chart of house prices versus number of houses sold — and is most useful in a line chart. To add a secondary axis, identify the data series you want to plot on the secondary axis according to index number, then write the statements *chartobject*. SeriesCollection(*seriesindex*).Select and *chartobject*.SeriesCollection(*seriesindex*). AxisGroup = 2.

Synchronize Two Charts

Y ou can write a macro to display two embedded charts for similar data from separate data ranges. If the charts are displayed side-by-side on a worksheet, they can be easily compared. However, if the data are dissimilar enough that the charts have different value axis scales, the charts give misleading visual information.

You can set the value axis scales in two charts to be the same — no matter what the value axis scale is — so that the data on the two charts is truly comparable. To set the value axis scales in two charts to be the same, set the

value axis in the first chart to automatic with the statement `chartobject.Axes(xlValue).MaximumScaleIsAuto = True`. Then set the `MaximumScale` in the second chart equal to the `MaximumScale` in the first chart.

This macro assumes that you have two embedded chart objects displayed on the same worksheet, and that you have named the chart objects for easy identification in your code. You can name a chart when you create the chart by using the statement `chartobject.Name = "chartname"`. For more information about embedded charts, see Chapter 17.

Synchronize Two Charts

① Arrange your editor and Excel windows so you can see both windows.

Note: To arrange the Excel and editor windows, see Chapter 5.

② Type **Sub** and the macro name, then press Enter to start a new macro.

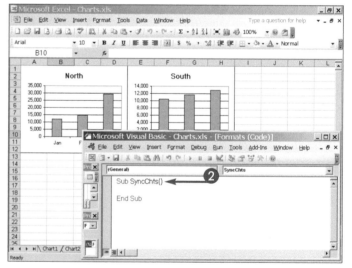

③ Type **dim** *variable* **as chart,** *variable2* **as chart**, replacing *variable* with the first chart variable and *chart2* with the second chart variable.

④ Type **set** *variable* **= sheetobject.chartobjects ("***chartname***").chart**, replacing *variable* with the first chart variable and *chartname* with the first chart name.

⑤ Repeat step **4** for the second chart.

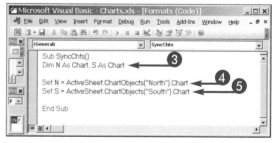

296

⑥ Type *variable*.**axes(xlvalue)** **.maximumscaleisauto = true**, replacing *variable* with the first chart variable.

⑦ Type *variable2*.**Axes(xlValue).MaximumScale** **= *variable*.Axes(xlValue).MaximumScale**, replacing *variable2* with the second chart variable and *variable* with the first chart variable.

⑧ Click ▶ to run the macro.

● The charts have the same value axis scales. The data can be easily compared.

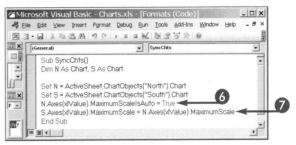

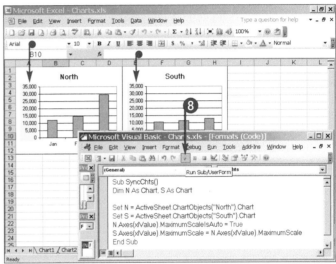

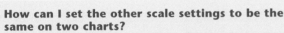

How can I set the other scale settings to be the same on two charts?

▼ You can use similar statements to set the other scale settings to be the same between the two charts. For example, to set the same minimum scale value for each chart's value axis, write the statement `firstchartobject.Axes(xlValue).MinimumScale = secondchartobject.Axes(xlValue).MinimumScale`. Some other scale properties include `HasMajorGridlines` and `HasMinorGridlines`, which have `True` or `False` values, and `MajorGridlines` and `MinorGridlines`, which have `Border` and `Color` properties. To find all the `Axis` object properties, open the Object Browser and click Axis in the Classes list. For more information about the Object Browser, see Chapter 6.

How can I format all my charts the same?

▼ You can format all your charts the same by formatting one chart, saving the chart format as a custom format, and then applying the custom format to other charts. To create a custom format, format the chart, then write the macro statments `chartobject.Activate` and `Application.AddChartAutoFormat Chart:=ActiveChart, Name:="formatname"`. Replace *formatname* with the new custom format name. This macro saves and names the custom format. To apply the custom format to another chart, write a new macro with the statement `chartobject.ApplyCustomType ChartType:=xlUserDefined, TypeName:="formatname"`, replacing *formatname* with the custom format name.

Add a Series Trendline

You can write a macro statement to add a trendline to a data series. Trendlines show a variety of different types of trends in data values, including the most common — linear — and logarithmic, polynomial, exponential, power, and moving average. The kind of data you are charting determines which type of trendline is appropriate.

You can add a trendline to a specific series of data by using the Trendlines.Add method for the SeriesCollection object. You must identify the series to which you want to add the trendline according to either index number or series name, and then define the type of trendline and other trendline properties in the Add arguments.

Trendlines in a chart are graphical representations of a line equation based on the data values in the series. You can display the line equation by setting the DisplayEquation argument to True, and display the R-squared value by setting the DisplayRSquared argument to True. For a trendline in scientific data, these two arguments display valuable information on the chart.

The trendline constant values for the Type argument are xlLinear, xlLogarithmic, xlExponential, xlPolynomial, xlMovingAvg, or xlPower. The Type argument is optional. If you do not enter a type argument, the default value is xlLinear.

Add a Series Trendline

① Type **Sub** and the macro name, then press Enter to start a new macro.

② Type **dim** *variable* **as chart**, replacing *variable* with your variable.

③ Type **set** *variable* = *chartobject*, replacing *variable* with your variable and *chartobject* with your chart object.

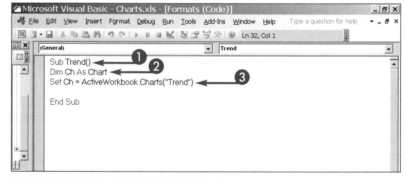

④ Type *variable*.**seriescollection**(*index*). **trendlines.add**, replacing *variable* with your variable and *index* with the series index number or name.

A series name must be enclosed in quotes.

⑤ Type **type:=***trendlineconstant*.

The type argument is optional. The default type is xlLinear.

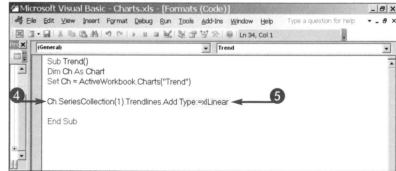

⑥ Type other trendline arguments.

⑦ Click ▶ to run the macro.

⑧ Click 🗷 to switch to Excel.

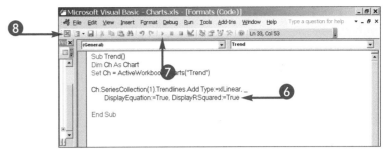

● Excel adds a trendline to the specified data series.

● This trendline displays an equation and R-squared value.

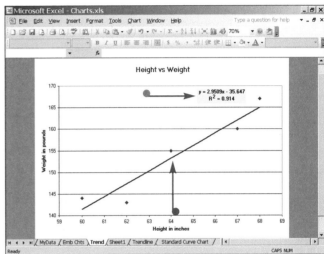

How can I extend a trendline forward or backward to extrapolate uncharted values?

▼ You can extend a trendline forward or backward to extrapolate uncharted values, or to display what you expect values outside the data range to be based on the trend, by using the `Forward` and `Backward` arguments in the `Trendlines.Add` method. You can set the value of the `Forward` or `Backward` argument to the number of series points to which you want to extend the trendline. For example, the statement `SeriesCollection(n).Trendlines.Add Forward:= 3` extends a linear trendline forward by three series points.

How can I add a moving average trendline to a data series?

▼ You can add a moving average trendline to a data series to smooth out fluctuations over time by setting the `Type` argument to `xlMovingAvg`. For a moving average trendline, the *period*, or the number of values that are averaged to calculate a point on the moving average line, must be an integer greater than 1 and less than the number of data points in the series. The period argument `Period:= integer` is required for a moving average trendline.

Create a PivotTable

You can write a macro that creates a PivotTable. A PivotTable displays data from a two-dimensional database and can be manipulated, or pivoted, by the user to display the data in whatever configuration is most useful.

The macro code for a PivotTable can be lengthy and complex, so it is often more efficient to record a macro that creates the PivotTable you want, and then edit the VBA code of the recorded macro for any changes you want.

To create a PivotTable, you first create a data *cache*, or store, that contains all the data for the PivotTable. The PivotCache is part of the workbook, so you use the statement `ActiveWorkbook.PivotCaches.Add` to create a

new cache. The `Add` method has two arguments, `SourceType` and `SourceData`, and is followed by the `CreatePivotTable` method, which has two arguments, `TableDestination` and `TableName`. These statements create the PivotCache and PivotTable, and are followed by a `With` block that creates the starting PivotFields. For example, the statement
`sheetobject.PivotTables("tablename").`
`PivotFields("fieldname").Orientation =`
`xlDataField` creates a data field in the PivotTable for the *fieldname* field in the database.

The macro creates a PivotTable on the active worksheet, after which the PivotTable can be manipulated on the worksheet.

Create a PivotTable

① Type **Sub** and the macro name, then press Enter to start a new macro.

② Type **activeworkbook.pivotcaches.add**.

③ Type **(sourcetype:=xldatabase, sourcedata:="***datarange***")**, replacing *datarange* with your worksheet and range reference.

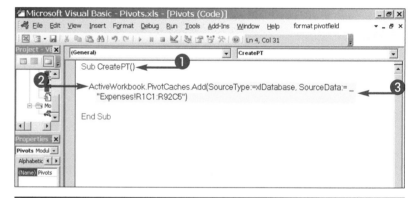

④ Type **.createpivottable tabledestination: =range("***cellreference***"), tablename: ="***tablename***"**, replacing *cellreference* with the cell reference for the upper-left corner of the new PivotTable and *tablename* with your PivotTable name.

⑤ Type **with**.

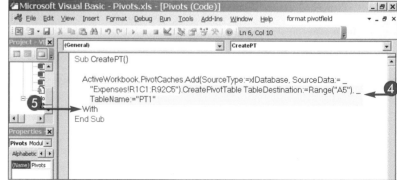

6 Type **activesheet.pivottables(**"*tablename*"**)**, replacing *tablename* with your PivotTable name.

7 Type **.pivotfields(**"*fieldname*"**).orientation =** *orientation*, replacing *fieldname* with a field name in the original database and *orientation* with an orientation constant.

8 Repeat step **7** to add other fields and orientations.

A PivotTable needs a data field with data that can be calculated. By default, the Data field calculation is Sum.

9 Type **end with**.

10 Click the View Microsoft Excel button (⊠) to switch to Excel.

11 Run the macro.

Note: To run a macro, see Chapter 2.

● Excel creates a new PivotTable.

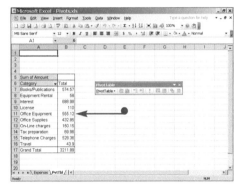

How can I find the list of orientation constants?

▼ There are five constants: xlColumnField, xlDataField, xlHidden, xlPageField, and xlRowField.You can find this list of xlPivotFieldOrientation constants in the VBA Help files. Type **xlPivotFieldOrientation constants** in the Ask A Question box and press Enter. Click the Orientation Property link in the Search Results pane, and then click the Orientation Property as it applies to CubeField and PivotField Objects link in the Help window. Finally, click the xlPivotFieldOrientation link in the Help window.

How can I change the layout of the PivotTable after I create it?

▼ You can change the layout of the PivotTable most easily by changing it in the worksheet. Right-click in the PivotTable and click Wizard. In the Step 3 of 3 dialog box of the PivotTable and PivotChart Wizard, click the Layout button. The PivotTable and PivotChart Wizard Layout dialog box shows all the database fields and the current PivotTable layout. You can drag field buttons to the layout positions you want and click OK. Click Finish in the PivotTable and PivotChart Wizard's Step 3 of 3 dialog box to change the PivotTable field layout.

Add PivotTable Fields

Y ou can add fields to an existing PivotTable by using the `AddFields` method with the orientation and `AddToTable` arguments, as in the statement `PivotTablevariable.AddFields RowFields:="Vendor", addtotable:=True`, which adds the database field named Vendor to the PivotTable in the row field orientation.

The PivotTable object consists of the worksheet reference where the PivotTable is located, and the PivotTable name that was assigned to the PivotTable when it was created.

Because this is a long statement, if you need to add more than one field, creating a variable for the PivotTable object and using a `With` block to list the added fields is more efficient. If you only want to add a single field, a single statement does not need a `With` block.

When you add a field, you assign it an orientation with the orientation argument in the `AddFields` method. There are three orientation arguments: `RowFields`, `ColumnFields`, and `PageFields`. The `AddToTable` argument has a value of `True` or `False`.

Add PivotTable Fields

① Type **Sub** and the macro name, then press Enter to start a new macro.

② Type **dim** *variable* **as pivottable**, replacing *variable* with your variable.

Replace *variable* with your variable throughout this macro.

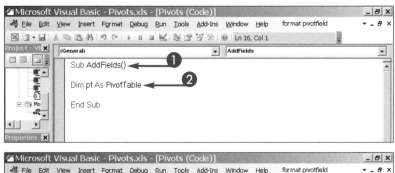

③ Type **set** *variable* = **worksheets(**"*sheetname*"**).pivottables(**"*pivottablename*"**)**, replacing *sheetname* with the worksheet name where the PivotTable is located, and *pivottablename* with the PivotTable name.

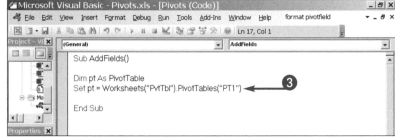

302

④ Type *variable*.**addfields** *orientation*:=**"*fieldname*"**, **addtotable:=true**, replacing *orientation* with the orientation argument constant and *fieldname* with the field name you want to add.

⑤ Click 🖾 to switch to Excel.

⑥ Run the macro.

Note: To run a macro, see Chapter 2.

● Excel adds the field to the PivotTable in the specified orientation.

How can I remove a PivotTable field?

▼ You can remove a field from a PivotTable by using the `PivotTableFields.Orientation = xlHidden` statement, as in `pivottableobject.PivotFields("fieldname").Orientation = xlHidden`. You hide fields that are part of a PivotTable rather than deleting them. To return a field to the PivotTable again, you use the AddFields method. For more information about hiding a field, see the section "Hide Pivot Fields in a PivotTable."

How can I find the name of the PivotTable I want to change?

▼ You can find the name of the PivotTable you want to change by using the Immediate window. In the Visual Basic Editor, click View→Immediate Window. In the Immediate window, type **?worksheets ("*sheetname*").pivottables(*index*).name**. If the worksheet contains only one PivotTable, the *index* number is 1. Press Enter. The name of the PivotTable appears on the next line in the Immediate window. For more information about the Visual Basic Editor windows, see Chapter 5.

Move PivotTable Fields

You can move PivotTable fields from one orientation to another within the PivotTable by using the `PivotFields.Orientation` method with the orientation constant to which you want to move the field. For example, to move a field named Vendor from the row orientation to the page orientation, you can write the statement *worksheetreference*`.PivotTables` *("pivottablename")*`.PivotFields("Vendor").Orientation = xlPageField`.

You can move all the fields to different orientations in a PivotTable by creating a `With` block that lists all the fields and their new orientations. For more information about using `With` blocks, see the section "Simplify Loops with a With Block" in Chapter 15.

To change the orientation of a field, you can use the `PivotFields.Orientation = orientationconstant` statement and give the field a different orientation constant — xlPageField, xlColumnField, or xlRowField. You can also remove a field from a PivotTable by hiding the field with the xlHidden constant. For more information about hiding fields, see the section "Hide PivotFields in a PivotTable."

Move PivotTable Fields

① Type **Sub** and the macro name, then press Enter to start a new macro.

② Type **with worksheets(*"sheetname"*).pivottables (*"tablename"*)**, replacing *sheetname* with the worksheet name and *tablename* with the PivotTable name.

You can identify the PivotTable by index number or by name.

③ Type **.pivotfields(*"fieldname"*). orientation = *orientationconstant***, replacing *fieldname* with the field name you want to move and *orientationconstant* with the new orientation constant.

The orientation constants are xlColumnField, xlDataField, xlHidden, xlPageField, and xlRowField.

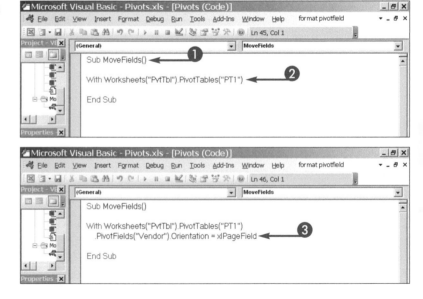

Unable

④ Repeat step **3** for other fields you want to move.

⑤ Type **end with**.

⑥ Click the Run Sub/UserForm button (▷) to run the macro.

⑦ Click ⬛ to switch to Excel.

● Excel moves the fields to new orientations in the PivotTable.

How can I identify the PivotTable I want to rearrange?

▼ You can identify the PivotTable by index number or by name. If the worksheet has only one PivotTable, the index number is (1). You can find the name of the PivotTable you want to change by using the Immediate window. In the Visual Basic Editor, click View→Immediate Window. In the Immediate window, type **?worksheets(***sheetname***)**. **pivottables(***index***).name** and press Enter. The name of the PivotTable appears on the next line in the Immediate window. For more information about the Visual Basic Editor windows, see Chapter 5.

How can I prevent the PivotTable toolbar from appearing after the macro runs?

▼ You can prevent the PivotTable toolbar from appearing after the macro runs by adding the statement `Application.CommandBars ("pivottable").Visible = False` to the end of the macro. The `CommandBars.Visible` method is applied to the `Application` object, which means that Excel hides the PivotTable toolbar for all PivotTables in all workbooks until the program is closed and restarted. To display the PivotTable toolbar again, open the worksheet and display the toolbar the way you would display any toolbar. To display the toolbar programmatically, use the statement `Application.CommandBars ("pivottable").Visible = True`.

Change PivotField Functions

Y ou can write a macro statement to change the calculation function of a PivotTable data field by using the statement Worksheets ("*sheet*"). PivotTables ("*pivottablename*").PivotFields ("*fieldname*").Function = *calculation*. You can identify the worksheet using any method you prefer, and you can identify the PivotTable according to name or index number. The PivotField must be identified by its current name or by index number, and the calculation is a VBA xlConsolidationFunction constant. For more information about worksheet references, see Chapter 9.

The name of a data field is determined in part by the calculation function the field performs, and each time you change the data function, the name of the field changes. For example, if a data field named Amount has the function Sum, the name of the field is Sum of Amount. To change the calculation function, you must reference the current field name in the statement.

To make the macro more efficient and easier to read, declare a variable for the PivotTable and set the variable equal to the worksheet reference and PivotTable name.

① Type **Sub** and the macro name, then press Enter to start a new macro.

② Type **dim** *variable* **as pivottable**, replacing *variable* with your variable.

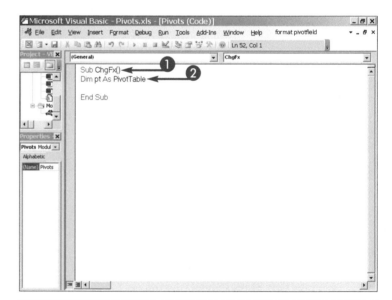

③ Type **set** *variable* = **worksheets("***sheetname***").pivottables("***pivottablename***")**, replacing *sheetname* with the worksheet name and *pivottablename* with the PivotTable name.

Both the worksheet and the PivotTable can be identified by index number or by name.

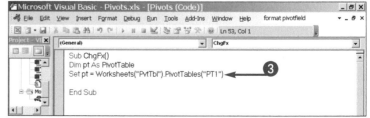

④ Type *variable***.PivotFields(** *"datafieldname"***).
Function** = *functionconstant*, replacing *variable* with your PivotTable variable, *datafieldname* with your data field name, and *functionconstant* with your xlConsolidationFunction constant for calculation.

Remember to use the current field name for the data field in which you want to change the function.

⑤ Click ▶ to run the macro.

⑥ Click 🗷 to switch to Excel.

● The calculation and the data field name change.

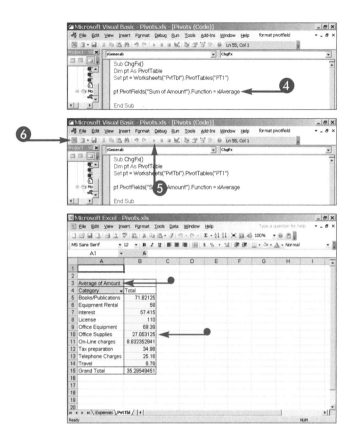

How can I find the source data for a PivotTable?

▼ You can find the source data for a PivotTable by using the Immediate window to find the source data for the PivotTable's PivotCache. Make sure the workbook with the PivotTable is the active workbook. In the Visual Basic Editor, click View➔ Immediate Window. Type **?activeworkbook. PivotCaches(index).sourcedata** in the Immediate window and press Enter. The worksheet and range for the source data appear on the next line in the Immediate window. For more information about the Immediate window, see Chapter 5.

How can I find the constants for the calculation functions?

▼ You can find the constants for the calculation functions in the VBA Help files. In the Visual Basic Editor, type **xlConsolidationFunction** in the Ask A Question box and press Enter. In the Search Results pane, click the ConsolidationFunction Property link. In the Help window that appears, click the blue xlConsolidationFunction link. The list of xlConsolidationFunction constants appears.

PART VI

Hide Pivot Fields in a PivotTable

You can hide a field to remove it from a PivotTable, using the `xlHidden` constant value for the `PivotFields.Orientation` property for the field you want to hide.

Hiding fields is part of the process of programmatically changing the layout of a PivotTable. You can change the layout of a PivotTable by giving the fields different orientations, like changing a column field orientation that displays data in columns to a row field orientation that displays data in rows. When you want to remove a field from the PivotTable display completely, you hide that field.

When you hide a field, you do not delete it. The field data remains part of the PivotCache and is available when you want to display the data in the table again. If you hide all the fields except the calculated data field, Excel reduces the PivotTable to a single row labeled Total, and shows the total amount for the PivotTable in terms of the function assigned to the data field.

To change the orientation of a field without hiding it, you can use the same `PivotFields.Orientation = orientationconstant` statement and give the field a different orientation constant — `xlPageField`, `xlColumnField`, or `xlRowField`.

Hide PivotFields in a PivotTable

① Type **Sub** and the macro name, then press Enter to start a new macro.

② Type **dim** *variable* **as pivottable**, replacing *variable* with your variable.

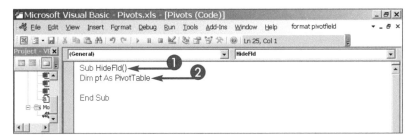

③ Type **set** *variable* = **worksheets** (*"sheetname"*).**pivottables** (*"pivottablename"*), replacing *variable* with your variable, *sheetname* with the worksheet name, and *pivottablename* with the PivotTable name.

You can also identify the worksheet and PivotTable by their index numbers.

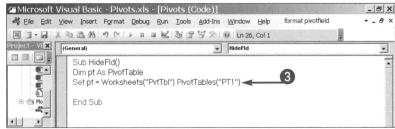

④ Type *variable*.**pivotfields**(*"fieldname"*).**orientation = xlhidden**, replacing *variable* with your variable and *fieldname* with the field name you want to hide.

⑤ Click ▶ to run the macro.

⑥ Click ☒ to switch to Excel.

● Excel removes and hides the field from the PivotTable.

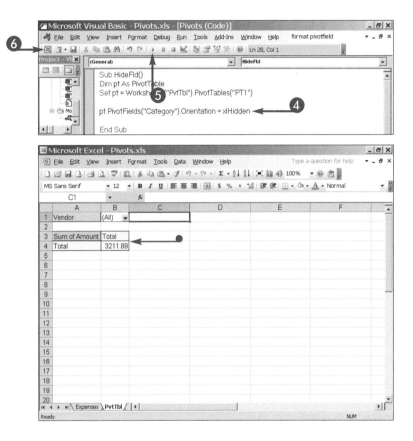

I hid my data field and now my PivotTable is empty. How can I display the data again?

▼ You can display the data again by displaying the data field first. A hidden data field is referred to with its calculated name, as in "Sum of Amount." But when you display the data field again, you refer to it using its original database field name, as in "Amount." Run a macro with the statement `pivottableobject.PivotFields ("datafieldname").Orientation = xlDataField`. This statement replaces the calculable data field in the Data Field orientation and restores the PivotTable to the layout before the data field was hidden.

How can I hide a single item in a field?

▼ You can hide a single item in a field by writing a macro that sets the Visible property for that PivotItem to False. You must designate the `PivotTable` object and the `PivotField` object, and then set the `Visible` property of the `PivotItem` object. For example, the statement `Worksheets("PvtTbl").PivotTables("PT1").PivotFields ("Category").PivotItems("Interest").Visible = False` hides the item labeled "Interest" which is in the field labeled "Category" which is in the PivotTable named "PT1" on the worksheet named "PvtTbl." You can show the item again by running the same macro and setting the `Visible` property to True.

Format Data Fields

Y ou can format a PivotTable quickly by formatting the entire PivotTable object with one of the built-in report or table formats. You can also format a specific field individually, as in setting a different number format in your data field.

To format a PivotTable with a built-in report or table format, use the statement *pivottableobject*.Format *formatconstant*. When you type the statement *pivottableobject*.Format and press the spacebar, an Auto List of report and table format constants appears. You can select the constant you want and run the macro to format the PivotTable.

You can also format the data field with a number format other than the format that the built-in report or table format applies. You can set your own number format for the data field by using the statement *pivottable object*.PivotFields(*"datafieldname"*).Number Format = *"numberformat"*. Type the number format you want between quotes. For example, "$#,##0" formats numbers as currency in whole dollars. You can use any custom format you want in the NumberFormat property.

① Type **Sub** and the macro name, then press Enter to start a new macro.

② Type **dim** *variable* **as pivottable**, replacing *variable* with your variable.

Replace *variable* with your variable throughout this macro.

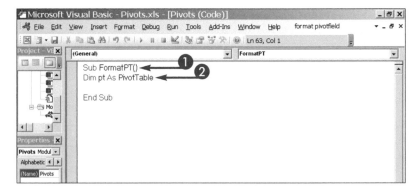

③ Type **set** *variable* = **worksheets** (*"sheetname"*).**pivottables**(*"pivottable name"*), replacing *sheetname* with your worksheet name and *pivottablename* with your PivotTable name.

④ Type *variable*.**format** and a space character.

⑤ Click a report or table constant in the Auto List.

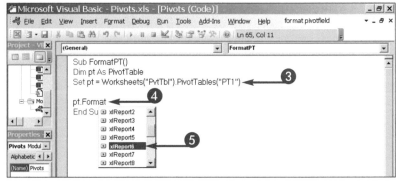

6 Type *variable*.**pivotfields**(*"datafieldname"*). **numberformat** = *"numberformat"*, replacing *datafieldname* with your data field name and *numberformat* with your number format.

Make sure you use the current data field name with the data calculation.

7 Click ⊠ to switch to Excel.

8 Run the macro.

Note: To run a macro, see Chapter 2.

● Excel formats the PivotTable and data field.

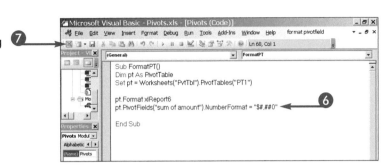

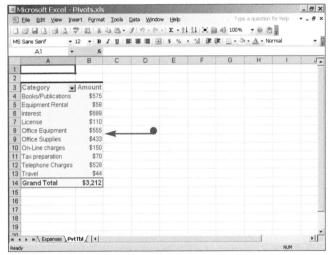

How can I find a list of custom number formats?

▼ You can find a list of custom number formats by opening a worksheet and selecting a cell that contains a number value. Click Format→Cells, then click the Number tab. In the Category list, click Custom. All the format patterns for built-in and custom formats are displayed in the Type list, and the Sample box displays the selected cell's number in the selected format type. You can also create your own custom formats by typing the appropriate characters in the Type box or between the quotes in the macro statement.

How can I refer to my PivotTable object by something other than worksheet and PivotTable names?

▼ You can refer to your PivotTable object worksheet by using the worksheet name between quotes, using the codename, or using the Sheets or Worksheets object index number. You can refer to the PivotTable object's PivotTable by using the PivotTable name that was assigned to the PivotTable when it was programmatically created, or by using the PivotTables object index number. Because a worksheet rarely has more than a single PivotTable, the PivotTables object index number is probably (1).

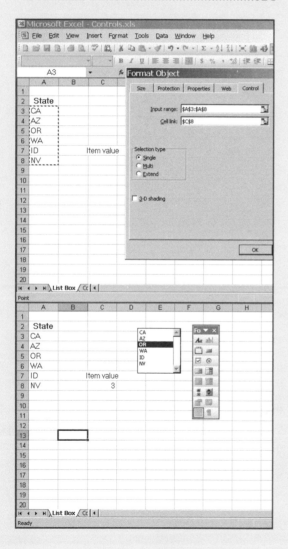

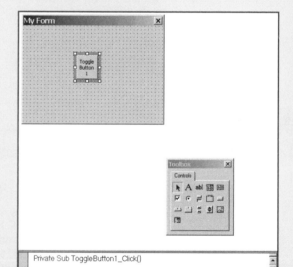

PART VII
USING FORMS AND CONTROLS

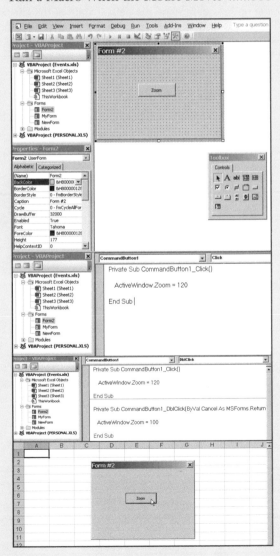

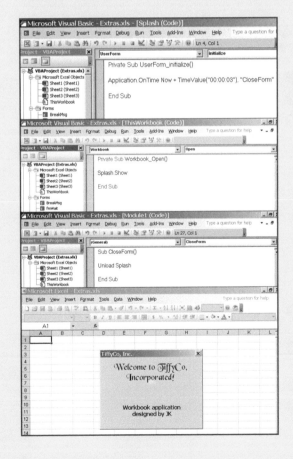

Create a Check Box on a Worksheet

Y ou can create an interactive worksheet without using VBA by creating form controls directly on the worksheet. For example, on a worksheet you can place a check box that, when clicked, enters the value True or False in a specified cell.

The check box enables a user to set the value of a cell to True or False, and you can use that value in other worksheet formulas. For example, you can create a check box on an invoice for overnight shipping, and use the resulting True or False value in a formula that calculates the shipping cost for the order.

When you format the Control properties for the check box, you enter the cell reference in the Cell link box as an absolute reference. You can also click in the Cell link box and then click the worksheet cell you want to enter. You can locate the linked cell as far from the user view as you want.

The Value options determine the default state of the check box. The Mixed option creates a default state that is neither checked nor unchecked, and the value of the linked cell is #N/A until you click the check box.

Create a Check Box on a Worksheet

① Click View.

② Click Toolbars.

③ Click Forms.

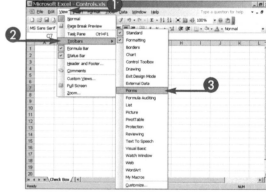

● The Forms toolbar appears on the worksheet.

④ On the Forms toolbar, click the Check Box button (☑).

⑤ Click in the worksheet where you want to paste the new check box.

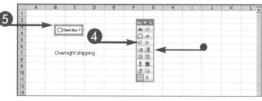

⑥ Right-click the check box.

⑦ Click Format Control.

The Format Control dialog box appears.

8 Click the Control tab.

9 Type the absolute reference for the cell in which you want to enter the value `True` or `False`.

● You can also click the cell you want to enter rather than typing the reference.

10 Click OK.

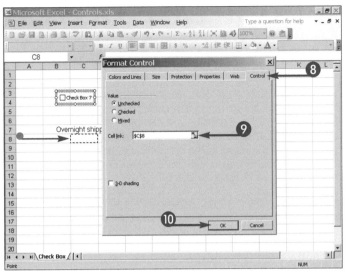

11 Click in the worksheet.

The check box is deselected.

12 Click the check box repeatedly.

● When the check box is marked, the linked cell displays True. When the check box is empty, the linked cell displays False.

How can I rename the check box label?

▼ You can rename the check box label to something more user friendly by right-clicking the check box and clicking Edit Text in the shortcut menu. The insertion point blinks in the check box label. Select the label text and type your new label. To resize the check box to accommodate the new label, you can drag a corner of the dotted border, and you can drag the dotted border to move the entire check box. Click another cell in the worksheet to deselect the check box when you are finished.

How can I change the look of a check box?

▼ You can change the look of a check box by right-clicking the check box and then clicking Format Control on the shortcut menu. You can use the settings on the Colors and Lines tab to change the look of the check box, including the background color behind the label, and the settings for the line around the check box and label. You can also mark the 3-D shading check box on the Control tab to make the check box look three-dimensional.

Build a List Box on a Worksheet

Y ou can create an interactive worksheet without using VBA by creating form controls directly on the worksheet. For example, you can place a list box on a worksheet that enters a numeric value in a specified cell when one of the items in the list is clicked, and then use that value in a formula or macro to return the actual item from the input range list.

When you format the `Control` properties for a list box, you enter the cell reference where the value is entered in the Cell link box. You can locate the linked cell as far from the user view as you want. You enter the range of values for the list box in the Input range box.

Under Selection type, if you select the Single option, the cell in the Cell link box returns the list position of the item that is clicked in the list box. For example, if the first item in the box is clicked, the linked cell returns the value 1. If you select the Multi or Extend option, the cell in the Cell link box is ignored. These options are not usable in a worksheet control.

Build a List Box on a Worksheet

① Click View.

② Click Toolbars.

③ Click Forms.

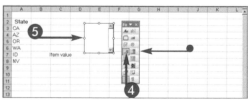

- The Forms toolbar appears on the worksheet.

④ On the Forms toolbar, click the List Box button (🔲).

⑤ Click in the worksheet where you want to paste the list box.

⑥ Right-click the list box.

⑦ Click Format Control.

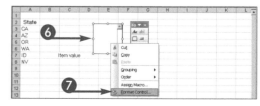

The Format Control dialog box appears.

8 Click the Control tab.

9 In the Cell link box, enter the cell in which you want the numeric value of the list box item returned.

10 Click in the Input range box.

11 Drag to select the range of list entries in the worksheet.

12 Click OK.

The entries appear in the list box.

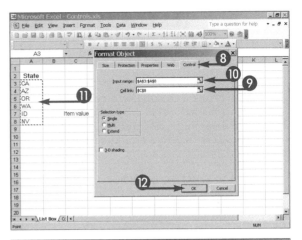

13 Click in the worksheet to deselect the list box.

14 Click each list box item in turn.

- When you click an item, the linked cell displays the value of that list box item.

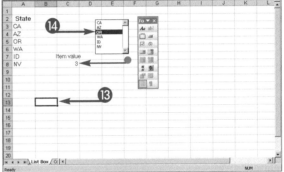

How can I change or add items to my list box list?

▼ You can change list box items by making the changes in the worksheet range. When you change the spelling of an item in the Input range, the list box is automatically updated with the change. You can add more items to your list box list by right-clicking the list box and clicking Format Control. Delete the entry in the Input range box, then drag on the worksheet to select the new range containing the added items. Click OK, and click in the worksheet to deselect the list box.

How can I use the linked cell value in a macro?

▼ You can use the linked cell value in a macro just like a range value. For example, you can write a `Select Case` statement that performs a different macro action depending on the value in the linked cell. You can create a list box of state names, and write a Select Case macro that applies a different sales tax rate depending on the linked cell value that is returned by the selected state. For more information about `Select Case` statements, see Chapter 14.

Build a Combo Box on a Worksheet

Y ou can create a combo box on a worksheet that enters a numeric value in a specified cell when one of the items in the list is clicked, and then use that value in a formula or macro to return the actual item from the input range list.

Though similar to a list box, a combo box takes less space on a worksheet because the list drops open when needed. When you format the Control properties for a combo box, you enter the cell reference where the value is entered in the Cell link box. You enter the range of values for the combo box list in the Input range box.

You can control the length of the combo box list by typing a number in the Drop down lines box. If the number of drop down lines is more than the number of items in the list, the list displays only the items in the list. But if the list contains many items, you can limit the number of items displayed and the user can scroll through the list to see all the items.

① Click View.

② Click Toolbars.

③ Click Forms.

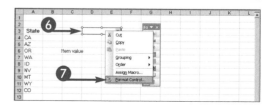

● The Forms toolbar appears on the worksheet.

④ On the Forms toolbar, click the Combo Box button (▦).

⑤ Drag to draw the combo box in the worksheet.

You must draw a horizontal box to create the combo box shape.

⑥ Right-click the combo box.

⑦ Click Format Control.

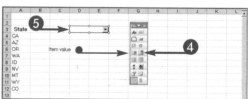

The Format Control dialog box appears.

⑧ Click the Control tab.

⑨ In the Cell link box, enter the cell in which you want the numeric value of the clicked item returned.

⑩ Click in the Input range box.

⑪ Drag to select the range of list entries in the worksheet.

⑫ Click OK.

The entries appear in the combo box.

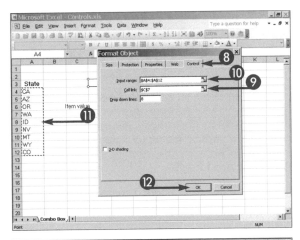

⑬ Click in the worksheet to deselect the combo box.

⑭ Click ⬝ on the combo box.

⑮ Click a combo box item.

- The linked cell displays the value of the clicked combo box item.

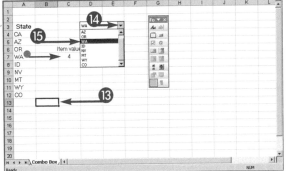

How can I change or add items to my combo box list?

▼ You can change combo box items by making the changes in the worksheet range. When you change the spelling of an item in the Input range, the combo box is automatically updated with the change. You can add more items to your combo box list by right-clicking the combo box and clicking Format Control. Delete the entry in the Input range box, then drag on the worksheet to select the new range containing the added items. Click OK, and click in the worksheet to deselect the combo box.

How can I change the shape of a combo box?

▼ You can change the shape of a combo box by right-clicking the combo box and then clicking in the combo box when the shortcut menu appears. The shortcut menu disappears and the combo box displays handles. You can drag a handle to change the size or shape of the combo box, and you can drag the center of the combo box to move it to a new location on the worksheet. Click in the worksheet to deselect the combo box when you finish.

PART VII

Use Option Buttons on a Worksheet

Y ou can create an interactive worksheet without using VBA by creating form controls directly on the worksheet. For example, you can place option buttons on a worksheet that enter a numeric value in a specified cell when one of the buttons is clicked, and then use that value in a formula.

You can use option buttons when you want the user to select one option from a list of two or more exclusive choices. Only one option can be selected at a time. Multiple option buttons used on the same worksheet are all automatically linked to the same cell; clicking any of the buttons changes the value in the linked cell. The first option button you create enters the value 1 in the linked cell, the second option button you create enters the value 2, and so on.

When you format the `Control` properties for option button, you enter the cell reference in the Cell link box. You can also click in the Cell link box and then click the worksheet cell you want to enter. You can locate the linked cell as far from the user view as you want.

Use Option Buttons on a Worksheet

① Click View.

② Click Toolbars.

③ Click Forms.

● The Forms toolbar appears on the worksheet.

④ On the Forms toolbar, click the Option Button button (⊙).

⑤ Click in the worksheet where you want to paste the new option button.

⑥ Repeat steps **4** to **5** to create more option buttons.

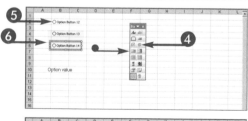

⑦ Right-click any option button.

⑧ Click Format·Control.

320

The Format Control dialog box appears.

9 Click the Control tab.

10 In the Cell link box, type the absolute reference for the cell in which you want to enter the numeric value of the option button.

● You can also click the cell you want to enter rather than typing the reference.

11 Click OK.

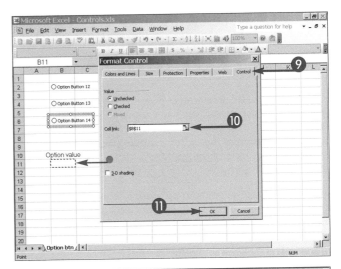

12 Click in the worksheet.

The option buttons are deselected.

13 Click each option button in turn.

● When an option button is marked, the linked cell displays the value of that option button.

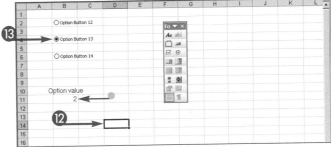

How can I rename an option button label?

▼ You can rename an option button label to something more user friendly by right-clicking the option button and clicking Edit Text in the shortcut menu. The insertion point blinks in the option button label. Select the label text and type your new label. To resize the option button to accommodate the new label, you can drag a corner of the dotted border, and you can drag the dotted border to move the entire option button. Click another cell in the worksheet to deselect the option button when you are finished.

How can I change the look of an option button?

▼ You can change the look of an option button by right-clicking the option button and then clicking Format Control on the shortcut menu. You can use the settings on the Colors and Lines tab to change the look of the option button, including the background color behind the label, and the settings for the line around the option button and label. You can also mark the 3-D shading check box on the Control tab to make the option button look three-dimensional.

Build an Option Group on a Worksheet

Y ou can create an interactive worksheet without using VBA by creating form controls directly on the worksheet. For example, you can place option buttons on a worksheet that enter a numeric value in a specified cell when one of the buttons is clicked, and then use that value in a formula.

All the option buttons created on a worksheet are automatically linked to the same cell; but you can use more than one group of option buttons on a worksheet if you place a group of option buttons in a group box. All the option buttons in a group box are automatically linked to the same cell, but are separate from any other option buttons on the worksheet.

The option buttons in a group box work just like the option buttons on a worksheet: they enable the user to select one choice from a list of two or more choices within the same group box, and you can then use the value entered by the selected option button in worksheet formulas. For more information about option buttons, see the section "Use Option Buttons on a Worksheet."

Build an Option Group on a Worksheet

① Click View.

② Click Toolbars.

③ Click Forms.

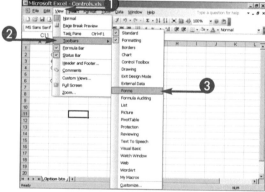

- The Forms toolbar appears on the worksheet.

④ On the Forms toolbar, click the Group Box button (▣).

⑤ Drag to draw the group box in the worksheet.

You can draw an empty group box and create new option buttons inside it, or draw a group box around an existing group of option buttons.

⑥ Right-click any option button in the group box.

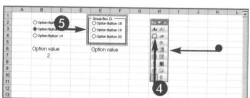

⑦ Click Format Control.

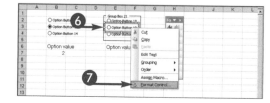

The Format Control dialog box appears.

⑧ Click the Control tab.

⑨ In the Cell link box, type the absolute reference for the cell in which you want to enter the numeric value of the option button.

● You can also click the cell you want to enter rather than typing the reference.

⑩ Click OK.

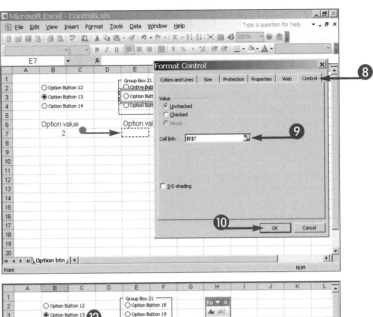

⑪ Click in the worksheet.

The option button is deselected.

⑫ Click each option in the group box button in turn.

● When an option button is marked, the linked cell displays the value of that option button.

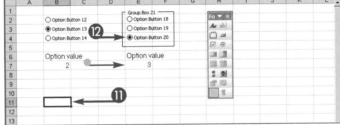

How can I rename a group box label?

▼ You can rename a group box label to something more user friendly by right-clicking the group box and clicking Edit Text in the shortcut menu. The insertion point blinks in the group box label. Select the label text and type your new label. You can also resize the group box by dragging a corner of the dotted border, and you can drag the dotted border to move the entire group box. Click another cell in the worksheet to deselect the group box when you are finished.

How can I use group boxes with other controls?

▼ You can place other controls, such as check boxes and list boxes, inside group boxes to group the controls visually, for better user understanding, but group boxes only affect the behavior of the option buttons on a worksheet. You can have more than one group box of option buttons on a worksheet, and each group of option buttons functions independently. Any option buttons that are not in a group box function together as another group.

PART VII

Attach a Macro to a Worksheet Command Button

On a worksheet, you can create a command button that runs a macro. You can find the Command Button button on the Forms toolbar. Unlike most of the other controls on the Forms toolbar, a command button's only function is to run a macro.

After you create a command button, you can assign a macro to the button immediately, or you can format the button text and then assign a macro to the button. If you plan on editing or formatting the button label or changing the size or shape of the button, selecting the button before you assign a macro is much easier. Before a macro is assigned, you can select the button for formatting by clicking it. After a macro is assigned, you can only select the button for formatting by right-clicking it and then either choosing a command from the shortcut menu or clicking the button's dotted border.

When you are ready to assign a macro, you can right-click the button and click Assign Macro on the shortcut menu.

Attach a Macro to a Worksheet Command Button

1 Click View.

2 Click Toolbars.

3 Click Forms.

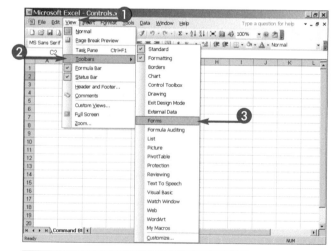

- The Forms toolbar appears on the worksheet.

4 Click the Command Button button (▣).

5 Drag to draw a button on the worksheet.

- When you release the mouse button, the Assign Macro dialog box appears.

6 Click Cancel.

You can format the button now and assign a macro later.

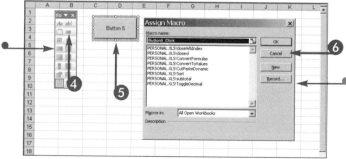

7 Drag to select the button text.

8 Format your label using buttons on the Formatting toolbar.

9 Type your label text.

10 Click in the worksheet.

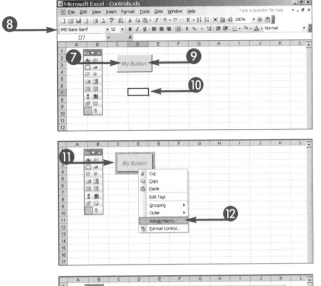

11 Right-click the button.

The shortcut menu appears.

12 Click Assign Macro.

The Assign Macro dialog box appears.

13 Click the macro you want to assign.

14 Click OK.

● The command button is complete.

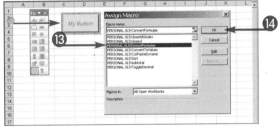

How can I set a command button to print with the worksheet?

▼ By default command buttons do not print when a worksheet prints, but you may want to print a worksheet with its command buttons for purposes of design review. To set a command button to print with the worksheet, right-click the command button and click Format Control in the shortcut menu that appears. Click the Properties tab. Click the Print object check box (☐ changes to ☑), then click OK. Repeat this procedure for each command button you want to print.

How can I assign different formatting to characters in a button label?

▼ You can assign different formatting to characters in a label by selecting the individual characters and using the buttons on the Formatting toolbar to format their font, size, and color, or to apply italics, bold, and underline. You can also format individual characters as superscript, subscript, or strikethrough by right-clicking the selected characters and clicking Format Control. The Format Control dialog box displays a Font tab containing these settings when individual characters are selected. When the entire button is selected, an Alignment tab enables you to set text alignment and orientation.

Understand Forms

Y ou can create custom dialog boxes, or *forms*, that a user can interact with in a workbook. Forms are a powerful programming tool, enabling you to get input from the user in a controlled manner. A form consists of three parts: the form, the controls, and the VBA code. All three parts relate closely to each other.

Interactive Forms

The form itself is the container for the controls with which a user interacts. The form is a UserForm object. You display a form by writing a macro with the statement `formname.Show` in a project module. You can run the macro to display a specific form by any means appropriate to your workbook. You can run the macro from the Macro dialog box, or by attaching the form-display macro to a toolbar button or graphical object, or by calling the form-display macro from another macro, or by triggering the form-display macro with an event such as `Workbook_Open`.

You can make the form remain visible while a user works in a worksheet by including the modal property False in the statement to open the form `formname.Show False`. When a form is *modal*, it retains the *focus* as long as it is open. Focus means that an object is ready to receive user input, and when a form is modal it does not allow any other object to receive user input. A good example of this is Excel's Options dialog box — as long as it is open, you can make choices in the dialog box, but you cannot work in the worksheet until you close the dialog box. The default modal property of a UserForm object is True, meaning the form is modal.

Form Controls

The controls on the form are the objects with which the user interacts. The controls run their own macros, which are written in the form Code window. You can switch between the form and the form Code window by clicking the View Object and View Code buttons. You can start a macro for a new control by double-clicking the control. There are useful standard conventions for naming controls and forms to make them easy to identify. Typically control and form names begin with three lower-case letters that identify the type of object. For example, button names begin with the letters *btn* or *cmd*. Form names typically begin with *frm*. Check box names begin with *chk*, and so forth. These naming conventions are optional, but can make your code easier for other users to read and understand quickly.

VBA Code

The VBA code is part of the form. The form itself is opened with a macro in a module, but the functionality of the open form is controlled by VBA code in the form Code window. The form Code window is opened by double-clicking the form or any control on the form, or by clicking the View Code button above the Project window.

Most of the controls in a form respond to *events*, actions such as clicking the object with a mouse or changing a selection. For more information about events, see Chapter 22.

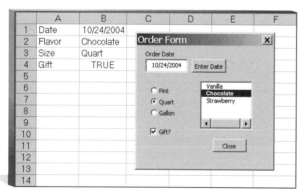

Parts of the UserForm Window in the Visual Basic Editor

Ⓐ View Code

Click to view the form Code window containing the macros for the UserForm and all the controls in that form.

Ⓑ View Object

Click to view the form and controls.

Ⓒ Project Window

Lists under the Forms folder icon all the forms that are part of a workbook project.

Ⓓ Form Icons

Double-click a form icon to open that form. You can name a form in the form's Name property in the Properties window.

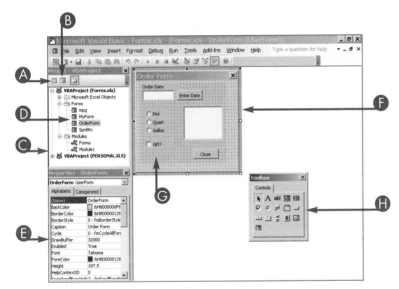

Ⓔ Properties Window

Displays the properties for the currently selected object, either the form itself or a control on the form.

Ⓗ Toolbox

Source of the controls you place on the form. You can click a Toolbox button, then click or drag to draw the tool in the form.

Ⓖ Controls

Objects that give the form its functionality. A user interacts with the controls on a form.

Ⓕ User Form

Background form on which you place controls that run macros.

Create a
Custom Form

Y ou can create custom forms, or dialog boxes, that you can use to run macros or ask for user input in a worksheet. Forms give the user a graphical interface in which they can click buttons or type input values for the macros to use.

You can create a form in the Visual Basic Editor by inserting a UserForm. When you create a new UserForm, a Forms folder appears in the workbook project tree in the editor's Project window. You can change the name of a UserForm to something more recognizable in a macro by changing the

Name property in the Properties window. For more information about Visual Basic Editor windows, see Chapter 5.

You can customize a UserForm by resizing it, changing its caption and font, adding pictures, and adding controls from the Toolbox to run your macros and accept user input. You can do all of the UserForm customizing by changing the properties in the Properties window and by adding controls from the Toolbox.

Create a Custom Form

① Select the VBAProject in which you want to create a new form.

Note: To open the Project and Properties windows, see Chapter 5.

② Click Insert.

③ Click UserForm.

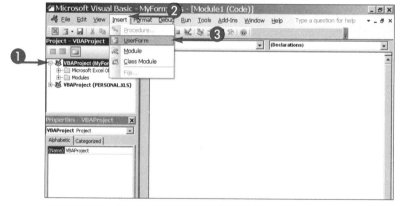

The editor creates a new form with the default name and caption UserForm1.

④ In the Name field in the Properties window, type a new name for the form.

The Name is not the caption. The Name identifies the form as an object and has the same naming rules as a macro.

⑤ Type a caption in the Caption field in the Properties window.

● The Caption appears on the form.

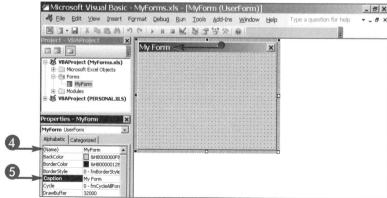

328

6 Click in the form.

● The Toolbox appears.

7 Add controls to the forms using the Toolbox.

Note: To create controls on forms, see the other sections in this chapter.

8 Click the Run Sub/UserForm button (▶) to switch to Excel and display the form.

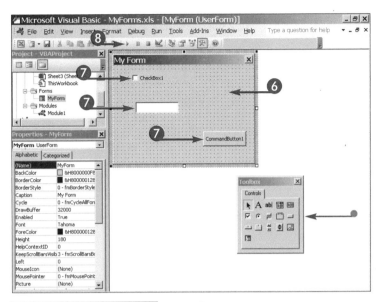

● Excel displays the form.

● You can click the close button in the upper-right corner of the form to return to the Visual Basic Editor.

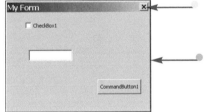

How can I open the form from within a worksheet?

▼ You can create a macro that shows the form and runs the macro from the worksheet. You can also call the form from within any macro. To show the form, you can write the statement *formname*.Show. The Show method has a Modal argument that is set to True by default. When a form is modal, the form retains the focus and you cannot work in the worksheet with the form open. To make the form nonmodal, so that you can work in the worksheet with the form open, write the statement *formname*.Show False.

How can I close the form with a button?

▼ You can create a command button that cancels the form. The command button runs the macro statement Unload Me and an event handler that runs when the button is clicked. The keyword Unload removes a form from memory, and the keyword Me refers to the current form. For more information about command buttons, see the section "Add a Command Button to a Form." For more information about events, see Chapter 22.

Save a Custom Form Template

Y ou can create a custom form template to save yourself time and effort when you create many similar custom forms, including those in other workbook projects. Custom forms reside in the workbook project in which you create the form. You can copy a custom form to another project if both projects are open, and then change all the settings for the controls in the copied form. But you can copy a custom form more efficiently if you create a new custom form with no macros attached to the controls, and then save the form by exporting it to a file on your hard drive. You can then import the custom form template into any project and customize the controls with macros in that project.

You can use the custom form template in a different project by importing the file in which you saved the template. When you import a form template, the Visual Basic Editor creates a new UserForm and assigns the UserForm a sequentially numbered name that you can change.

Save a Custom Form Template

① Create a new UserForm as your template.

Note: *To create a custom form, see the section "Create a Custom Form."*

② Click File.

③ Click Export File.

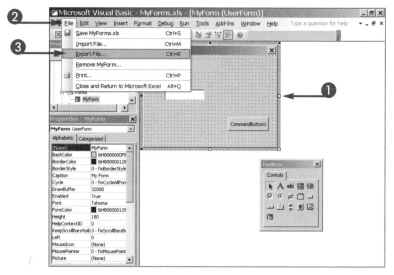

The Export File dialog box appears.

④ Click ⊡ to navigate to the folder where you want to save the file.

⑤ Type the form file name in the File name box.

⑥ Click Save.

The custom form template is a file saved in the specified folder.

Import a Custom Form Template

① In the Project window, click the project into which you want to import the form.

Note: For more information about editor windows, see Chapter 5.

② Click File.

③ Click Import File.

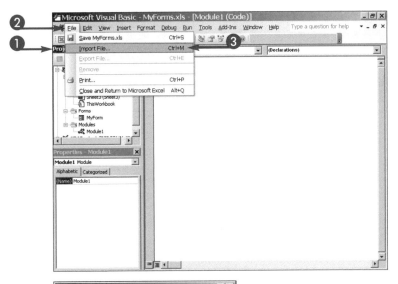

The Import File dialog box appears.

④ Click ⏷ to navigate to the folder where you saved the file.

⑤ Click the name of the custom form template file.

⑥ Click Open.

The Visual Basic Editor adds the imported form to the current project.

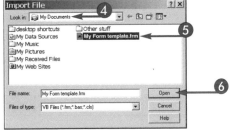

How can I export and import the macros that accompany the form template?

▼ You can export and import the macros that accompany the form template by exporting and importing the module that contains the macros. The macros that are attached to the controls on the form, such as the `button_Click` macro `Unload Me` in a Cancel button, travel with the controls. The macros associated with the form can be written in a specific module which is exported and imported along with the custom form. For more information about exporting a module, see the section "Share Macros by Exporting a Module" in Chapter 23.

What other properties travel with a custom form template?

▼ A custom form template carries with it all the code and properties that are directly attached to the form and controls, including the control tab order and all event handlers. *Tab order* is the order in which the focus moves from control to control when the user presses the Tab key, and *event handlers* are macros that run in response to events such as clicking. For more information about tab order, see the section "Set the Tab Order for Form Controls." For more information about events, see Chapter 22.

Add a Command Button to a Form

You can add command buttons that run macros in a form. Typically, forms include a command button to close the form, but they can also include command buttons to perform other functions such as printing a worksheet, showing a subtotaled view, or any other procedure for which a macro exists.

Command buttons typically run their procedures at a `Click` event. When the button is clicked, the macro you wrote for that button runs. When the button has the focus, indicated by a dotted line just inside the button border, pressing the Enter key has the same effect as clicking the mouse button.

To create the macro that a command button runs, you double-click the button in the form in the Visual Basic Editor. A new macro with a `Click` event opens, and you can type your statements between the Sub and End Sub lines. The macro to close a form is Unload Me. Unload and Me are both keywords that VBA recognizes. You can also create command buttons to run any macro. You can type an entire macro, or you can call the macro by name if the macro resides in the same workbook project.

Add a Command Button to a Form

① Create or open a custom form.

Note: *To create a form, see the section "Create a Custom Form."*

② In the Toolbox, click the Command Button button ( ).

③ Click in the form to paste the command button.

④ Double-click the new command button.

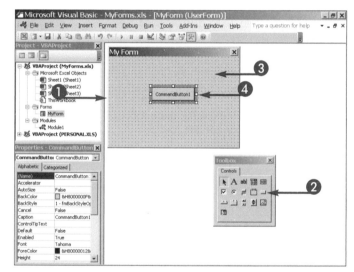

The Code window opens with a Private macro for the command button. The button is activated by the Click event.

⑤ Type the statement **unload me**.

This example macro closes the form when a user clicks the button. You can type any macro you want the button to run when clicked.

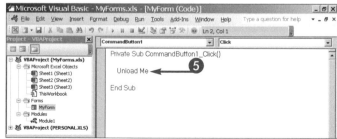

6 Click the View Microsoft Excel button (⊠) to switch to Excel.

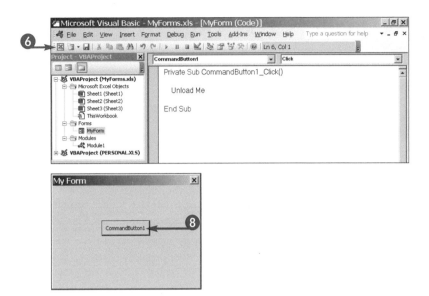

7 Run the macro that displays the custom form.

Note: *You can display the form with the macro* formname.Show. *For more information about forms, see "Create a Custom Form."*

8 Click the new Command button.

The command button macro runs. In this example, the form disappears.

How can I format a command button?

▼ You can format a command button by clicking the command button to select it and setting the properties in the Properties window. You can set and change properties such as BackColor and Font, and resize the button by dragging the handles around the sides and borders of the button. You can change the button label by dragging to select the text and typing new text, or by changing the Caption property. For help on any property, click the property name and press F1.

How can I show a form by clicking a toolbar button?

▼ You can show a form by clicking a toolbar button if you create a custom toolbar button and assign a macro to the new button. The macro consists of a single statement, formname.Show. If you want the form to remain open while you work in the worksheet, you can make it a nonmodal form by writing formname.Show False. The macro to show the form is written in the module for the workbook, and is available whenever the workbook is open. For more information about custom toolbar buttons, see Chapter 2.

Add a Check Box to a Form

Y ou can add a check box to a custom form when you want to enter a value of True or False in response to user input. You can enter the check box value in a worksheet cell or in a macro, and the user decides whether the entry is True or False by clicking the check box. When the user marks the check box, the value is True, and when the user clears the check box, the value is False.

A check box control has a label adjacent to the check box. You can change the label by either dragging to select the label in the control, or by changing the Caption property

in the Properties window. You can change the Name property of the check box to make the control more identifiable in your macros.

You can most easily change the size and shape of a selected check box by dragging the handles on the sides and corners of the check box border, and you can move the entire check box by dragging the center of the control. You can change the Font, Font Style, and Font Size by clicking the ellipsis button in the Font property in the Properties window.

Add a Check Box to a Form

① Create or open a custom form.

Note: To create a form, see the section "Create a Custom Form."

② In the Toolbox, click the CheckBox button (☑).

③ Click in the form to paste a check box.

④ Double-click the new check box.

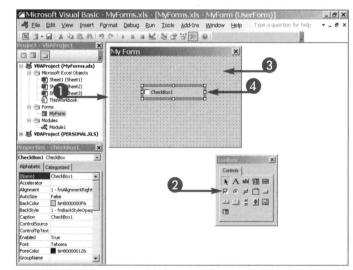

● The Code window opens with a new macro and the Click event.

⑤ Type **dim *R* as range**, replacing *R* with your range variable.

⑥ Type **set *R* = *sheet*.*range***, replacing *sheet* with a worksheet reference and *range* with a range reference.

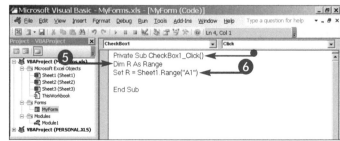

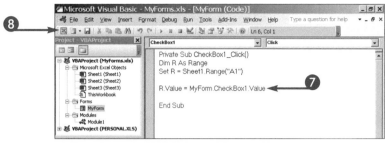

7 Type *R*.**value** = *formname*.**checkbox1** .**value**, replacing *formname* with your form name.

8 Click ⊠ to switch to Excel.

9 Run the macro that displays the form.

Note: To display a form, see the section "Create a Custom Form."

10 Click the check box.

● The value TRUE appears in the specified cell when the check box is marked. The value FALSE appears in the specified cell when the check box is cleared.

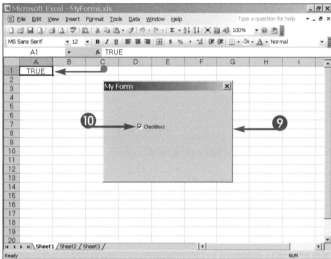

How can I use the check box value in a macro?

▼ You can use the check box value in a macro instead of in a worksheet cell by using the value returned by the check box in any statement that needs a True or False input. For example, you can use a check box value in a conditional statement such as

```
If MyForm.CheckBox1.Value = True Then
macro statements
End If
```

In this macro, if the check box is marked, the *macro statements* run. If the check box is not marked, the statements do not run.

How can I set up the check box to enter values other than True or False?

▼ You can set up the check box to enter values other than True or False with an If Then statement such as

```
If MyForm.CheckBox1.Value = True Then
R.Value = "You win!"
Else
R.Value = "You lose!"
End If
```

In this macro, if the check box is marked, the text string "You win!" replaces the text string "True," and if the check box is not marked, the text string "You lose!" replaces the text string "False."

Create a Text Box on a Form

You can add a text box to a form, enabling users to enter data in a worksheet. Text boxes are very useful when a worksheet or macro needs user input for information such as name, address, or telephone number. A text box enters a user's data into a cell that you specify in the text box macro.

After you create a new text box on a custom form, you double-click the text box to create a new macro for it. The new macro runs at the Change event by default, but you can select a different event from the Procedure box at the top of the Code window.

The macro enters the value typed in the text box into a cell you specify. Declaring variables for both the value in the text box and the cell range where you want the value entered is most efficient. Then you can set the cell range value equal to the text box value. By default text box objects are named with sequential numbers, but you can change the name for easier identification by using the Name property in the Properties window.

Create a Text Box on a Form

① Create or open a custom form.

Note: To create a form, see the section "Create a Custom Form."

② In the Toolbox, click the TextBox button (abl).

③ Click and drag to draw a text box in the form.

④ Double-click the new text box.

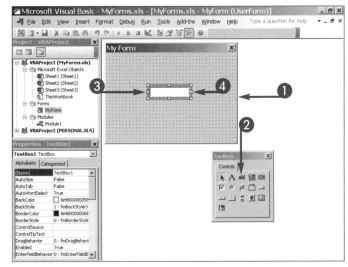

● The Code window opens with a new macro and the Change event.

⑤ Type **dim R as range**, replacing *R* with your variable.

⑥ Type **dim S as string**, replacing *S* with a second variable.

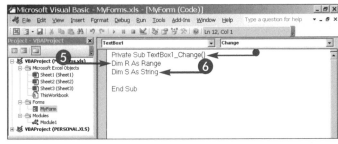

⑦ Type **set R = *sheet.range***, replacing *sheet* with a worksheet reference and *range* with a range reference.

⑧ Type **S = *formname*.textbox1.value**, replacing *formname* with your form name.

⑨ Type **R.value = S**.

⑩ Click ▨ to switch to Excel.

⑪ Run the macro to display the form.

Note: To display a form, see the section "Create a Custom Form."

⑫ Type an entry in the text box.

● The entry appears in the specified range.

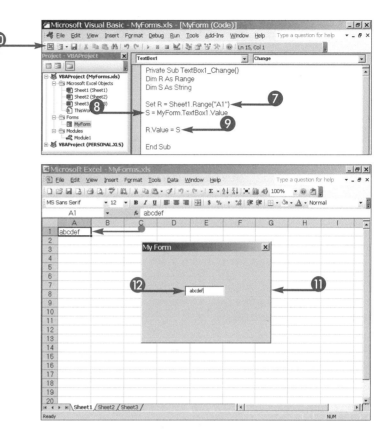

How can I add a label to identify the text box?

▼ You can add a label to the form to identify the text box by using the Label button in the Toolbox. Show the form in the Visual Basic Editor, then click the Label button in the Toolbox and click in the form where you want to paste the new label. You can drag to select the label text and type new text, and you can change the colors and font using the properties in the Properties window. You can also resize the label by dragging its handles.

How can I enter multiple lines in a text box?

▼ You can enter multiple lines in a text box by setting both the `MultiLine` and `EnterKeyBehavior` properties to True. Select the text box in the Visual Basic Editor, and in the Properties window set both the `MultiLine` property and the `EnterKeyBehavior` property to True. A user pressing the Enter key while typing in the text box enters a line break and starts a new line. Excel enters the typed data on multiple lines in the specified cell in the worksheet, with a line break character displayed.

Initialize a Text Box

You can set a starting entry in a text box, thus saving the user time. Setting a starting, or initial, entry in a text box is called *initializing* the text box. For example, if you want a user to use the current date in an order form, you can make the current date the initial entry in the text box. All controls that need to be initialized in a form are initialized in the form's `Private Sub UserForm_Initialize` macro in the form code window.

A text box typically functions with a `Change` event, which enters the data typed in the text box as the data is being typed. You write a Change event macro in the control's

macro code. But if you want the initial text box data entered in a worksheet or macro without the user typing it, you must give the form another means of using the data. One means of allowing the user to use the initial text box entry is a command button that, when clicked, runs the macro that uses the initial text box value.

For more information about command buttons, see the section "Add a Command Button to a Form."

For more information about command buttons, see the section "Add a Command Button to a Form."

Initialize a Text Box

① In the Visual Basic Editor, open a form that has a text box you want to initialize.

② Create a command button on the form.

Note: To create a command button, see the section "Add a Command Button to a Form."

③ Double-click the form background.

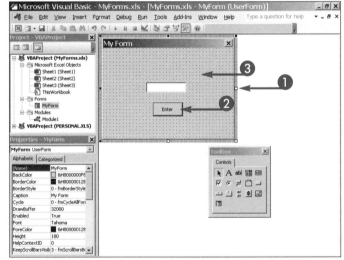

The form code window opens with a Private Sub `UserForm_Click` macro started.

④ In the Sub line, replace the word *Click* with the word *Initialize*.

⑤ Type **textbox1.value = date**.

The keyword Date initializes the text box with the current date.

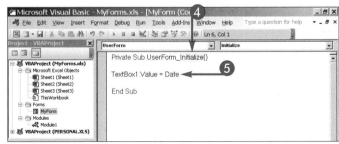

6 Click ⬝ in the Object box.

7 Click the command button object you created in step **2**.

A new `Private Sub CommandButtonobject_ Click` macro appears.

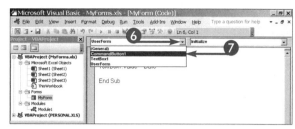

8 Type the code you want the button to run.

This example macro enters the text box value into a worksheet cell.

9 Click ⊠ to switch to Excel.

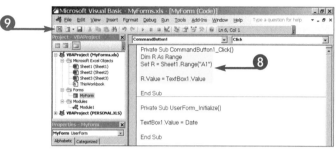

10 Open the form.

Note: To open a form, see "Create a Custom Form."

● Excel initializes the text box with the current date.

11 Click the command button.

● The command button macro runs.

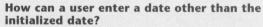
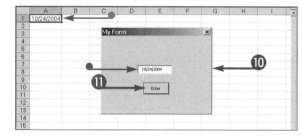

How can a user enter a date other than the initialized date?

▼ A user can enter a date other than the initialized date by typing a date in a recognizable date format, and then clicking the command button that enters the text box value into the worksheet or macro. Most date formats are recognizable, including Dec 3, 12-3-04, and 12/3. Because users typically press Enter after typing an entry, you should set the tab order to move to the command button after the text box. For more information about tab order, see the section "Set the Tab Order for Form Controls."

How can I use recognizable names for my controls?

▼ You can and should use recognizable names for your controls by giving each control a name in the `Name` property in the Properties window. You can then use the control names in all of the macros in the form code window. The one place where you cannot use an item's name is in the `Private Sub UserForm_Initialize` macro. You cannot use the form's name in the `Sub` line because this macro requires the name `UserForm`. You can, however, use the form's name in all macros in a module, such as macros that open the form.

Create Option Buttons on a Form

Y ou can add option buttons to a custom form when you want a user to choose one of two or more choices. All the option buttons on a form are linked together by default.

One of the many ways to use option buttons in a macro is to write a different macro for each button. The macro then runs when a user clicks that button. You can make your macros much easier to read if you give each option button a recognizable name in the Name property in the Properties window.

You can change an option button label directly in the control or by changing the Caption property in the Properties window. You can change the Font properties for the label by using the Font property in the Properties window. You can change the Name property of the option button to make the control more identifiable in your macros. You can change the size and shape of a selected option button by dragging the handles on the button's border, and you can move the option button by dragging the center of the control.

Create Option Buttons on a Form

① Create or open a custom form.

Note: To create a form, see the section "Create a Custom Form."

② In the Toolbox, click the OptionButton button.

③ Click in the form to paste an option button.

④ Repeat steps **2** to **3** to paste more option buttons.

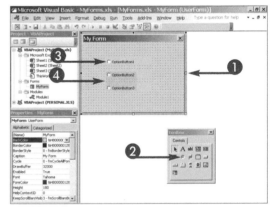

⑤ Double-click one of the new option buttons.

- The Code window opens with a new macro and the Click event for the option button you double-clicked.

⑥ Type **dim *R* as range**, replacing *R* with your range variable throughout this macro.

⑦ Type **set *R* = *sheet.range***, replacing *sheet* with a worksheet reference and *range* with a range reference.

⑧ Type ***R*.value** = *"textstring"*, replacing *textstring* with a text string to display when a user clicks the button.

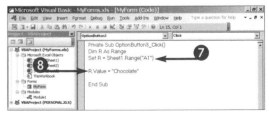

9 Repeat steps **5** to **8** for each button in the form.

● You can switch back to the form by clicking the View Object button above the Project window.

10 Click 🗷 to switch to Excel.

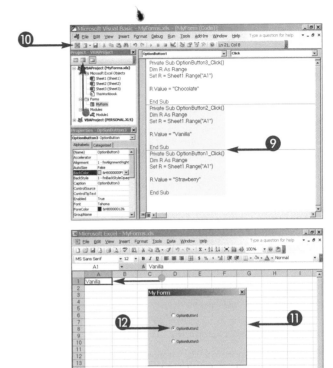

11 Run the macro to display the form.

Note: To display a form, see the section "Create a Custom Form."

12 Click each option button in turn.

● The macro for each option button runs when that button is clicked. In this example, the value you created for that option button is entered in the cell to specified in the macro code.

How can I make several option buttons match?

▼ You can make several option buttons match by aligning and resizing them as a group. You can align several option buttons by dragging the mouse to select the entire set of buttons and then right-clicking one of the selected option buttons. In the shortcut menu, you can click Align and then use the Align commands to align the option buttons. You can also click Make Same Size and use one of the Make Same Size commands to resize all the option buttons to match.

What are some other properties of options buttons?

▼ Some other properties of option buttons include background color, which you can set in the `BackColor` property in the Properties window; the ScreenTip text, which you can set in the `ControlTipText` property; and the font color, which you can set in the `ForeColor` property. You can make an option button unusable by setting its `Enabled` property to `False`. You can set the control's position in the tab order with the `TabIndex` property. For more information about control tab order, see the section "Set the Tab Order for Form Controls."

Add a Spin Button to a Form

Y ou can add a spin button to a form to allow a user to set incremental values in a worksheet cell or a form control, ensuring that only integer values within a range you set for the spin button value are entered. You must show the spin button value to the user, in a cell or a form text box.

A spin button increments and decrements numbers when a user clicks one of the two arrow buttons. A spin button returns an integer value, and you can use that value in a

macro or worksheet formula. For example, you can set up a loan payment formula in a worksheet and use spin buttons to set and change the entries in the loan amount and term cells. By using a spin button, you can restrict the entry in those cells to valid values. You can set minimum and maximum values for a spin button in the `Min` and `Max` properties in the Properties window.

You can also use spin button values in conditional statements, such as `Select Case` statements. For more information about conditional statements, see Chapter 14.

Add a Spin Button to a Form

① Create or open a custom form.

Note: To create a form, see the section "Create a Custom Form."

② In the Toolbox, click the SpinButton button (⊡).

③ Drag to draw a spin button in the form.

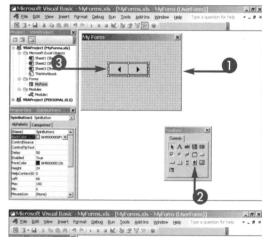

④ With the spin button selected, click in the `Max` property in the Properties window.

⑤ Type a maximum value for the spin button.

The spin button changes value incrementally between the `Min` value to the `Max` value when you click the buttons.

⑥ Double-click the new spin button.

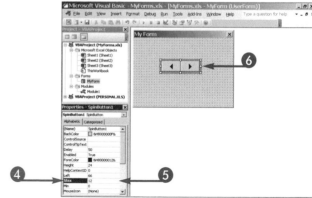

- The form Code window opens with a new `Private Sub SpinButton1_Change` macro.

7 Type your macro code.

This example enters the spin button value in a worksheet cell.

8 Click ⊠ to switch to Excel.

9 Run the macro to display the form.

Note: To display a form, see the section *"Create a Custom Form."*

10 Click the spin button repeatedly.

- The spin button value increases incrementally each time you click the button.

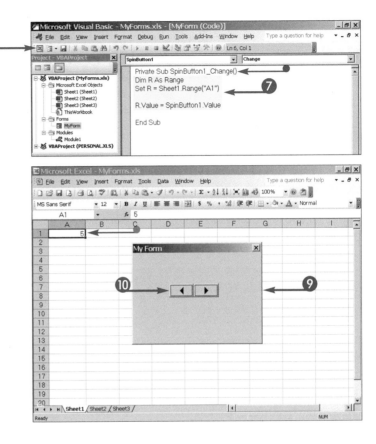

How can I show the spin button value in a text box?

▼ You can show the spin button value in a text box by placing a text box in the form and then writing the spin button macro statement *spinbuttonname.* `Value` = *textboxname.* `Value`. This statement sets the text box value equal to the spin button value. You do not write a macro for the text box, and you can use either control's value in other macros.

How can I change the increment of the spin button value?

▼ You can change the increment of the spin button value by typing the increment in the `SmallChange` property in the Properties window. Spin button values can only be integers, not decimals. For example, if you want the value to change by 2 each time a user clicks one of the buttons, type **2** in the `SmallChange` property.

How can I create a vertical spin button?

▼ You can create a vertical spin button by dragging to draw a vertical rectangle when you create the `SpinButton` control on the form. You can also change an existing horizontal spin button into a vertical spin button by selecting the spin button and then dragging a corner handle to change the shape to a vertical rectangle.

Use a Toggle Button on a Form

Y ou can add a toggle button to a form to run each of a set of two macro statements: one for the toggle setting True, or depressed, and the other for the setting False, or not depressed. Typically toggle buttons run at the `Click` event.

A toggle button has two values: True and False. When a user clicks a toggle button, the button appears depressed, or pushed in, and has a value of True. When the user clicks

the button again, the button appears normal and has a value of False. You can use an `If Then Else` statement to write the macros for the two toggle button states. For more information about `If Then Else` statements, see Chapter 14.

One useful thing you can do in your toggle button macro statements is change the caption of the toggle button to show the status of the button's macros, or to tell the user to click the button to perform some action.

Use a Toggle Button on a Form

① Create or open a custom form.

Note: To create a form, see the section "Create a Custom Form."

② In the Toolbox, click the ToggleButton button (☐).

③ Click in the form to paste a toggle button.

④ Double-click the new toggle button.

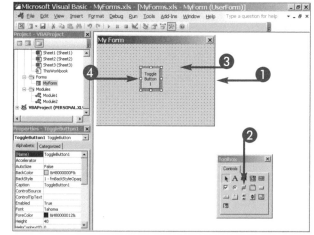

● The form Code window opens with a new macro and the `Click` event.

⑤ Write your macro statements for the toggle button.

This example shows and hides a logo in the active worksheet and changes the button caption.

⑥ Click ☒ to switch to Excel.

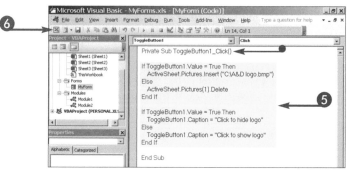

7 Run the macro that displays the form.

Note: To display a form, see the section "Create a Custom Form."

8 Click the toggle button.

- The button is depressed and the part of the macro's code associated with the `True` value is executed.

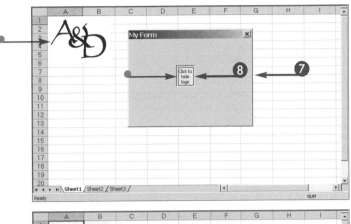

9 Click the toggle button again.

- The button is not depressed and the part of the macro's code associated with the `False` value is executed.

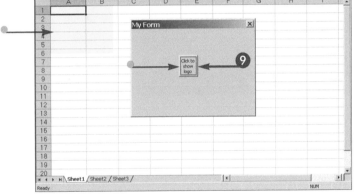

How can I find the code for a specific control in the form code window?

▼ You can find the code for a specific control in the form code window by clicking ⊡ on the Object box, above the Code window, and then clicking the name of the control. You can also limit the Code window display to a single macro by clicking the Procedure View button in the lower-left corner of the Code window.

How can I make the form open with a user-friendly caption in the toggle button?

▼ You can make the form open with a user-friendly caption in the toggle button in one of two ways. You can write a `ToggleButton1.Caption = "caption"` statement in the `Private Sub UserForm_Initialize` macro to set the caption when the form opens, or you can change the button caption in the `Caption` property in the Properties window.

How can I change the font in the toggle button caption?

▼ You can change the font to make the toggle button caption easier to read by selecting the toggle button control and then, in the Properties window, click in the `Font` property and click the Ellipsis button that appears. In the Font dialog box that opens, you can change the Font, Font style, and Size of the toggle button caption.

Build a List Box on a Form

On a custom form, you can create a list box from which a user can select an item from a list, and then you can use that item in macro code or enter the item in the worksheet. Creating a list box requires three separate macros: one macro opens the form, the second macro *initializes*, or sets up, the list box in the form, and the third macro tells VBA what to do with the user's selection in the list box.

To create the macro that opens the form, create the form and then write a macro in a project module with the single statement *formname*.Show False. The keyword False

allows the form to remain open when you click in the worksheet. For more information about creating a custom form, see the section "Create a Custom Form."

You write the second macro in a Private Sub UserForm_Initialize macro in the form code window. This macro uses the ListBox.AddItem method to initialize the list box with the values you want the user to select.

The third macro is a Private Sub ListBox1_Click() macro in the form code window that tells VBA what to do when an item is selected. This example macro enters the form's ListBox.Value into the worksheet cell you specify.

Build a List Box on a Form

① Create or open a custom form.

Note: To create a form, see the section "Create a Custom Form."

② In the Toolbox, click the ListBox button.

③ Click in the form to paste a list box.

④ Double-click the new list box.

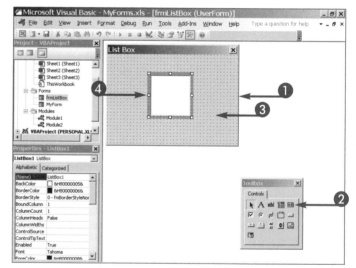

● A new macro for ListBox1_Click opens in the form code window.

⑤ Type **dim R as range**, replacing *R* with your variable throughout this macro.

⑥ Type **set R = *sheet.range***, replacing *sheet* and *range* with your worksheet and range reference.

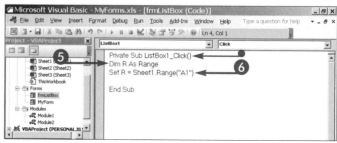

7 Type *R*.**value** = *formname*.**listbox1**.**value**, replacing *formname* with your form name.

8 Click the View Object button (🖼).

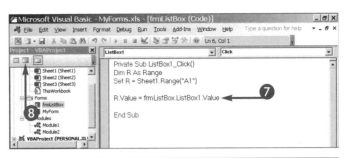

The form appears.

9 Double-click the form background.

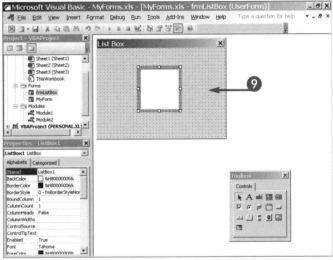

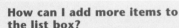

How can I add more items to the list box?

▼ You can add more items to the list box by opening the `UserForm_Initialize` macro and adding more `ListBox .AddItem "item"` statements to the macro. To open the `UserForm_Initialize` macro, double-click the Form icon in the Project window and then double-click the form background. All the form and control macros appear in the form code window.

How can I make changes to the list box code?

▼ You can make changes to the list box code by opening the form code window and editing the code for the control, which tells VBA what to do when a user clicks an item. To open the form code window, you can double-click the form background or any control in the form, or you can click the View Code button above the Project window.

How can I remove a list box from a form?

▼ You can remove a list box from a form by deleting the control. Double-click the form icon in the Project window to display the form. You can right-click the list box control and click Delete on the shortcut menu, or you can click the control to select it and then press the Delete key. Deleting the control does not delete any code in the form code window.

continued

PART VII

Build a List Box on a Form *(Continued)*

A combo box control is very similar to a list box control, but a combo box control takes less space in the form by showing a list of items only when a user clicks the down arrow in the combo box.

You can create a combo box control using exactly the same procedures as you use to create a list box control. You create and name the form, and then write a macro in a module to show the form, using the statement `formname.Show False`. Then you create a combo box in the form with the ComboBox button in the Toolbox.

Next, you write a `Private Sub UserForm_Initialize` macro in the form code window to add the entries to the combo box list when the form opens, and add the entries using the `ComboBox1.AddItem "item"` statement for each item in the list.

Finally, you write a `Private Sub ComboBox1_Change` macro that tells VBA what to do when a user selects an item in the combo box list. You can start this macro by double-clicking the combo box control in the form in the Visual Basic Editor.

Build a List Box on a Form *(continued)*

- A new macro for `UserForm_Click` appears in the form code window.

⑩ Select the word *Click* and type **Initialize** to replace it.

⑪ Type **with listbox1**.

⑫ Type **.additem** *"itemtext"*, replacing *itemtext* with your item text.

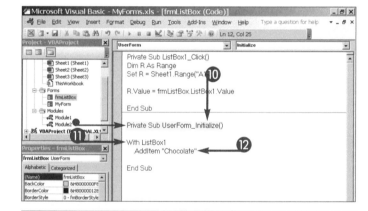

⑬ Repeat step **12** to add all your list box items.

⑭ Type **end with**.

⑮ Double-click a module icon in the Project window.

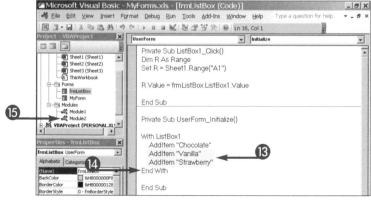

348

⑯ Start a new macro.

⑰ Type *formname*.**Show False**, replacing *formname* with your form name.

⑱ Click ☒ to switch to Excel.

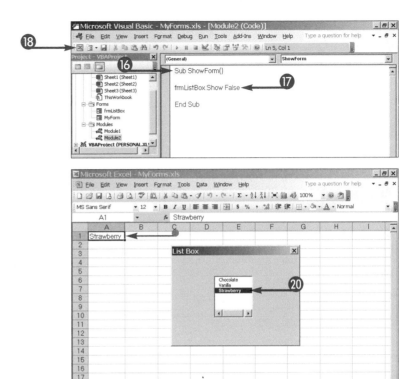

⑲ Run the macro to open the form.

Note: To run a macro, see Chapter 2.

⑳ Click each item in turn to test the list box.

● Excel enters the clicked item value in the specified cell.

How can I create a label for the list box?

▼ You can create a label for a list box with the Label button. Display the form in the Visual Basic Editor, then click the Label button in the Toolbox. Click in the form where you want to place the label. You can change the label text by editing the text directly in the label or by changing the Caption property. You can move the label by dragging it, and change the size by dragging the selection border handles. You can also add a border and set the border color.

How can I get more information about list boxes?

▼ You can get more information about list boxes by clicking on the control in the form to select it, and then pressing F1 to open a Help file about list boxes. In the List Box Control Help window, you can click the various links to explore all the Help files information. You can also press F2 to open the Object Browser, and then click ListBox in the Classes list. Click an item in the Members list and click the Help button in the Object Browser to open more Help files.

PART VII

Add a Picture to a Form

You can add a picture to a custom form by creating an Image control and then specifying a picture from your hard drive to display in the control. Typically a picture displays a company logo or a product image, but the picture can be anything you want, such as employee photographs in personnel forms. The Image control supports the file formats BMP, CUR, GIF, ICO, JPG, and WMF.

You can use an Image control to run a macro if you write a `Private Sub` *imagecontrol*`_Click` macro in the form code window. For more information about events, see Chapter 22.

You can change the picture in an Image frame by selecting a different picture in the Picture property. You can delete a picture from an Image frame by clicking in the Picture property and pressing the Delete key. Excel replaces the Picture property with (None). You can delete the Image control from the form by right-clicking the control and clicking Delete in the shortcut menu, or by clicking the control to select it and then pressing the Delete key.

Add a Picture to a Form

1 Create or open a custom form.

Note: *To create a form, see the section "Create a Custom Form."*

2 In the Toolbox, click the Image button ( ).

3 Click or drag in the form to draw an image frame in which to open a picture.

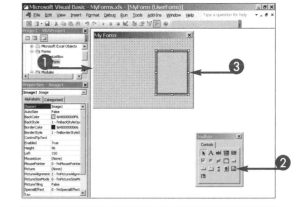

4 In the Properties window, click the Picture property.

5 Click the ellipsis button that appears.

The Load Picture dialog box appears.

6 Navigate to the picture you want to display in the form.

7 Click Open.

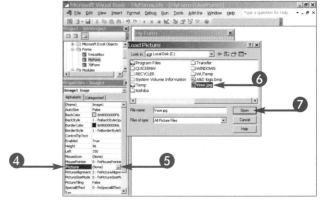

The picture appears in the Image frame.

⑧ Click in the `PictureSizeMode` property box.

⑨ Click ☑ and select 3 — `fmPictureSizeModeZoom`.

The picture fits the image frame.

⑩ Click ☒ to switch to Excel.

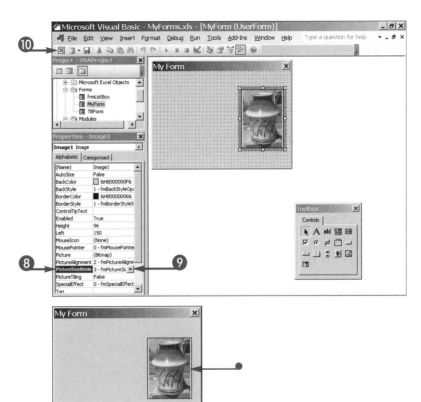

⑪ Run the macro that displays the form.

Note: To display a form, see the section "Create a Custom Form."

● Excel displays the picture in the form.

How can I display the entire picture in the frame?

▼ You can display the entire picture in the frame by setting the PictureSizeMode property to 3 — fmPictureSizeModeZoom. The Zoom property zooms in or out on the picture so that the entire picture is displayed in the Image frame. The other properties are 0 — fmPictureSizeModeClip and 1 — fmPictureSizeModeStretch. The Clip property trims the picture at its original resolution and displays the portion that fits in the frame, and the Stretch property stretches the picture to fill the frame completely but often skews the proportions.

How can I place other controls on top of the picture?

▼ You can place other controls on top of the picture by dragging existing controls onto the picture or by creating new controls and placing them on the picture. You can also make the entire form background a picture by clicking the form background to select it and then selecting a picture in the Picture property in the Properties window. Remember to set the PictureSizeMode property to Clip, Stretch, or Zoom to control how your picture is displayed.

Use a Multi-Page Control on a Form

Y ou can place more controls into a small form if you use a MultiPage control to create multiple pages in a form. A MultiPage control has different pages, each of which contains a different set of controls. For example, you can use a MultiPage to display information from an employment application. One page may contain personal information such as name and address, and another page may list previous employers.

When you use a MultiPage in a form, you create the MultiPage first, typically drawing it large enough to cover the entire form background. You then click a page tab to

select a page and you place controls on the page. Then you click a different page tab to select a different page and you place controls on that page.

After you place controls on a page of a MultiPage control, you set control properties and write macros to make each control functional, just as if the controls were on a form background. Placing a command button on each page to close the form is a good idea. The Close command buttons can all run the same macro, Unload Me.

Use a Multi-Page Control on a Form

① Create or open a custom form.

Note: To create a form, see the section "Create a Custom Form."

② In the Toolbox, click the MultiPage button (▨).

③ Drag to draw a MultiPage control that covers the form background.

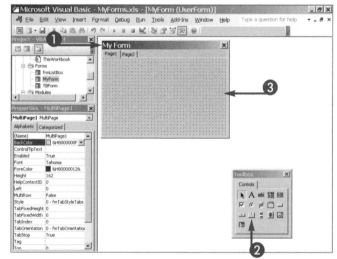

④ Click the left tab of the MultiPage.

⑤ Place controls on the page.

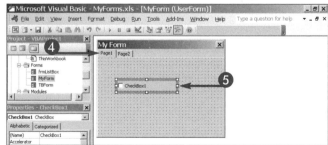

6 Click the right tab of the MultiPage.

7 Place controls on the page.

8 Click 🔣 to switch to Excel.

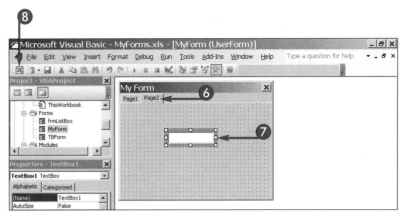

9 Run the macro that displays the form.

Note: To display a form, see the section "Create a Custom Form."

10 Click each page tab in turn to display the controls on that page.

● Excel displays the page controls.

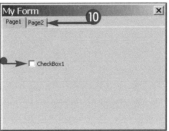

How can I add more page tabs?

▼ You can add more page tabs by using the page tab shortcut menu. In the Visual Basic Editor, show the form. Right-click any existing page tab and click New Page on the shortcut menu. Excel adds a new page to the multipage control. You can also right-click a specific page tab and click Delete Page to remove that page and all its controls.

How can I name the page tabs?

▼ You can name the page tabs with user-friendly and recognizable names by right-clicking the page tab and clicking Rename. In the Rename dialog box, you can type a new caption and also an optional accelerator key and Control Tip Text. Control Tip Text is the ScreenTip that appears when you position the mouse ⌖ over the tab.

How can I control which page is displayed when the form opens?

▼ You can control which page is displayed when the form opens by leaving that tab selected in the form in the Visual Basic Editor. For example, if you want to have the leftmost page displayed when the form opens, open the form in the Visual Basic Editor and click the leftmost tab to make it active.

Layout the Controls on a Form

Y ou can layout the controls on a form in a logical and convenient way, so that users can enter data more quickly and with fewer errors. To layout form controls, consider how the user is likely to enter data. For example, if the user is entering data from a handwritten form such as an application, data entry is faster if the Excel form is laid out similarly to the handwritten form. Make sure the tab order in the form follows the flow of the items in the handwritten form. For more information about tab order, see the section "Set the Tab Order for Form Controls."

You can reposition controls by dragging the center of the selected control, and you can resize or reshape a selected control by dragging the handles on the control border. You can also resize and reshape the entire form by dragging the handles on its border.

You can align similar controls by dragging to draw a rectangle around them, right-clicking one of the selected controls, and then using the Align command to align them with one another and the MakeSameSize command to make them the same size.

Layout the Controls on a Form

① Create or open a custom form with controls.

Note: To create a form, see the section "Create a Custom Form."

② Click a control and drag it to a new position on the form.

The upper-left corner of the control snaps to the grid dots. You can use the grid dots to align controls.

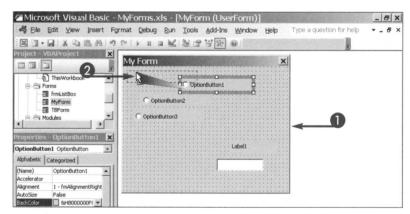

③ Click and drag a handle on the selected control border to change the size or shape of the control.

The handles do not snap to the grid dots.

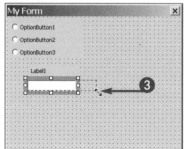

④ Click the form background.

⑤ Click and drag a handle on the form border to change the size or shape of the form.

⑥ Click ⊠ to switch to Excel.

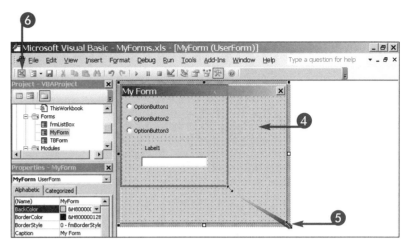

⑦ Run the macro that displays the form.

Note: To display a form, see the section "Create a Custom Form."

● Excel lays out the form controls the way you set them.

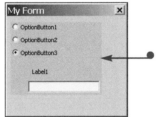

How can I change the startup location for a form?

▼ You can change the startup location for a form when it opens by setting the value of the `StartUpPosition` property. Click the form background to select it, then click the `StartUpPosition` property in the Properties window. Click the down arrow that appears in the property box and then click a built-in property. `1 — CenterOwner` opens the form in the center of the Excel window, `2 — CenterScreen` opens the form in the center of the computer screen, and `3 — WindowsDefault` opens the form in the upper-left corner of the computer screen.

How can I move or resize several controls together?

▼ You can move or resize several controls together if you first drag to draw a selection rectangle around all the controls. When you move one of the selected controls, all the controls move together as a group. When you drag a handle on one control, all the controls are resized together. You can right-click one of the selected controls and use the `Align` commands from the shortcut menu to align the controls with one another, and use the `Make Same Size` command to make all the controls the same height, width, or shape.

Set the Tab Order for Form Controls

You can set the order in which the focus moves from control to control in a form by setting the tab order for the form. The tab order is the order in which controls are selected when the user presses the Tab key. By default the tab order is the order in which you add controls to the form, but this is often not a logical order for a user.

Controls have two properties for tab order: The `TabIndex` property, designated by a value between 0 and the total number of controls, indicates the control's position in the

tab order. The `TabStop` property controls whether the focus stops on a control. If the `TabStop` property for a control is set to False, the tab order skips that control.

Both properties can be set in the Properties window, but setting the tab order, the `TabIndex` property, in the Tab Order dialog box is much easier. You can click View→Tab Order to show the Tab Order dialog box. In the dialog box, you can click a control and click the Move Up or Move Down buttons to reposition the control in the tab order.

Set the Tab Order for Form Controls

① Open the form in the Visual Basic Editor.

② Click View.

③ Click Tab Order.

   The Tab Order dialog box appears.

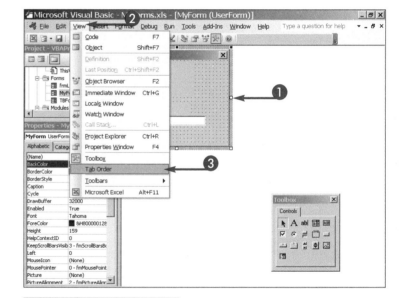

④ Click a control you want to move.

⑤ Click the Move Up button or the Move Down button to reposition the control in the tab order.

6 Click OK.

7 Click ⊠ to switch to Excel.

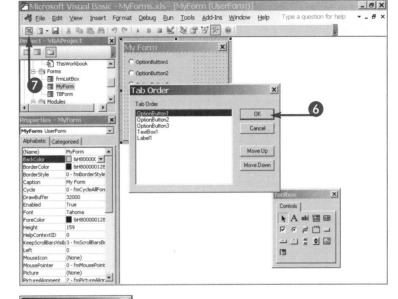

8 Run the macro that displays the form.

Note: To display a form, see the section "Create a Custom Form."

9 Press the Tab key repeatedly to test the tab order.

● The controls gain focus in the tab order you set.

How can I set the tab order to skip a control?

▼ You can set the tab order to skip a control by setting the `TabStop` property for that control. To set the `TabStop` property, click the control to select it, then set the `TabStop` property in the Properties window to False. Because it has only a True or False value, you can double-click the `TabStop` property to switch between True and False. You can also click in the property box, click the ⊡ that appears, and click the setting you want.

How can I redesign the control layout on a form?

▼ You can redesign the control layout on a form by dragging the controls, moving them to new positions and giving them new shapes and sizes that fit more neatly into your form. You can reshape and resize a control by clicking it and then dragging the handles on its sides and corners. After you redesign the control layout, you may need to reset the tab order so the focus moves logically in the new layout. For more information about control layout, see the section "Layout the Controls on a Form."

Run a Macro When a Workbook Opens

You can run many macros when a workbook opens. The most typical are macros that open a custom toolbar, activate a specific worksheet, display instructions or custom forms, or open other workbooks.

You can run a macro when a workbook opens by writing the macro statements in a `Private Sub Workbook_Open` macro. This macro is triggered by the Open event. For example, the statement `formname.Show` opens the custom form named `formname` when the workbook opens. The statement `Worksheets("Sheet3").Activate`

activates the worksheet named Sheet3 when the workbook opens. The statement `Application.CommandBars ("toolbarname").Visible = True` displays the toolbar named `toolbarname` when the workbook opens.

The `Workbook_Open` macro can run statements you write in the macro, or it can call and run macros contained in other modules. To call a macro from another module, you type the name of the macro as a statement. The called macro must be in a module in the same workbook project. For more information about calling macros, see the section "Create a Macro That Runs Other Macros" in Chapter 6.

Run a Macro When a Workbook Opens

① Double-click the Microsoft Excel Objects icon in the workbook project.

② Double-click the ThisWorkbook icon.

The ThisWorkbook Code window opens.

③ Click ⬇ in the Object box.

④ Click Workbook.

   ● Excel creates the default Private Sub Workbook_Open macro.

⑤ Type your macro statements.

This example macro displays a custom toolbar.

⑥ Click the Save button (🖫).

⑦ Click the View Microsoft Excel button (🖾) to switch to Excel.

⑧ Click File.

⑨ Click Close.

The workbook closes, but Excel remains open.

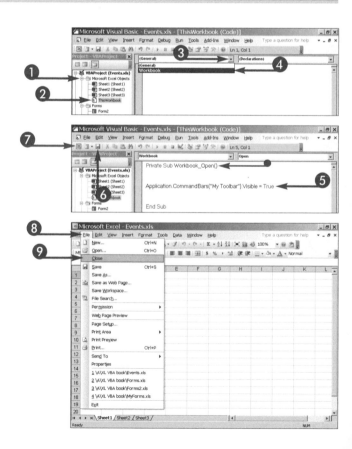

10 Click File.

11 Click the workbook name.

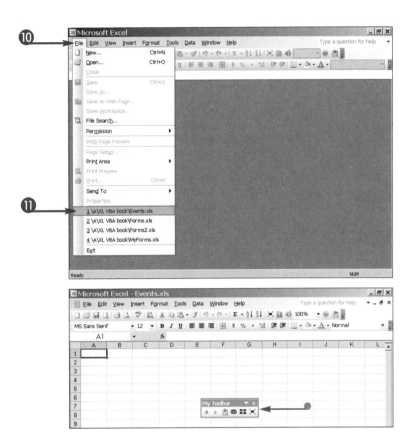

The macro runs just after the workbook opens.

● In this example, Excel displays the custom toolbar.

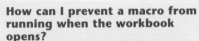

How can I prevent a macro from running when the workbook opens?

▼ You can prevent a macro from running when the workbook opens by holding down the Shift key while opening the workbook. You must press and hold the Shift key while you click the button or menu command that opens the file. This is useful when you need to open a file but do not need to perform the Workbook_Open macro action.

How can I remove a custom toolbar when the workbook closes?

▼ You can remove a custom toolbar when the workbook closes by writing the statement `Application.CommandBars ("toolbarname").Visible = False` in a `Private Sub Workbook_BeforeClose` macro in the ThisWorkbook module. When the workbook closes and hides the toolbar, the toolbar is no longer available to other workbooks. For more information about `Workbook_ BeforeClose` macros, see the section "Run a Macro When a Workbook Closes."

What other events can I run at the workbook level?

▼ Another event at the workbook level is the `BeforePrint` event, which runs when you click File➜Print or click the Print toolbar button. If you click File➜Print, the Print dialog box appears after the `BeforePrint` macro runs; and after you click the Print toolbar button, the data goes to the printer immediately after the `BeforePrint` macro runs.

Run a Macro When a Workbook Closes

You can run a macro when a workbook closes by writing a `Private Sub Workbook_BeforeClose` macro in the ThisWorkbook module. You can automatically run any macro you want when the active workbook closes.

A `Workbook_BeforeClose` macro is a convenient place to automatically save a workbook quietly, without asking a user if they want to save the workbook. To automatically save a workbook without user input, you can write the

statement `ActiveWorkbook.Save`. This statement saves the active workbook with the current file name and location and, because the `Workbook_BeforeClose` macro contains the statement, runs immediately prior to the workbook closing.

You can run a macro to make a backup copy of the workbook file just before closing. You can also ask the user whether the current name is correct for saving the file by using a message box that gives the user the opportunity to respond Yes or No.

Run a Macro When a Workbook Closes

① Double-click the Microsoft Excel Objects icon in the workbook project.

② Double-click the ThisWorkbook icon.

The ThisWorkbook Code window opens.

③ Click ⊡ in the Object box.

④ Click Workbook.

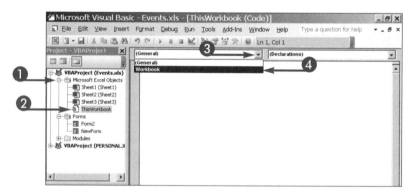

● Excel creates a new `Private Sub Workbook_Open` macro.

⑤ Click ⊡ in the Procedure box.

⑥ Click BeforeClose.

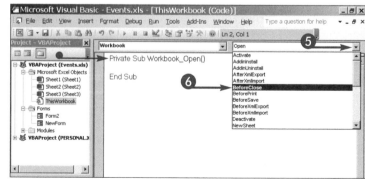

- Excel creates a new `Private Sub Workbook_BeforeClose` macro.

7 Delete the `Private Sub Workbook_Open` macro created in step **5**.

8 Type your macro statements in the new `Workbook_BeforeClose` macro.

9 Click ⊠ to switch to Excel.

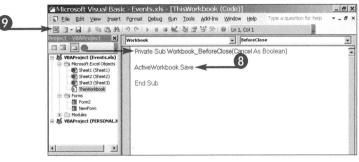

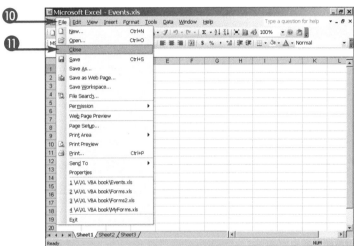

10 Click File.

11 Click Close.

The workbook file saves any changes and closes quietly.

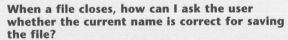

When a file closes, how can I ask the user whether the current name is correct for saving the file?

▼ You can ask the user whether the current name is correct for saving the file by writing the statements

```
Dim reply As Integer
reply = MsgBox("Close " &
ActiveWorkbook.Name & "?", vbYesNo)
If reply = vbNo Then
Cancel = True
End If
```

A message box appears and the user can click Yes to save normally, or No to stop the closure. Write the statement `ActiveWorkbook.Save` at the end of the macro to continue the closure and save the workbook quietly if the user clicks Yes.

How can I run a macro to make a backup copy of the workbook file just before closing?

▼ You can run a macro to make a backup copy of the workbook file just before closing by writing the statement `ThisWorkbook.SaveCopyAs "driveletter:\folder\" & ThisWorkbook.Name` in the `Workbook_BeforeClose` macro. This statement creates a copy of the file in a folder named *folder* on the *driveletter:* drive. Make sure you use the correct drive and path in your macro. Also make sure you write the statement `ActiveWorkbook.Save` at the end of the macro to continue the closure and save the workbook quietly.

Launch a Form with an Event

You can launch, or open, a custom user form with an event rather than running a separate macro to open the form. For example, you can launch a form when the user activates a specific worksheet; such a form would not be available until the worksheet that requires user input through the form is active.

You can launch a form from any event by writing the statement *formname*.Show in the event macro. If you want to keep the form open while the user works in the worksheet, remember to include the modal argument False, making the statement *formname*.Show False.

You can make the event that launches the form a worksheet event, a workbook event, or a control event. For any instance in which you want the form displayed automatically, you can create a logical event, such as a Worksheet_Activate event, that launches the form. If you want to close or hide the form automatically, you can create another logical event, such as a Worksheet_Deactivate event, to run the macro *formname*.Hide.

Launch a Form with an Event

① In the Project window, double-click a worksheet in the project.

A Code window for the worksheet opens.

② Click 🔽 in the Object box.

③ Click Worksheet.

A new Private Sub Worksheet_SelectionChange macro appears.

④ Click 🔽 in the Procedure box.

⑤ Click Activate.

A new Private Sub Worksheet_Activate macro appears.

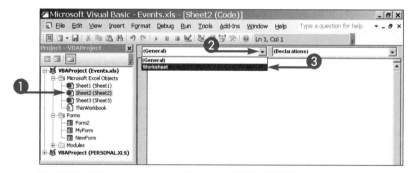

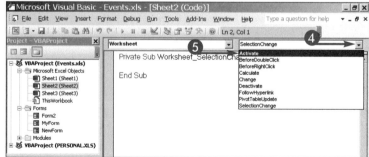

⑥ Select and delete the first macro from step **3**.

⑦ Type *formname*.**show false**, replacing *formname* with your form name.

⑧ Click 🔲 to switch to Excel.

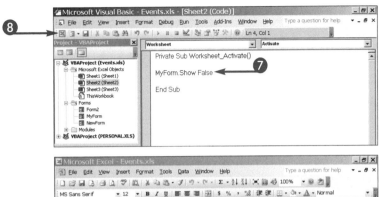

⑨ Click the tab of the worksheet for which you created the event.

● The form appears.

You may need to activate the event worksheet by selecting a different worksheet and then selecting the event worksheet.

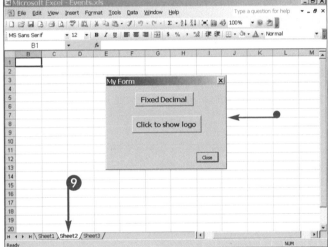

How can I close the form when I switch worksheets?

▼ You can close, or hide, the form when you switch to a different worksheet by writing a `Deactivate` event for the same worksheet. In the worksheet Code window, select Deactivate from the Procedure box. A new `Private Sub Worksheet_Deactivate` macro appears in the Code window. Type the statement *formname*.`Hide` in the macro. When you activate a different worksheet, Excel deactivates the event worksheet and hides the form.

What other events can I use to launch forms automatically?

▼ You can launch forms automatically from any event triggered by any object in a workbook project. For example, you can launch a form when the user clicks a button (including a button in another form), opens or closes a workbook, changes data in a worksheet, and so forth. To see the list of events you can use for a specific object, open the Code window for the form, worksheet, or workbook, select the object in the Object box, and then open the Procedure list.

Run the Same Macro on All Worksheets

You can write a `Private Sub Workbook_SheetActivate` macro in the workbook Code window to run the same macro when a user activates any worksheet in a workbook. If you want to run the same macro on every worksheet, a workbook-level macro saves you the time and effort of copying the same macro to every worksheet and every added worksheet in the workbook.

Activating any sheet in the workbook, including new sheets added to the workbook, triggers the `Workbook_Sheet Activate` event. For example, you can run macros to launch a form, show a message box, or save the data quietly every time the user activates a different worksheet.

You write the `Private Sub Workbook_SheetActivate` macro in the workbook code module, which opens when you double-click the ThisWorkbook icon in the Project window. You add the Workbook object from the Object box, and then select the `SheetActivate` event in the Procedure box.

You can write a complete set of statements in the `Workbook_SheetActivate` macro, or you can call another macro from the `Workbook_SheetActivate` macro. You can call any public macro from any module in any open workbook.

Run the Same Macro on All Worksheets

① In the Project window, double-click the ThisWorkbook icon in the project.

A Code window for the workbook opens.

② Click 〔▪〕 in the Object box.

③ Click Workbook.

A new `Private Sub Workbook_Open` macro appears.

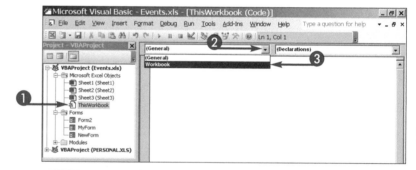

④ Click 〔▪〕 in the Procedure box.

⑤ Click SheetActivate.

A new `Private Sub Workbook_SheetActivate` macro appears.

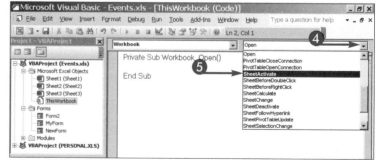

364

Controlling Macros with Events chapter **22**

⑥ Select and delete the `Private Sub Workbook_Open` macro from step **3**.

⑦ Type your macro statements.

This example macro shows a message box with the name of the selected sheet.

⑧ Click ⊠ to switch to Excel.

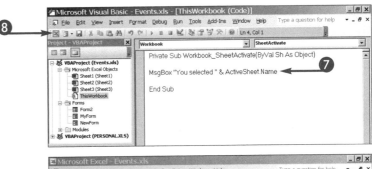

⑨ Click a sheet tab.

● The macro runs each time you click a sheet tab.

In this example macro, you must click the OK button to remove the message box.

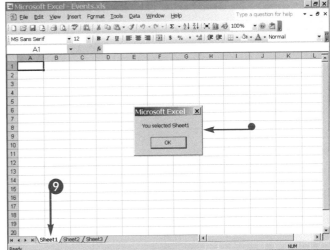

How can I run a macro on just one worksheet?

▼ You can run a macro on just one worksheet by writing the macro in the specific worksheet module. In the Project window, double-click a sheet icon. Select Worksheet in the Object box, and then select Activate in the Procedure box. Excel creates a new `Worksheet_Activate` macro, and the statements you write in that macro run every time a user activates that specific worksheet. Another worksheet-level macro you can run is `Worksheet_Calculate`. For example, the statement `Columns("A:F").AutoFit` in a `Worksheet_Calculate` macro AutoFits the specified columns every time the worksheet recalculates.

How can I show a custom toolbar on just one worksheet?

▼ You can show a custom toolbar on just one worksheet by writing a pair of macros, for the `Activate` and `Deactivate` events, for that worksheet. In the Project window, double-click the worksheet icon. Create a `Private Sub Worksheet_Activate` macro, and write the statement `Application.CommandBars ("toolbarname").Visible = True`. Then create a `Private Sub Worksheet_Deactivate` macro, and write the statement `Application. CommandBars("toolbarname").Visible = False`. The named toolbar appears when you activate the worksheet and disappears when you switch to a different worksheet.

Assign Two Events to the Same Control

You can assign two events to the same control to save space on a custom form. For example, you can assign both a `Click` and a `DblClick` event to a command button so that the same button can run two different macros: one when a user clicks the button, and the other when a user double-clicks the button.

To assign two events to the same control, you write two macros in the form Code window for that control. You can select the control from the Object box and the event from the Procedure box; both boxes are located at the top of the form Code window. When one event macro exists for a control, you can create another event macro for the control by clicking in the first event macro and then selecting a different event from the Procedure box.

Make sure you give the user instructions on how to use the two-event control. For example, you can create a label in the form that tells the user how to use the button, or you can incorporate the instructions into the button label.

Assign Two Events to the Same Control

① Create a control on a custom user form.

Note: To create a custom user form or command button, see Chapter 21.

② Double-click the control.

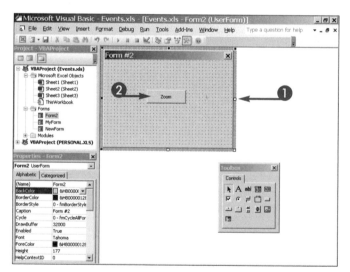

The form Code window opens with a default `Click` event for the control.

③ Type your macro code.

This example macro zooms the active window to 120% magnification when a user clicks the button.

④ Click in the existing macro.

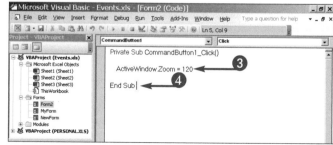

⑤ Click ⬛ on the Procedure box.

⑥ Click a different event.

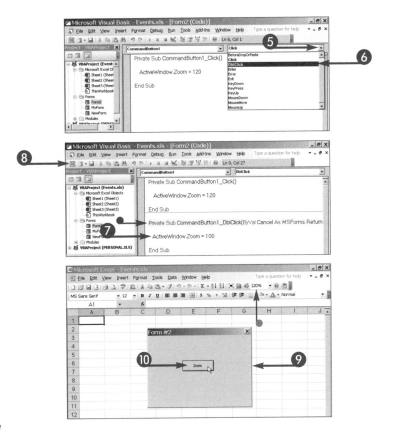

● Excel creates a new macro for the existing control and a new event.

⑦ Type your alternate macro code.

⑧ Click ⬛ to switch to Excel.

⑨ Show the form.

Note: To show a form, see Chapter 21.

⑩ Test the events you assigned to the control.

● The macros run at each event.

This example macro zooms in when the button is clicked and zooms out when the button is double-clicked.

Note: If you have problems with the double-click event, try changing your mouse speed setting in the Control Panel to a faster speed.

How can I create a label with instructions for using a two-event command button?

▼ You can create a label with instructions for a user with the Label control in the Toolbox. Show the form in the Visual Basic Editor and click the Label button in the Toolbox. Drag to draw a label in the form. Click in the label to switch the dotted border to a hatched border so you can edit the text. Delete the existing caption and type your instructions. Then drag a corner handle to resize the label and force the lines of text to break where you want.

How can I prevent the shortcut menu from appearing when a cell is right-clicked?

▼ You can prevent the shortcut menu from appearing when a cell is right-clicked by writing a `Private Sub Worksheet_BeforeRightClick` macro with the statement `Cancel = True`. The Cancel statement in a worksheet's BeforeRightClick event cancels the event, meaning that no right-click events occur. The display of shortcut menus upon right-clicking a cell is a built-in event in Excel, and you can cancel that built-in event with the Cancel statement. You can cancel any event, including built-in events, by writing a Cancel statement for that event.

Run a Macro When the Mouse Moves

Y ou can run a macro in response to mouse movement over a form, or over a control or label on a form. When the object detects mouse movement, the macro runs. To trigger a macro in response to mouse movement, you use the MouseMove event.

An object recognizes a MouseMove event whenever a user positions the mouse ⬩ within the object's borders, and MouseMove events are triggered continually as the mouse ⬩ moves across the object. As the mouse moves, the macro is triggered repeatedly, so you must make sure the macro is one that can run repeatedly without causing

problems. For example, if a MouseMove macro inserts a picture in a worksheet, Excel inserts many new copies of the picture while the mouse moves over the control. But if the macro performs an action that can be performed repeatedly without causing problems in the workbook or worksheet — such as changing the window magnification to a specified new level of magnification — it does not matter if the macro runs repeatedly while the mouse moves over the control.

You can create two controls with MouseMove events to perform opposite actions, such as increasing and then decreasing worksheet magnification.

Run a Macro When the Mouse Moves

① Create a command button in a user form.

Note: *To create a form or a command button on a form, see Chapter 21.*

② Type a caption for the command button in the Caption property.

③ Double-click the new command button.

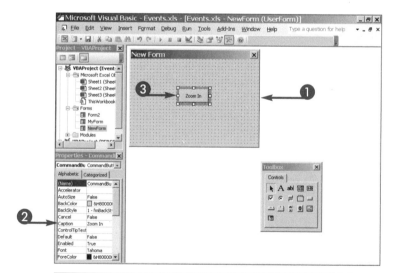

● The form Code window opens and a new `Private Sub CommandButton1_Click` macro appears.

④ Click ⬩ in the Procedure box.

⑤ Click MouseMove.

Excel creates a new `Private Sub btnHide_MouseMove` macro.

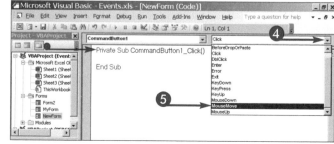

6 Select and delete the
`CommandButton1_Click` macro.

7 Type your macro.

In this example, the statement
`ActiveWindow.Zoom = 120` zooms the
window to 120% magnification.

8 Click ⊠ to switch to Excel.

9 Show the form.

Note: To show a form, see Chapter 21.

10 Position the mouse ⬚ over the button.

● The macro runs. The worksheet zooms to
120% magnification.

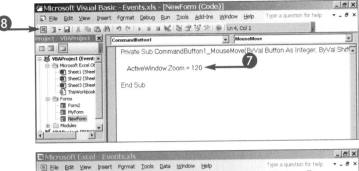

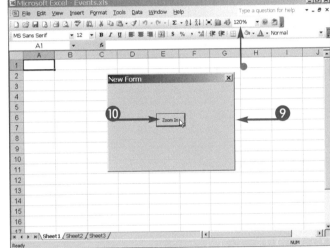

How can I write a MouseMove macro to zoom out again?

▼ You can write a `MouseMove` macro to zoom the worksheet magnification out again, back to 100% or to any level you want, by creating another command button with a `MouseMove` event and then writing the macro `ActiveWindow.Zoom = zoomlevel`. A *zoomlevel* of 100 returns the window to 100% magnification. You can create this macro easily by copying the first `MouseMove` macro, pasting it in the form Code window, and then changing both the button name and the Zoom method value.

How can I color a command button?

▼ You can color a command button, or any control, by writing a *controlname*`.BackColor =` `RGB (`*red,green,blue*`)` statement in the `UserForm_Initialize` macro in the form Code window for the form. The `RGB` arguments for *red*, *green*, and *blue* are integer values between 0 and 255. The 0 value is a complete absence of that color, and 255 is the highest intensity of that color. You can get pale colors by mixing high values of all three colors. For example, the property `RGB` `(250,200,250)` gives a pale pink.

Stop Screen Flicker

Y ou can make a long macro run faster and more neatly by adding statements that halt screen flicker to the macro. Screen flicker happens as Excel continuously repaints the computer screen while executing code statements.

Some macros, especially recorded macros, include commands such as `Select`, `Activate`, `LargeScroll`, and others that cause Excel to update and repaint the computer screen. The macro does not need to have the screen updated while carrying out its actions, and in fact the process of repainting the screen slows down the macro and looks unsightly. The problem becomes more pronounced the longer the macro runs.

You can write the macro to run without any screen repainting by writing the statement `Application.ScreenUpdating = False` at the beginning of the macro. You should include the statement `Application.ScreenUpdating = True` at the very end of the macro to ensure that Excel's screen repainting is turned back on after the macro runs.

You may find that screen flicker returns during a long macro (especially a recorded macro) that contains many Select actions. In that case you can insert a few more `Application.ScreenUpdating = False` statements in the macro.

Stop Screen Flicker

1 Open the macro that takes a long time to run.

2 At the beginning of the macro, type **application.screenupdating = false**.

3 At the end of the macro, type **application.screenupdating = true**.

4 Click the View Microsoft Excel button (⊠) to switch to Excel.

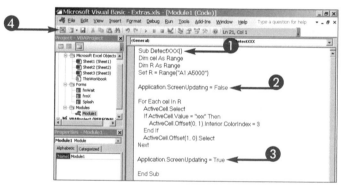

5 Run the macro.

Note: To run a macro, see Chapter 2.

● The macro runs quickly with no screen flickering.

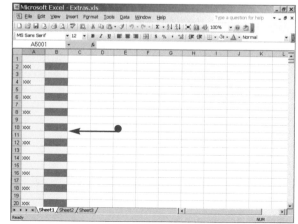

Show a Please Wait Message

If a macro is likely to run a long time and make a user wonder if the macro has locked up, you can show a message to reassure them that the macro is still running. The many ways to show a "Please Wait" message include Excel progress meters and code that displays drawn graphical objects; but the quickest and easiest way is to create a user form resized to show only the title bar, and then type your "Please Wait" message text in the form caption. For more information about creating user forms, see Chapter 21.

You can write a *formname*.Show False statement at the beginning of your lengthy macro to show the form before the macro starts, and write a *formname*.Hide statement at the end of the macro to hide the form when the macro is complete. The False argument in the *formname*.Show False statement is necessary in this case because the argument allows the form to remain in view while the macro runs.

Show a Please Wait Message

① At the beginning of the macro, type *formname*.**show false**, replacing *formname* with your message form name.

② At the end of the macro, type *formname*.**hide**, replacing *formname* with your message form name.

③ Click ⊠ to switch to Excel.

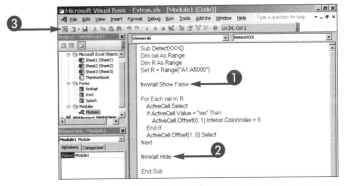

④ Run the macro.

Note: *To run a macro, see Chapter 2.*

● The message form displays while the macro runs, and disappears when the macro completes.

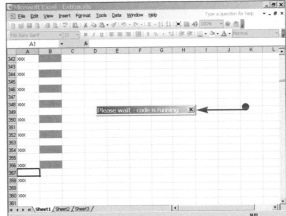

Run a Macro at a Specific Time

You can write an `Application.OnTime` macro, which runs another macro, like a pop-up reminder, at a specific time. You can trigger the macro using a `Workbook_Open` macro, so that when the user opens a specific workbook, the `Application.OnTime` macro launches and runs the automatic macro at the time you specify. The sequence of events starts with opening the workbook, at which point the `Workbook_Open` macro runs and triggers the `Application.OnTime` macro, which then calls the macro you specify at the times you set.

The `Application.OnTime` macro has four arguments, but only the first two are required. The `EarliestTime` argument specifies when the macro is called, and the `Procedure` argument is the macro that is called. The optional `LatestTime` argument specifies the latest time at which the argument can run, and the optional `Schedule` argument schedules the `OnTime` macro to run again at the specified time.

The `Application.OnTime` macro can be run from any macro in any Code window, but the `Workbook_Open` macro ensures that the `Application.OnTime` macro runs when the workbook opens.

Run a Macro at a Specific Time

① In the Projects window, double-click the ThisWorkbook icon.

The ThisWorkbook Code window opens.

② Click ▾ in the Object box.

③ Click Workbook.

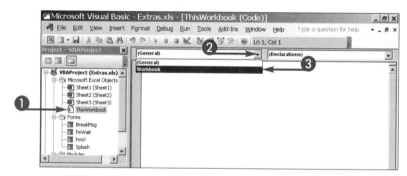

- Excel creates a new `Private Sub Workbook_Open` macro.

④ Type **application.ontime**.

⑤ Type **timevalue**.

⑥ Type (*"timeexpression"*), replacing *timeexpression* with a valid time expression.

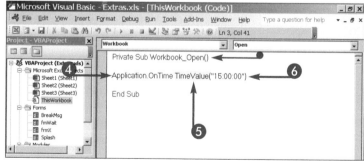

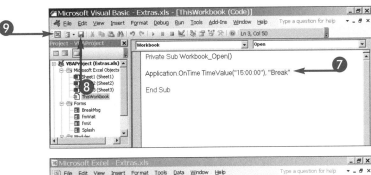

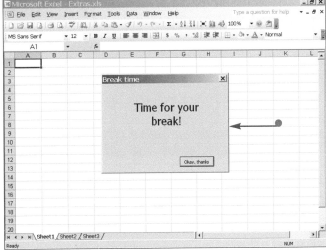

7 Type a comma and the name of the macro to call.

Make sure to put the macro name in quotes. In this example, the called macro shows a form.

8 Click the Save button (💾).

9 Click 🗵 to switch to Excel.

10 Close the workbook.

11 Open the workbook.

The workbook opens and the `Workbook_Open` macro runs.

● At the specified time, the `Application.OnTime` macro runs the called macro.

How can I run the Application.OnTime macro without opening a specific workbook?

▼ You can write the `Application.OnTime` macro in a `Workbook_Open` macro in your Personal Macro Workbook. Every time you start Excel, the Personal Macro Workbook opens and any code in its `Workbook_Open` macro runs. An `Application.OnTime` macro written in the `Workbook_Open` macro runs every time you start Excel. To write a `Workbook_Open` macro in the Personal Macro Workbook, double-click the ThisWorkbook icon in the VBAProject (PERSONAL.XLS) project in the Project window, and create your `Workbook_Open` macro.

How can I set a macro to run after a specific amount of time has passed?

▼ You can set a macro to run after a specific amount of time has passed by using the string `Now + TimeValue("timeexpression")` in the `EarliestTime` argument. `Now` is a built-in VBA function that returns the current time, so this argument runs the called macro at a specific elapsed time from when the `Workbook_Open` macro runs. For example, in a `Workbook_Open` macro, you can write the statement `Application.OnTime Now + TimeValue ("00:30:00"), "macro"` to run the called macro 30 minutes after the workbook opens.

Open a Workbook with a Splash Screen

You can add polish to a workbook and keep users entertained by creating a splash screen that displays automatically while the workbook opens and then closes itself automatically. You can create a splash screen by making a custom form with an informational caption and labels, formatting each label with font properties in the Properties window.

To make the form functional as a splash screen, you write three macros: In a `Private Sub Workbook_Open` macro, you write the statement `formname.Show`, which displays the form when the workbook opens. In a `Private Sub UserForm_Initialize` macro, you write the statement

`Application.OnTime Now + TimeValue(00:00:05), "CloseForm"`, which runs a macro named `CloseForm` five seconds after the form opens. Last, you write the public macro named `CloseForm` with the statement `Unload formname`, which removes the form when called by the `UserForm_Initialize` macro. You can set the `TimeValue` to any length of time you want, and you can name the `CloseForm` macro any name you want.

For more information about custom forms, see Chapter 21. For more information about the `Application.OnTime` statement, see the section "Run a Macro at a Specific Time."

Open a Workbook with a Splash Screen

① Create a custom form for your splash screen.

Note: To create a custom form, see Chapter 21.

② Double-click in the form background.

The form Code window opens with a `Private Sub UserForm_Click` macro.

③ Replace the word Click with **initialize**.

④ Type **application.ontime now + timevalue ("displaytime"), "macro"**, replacing *displaytime* with your display time and *macro* with your macro name.

You create the *macro* in step 9.

⑤ Double-click the ThisWorkbook icon.

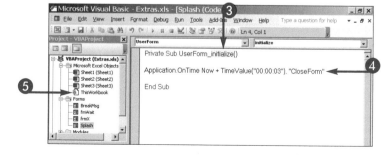

⑥ Create a new `Private Sub Workbook_Open` macro.

Note: To create a Workbook_Open macro, see Chapter 22.

⑦ Type *formname*.**show**, replacing *formname* with your form name.

⑧ Double-click a module icon.

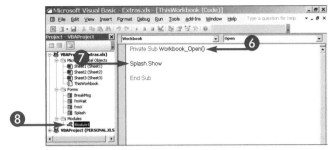

⑨ Create a new macro with the *macro* name from step 4.

⑩ Type **unload** *formname,* replacing *formname* with your form name.

⑪ Click 🖫 to save.

⑫ Close the workbook.

⑬ Open the workbook.

● When the workbook opens, Excel displays the splash screen for the specified time period.

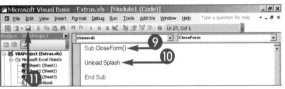

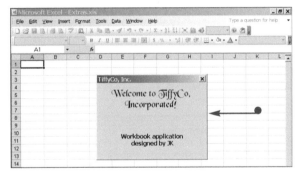

How can I use informational forms in other ways?

▼ One way you can use informational forms is to create a worksheet with command buttons that show instructional forms. For example, a command button can show instructions for filling out a worksheet. Each command button uses the `Private Sub buttonname_Click` macro with the statement *formname*.`Show` to show the specific informational form. To set the workbook to open with a specific worksheet that contains instructional command buttons displayed, write a `Private Sub Workbook_Open` macro with the statement *sheetname*.`Activate`. Opening to a specific worksheet ensures that the user sees the instructions.

How can I color the splash screen?

▼ You can color a splash screen by writing a `Me.BackColor = RGB (`*red,green,blue*`)` statement in the `UserForm_Initialize` macro for the form. The `RGB` arguments for *red*, *green*, and *blue* are integer values between 0 and 255. The 0 value is a complete absence of that color, and 255 is the highest intensity of that color. For example, the property `RGB (`*250,250,100*`)` gives a bright yellow. You can also use a picture in the form. For more information about pictures in forms, see Chapter 21.

Print All Cell Comments to a File

You can write a macro that copies all the cell comments in a workbook to a text file on your hard drive. Although you can set workbook properties both in Excel and in VBA to print cell comments as the last page in a workbook printout, you can also programmatically create a list of cell comments and addresses in a separate file and open that file for review or printing in any text editor program.

To copy all the comments in a workbook to a text file, you first create the text file on your hard drive. A simple program such as Windows Notepad works well. Make sure you remember the path to the file because you must type the path in the macro.

You use a nested `For Each` loop that loops through each worksheet in the workbook and each comment in each worksheet, and lists each comment with its sheet name, cell address, and comment text. This macro uses variables for the comments, the worksheets, and the file number of an unused file into which to paste the comments. The VBA function FreeFile returns an integer representing the next file number available for use.

Print All Cell Comments to a File

① Type **Sub** and the macro name, then press Enter to start a new macro.

② Type **dim *cmt* as comment**, replacing *cmt* with your comment variable throughout the macro.

③ Type **dim *sh* as worksheet**, replacing *sh* with your worksheet variable throughout the macro.

④ Type **dim *fn* as integer**, replacing *fn* with your file number variable throughout the macro.

⑤ Type *fn* = **freefile**.

⑥ Type **open *"pathandfile"* for output as #*fn***, replacing *pathandfile* with the path and file name of the text file.

Make sure you type the file name extension **.txt**.

⑦ Type **for each *sh* in worksheets**.

⑧ Type **for each *cmt* in worksheets(*sh*.name).comments**.

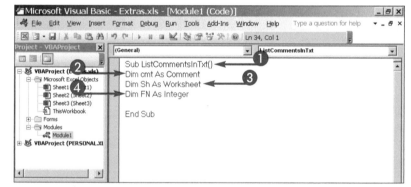

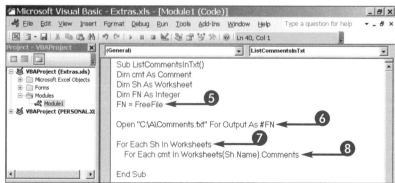

376

9 Type **print #*fn*, "Sheet " & *cmt*.parent .parent.name & " Cell " & *cmt*.parent.address & " " & *cmt*.text**.

The space characters within the quotes separate the sheet name, cell address, and comment text.

You can break the long statement with underscore characters (_) to make it more readable.

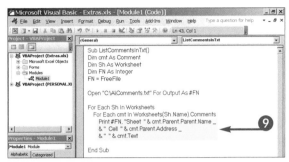

10 Type **next *cmt***.

11 Type **next *sh***.

12 Type **close #*fn***.

13 Click the Run Sub/UserForm button (▶) to run the macro.

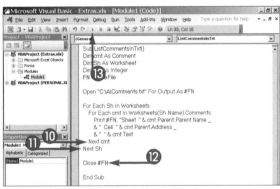

14 Open the text file.

● Excel lists the comments with their sheet and cell addresses.

MASTER IT

Why does my macro not put the comments in the text file?

▼ If the text file is open when you run the macro, the comments are not listed in the text file because the first action in the macro is to open the text file. Close the text file and run the macro. The comments are then listed when you open the text file.

What is the rectangular character that appears in each line in the text file list?

▼ The rectangular character in each comment just after the username is a line break character. The line break character allows the comment text to be typed on the next line below the username. If you open the file in Word or WordPad, the lines are broken but no line break characters appear.

How can I list comments in a separate Excel file instead of a text file?

▼ You can list comments in a separate Excel file instead of a text file by writing the same macro as above, but using an Excel file in the path and file name instead of a text file. Remember to create and save the Excel file before you run the macro.

Add Excel's Calendar Control to a Worksheet

You can allow a user to enter a date in a worksheet cell by selecting the date from a Calendar. The `Calendar` control allows a user to easily select a date and ensures that the date entered in the worksheet is a valid date format.

The `Calendar` control is an embedded object in the worksheet to which it is added, and is available in a list of additional controls that you can access by right-clicking the Control Toolbox toolbar. You create a new `Calendar` control and

write a short statement such as `ActiveCell = Calendar1.Value` in the `Private Sub Calendar1_Click` macro in the Worksheet Code window. The statement tells VBA where to enter the selected date in the worksheet.

The `Calendar` control is an *ActiveX control*, which are controls for which you can write macros. They are found on the Control Toolbox toolbar. For more information about ActiveX controls, look up "activex controls" in the Excel Help files.

The `Calendar` control is already set up any date between the years 1900 and 2100 and needs no further programming to function.

Add Excel's Calendar Control to a Worksheet

① Click View.

② Click Toolbars.

③ Click Control Toolbox.

   The Control Toolbox toolbar appears.

④ Click More Controls (🖼).

⑤ Click Calendar Control.

⑥ Click in the worksheet.

   A new `Calendar` control appears in the worksheet.

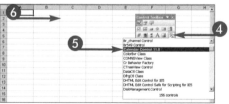

⑦ Right-click the Calendar.

⑧ Click View Code.

   Excel creates a new `Private Sub Calendar1_Click` macro in the Worksheet Code window.

9 Type **activecell = calendar1.value**.

10 Click ⊠ to switch to Excel.

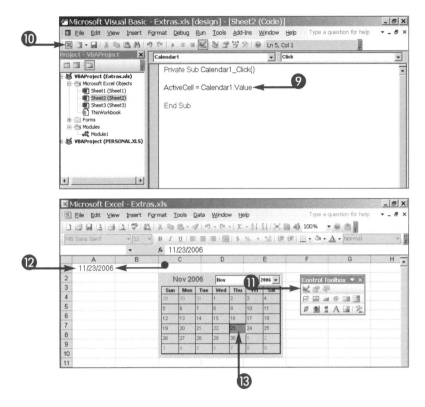

11 In the Control Toolbox, click Exit Design Mode.

12 Click a cell where you want to insert the date.

13 Click a date in the Calendar.

● Excel enters the date in the active cell.

How can move or edit the calendar?

▼ You can edit or move the control in the worksheet if you turn on Design Mode. Click the Design Mode button in the Control Toolbox toolbar to move and resize the calendar and edit the control code. For example, you can edit the cell in which the date is entered by writing the statement `Range("celladdress") = Calendar1.Value` in the `Calendar1_Click` macro. You can also change properties such as the `GridFontColor` by right-clicking the control and clicking Properties. Click the Design Mode button again to return the control to full functionality.

How can I create a Calendar in a custom form?

▼ You can create a form Calendar using the techniques you use for other form controls. To add the `Calendar` control to the form Toolbox, you right-click the Toolbox in the form window, click Additional Controls, click Calendar Control, and Click OK. You draw a `Calendar` control on a form and write two macros. One macro is `Private Sub Calendar1_Click` with a statement such as `ActiveCell = Calendar1.Value`, and the other is `Private Sub UserForm_Activate` with a statement such as `Me.Calendar1.Value = Date` to initialize the calendar with the current date.

Share Macros by Exporting and Importing a Module

You can share macros with other users, or between your own workbooks, by exporting the module that contains those procedures. You can also export a module from a workbook when you no longer need that module in the workbook, but you want to save the macros in that module for future use.

You can export a module by right-clicking the module name in the Project window and clicking Export File. When you export a module, the module code is saved in a file with the extension .bas. You can import the .bas file to a

new workbook project or back into the original project any time you need access to the code that file contains. If you want to share your code with other Excel developers, you can e-mail the .bas file to them and they can import the file into their workbook projects.

You can import a module by right-clicking anywhere in the Project window of the workbook project and clicking Import File. When you import a module into a new workbook, you may have to do some debugging in the code for objects such as specific sheet names, range names, and so forth.

Export a Module

① In the Project window, click the name of the module you want to export.

You can also right-click the module name.

② Click File.

③ Click Export File.

The Export File dialog box appears.

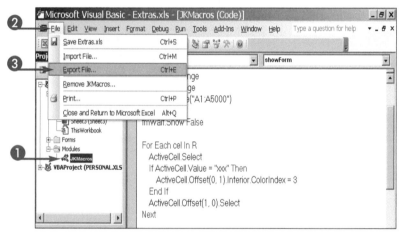

④ Navigate to the folder where you want to save the module file.

⑤ Type a name for the file or accept the name that is offered.

⑥ Click the Save button.

Excel saves the module file.

Import a Module

① Click any icon in the project into which you want to import the module file.

You can also right-click any icon in the project.

② Click File.

③ Click Import File.

The Import File dialog box appears.

④ Navigate to the folder where the file is saved.

⑤ Click the file name.

⑥ Click Open.

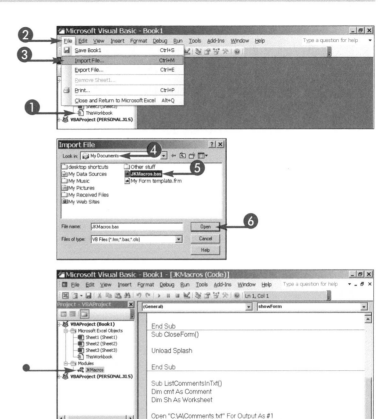

● Excel imports the module into the workbook project.

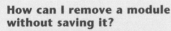

How can I remove a module without saving it?

▼ You can remove a module without saving it by right-clicking the module icon in the Project window and then clicking Remove *modulename*. Click No in the message that reads "Do you want to export *modulename* before removing it?" Excel deletes the module from the workbook project.

How can I rename a module?

▼ You can rename a module with a recognizable name by clicking the module icon in the Project window and then typing a new name in the Name box in the Properties window. After you type the new name, click anywhere outside the Name box. For more information about modules, see Chapter 7.

How can I export a module to a text file?

▼ You can export a module to a text file, in which you can read the code or copy the code for a single macro into another module, by exporting the module and selecting All Files (*.*) in the Save as type box in the Export File dialog box. When you type the file name, make sure you include the extension **.txt** to save a file that can be opened in any text program.

Distribute Macros with an Add-In

You can distribute a macro's functionality without distributing the workbook if you create an add-in. An add-in is a workbook that is saved as an add-in. When an add-in is installed, the add-in's workbook is hidden and can only be seen in the Project window in the Visual Basic Editor. It cannot be unhidden like the Personal Macro Workbook, and cannot display data or charts.

Add-in macros are not visible in the Macros dialog box, but you can make the macros available by running them from a custom toolbar that only appears when the add-in is installed; when the add-in is uninstalled, the custom toolbar remains hidden.

You can create a custom toolbar and add buttons to run your workbook macros. Then you create a `Workbook_Open` macro with the statement `Toolbars("toolbarname").Visible = True` to display the toolbar when the add-in is installed. You should write a `Workbook_BeforeClose` macro with the statement `Toolbars("toolbarname").Visible = False` to hide the custom toolbar when the add-in is uninstalled.

For more information about custom toolbars and custom toolbar buttons, see Chapter 2. For more information about `Workbook_Open` and `Workbook_BeforeClose` macros, see Chapter 22.

Distribute Macros with an Add-In

① Create a custom toolbar and add custom buttons to run your workbook macros.

② Click Tools.

③ Click Macro.

④ Click Visual Basic Editor.

The Visual Basic Editor opens.

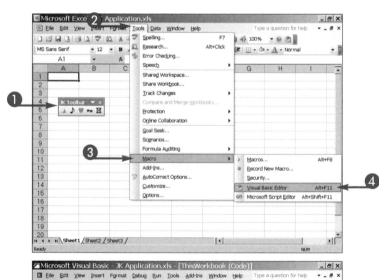

⑤ Double-click the ThisWorkbook icon.

⑥ Create a `Private Sub Workbook_Open` macro.

⑦ Type **toolbars("***toolbarname***").visible = true**, replacing *toolbarname* with your custom toolbar name.

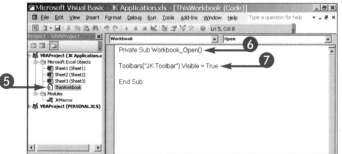

8 Create a `Private Sub Workbook_BeforeClose` macro.

9 Type **toolbars(***"toolbarname"***).visible = false**, replacing *toolbarname* with your custom toolbar name.

10 Click 🖫 to save.

11 Click 🔀 to switch to Excel.

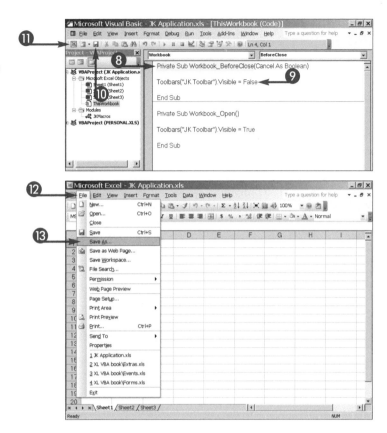

12 Click File.

13 Click Save As.

The Save As dialog box appears.

How can I prevent a user from changing the add-in code?

▼ You can prevent a user from changing your add-in code by locking the add-in project and protecting it with a password. Before you save the workbook as an add-in, right-click the workbook project icon in the Project window and click VBAProject Properties. Click the Protection tab and click to mark the check box labeled "Lock project for viewing." Type a password in the Password and Confirm password dialog boxes, and click OK. For more information about locking and protecting macro code, see Chapter 4.

How can I include a custom function in an add-in?

▼ You can include a custom function in an add-in by creating the custom function in the workbook project before you save the project as an add-in. In a VBA module, write the macro `Public Function functionname` followed by the statement of the function and the `End Function` statement. When the add-in is installed, any public functions it contains are available in the Insert Function dialog box, in the User-Defined category. For more information about function procedures, see the section "Write a Function Procedure" in Chapter 13.

Distribute Macros with an Add-In *(Continued)*

To create the add-in, you save the workbook as an Add-In (*.xla) file. You can then install and uninstall the add-in from Excel's Tools/Add-Ins dialog box. To locate the add-in easily for installation, save it in the default Documents and Settings/*username*/Application Data/Microsoft/AddIns folder. If you save the add-in in a different folder, you can browse for the file in the Add-Ins dialog box. After you install the add-in one time, it remains listed in the Add-Ins dialog box and you do not need to browse for it again.

When you distribute the add-in to other users, you send them the add-in (*.xla) file. Users can save the file in their Documents and Settings/*username*/Application

Data/Microsoft/AddIns folder, or save it in a different folder and browse for the file in the Add-Ins dialog box.

If your add-in remains installed when Excel closes, it opens automatically when Excel starts again, and any macros in the `Workbook_Open` macro run at startup. To keep the add-in from opening the next time Excel starts, you must uninstall the add-in before closing Excel. Click Tools, click Add-Ins, click the add-in file check box, and then click OK.

⑭ Click ⏷ in the Save as type box.

⑮ Click Microsoft Excel Add-In (*.xla).

● The Save in box navigates to the AddIns folder.

⑯ Click Save.

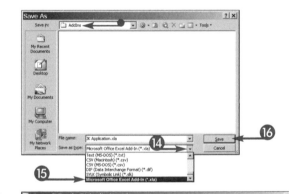

⑰ Click File.

⑱ Click Exit.

Excel closes.

⑲ Start Excel.

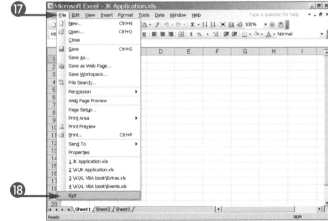

20 Click Tools.

21 Click Add-ins.

22 Click the check box for your add-in
(☐ changes to ☑).

23 Click OK.

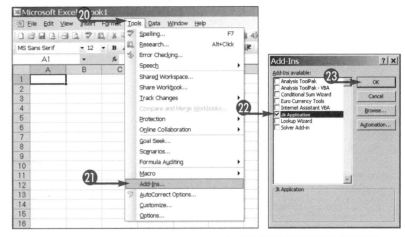

● Your add-in installs and opens.
Excel displays your custom toolbar.

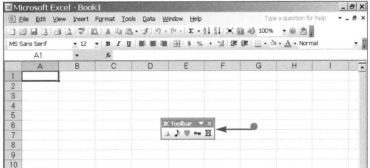

How can I show a description of the add-in the Add-Ins dialog box?

▼ When you save the Excel file as an add-in, you see a Properties dialog box after you click the Save button. Type a title for the add-in file in the Title box and a description of the add-in function in the Comments box, then click OK to complete saving the file as an add-in. When you open the Tools/Add-Ins dialog box and click the name of the add-in, your title and description appear in the lower half of the dialog box.

How does an add-in differ from a workbook?

▼ An add-in differs from a workbook in a number of ways. An add-in workbook window is hidden and cannot be unhidden. The Macros dialog box does not display macros contained in add-ins. An add-in must have at least one worksheet, but because the add-in is hidden, you cannot display any data on that worksheet to a user. Although holding down Shift while opening a workbook bypasses the `Workbook_Open` macro, holding down Shift has no effect on an add-in.

Use Your Personal Macro Workbook on a Network

Y ou can store your macros in a Personal Macro Workbook by creating an alternate startup directory in which to store your Personal Macro Workbook You can do this even if you use a shared installation of Excel on a network.

The Personal Macro Workbook is a hidden workbook that starts every time you start Excel. Because it is always open, the Personal Macro Workbook is a good place to store macros that you want to always have available. Excel creates the Personal Macro Workbook and saves it in the XLSTART directory on your hard drive so that the workbook

opens when you start Excel. But if you work on a network with a shared installation of Excel, the XLSTART directory may be a shared, read-only directory to which you cannot make and save changes.

To make your Personal Macro Workbook available in a shared network environment, you can specify an alternate startup directory, either on your hard drive or in your private area of the network. You create the alternate startup directory in the Excel Tools/Options/General dialog box. A Personal Macro Workbook does not appear in the new startup folder until you record a macro, saving it in the Personal Macro Workbook.

Use Your Personal Macro Workbook on a Network

① Create a new folder, either on your hard drive or in your private area of the network.

Note: Do not save any files in this folder other than those you want to open automatically on startup.

② Click Tools.

③ Click Options.

The Options dialog box appears.

④ Click the General tab.

⑤ In the field labeled *At startup, open all files in,* type the complete path to the new folder from step **1**.

Note: In earlier versions of Excel, this is the Alternate startup file location box.

⑥ Click OK.

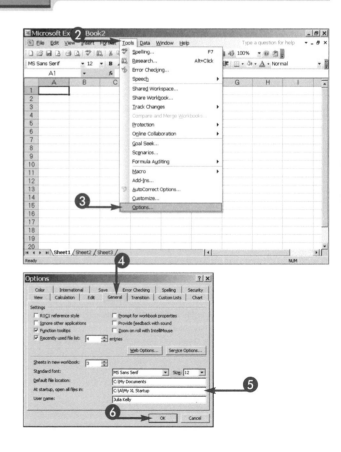

7 Click File.

8 Click Exit.

Excel and all open workbooks close.

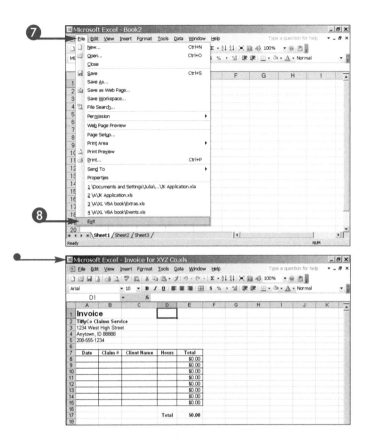

9 Start Excel.

● Excel starts and opens all files saved in the alternate startup folder.

You can record a macro and save it in the Personal Macro Workbook. Excel saves the new Personal Macro Workbook in the new alternate startup folder.

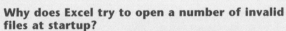

Why does Excel try to open a number of invalid files at startup?

▼ Excel tries to open a number of invalid files at startup because your new startup folder contains non-Excel files. When you start Excel, it attempts to open every file in its startup folder. To fix the problem, you must start Excel, click OK to each "Invalid File Type" message, close any files that open, and then create a different alternate startup file location in the Tools/Options/General dialog box. Do not store any files in this startup folder unless you want the files to open automatically every time you start Excel.

What else can I use a startup folder for?

▼ You can use the startup folder, whether it is the XLSTART folder in your computer or an alternate startup folder you create, to store Excel files and shortcuts to Excel files that you want to open automatically when you start Excel. Do not place a copy of a file in the startup folder, because changes you make to a copy of a file are saved in the copy, not in the original. You can place a shortcut to the file in the startup folder so that the original file remains easily accessible, and the shortcut opens the original file when Excel starts.

A

absolute references, 209
`Activate` method, 157
ActiveX controls, 378
`Add` method, 114, 274, 276, 298, 300
Add Procedure dialog box, 79, 90, 91
Add Watch dialog box, 271
`AddFields` method, 302
add-ins

code, locking, 383
creating, 384
custom functions in, 383
defined, 382
description, 385
distributing macros with, 382–385
installing, 382, 384
uninstalling, 382, 384
user change prevention, 383
workbooks versus, 385

Add-Ins dialog box, 384, 385
appending lists, 220–221
arguments

adding, 103
defined, 50
deleting, 50
help, 83

array references, 133, 137
Assign Macro dialog box, 25, 27, 28
Attach Toolbars dialog box, 21
Auto List

defined, 82
not getting, 289
spelling and, 103
turning on/off, 82
uses, 82

Auto Syntax Check, 77, 268, 269

AutoFit

columns, 37, 192
ranges, 192–193
rows, 193

`AutoFit` method, 192
axes

customizing, 294–295
data series, changing, 287
identifying, 294
scales, 296
secondary, 295
X/Y, 286

B

`BorderAround` method, 194
borders

color, 194
interior, 195
range, 194–195
style, 194, 195
weight, 194, 195

break points

colors, 267
debugging with, 266–267
defined, 266
setting up, 266–267

Button Editor, 25
buttons

clicks, return values, 239
command, 324–325
Commands list, 23
multiple, using, 239
option, 320–321, 340–341
spin, 342–343
toggle, 344–345

INDEX

continued

continued

continued